Truth and Justification

SLC

Books by Jürgen Habermas included in the series Studies in Contemporary German Social Thought
Thomas McCarthy, general editor

Philosophical-Political Profiles (1983)

Observations on "The Spiritual Situation of the Age" (editor, 1984)

The Philosophical Discourse of Modernity: Twelve Lectures (1987)

On the Logic of the Social Sciences (1988)

The New Conservatism: Cultural Criticism and the Historians' Debate (1989)

The Structural Transformation of the Public Sphere: An Inquiry into a Category of Bourgeois Society (1989)

Moral Consciousness and Communicative Action (1990)

Postmetaphysical Thinking: Philosophical Essays (1992)

Justification and Application: Remarks on Discourse Ethics (1993)

Between Facts and Norms: Contributions to a Discourse Theory of Law and Democracy (1996)

The Inclusion of the Other: Studies in Political Theory (1998)

On the Pragmatics of Communication (1998)

The Liberating Power of Symbols: Philosophical Essays (2001)

The Postnational Constellation: Political Essays (2001)

On the Pragmatics of Social Interaction: Preliminary Studies in the Theory of Communicative Action (2001)

Religion and Rationality: Essays on Reason, God, and Modernity (2002)

Truth and Justification (2003)

Truth and Justification

Jürgen Habermas

edited and with translations by Barbara Fultner

The MIT Press, Cambridge, Massachusetts

First MIT Press paperback edition, 2005

This edition © 2003 Massachusetts Institute of Technology
This work originally appeared under the title *Wahrheit und Rechtfertigung,* © 1999
Suhrkamp Verlag, Frankfurt am Main, Germany. Chapters 2 and 5 of the German
edition have been omitted; translations of both were included in the volume *On the
Pragmatics of Communication* (1998). In their place the author has included two new
essays (chapters 2 and 5 of this edition).

The translations of several chapters are based on earlier published translations, as
follows: A translation of chapter 1 by Hella Beiser was published in *German Philosophy
since Kant,* edited by Anthony O'Hear (Cambridge University Press, 1999). A translation of chapter 3 by Maeve Cooke was published in the *European Journal of Philosophy*
(December 2000). A translation of chapter 4 by Peter Dews was published in *European Journal of Philosophy* (August 1999).

MIT Press books may be purchased at special quantity discounts for business or sales
promotional use. For information, please email <special_sales@mitpress.mit.edu> or
write to Special Sales Department, The MIT Press, 55 Hayward Street, Cambridge,
MA 02142.

This book was set in New Baskerville by UG / GGS Information Services Inc. and
printed in the United States of America.

Library of Congress Cataloging-in-Publication Data

Habermas, Jürgen.
  [Wahrheit und Rechtfertigung. English]
  Truth and justification / Jürgen Habermas; edited and translated by Barbara Fultner.
    p. cm.—(Studies in contemporary German social thought)
  Includes bibliographical references (p.   ) and index.
  ISBN-13 978-0-262-08318-8 (hc: alk. paper), 978-0-262-58258-2 (pb)
  1. Philosophy. I. Fultner, Barbara. II. Title. III. Series.

1006160357

B3258.H323 W3413   2003
100—dc21   2002190859

10 9 8 7 6 5 4 3

Contents

Translator's Introduction

To write an introduction to a volume to which the author himself has already written a lengthy introduction may seem superfluous. However, it is perhaps the very length of Jürgen Habermas's own introduction to *Truth and Justification* that warrants a briefer preface. Moreover, given the nature of the essays collected in this volume, it is important to situate his work in relation to major current thinkers of the Anglo-American analytic—or, more aptly, postanalytic—tradition. This collection, perhaps more than any other by Habermas, is an intervention in and contribution to current debates in what he terms "theoretical philosophy," that is, in epistemology, metaphysics, and philosophy of language. At the same time, these essays elucidate the connection between Habermas's moral and practical philosophy and his epistemology and metaphysics. As such, the volume will be of interest to analytically oriented philosophers as much as to those who have followed Habermas's work in social theory and discourse ethics.

Habermas continues to be one of the few thinkers today aiming to develop a comprehensive philosophy. Although his main focus in this volume is on questions of knowledge and objectivity, these are always reconnected to issues of moral, social, and political theory that have occupied Habermas over the last several decades. The essays cover topics as wide-ranging as epistemological and moral cognitivism, cultural relativism, legal theory, practical reasoning, and human rights. Most important, Habermas shows how all these different issues impinge on one another and how a thoroughgoing pragmatism can provide a unified account of a vast array of phenomena. In doing so, he bridges the gap between so-called continental and analytic philosophy. On the one hand, he brings together the tradition of Humboldt, Hegel, and Heidegger with that of Frege, Quine, Davidson, and Dummett; on the other hand, he plays the two traditions against one another in order to identify their strengths and weaknesses. The result is a historically informed conceptual map and a trenchant diagnosis of the state of debate among contemporary pragmatists. Finally, the present collection of essays marks certain shifts in his thinking, in particular regarding his conception of truth.

A distinctive feature of Habermas's work has been his defense of enlightenment reason even in the age of what he himself has called "postmetaphysical thinking." He has always treaded the narrow path between objectivism and subjectivism—be it in his social theory and practical philosophy or, as here, in his epistemology and metaphysics. That is, on the one hand, he has sought to avoid reducing social situations or moral issues to mere objectively observable phenomena but instead to theorize them from a participant perspective. On the other hand, he has been critical of social or ethical theories that accord too much constitutive authority to the subject or the linguistic community.[1] Thus the purpose of the theory of communicative action has been to address problems of action coordination and social integration by developing an *intersubjectivist* theoretical framework that avoids the pitfalls of both objectivism and subjectivism. From the outset, Habermas has embraced the "linguistic turn" as the basis for such a framework: The theory of communicative action situates the roots of rationality in the structures of everyday communication and regards the critical power of reason to be immanent in ordinary language. Using the resources of speech act theory, Habermas understands communicative action in terms of the raising of criticizable validity claims. Following the publication of *The Theory of Communicative Action* in the early 1980s, he went on to develop a cognitivist moral theory in the form of discourse ethics. The core of this theory is the so-called Principle of Universalization, according to which a moral norm is justified if all those affected would assent to it under conditions of an ideal speech situation.[2] Moral norms, unlike ethical values, have a universal and unconditional validity. At the same time, moral rightness is an *epistemic* notion. That is, it is defined in terms of what rational agents would agree on under (approximately) ideal conditions.

In this collection, Habermas turns to the implications of the theory of communicative action—and, more broadly, of the linguistic turn—for epistemology and metaphysics. He returns to the problem of representation and objectivity, an issue he has not addressed in detail since writing *Knowledge and Human Interests*. In particular, he distinguishes a *nonepistemic* notion of objective validity from the above notion of moral validity. Having worked out the linguistic and pragmatic turns in practical philosophy, that is, in the theory of action and rationality and in ethics, he wants to do the same for ontology and epistemology. In taking this route, he reverses what he takes to be the dominant approach in both analytic and continental philosophy, namely, to give primacy to theoretical over practical philosophy and, consequently, to develop practical philosophy in the light of theoretical philosophy, rather than the other way round—or, more appropriately, rather than developing the two in tandem. His goal, as these essays make clear, is to steer a middle course between the Scylla and Charybdis of much contemporary thought shaped by the linguistic turn, namely, between a pragmatist contextualism that gives up all claims to objective knowledge and a reductive objectivism that fails to do justice to the participant perspective of agents in interaction. This raises two central problems: How can the ineluctable normativity of the perspective of agents interacting in a linguistically structured lifeworld be reconciled with the contingency of how forms of life evolve? And how can the assumption that there is an independently existing world be reconciled with the linguistic insight that we cannot have unmediated access to "brute" reality? Habermas wants to answer both questions from a thoroughly pragmatist perspective. Indeed, he believes that, for the most part, the pragmatic turn has still not been adequately realized, and that this failure accounts for the problems faced by other contemporary pragmatists, as his engagement with them here illustrates.

1   Toward a Postanalytic and Postcontinental Philosophy

A major theme of this collection of essays is Habermas's continuing effort to mediate between the analytic and continental traditions of philosophy, which he regards as complementary and without both of which his formal pragmatics would not be possible. Here we find him engaging the views of Heidegger, Gadamer, and Apel, on the continental side, and Frege, Dummett, Davidson, Putnam, and Brandom, on the analytic. Towering above all, of course, are Kant and Hegel as the two main historical figures informing contemporary debate. He identifies two major currents in twentieth-century philosophy in the wake of the linguistic turn. The first is represented by Wittgenstein and Heidegger and emphasizes linguistic world-disclosure, that is, the idea that our access to reality is always filtered and indeed made possible by our language or conceptual scheme. As already indicated, this strand jeopardizes the notion of objectivity since it puts us at the mercy, so to speak, of "Being" or of the grammar of our language games. The second is represented by Quine and Davidson and veers too far in the direction of objectivity; it embraces an empiricist outlook at the expense of doing justice to the participant perspective of language users (pp. 69ff., 112ff.). In addition, he identifies a third current, namely, that of Kantian pragmatism, represented by Putnam, Dummett, Apel, and others—including himself. This group takes the linguistic turn seriously not just as a methodological shift, but as a paradigm shift (p. 69). Proponents of this third strand seek to do justice both to the constitutive nature of language and to the objectivity of claims to truth.

The first essay explicitly takes up the complementarity of the analytic and continental traditions, with Wilhelm von Humboldt emerging in some sense as the historical hero of the collection. Although language has a constitutive function for Humboldt, he also emphasizes the possibility of cross-linguistic and cross-cultural communication and retains a notion of objective reference. Habermas does not make it explicit, but his reading of Humboldt—and especially of Humboldt's emphasis on the interchangeability of the dialogical roles of speaker and hearer—parallels on the continental side his earlier reading of Mead on the Anglo-American side.[3] Moreover, for

Habermas, Humboldt lays the foundations of the kind of Kantian pragmatism he defends. Both the hermeneutic and analytic traditions, however, limit themselves to what Habermas calls the "semantic aspects" of language (p. 62) and treat pragmatics as secondary. Insofar as Humboldt argued that there are three aspects or levels of language, namely, world-disclosure (taken up by hermeneutics), representation (taken up by formal semantics), and pragmatics, his account goes beyond these two traditions.

What is missing from the continental tradition is an adequate account of the representational function of language, of reference and propositional truth (p. 61). For this purpose, Habermas draws on the analytic tradition, particularly on the work of Hilary Putnam. He stresses that sameness of reference is a *formal pragmatic presupposition* of communication, and this presupposition is independent of the specific—and possibly divergent—descriptions that two speakers may associate with a term or referent. Indeed, for two speakers to disagree about the appropriate description of a referent presupposes that they are referring to the same thing.[4]

The most salient difference between analytic and continental thought, according to Habermas, is that the analytic tradition does not engage in cultural critique (p. 79). If we accept this characterization, then Habermas shows himself to be a decidedly continental thinker. Despite the focus on theoretical philosophy, there is a palpable sense of the political throughout the volume, starting with the introduction's concluding section of legal theory all the way to the final essay's observations on the relationship between theory and practice and on the philosopher's role as public intellectual. The connection between Habermas's epistemology and his social-political theory is increasingly foregrounded in the later essays. The final three essays are, albeit in different ways, intended to show how the main themes of the volume are connected to the bulk of Habermas's oeuvre in social theory and moral philosophy.

2 Kantian Pragmatism

Habermas is one of several contemporary "Kantian pragmatists." It is therefore not surprising that his debate with philosophers like

Hilary Putnam or Robert Brandom is cast in terms of how to "prag-matize" or, as he puts it, "detranscendentalize" Kant. What follows, in other words, from understanding the transcendental conditions of possibility of our experience as something *in* the world, of situat-ing them in our practices (pp. 18, 20ff.)? The first part of essay 2 contains a detailed account of his appropriation of Kant. On the one hand, Kant's necessary subjective conditions of objective experi-ence are transformed and given the "quasi-transcendental" role of *intersubjective* conditions of linguistic interpretation and communica-tion. Yet on the other hand, if taken too far, this detranscendental-ization leads to undesirable consequences. As the titles of essays 3 and 4 suggest, one might say that we must find a middle road be-tween Kant and Hegel. Habermas argues that Hegel was right to his-toricize reason, but that he subsequently went too far in the direction of an "objective idealism" according to which objectivity is ultimately reduced to intersubjectivity. When "spirit" (Hegel) or "Being" (Heidegger) or simply lifeworlds or linguistic frameworks are given too much constitutive authority, the result is linguistic de-terminism and cultural and epistemological relativism. Situating transcendental features of experience in local forms of life raises the problem of how to theorize an objective world existing indepen-dently of our conceptual schemes or practices. If what we know de-pends not merely on universal structures of the mind, but on the conceptual articulation of our language—since this articulation is what gives us access to "reality" in the first place—there are as many ways of knowing as there are languages. If these languages further-more are regarded as incommensurable, the concept of objectivity loses all bite and we are left with relativism. Even though Habermas, too, argues that we have no "uninterpreted" or direct access to real-ity, but that our grasp of how things are in the world is always medi-ated through language, he rejects relativism in epistemology as much as in moral theory.

Habermas argues the above problems follow not from the project of detranscendentalization per se, but from a (continued) privileging of the representational model of knowledge. According to this model, which has traditionally gone hand in hand with the correspondence theory of truth, knowledge is a matter of correctly *representing* the world. Habermas argues that this privileging is present even in authors who claim to have overcome this model. Indeed, Habermas makes the (strong) claim that even pragmatically oriented analytic philosophers from Quine and Davidson to Sellars and Brandom remain too caught up in the representational paradigm and thus do not fully take the linguistic-pragmatic turn (see his introduction, and essays 2 and 3). Even the most promising pragmatic approaches such as Brandom's inferentialism, he maintains, ultimately subscribe to what Habermas regards as an objectivist understanding of agency that does not do justice to the intersubjective, dialogical nature of communication (essay 4). The threats of relativism and its converse, objectivism, in other words, both follow from an insufficiently thorough pragmatism.

Habermas counters the representational model with a pragmatic conception of knowledge. The pragmatist deflation of Kantian transcendental analysis shows how the background structures of our lifeworld are embodied in our practices and activities and emphasizes the participant perspective. Just as Habermas's analysis of moral discourse involved the formal pragmatic presuppositions interlocutors must make, so the pragmatic presuppositions governing our epistemic practices play a central role here, first and foremost the presupposition of a single objective world that is the same for everyone. This presupposition lies at the core of our ability to refer to objects in the world at all and, as such, underlies the representational function of language. This representational function of language, however, for Habermas, must remain tied to "contexts of experience, action, and discursive justification" (p. 26). Thus a strictly causal theory of reference is unacceptable to him. More important, in the present context, it means that our empirical knowledge of the world and our linguistic knowledge must be regarded as interdependent. Not only does language make possible our access to reality, but our coping with the world in turn has the power to lead us to revise our linguistic practices (essay 6). Language does not (fully) determine what we can know of the world or what the world is for us. Rather, we learn from experience, and this empirical knowledge can lead us to revise the meanings of the terms we use. This is why Habermas refers to the world-disclosure of language as "weakly transcendental."

Crucial for accounting for the revisionary power of experience relative to language is the role Habermas accords to *problem solving*. It is the key activity underlying knowledge acquisition. We encounter the world first in our engaged coping, and—often—we encounter it as a source of resistance. That the world provides resistance when we deal with it means that "the way the world is" is not simply *up to us*. Rather, reality constrains our practices in tangible ways, and this provides the foothold for a robust notion of objectivity. This is crucial for *learning*. The resistance of the objective world is analogous to the resistance we may encounter when others criticize the claims we raise in discourse, and Habermas uses this analogy to argue for the unconditionality of moral validity (essay 6).

This pragmatist conception of knowledge has ontological implications. Working out an adequate notion of objectivity leads Habermas to endorse a "weak naturalism" to complement his epistemological realism. Weak naturalism is a form of *naturalism* insofar as it views nature and culture as continuous with one another. Culture evolves naturally. Here, too, learning is a central metaphor: Our sociocultural form of life has evolved from prior forms through natural learning processes. Habermas's is a *weak* naturalism because he wants to refrain from making any sort of reductionist claims about social practices (such as reducing them to merely observable behavior); they are to be analyzed from the participant perspective as norm-governed practices. Similarly, weak naturalism is supposed to be neutral with regard to the mind–body problem. The idea is that once we connect transcendental pragmatism with weak naturalism, we can give an account of how reality imposes constraints on our practices (p. 30). The paradigmatic representatives of "strong" naturalism, by contrast, are Quine and Davidson, who, according to Habermas, explain human behavior naturalistically, assimilating normative social and linguistic practices to observable events in the world. By seeking to eliminate all normative elements from its explanations, strong naturalism fails to do justice to the participant perspective, whereas weak naturalism takes seriously the normative self-understanding of agents in interaction.

3   Objective and Normative Validity: A Revised Conception of Truth

Most of Habermas's work following *The Theory of Communicative Action* in the 1980s and early '90s focused on developing discourse ethics. In terms of validity, this meant working out what is involved in raising and vindicating normative rightness claims. The focus, in other words, was on *normative validity* (*Sollgeltung*), on what one *ought* to do. The question of truth, in contrast, for him is a question about *objective validity* (*Wahrheitsgeltung*). Here, the issue of normativity becomes tricky. Of course, the question of objective validity has to do with what one ought to believe or take to be true, and to that extent, it makes sense to speak of truth as a "normative" concept. However, truth, for Habermas, must not be assimilated to (merely) holding true. Ultimately, objective validity is a matter of what is, in fact, *true,* not of what we take to be true (despite the fact that we can confidently say that some of our truths have replaced earlier beliefs that we now know were false, and the fallibilist insight that, for all we know, our own beliefs may be similarly replaced in the future). Truth, in contrast to normative rightness, in other words, is not an epistemic notion—a point to which I return below.

References to truth, objectivity, and the cognitive or representational dimension of language, to be sure, have always figured in Habermas's accounts of language and communication as well as in his critiques of other approaches. Thus, for example, he criticizes analytic philosophy of language and in particular truth-conditional approaches to semantics for privileging the representational dimension of language.[5] However, at least since writing "Wahrheitstheorien,"[6] Habermas has not addressed in further detail the question of the nature of truth. Rather, he has generally confined himself to the view that in raising a truth claim, a speaker claims that some state of affairs or fact obtains. In "Wahrheitstheorien," Habermas already rejected both correspondence and coherence theories of truth, and he does so still in essays 5 and 6. On the one hand, correspondence is too strong a notion inasmuch as it assumes the possibility of direct access to "brute" or "naked" reality. On the other hand, a coherence theory of truth fails to capture important aspects of our concept of truth, even though it looks to be one of the implications of the linguistic turn: Once we grant that there is no direct, but only linguistically mediated access to reality, it seems that any belief or statement can be corroborated only by other beliefs or statements and that thus a coherence theory of truth is the only kind available to us. Yet coherence is too weak a notion for truth inasmuch as, according to Habermas, statements are true not because they cohere with other statements we accept, but because the states of affairs they describe actually obtain (even though they can be *established* only by means of other statements).

In "Wahrheitstheorien," Habermas thus infamously coined the term "consensus theory of truth," which has caused a fair amount of confusion about and misunderstanding of his position. This early essay should be read as presenting not so much a theory of *truth* as a theory of *justification*.[7] Possibly fueling the confusion, Habermas himself did espouse what he subsequently called a "discursive" conception of truth until the mid- to late-1990s, according to which truth is ideal warranted assertibility—a view he shared with Hilary Putnam, among others. In response to criticism, Habermas has since abandoned this epistemic conception of truth. As he argues at length in essays 2 and especially 6, the discursive conception as formulated hitherto is inadequate. In particular, the discursive or consensus theory of truth misleadingly suggests that we take a proposition to be true because it is or can be agreed to by all those concerned, whereas in fact, we ought to agree to a proposition *because* it is true, not the other way around. This change of mind is in large part what has prompted him to return to epistemology and metaphysics in order to work out a better pragmatist conception of truth; he now takes it that "the discursive conception of truth is due to an overgeneralization of the special case of the validity of moral judgments and norms" ("Introduction," p. 8). The validity of the latter is *exhausted* by ideal warranted assertibility: A moral claim is normatively right if and only if all those affected would agree to it under approximately ideal conditions of discourse. There are no facts independent of the (ideal) community of those affected to which normative rightness claims purport to refer. But talk of truth, in contrast to that of normative rightness, has certain specific ontological connotations: It presupposes reference to a single objective world that exists independently of our descriptions and is the same for all of us. This realization has led Habermas to acknowledge the need for a theory of reference to supplement the theory of communicative action. Hence he endorses a direct theory of reference as developed by Hilary Putnam, which allows for sameness of reference under different descriptions. This, too, is clearly a necessary presupposition of discourse about whether what we say is true.

Truth figures at different levels in Habermas. On the one hand, truth plays a role in discussions of the nature of the theory of meaning. Habermas is drawn to the analytic tradition because it can provide a theory of meaning that, in particular, accounts for the representational dimension of language, which the continental linguistic tradition tends to neglect. Furthermore, Habermas especially applauds the recognition, since Frege, of the internal connection between meaning and validity. Although truth, as one of the three validity claims, is indispensable to the theory of communicative action, Habermas has argued against taking truth as a semantic primitive. Rather, it is but one dimension of validity. A truth-conditional semantics as developed by philosophers of language from Frege to Davidson is too narrow, in his view, for it privileges the representational dimension of language over its expressive and communicative dimensions.[8]

For Habermas, communication, action, and representation are equiprimordial. This has been a hallmark of his conception of speech acts since the 1970s: In performing a speech act, a speaker represents a state of affairs, establishes an intersubjective relation with a hearer, and expresses her intention. In other words, she raises three validity claims: a claim to truth, to normative rightness, and to sincerity. The insistence on these three mutually irreducible validity claims forms a cornerstone of Habermas's conceptual system. And it is this view that continues to set him apart from the analytic philosophers he discusses. In one way or another, it lies at the bottom of his critique of Quine and Davidson as well as of Brandom and even Putnam. All are seeking to find a common denominator or to level the conceptual landscape in ways that Habermas rejects. Quine and Davidson, in his view, err on the side of objectivism by turning the communicative actions of others into mere observable behavior; Brandom assimilates norms of rationality to norms of action; and Putnam levels the fact-value distinction by associating value judgments with "ought-implying facts."

On the other hand, Habermas also discusses truth at the level of metaphysics and ontology. This is the case, for instance, when he is trying to elucidate what is involved in truth as a validity claim. The question here is how should truth be defined? What *is* truth on a pragmatist account that nonetheless wants to embrace epistemological realism? For a pragmatist, of course, this very question is ill put. Indeed, one might argue that a major advantage of Habermas's present account over that he offered in "Wahrheitstheorien" is that he no longer provides a definition of truth or *equates* it with anything. Rather, not unlike Brandom in *Making It Explicit,* he directs our attention to how the concept of truth functions, both in everyday coping and in discourse. Whereas in the latter context, we are aware of the "cautionary" uses of the truth predicate and of the fallibility of our claims, the unconditionality of truth is most evident in practical contexts of ordinary coping. There, we presuppose certain truths, practical certainties, as unconditionally valid. As Habermas succinctly puts it, "We do not walk onto any bridge whose stability we doubt" (p. 39). This unconditional acceptance is the pragmatic corollary of a realist conception of truth.

Habermas is an epistemological realist in another respect as well: The objects we can refer to may fail to meet the descriptions we associate with them. This is the core of his fallibilism; it is also where he draws on Putnam's theory of reference. In defense of his version of a pragmatic conception of truth, he argues that the connection between truth and justification is epistemically, but not conceptually necessary (p. 38). In other words, truth may always "outrun" justified belief, even under (approximately) ideal conditions, but he nevertheless insists on the fact that from the agent's perspective, practical certainties are and must be taken to be true absolutely at the risk of incapacitation. It is only in discourse that such practical convictions come under a fallibilist proviso.

Finally, Habermas considers himself to be a "conceptual nominalist" rather than a conceptual realist (p. 31). This follows, first, from his commitment to the revisability of language by experience. But it also means, second, that the world does not consist of *facts* but of *things*. A fortiori, then, for Habermas, facts are not things. This view is clearly reminiscent of Davidson's claim that "nothing, *no thing*, makes our sentences true."[9] Although facts, for Habermas, are what is represented in true statements, he does not mean to reify or hypostatize the notion of fact. In a sense, both Davidson and Habermas allow that facts—that things are thus and so—are what make sentences true; both endorse realist views about truth; and both maintain that there is a mind- and language-independent objective world. Moreover, both are antireductionists: Like Habermas, Davidson defends the mutual irreducibility and equiprimordiality of subjectivity, objectivity, and intersubjectivity. Nonetheless, his epistemology is more strongly naturalistic and less pragmatic that Habermas's. On the other hand, he is more suspicious of "fact-talk" than Habermas and would rather do without it entirely. In this regard, Davidson is arguably more metaphysically abstemious if not postmetaphysical.

Much of the interest of the present volume lies in Habermas's clarification of the—often subtle—differences between his own position and similar approaches. One must, for this very reason, be careful to distinguish substantive differences from differences in emphasis between Habermas and his sparring partners. These are in a sense, to borrow Habermas's phrase, "domestic disputes." His and Robert Brandom's accounts of objectivity, for example, can and perhaps should be regarded as complementary. Brandom argues that there is a "structural objectivity" built into our practices of giving and asking for reasons; for him, the distinction between something's being true and being taken to be true is a pragmatic one, built into the structures of communication. To that extent, his account is compatible with Habermas's own pragmatic account of objectivity. According to the latter, the formal presupposition of a single objective world existing independently of us is, after all, also a structural feature of discourse.[10]

Another example is the disagreement with Putnam about truth. Habermas criticizes Putnam's account of the objectivity of value (as the inverse of the value-ladenness of facts) and his assertion that there are "ought-implying facts" and that, therefore, value judgments can be true or false. Against Putnam, Habermas argues that there are "different senses in which judgments can be correct" (p. 224). Norms must not be assimilated to facts, for the facts are not "up to us" in the way that moral or ethical norms are. The meaning of truth, as he puts it, is not exhausted by reaching consensus. At issue in this dispute is whether it is legitimate to allow for different *types* of truth that in turn require different types of justification or whether "truth" is a notion that applies to statements about the objective world only whereas moral judgments, though they have cognitive content, are subject to a different kind of validity. Some have argued along these lines that, in the moral domain, Habermas has been defending a peculiar brand of cognitivism, since he has consistently denied that moral claims are truth-evaluable when truth-evaluability is generally thought to be the hallmark of moral cognitivism. What difference it makes whether we talk about, say, moral or aesthetic *truth* or moral rightness and aesthetic authenticity, as long as we recognize that they are subject to justification in terms of different kinds of reasons, remains an open question.[11]

Perhaps a more salient point of disagreement between Habermas and Putnam in their ongoing debate is their respective understandings of pluralism, as this collection's essay and especially Putnam's response to it show.[12] Putnam seems to have an almost instrumentalist conception of the value of pluralism. For him, it involves more than mere tolerance. A consistent pluralist cannot hold that some other form of life, religious tradition, or sexual orientation is "wrong." Above and beyond this "minimal pluralism," however, he also claims that a pluralist must accept that other forms of life, religion, or sexual orientation may have insights available to them that are not available to her, but that may be of use to her and to her own community.[13] This sheds new light on Putnam's dictum to "let a thousand flowers bloom." The value of pluralism—rather like the value of pluralism in scientific inquiry—is that it can help us in our discovery of the good life. But a Habermasian, according to Putnam, can approach a value judgment from another community or culture in only two ways: She can ask either (a) whether it is deontologically admissible, that is, whether it violates any universal norms, or (b) whether it contributes to a collective form of life that is in the interest of all those affected.[14] This, however, is too narrow an understanding of cross-cultural dialogue according to Putnam. This is no doubt the case, but a Habermasian need not be confined to this narrow conception. Putnam does not consider Habermas's emphasis on learning processes, on the one hand, and on the dialogical nature of communication, be it intra- or intercultural, on the other. These at least prima facie surely allow for the possibility of our learning by interacting not only with the objective world, but also with others. Just as we are able to revise our linguistic knowledge in light of new empirical knowledge, so surely we must be able to revise our moral and ethical knowledge in light of our interactions with one another. Ultimately it is this ability that lies at the cognitivist heart of a realist epistemology and universalist moral theory.

Essays 1, 3, and 4 have been published elsewhere in translations by others. Habermas himself penned an English version of essay 7. While I have learned from each of these translations, I have revised all in an effort to give the volume unity of style and to correct for some discrepancies with the published German original. A few terms presented particular difficulties that should be mentioned here. (1) Habermas uses two terms for "validity," *Geltung* and *Gültigkeit*. There is a latent attempt to use them to mark two distinctions, namely, on one hand, between the objective validity of a claim and its de facto "validity for us," its social acceptance or force, and, on the other, between objective and normative validity. The latter, in other words, is a distinction *within* the dimension of validity in general. However, Habermas does not draw either distinction systematically. (2) For the most part, I have rendered *Aussage* as "statement," though sometimes "proposition" or "assertion" were more appropriate. Thus, for example, Habermas distinguishes between *moralische Aussagen* and *empirische Aussagen*, but also associates truth with *propositions* (*Propositionen*) and assertions as distinct from normative rightness and normative claims, which he explicitly distinguishes from assertions. As a result, it is somewhat awkward to speak of "moral propositions" rather than moral claims or statements. (3) The rather different connotations or, to put it in terms of the Brandom–Habermas debate, inferential relations of terms like *practical commitments* and *praktische Vorhaben* ("practical projects" or "undertakings") potentially lead to confusion in transposing a philosophical debate from one language into another, one philosophical culture into another, even challenging one's faith in the principle of translatability. For the sake of the English-speaking audience who may be familiar with Brandom's work, I have tried to cast the debate as much as possible in Brandom's original terms without distorting Habermas's criticisms.

I am grateful to Gary Davis, Cristina Lafont, Sid Maskit, Christoph Menke, Bill Rehg, and especially Jonathan Maskit for their advice and assistance with various parts of this manuscript. Finally, I would like to thank Jürgen Habermas for generously clarifying a number of points in the text.

Introduction: Realism after the Linguistic Turn

The present volume brings together philosophical essays that were written between 1996 and 2000 and pick up on a line of thought that I had set aside since *Knowledge and Human Interests*. With the exception of the final essay ("The Relationship between Theory and Practice Revisited"), they deal with issues in theoretical philosophy that I have neglected since then. Of course, the formal pragmatics that I have developed since the early 1970s cannot do without the fundamental concepts of truth and objectivity, reality and reference, validity and rationality. This theory relies on a normatively charged concept of communication [*Verständigung*], operates with validity claims that can be redeemed discursively and with formal-pragmatic presuppositions about the world, and links understanding speech acts to the conditions of their rational acceptability. However, I have not dealt with these themes from the perspective of theoretical philosophy. I have pursued neither a metaphysical interest in the being of Being, nor an epistemological interest in the knowledge of objects or facts, nor even the semantic interest in the form of assertoric propositions. The linguistic turn did not acquire its significance for me in connection with these traditional problems. Rather, the pragmatic approach to language [*Sprachpragmatik*] helped me to develop a theory of communicative action and of rationality. It was the foundation for a critical theory of society and paved the way for a discourse-theoretic conception of morality, law, and democracy.

This explains a certain one-sidedness of my theoretical strategy, which the essays in this volume are meant to redress. They revolve around two fundamental questions of theoretical philosophy. On the one hand, I here take up the ontological question of naturalism: As subjects capable of speech and action, we "always already" find ourselves in a linguistically structured lifeworld. How can the normativity that is unavoidable from the perspective of the participants in this lifeworld be reconciled with the contingency of sociocultural forms of life that have evolved naturally? On the other hand, I turn to the epistemological question of realism: How can we reconcile the assumption that there is a world existing independently of our descriptions of it and that is the same for all observers with the linguistic insight that we have no direct, linguistically unmediated access to "brute" reality? Needless to say, I deal with these topics from within the formal-pragmatic perspective.

I Communication or Representation?

Once Frege replaced the mentalistic *via regia* of analyzing sensations, representations, and judgments with a semantic analysis of linguistic expressions and Wittgenstein radicalized the linguistic turn into a paradigm shift,[1] Hume and Kant's epistemological questions could have taken on a new, pragmatic significance. In the context of lived practices, of course, they then would have lost their primacy over questions in the theory of communication and action. Yet even within philosophy of language, the traditional order of explanation has persisted. As ever, theory takes precedence over practice, representation over communication; and the semantic analysis of action depends on a prior analysis of knowledge.

Still caught up in the tradition of Platonism, the philosophy of consciousness privileged the internal over the external, the private over the public, the immediacy of subjective experience over discursive mediation. Epistemology rose to the rank of a First Philosophy, while communication and action were relegated to the realm of appearances, thus retaining a derivative status. After the transition from philosophy of consciousness to philosophy of language, it seemed to make sense not to turn the hierarchy of explanatory moves upside-down, but rather to level it. After all, language is used to communicate as much as to represent, and a linguistic utterance is itself a form of action, which is used for producing interpersonal relationships.

After the linguistic turn, the relation between proposition and fact replaces the relation between representation and object. Charles Sanders Peirce already eschewed focusing too narrowly on semantics and expanded this two-place relation into a three-place relation. Thus the sign, which refers to an object and expresses a state of affairs, must be interpreted by a speaker and hearer.[2] Subsequently, speech act theory following Austin showed how, in the normal form of a speech act (Mp), the propositional component's reference to the world and to objects is interlinked with the illocutionary component's reference to other interlocutors. By creating an intersubjective relationship between speaker and hearer, the speech act simultaneously stands in an objective relation to the world. If we conceive of "communication" [*Verständigung*] as the inherent telos of language, we cannot but acknowledge the equiprimordiality of representation, communication, and action. As representation and as communicative act, a linguistic utterance points in both directions at once: toward the world and toward the addressee.

Nonetheless, even after the linguistic turn, the analytic mainstream held fast to the primacy of assertoric propositions and their representational function. The tradition of truth-conditional semantics founded by Frege, the logical empiricism of Russell and the Vienna Circle, the theories of meaning from Quine to Davidson and from Sellars to Brandom all start from the premise that the proposition or assertion is paradigmatic for linguistic analysis. Aside from the important exception of the later Wittgenstein and his unorthodox students (such as Georg Henrik von Wright),[3] analytic philosophy has meant the continuation of epistemology by other means. Questions pertaining to theories of communication, action, morality, and the law were as ever considered to be of secondary importance.

In the face of this fact, Michael Dummett explicitly raises the question of the relationship between representation and communication:

Language, it is natural to say, has two principal functions: that of an instrument of communication, and that of a vehicle of thought. We are therefore impelled to ask which of the two is primary. Is it because language is an instrument of communication that it can also serve as a vehicle of thought? Or is it, conversely, because it is a vehicle of thought, and can therefore express thoughts, that it can be used by one person to communicate his thoughts to others?[4]

For Dummett, this question is based on a false dichotomy. On the one hand, (a) the communicative function of language must not be rendered independent of its representational function since this would yield a distorted intentionalistic picture of communication. On the other hand, (b) the representational function can no more be conceived independently of the communicative function since this would mean losing sight of the epistemic conditions for understanding propositions.

(a) By asserting Kp a speaker does not merely express her intention (in Grice and Searle's sense) of making her interlocutor recognize that she takes p to be true and that she wants him to know this. Instead of her own thought p, she wants to communicate the fact *that p* to him. The speaker's illocutionary goal is that the hearer not only acknowledge her belief, but that he come to the *same* opinion, that is, to *share* that belief. But this is possible only on the basis of the intersubjective recognition of the truth claim raised on behalf of p. The speaker can realize her illocutionary goal only if the cognitive function of the speech act is also realized, that is, if the interlocutor accepts her utterance as valid. To this extent, there is an *internal* connection between successful communication and factual representation.[5]

(b) This intentionalist emancipation of the communicative function of language mirrors the truth-theoretic privileging of its cognitive function. According to this conception, we understand a sentence or proposition if we know the conditions under which it is true. However, language users do not have direct access to truth conditions not requiring interpretation. Hence Dummett insists that we must have knowledge of the conditions under which an interpreter is able to *recognize* whether the conditions that make a sentence true obtain. With this epistemic turn, understanding shifts from solipsistically accessible truth conditions to conditions under which the sentence to be interpreted can be asserted as true and thus can be justified publicly as rationally acceptable.[6] Knowing a sentence's assertibility conditions is connected to the sorts of reasons that can be cited in support of its truth. To understand an utterance is to know how one *could* use it in order to reach an understanding with someone about something. If, however, we are able to understand a sentence solely with regard to its conditions of use in rationally acceptable utterances, then there must be an *internal* connection between the representational function of language and the conditions of successful communication.[7]

It follows from (a) and (b) that the representational and communicative functions of language mutually presuppose one another, in other words, that they are equiprimordial. Although Dummett shares this view, even he follows the prevailing spirit of contemporary analytic philosophy. The purpose of his own theory of meaning is essentially to translate the classical questions of epistemology into the linguistic paradigm. In spite of Dummett's remarkable political engagement, questions of practical philosophy, in any case, recede into the background.[8] This choice of emphasis can be explained as a result of understandable reservations regarding the later Wittgenstein's rejection of theory. The latter connected the pragmatic turn away from truth-conditional semantics with a rejection of any systematic philosophy of language whatsoever. Yet a pragmatics that takes into account the linguistic structure of the lifeworld as a whole and takes the various functions of language equally into consideration need not be antitheoretical. It need neither limit itself to the piecemeal therapeutic handiwork of a linguistic phenomenology (as did Wittgenstein's followers) nor aim at the epochal transcendence of a Platonistically alienated culture (as did the followers of Heidegger).

The same primacy of theoretical questions that characterizes orthodox analytic philosophy has also made its mark on the hermeneutic branch of philosophy of language. This is surprising to the extent that hermeneutics starts from the dialogue of the interpreter with formative traditions and hence is interested in language less as a means of representation than as a vehicle of communication. Thus hermeneutics followed in the path of rhetoric since the Renaissance.

But even on this side the interest in the representational function of language has acquired priority, ever since Dilthey sought to ground the objectivity of understanding in the human sciences in their methodology. Heidegger's questioning of the existential condition of a being characterized by the distinctive feature of understanding finally brings into play a semantic interest in the linguistically articulated preunderstanding of the world as a whole. Innerworldly aspects of language use recede behind the world-disclosing function of language.

The limitation of philosophy of language begins with Frege and Russell's focus on the semantics of assertion. On the hermeneutic side, a parallel limitation takes place in the focusing on a semantics of linguistic worldviews. Such a semantics guides the preontological interpretation of the world of a given linguistic community along categorially predetermined tracks. In *Truth and Method,* Gadamer criticizes Dilthey's methodology of "understanding" in the human science from the perspective of the later Heidegger's conception of the history of being. The authentic appropriation of an authoritative tradition is supposed to depend on a prior interpretation of the world that unites the interpreter with her object *a tergo.* Apel and I have confronted this emancipation of the world-disclosing function of language with a theory of epistemic interests, which was supposed to return hermeneutics to a metaphysically abstemious role.[9] Admittedly, even *Knowledge and Human Interests* was shaped by the primacy of epistemological issues and problems.

Thus the latter work contained themes that receded into the background along the way to the *Theory of Communicative Action.*[10] *Knowledge and Human Interests* answered the basic questions of theoretical philosophy in terms of a weak naturalism and a transcendental-pragmatic epistemological realism. However, these topics have faded ever since the desideratum of an epistemic justification of a critical social theory was rendered superfluous by the attempt to formulate a direct linguistic-pragmatic justification.[11] Since then I have analyzed the pragmatic presuppositions of action aimed at reaching mutual understanding independently of the transcendental conditions of knowledge.

Yet in light of the premises of this theory of language, I now wish to return to the problems associated with a Kantian pragmatism that I had set aside. As already mentioned, formal pragmatics arose from the needs of a sociological theory of action; it was meant to elucidate the socially integrating and binding force of speech acts with which speakers raise validity claims that are subject to critique and with which they make their hearers take a rationally motivated stance. Therefore the formal-pragmatic analysis of the representational function of language remained at a relatively low level of explication. However, it can avail itself of a broader research perspective than those theories of meaning that have evolved out of Fregean truth-conditional semantics. It has the advantage of taking all functions of language equally into consideration and of placing in the right light the critical role that the second person plays in taking a stance on reciprocally raised validity claims.

II   Content and Guiding Themes

The following essays express a renewed interest in issues of a pragmatic epistemological realism that follows in the path of linguistic Kantianism.[12] While the first essay, "Hermeneutics and Analytic Philosophy," retraces how we get from hermeneutics to formal pragmatics, the second, on Kant's ideas of pure reason, is an attempt to provide a conceptual history of the genesis of the basic concepts and assumptions of formal pragmatics in the light of the Kantian doctrine of ideas. In performing speech acts, speakers trying to reach an understanding with one another must "unavoidably" undertake certain idealizations. It has been my experience that, particularly in the Anglo-American context, the pragmatic conception of these idealizations is often misunderstood. This has prompted me to offer a genealogy that draws attention to the differences between the Humean and the Kantian heritage of contemporary philosophy of language (Davidson vs. Dummett and Brandom) and incorporates formal pragmatics into the lineage of "linguistic Kantianism." In the next essay, "From Kant to Hegel: Robert Brandom's Pragmatic Philosophy of Language," I engage with the theory representing, in my view, the state of the art of pragmatic approaches in analytic philosophy of language. Brandom combines Wilfrid Sellars's inferentialist semantics step by step with a pragmatics of discourse in order to explain the objectivity of conceptual norms from the perspective of the intersubjectively shared "practice of giving and asking for reasons." In the end, Brandom is able to do justice to the intuitions underlying epistemological realism only at the price of a conceptual realism that obliterates the distinction between the intersubjectively shared lifeworld and the objective world. This assimilation of the objectivity of experience to the intersubjectivity of communication is reminiscent of an infamous Hegelian move. Thus, in the following essay, "From Kant to Hegel and Back Again," I take up the question of why and how Hegel paved the way for detranscendentalizing the knowing subject, yet then himself made the move to objective idealism. By way of a metacritical engagement with Hilary Putnam in "Norms and Values," I would like to illustrate how, even after the linguistic-pragmatic turn, one can continue to be a realist regarding questions of epistemology without assuming the burdens of moral realism. For reasons similar to Putnam's, I have given up an epistemic conception of truth and have sought to distinguish more clearly between the truth of a proposition and its rational assertibility (even under approximately ideal conditions).[13] In retrospect, I see that the discursive conception of truth is due to an overgeneralization of the special case of the validity of moral judgments and norms. A constructivist conception of the moral "ought" does require an epistemic understanding of normative rightness. But if we want to do justice to realist intuitions, the concept of propositional truth must not be assimilated to this sense of rational acceptability under approximately ideal conditions. This leads me in the following essay, "Rightness versus Truth," to a more precise differentiation between "truth" and "rightness."[14]

Kantian pragmatism—an orientation I share with Hilary Putnam[15]—relies on the transcendental fact that subjects capable of speech and action, who can be affected by reasons, can learn—and in the long run even "cannot not learn." And they learn just as much in the moral-cognitive dimension of interacting with one another as they do in the cognitive dimension of interacting with the world. By the same token, the transcendental formulation of the issue expresses the postmetaphysical awareness that even the best results of these fallible learning processes remain, in a significant sense, *our* insights. Even true assertions can realize only those ways of knowing that our sociocultural forms of life make available to us. This insight teaches us the limits of philosophical thought after metaphysics. If we abandon Hegelian versions of the philosophy of history, the relationship between theory and practice, too, is transformed, as is shown in the final essay, "The Relationship between Theory and Practice Revisited."[16] This further enjoins philosophy to respect the limits that the division of labor of a democratically constituted, complex society imposes on its legitimate public activism.

Collected essays are naturally more unwieldy than chapters of a monograph written in a single mold. Therefore I would at least like to comment in this introduction on issues that would have deserved a more systematic treatment. When I responded to critiques of *Knowledge and Human Interests* in the appendix to the paperback edition in 1973,[17] the turn toward a postempiricist philosophy of science had already been initiated by Thomas Kuhn. However, I had not yet fully realized the philosophical implications of a consistent contextualism. Only six years later Richard Rorty precipitated a pragmatic turn in epistemology,[18] in which, despite all our differences, I was able to discern some of my own intentions. Against this background, I would first like to sketch how this turn has transformed Kant's transcendental problematic (III).

This transformation particularly affects the idealist background assumptions that for Kant ensured the status of the unavoidable conditions of the possibility of cognition as rational and as atemporal. Yet if the transcendental conditions are no longer "necessary" conditions of cognition, it cannot be ruled out that they are based on an anthropocentrically contingent and perspectively curtailed view of the world. And if they have a beginning in time, the difference between the world and what is innerworldly, which is crucial for the architectonic of his theory, is blurred (IV).

The classical pragmatists already wanted to reconcile Kant with Darwin. According to G. H. Mead and John Dewey, the detranscendentalized conditions of problem-solving behavior are embodied in practices. These practices are characteristic of our sociocultural forms of life, which have evolved naturally. But then the problem has to be formulated in a way that is compatible with this naturalist perspective (V).

The ontological assumption of the genetic primacy of nature further requires an epistemologically realist assumption of a mind-independent objective world. Yet within the linguistic paradigm the classical form of realism that relies on the representational model of cognition and on the correspondence between propositions and facts is no longer viable. On the other hand, even after the linguistic-pragmatic turn, a realist approach requires a concept of reference that explains how we can refer to the same object (or objects of the same kind) under different theoretical descriptions (VI). Moreover, it requires a nonepistemic conception of truth that explains how we can preserve the difference between the truth of an assertion and justified assertibility under ideal conditions given the premise that our dealings with the world are permeated by language (VII).

In moral and legal theory, however, we must preserve an epistemic concept of normative rightness. Discourse ethics, like the Kantian tradition in general, is subject to familiar objections against ethical formalism. In the context of moral epistemology, this cannot be the subject of discussion.[19] Here I shall confine myself to a problem that becomes acute when Kantian ethics is detranscendentalized. I have in mind the question of what can provide the moral orientation for the very practice whose goal it is to determine the conditions for rational judgment formation and for the reasonableness of moral action. In conclusion I therefore revisit the topic of the relation between theory and practice once more with reference to the political uncertainties of *morally self-reflective* action. This will afford me the opportunity to engage at a metacritical level with Karl-Otto Apel's proposal on this topic (VIII).

III The Transcendental Problem—After Pragmatism

Transcendental philosophy, as the famous phrase has it, "deals not so much with objects as rather with our way of cognizing objects in general insofar as that way of cognizing is to be possible a priori."[20] It takes itself to be reconstructing the universal and necessary conditions under which something can be the object of experience and cognition. The significance of this transcendental problematic can be generalized by divorcing it from the basic mentalistic concept of self-reflection as well as from a foundationalist understanding of the conceptual pair a priori–a posteriori. After the pragmatist deflation of Kantian conceptuality, "transcendental analysis" refers to the search for presumably universal but only *de facto* unavoidable conditions that must be fulfilled in order for fundamental practices or achievements to emerge. All practices for which there are no functional equivalents because they can be substituted only by practices *of the same kind* are "foundational" in this sense.

The reflexive self-reassurance by an active subjectivity *in foro interno*, outside space and time, is replaced by the explication of a practical knowledge that makes it possible for subjects capable of speech and action to participate in these sorts of practices and to attain the corresponding accomplishments. At issue are no longer only empirical judgments, but grammatical propositions, objects of geometry, gestures, speech acts, texts, calculations, logically connected propositions, actions, social relations or interactions—in short, basic types of rule-governed behavior in general. Wittgenstein's notion of "rule-following" provides the key for the analysis of these kinds of fundamental practices or "self-substituting orders" (Luhmann). This intuitive and habitual know-how—the practical understanding of generative rules or mastery of a practice—enjoys primacy over explicit knowledge of rules. Implicit knowledge of such "skills" supports the totality of the web of basic practices and activities of a community that articulate its form of life. Because of the implicit and, in a certain sense, holistic nature of this know-how, Husserl already described the intersubjectively shared lifeworld as an unthematically concomitant "background."

The object of transcendental philosophy is thus no longer "consciousness *überhaupt*," which is without origin and forms the common core of all empirical minds. Rather, the investigation now aims to discover deep-seated structures of the background of the lifeworld. These structures are embodied in the practices and activities of subjects capable of speech and action. Transcendental philosophy seeks to discover the invariant features recurring in the historical manifold of sociocultural forms of life. The perspectives of this investigation are broadened accordingly while the transcendental approach is maintained. Because (a) the concept of experience is understood pragmatically, (b) knowledge is seen as a function of learning processes, which (c) are enriched by the entire spectrum of lifeworld practices; (d) this gives rise to an architectonic of lifeworld and objective world, which (e) corresponds to a methodological dualism of understanding [*Verstehen*] and observation.

(a) Experience, which is represented in empirical propositions, is no longer derived introspectively, by way of self-observation on the part of the knowing subject, from the subjective capacity for "sensibility." It is now analyzed from the participant perspective of an actor, in the context of confirmation where actions are guided by experience. Mentalism lived off the "Myth of the Given." After the linguistic turn, we no longer have access to an internal or external reality that is not linguistically mediated. The presumed immediacy of sense impressions no longer serves as an infallible court of appeal. Absent the possibility of a recourse to uninterpreted sense data, sense experience loses its unquestioned authority.[21] In its place, there is the authority of "second-order experience" that is possible only for an *acting* subject.

In the context of goal-oriented action, reality manifests itself differently as soon as either a habitual practice or an explicit attempt at intervention *fails,* for such failures indirectly call into question the experiential content of the belief *motivating* the action. Peirce already highlighted the epistemological significance of "success-controlled action" (Gehlen) with his "belief-doubt" model. The experience of performative failure in the face of reality, of course, can only unsettle unthematized concomitant assumptions; it cannot refute them. Controlling actions in terms of whether they are successful does not replace the authority of the senses in terms of their function to warrant truth. Nonetheless, the empirical doubts triggered by disturbances in the course of action may set in motion discourses leading to correct interpretations.

(b) This pragmatist conception of experience changes not only how we view the basis of experience, but also how we describe the phenomenon of cognition that we are trying to explain. As Popper already emphasized, the objectivity of an experience is no longer assessed in terms of how it came to be "in the mind," that is, in terms of how judgments are constructed based on sense data. Rather, creative problem solving, caused by disturbances in routine practices, is what makes us change our beliefs. These beliefs in turn are fallible and subject to confirmation. From a pragmatist point of view, "cognition" results from the intelligent processing of performatively experienced frustrations. Nor is this contradicted by the "purposeless" mode of scientific knowledge that exists owing to the institutionalization of learning as trial and error. This institutionalization is itself based on a rich set of presuppositions. Scientific learning processes can be advanced by the dynamics of *self-generated* problems only to the extent that they are uncoupled from the everyday pressures of decision making.

The phenomenon we need to explain is no longer the elementary layer of sensations organized into perceptions, on which judgments and inferences are subsequently based. Rather, epistemology must explain the deeply complex learning process that sets in when the expectations that guide our actions are problematized. This makes the totality of practices that are woven together into a form of life epistemologically relevant. On the one hand, all aspects of the lifeworld can be sucked into the pull of problematization; on the other hand, which practices contribute to the solution of any given problem differs from case to case. The epistemic dimension so permeates all nonepistemic domains of action that the transcendental formulation of the problem must extend to the supporting structures of the lifeworld as a whole.

(c) The lifeworld comprises different types of rule-governed action. Discourses and speech acts can be differentiated by whether language is being used essentially to communicate or to represent. Nonlinguistic practices, too, are characterized by the propositional structure of language, but unlike linguistic practices, they are not used in order to attain illocutionary goals. In addition, actions are either social or nonsocial. Social action consists either in norm-governed interaction between communicative actors or in attempts on the part of agents to influence one another strategically. Instrumental action is embedded in social contexts of action, but is essentially used for goal-oriented interventions in a world of causally connected things and events. These types of rule-governed *action* in turn form a mere subset of rule-governed *behavior*. This includes parlor games, which Wittgenstein used as a model for investigating how we form numerical series, geometrical constructs, grammatical expressions, logical connections, and so on. "Operations" of this sort are normally performed as part of other actions and constitute something like the infrastructure of actions at the macrolevel that "touch the world," as it were.[22] These types of rule-governed behavior can be differentiated according to the status of the rules that are embodied in such practices.

In general, an actor who obeys—or violates—a norm at least intuitively has to base her actions on the concept of a rule. As Kant already realized, an actor can conform her will only to those maxims that she *conceives* as such. But not all norms are in and of themselves conceptual norms. There is no unified "deontological" sense of normative obligation [*Verbindlichkeit*]. The rules of logic, geometry, and arithmetic, rules of physical measurement, grammar, or the pragmatics of language are used in the production and syntactic ordering of symbolic forms: signs, figures, numbers, calculi, sentences, arguments, and so on. These rules, which are in a broad sense conceptual,[23] are constitutive of certain practices. Insofar as these practices do not refer to anything external to themselves, rule violations have but internal consequences. Someone who has not mastered the rules of chess may move the figures on the board in a way that accords contingently with the rules of the game, but she is not playing chess. If we ignore or mistake the "logic" or particular meaning of such a practice, our incompetence in a sense leads us to falter on the rules themselves. But no one and no thing sanctions us—neither our own conscience, nor society, nor nature.

In contrast, social norms of action have the "deontological" force of obligating the addressee to follow the rules, though the type of sanctions varies depending on the type of rules; we may transgress moral or legal norms, violate habits or conventions, or deviate from social roles. Such norms regulate interpersonal relations among actors who communicate with one another and engage in shared practices. These practices form immediate components of the symbolic context of the lifeworld. At the same time, they dovetail with the "hardware" of our natural environment. The same calculation can be jotted down with a piece of chalk on a blackboard or with a keyboard on a computer screen. Of course this ontic relation between a practice and the material substrate that supports it is different from the semantic relation speakers establish to something in the objective world by making assertions.

(d) Practical interventions, when actors employ their knowledge of technical rules in order "to cope with reality," also requires referring to entities in a way similar to how we refer to them in speech acts. A particular kind of normativity is implicated with "technologies" in a broader sense: cognitive normativity against which the empirical content and epistemic cogency of the beliefs that are at work is assessed. Rules that govern our attempts instrumentally to intervene in or strategically to influence the course of events sometimes make us "run up against reality" because we do not master them properly or misapply them. What is more interesting, however, are cases where the technologies are misdesigned and ineffective. These kinds of mistakes ultimately belie a shortfall of reliable empirical knowledge. In this sense, the normativity of rules governing success-controlled action mirrors the validity of our knowledge about something in the objective world. Successful reference and the truth of propositions contribute to the normativity of successful coping. With respect to this relation to truth and the world, Peirce developed the view that there is a transcendental relationship between certain formal properties of instrumental action, on the one hand, and the necessary conditions of experience of objects we encounter in these performative interventions, on the other.[24]

This performatively established relation to objects that actors can affect is connected to the semantic relation to objects that interlocutors establish in asserting facts about them. In negotiating practical challenges, actors have to make the same pragmatic presupposition as language users in communicating about states of affairs. They presuppose a shared objective world as the totality of objects to be dealt with and judged. Whether they are acting instrumentally or communicatively, participants must formally presuppose one and the same world. This is what makes it possible to preserve reference and to transform practical certainties about what is "ready to hand" that have become problematic into explicit assertions about what is "present at hand." Once the transition from communicative action to discursive practice has been made, the truth claims raised in assertions can be treated hypothetically and evaluated in the light of reasons. We can learn from the performative experience of reality and its resistance to us only to the extent that we thematize the beliefs that are implicitly challenged by such experiences and learn from the objections raised by other participants in discourse. The "ascent" from action to discourse means that the full range of resources available in the lifeworld for cognitively processing problems we encounter in our practical coping with the world can be mobilized.

In both our practical and our semantic relationship to objects, we are confronted with "the" world, whereas in claiming that the statements we make about objects are true, we are confronted with the opposition of "others." The vertical view of the objective world is interconnected with the horizontal relationship among members of an intersubjectively shared lifeworld. The objectivity of the world and the intersubjectivity of communication mutually refer to one another. This changes the picture of the transcendental subject standing, as it were, opposite to objects that appear to it in a world it has constituted. Subjects engaged in their practices refer *to* something in the objective world, which they suppose as existing independently and as the same for everyone, from *within* the horizon of their lifeworld. This presupposition also gives expression to the facticity of all challenges and contingencies that simultaneously provoke and limit our routine understandings and actions.

(e) This architectonic of "lifeworld" and "objective world" goes hand in hand with a methodological dualism of understanding and observation. This dualism more or less echoes the distinction between transcendental and empirical cognition. Philosophy of consciousness altogether was dominated by the methodological distinction between first- and third-person perspectives—between a person's introspection or self-observation the object of which are her own representations, on the one hand, and a person's observation as she turns to objects themselves in an objectifying attitude, on the other. This classical distinction is replaced by a dualism between second- and third-person perspectives—between an interlocutor's interpretive achievements and an observer's perception of an object. As observers, we relate to objects in the world "from without," as it were, whereas the rule-governed practices of the lifeworld can be disclosed only to the hermeneutic understanding [*Verständnis*] of participants from within a performative attitude. The intuitive knowledge of how to follow a rule and of what it is to violate a rule is inherently normative. This cannot be captured by a notion of observation limited to empirical regularities. Furthermore, analyzing language use oriented toward reaching mutual understanding from the participant perspective provides the key to the entire web of lifeworld practices because all symbolic structures of the lifeworld are differentiated through the medium of language.

IV Two Fall-Out Problems: Endangering the Objectivity of Cognition and Blurring the Difference between the World and What Is Innerworldly

Detranscendentalization alters the very concept of the transcendental. Transcendental consciousness loses the connotations of an "otherworldly" dimension rooted in the realm of the intelligible. It has come down to Earth in the form of everyday communicative practice, which is no longer sublime. Thus, the profane lifeworld has usurped the transmundane place of the noumenal. Although pragmatism retains the transcendental framing of the issue, it defuses the tension between the transcendental and the empirical. To be sure, communicative language use still commits participants to strong idealizations. By orienting themselves to unconditional validity claims and presupposing each other's accountability, interlocutors aim beyond contingent and merely local contexts. But these counterfactual presuppositions are rooted in the facticity of everyday practices. Subjects capable of speech and action learn the practices that maintain their lifeworld and acquire the corresponding knowledge of rules in the course of their socialization. As long as communication and communicative action, which reproduce the lifeworld, are to prevail, interlocutors cannot but undertake such idealizations. Yet the social facts themselves are characterized by the dual nature of the normative terrain.

Deflating our original understanding of the transcendental has significant consequences. If transcendental rules are no longer something rational outside the world, they mutate into expressions of cultural forms of life and have a beginning in time. As a consequence, we may no longer without qualification claim "universality" and "necessity," that is, objectivity for empirical cognition the possibility of which has been established transcendentally (1). And the transcendental conditions under which we have epistemic access to the world themselves must be conceived as something *in* the world (2).

(1) M. Sacks describes the move from the detranscendentalization of Kantian idealism as a transition from the classical concept of the transcendental (T_1) to a Wittgensteinian conception of this concept (T_2):[25]

T_1: There are transcendental constraints imposed by the mind on what can count as an object in experience, such that we can know objects only in conformity with these constraints. (p. 167)

On a strong reading of the transcendental, this means that the world of objects that can be experienced *receives* its form from the structures of our mind. The weaker reading requires only that the world, insofar as we are to be able to know its objects at all, *conforms* to the structures of our mind. Given this premise, of course, we cannot know to what extent there is an ontological correspondence between the structures of the mind and the world itself. The world that is disclosed to us by the structures of our mind could be a selective and distorted segment of the world. On this weaker reading, subjective idealism could open the gate to a Kleistian skepticism:[26] We could never be certain that the transcendentally established cognition of a world that is objective "for us" is universal and necessary. This doubt is met—in accordance with Kant's "first principle"— by the strong reading, according to which the transcendental generation of the world of objects of possible experience is rooted in the world-generating spontaneity of a subjectivity without origin. This subjectivity guarantees the objectivity of possible empirical knowledge.

By making the metaphysical assumption that transcendental consciousness has intelligible status, Kantian epistemology does live up to its name: transcendental *idealism.* It is not compatible with the realist presupposition of a mind-independent world that places constraints not only on judgments of experience but also on the learning processes of the judging subjects. Sacks opposes this Kantian idealism with a Kantian pragmatism, which he gleans from Wittgenstein's *Philosophical Investigations.* Spontaneity shifts from the constitution of the world to the grammar of language games and forms of life, and this renders transcendental consciousness simultaneously social and manifold.

T_2:   Anything that is a possible object of experience is ultimately an expression of our activity—where that is taken to include human concerns, interests, actions, and beliefs. (p. 171)

Accordingly, the transcendental "constraints" that the mind imposes on the world of possible objects of experience (by T_1) are transformed into transcendental "features" of local forms of life situated in space and time. These forms of life determine the modes of possible experience by their values, interests, and forms of action. For members of a given form of life, these transcendental features retain the status of unavoidable epistemic presuppositions under which they can encounter anything in the objective world. However, the experience that is thus made possible can no longer be said to be universal or necessary. Each form of life has as its correlate an objective world that cannot be transcended from within that form of life, that is, from within its own horizon. For the transcendental features of a form of life are still embodied in types of rule-governed behavior that its members cannot intelligibly imagine to be otherwise: "they are presuppositional features relative to the world we can experience and describe, such that they cannot be established to obtain in the manner of empirical facts."[27]

The strong, idealist reading of the transcendental was supposed to allay doubts about the objectivity of cognition. Yet these doubts resurface in light of the multiplicity and contingency of world-generating grammars. The pluralism of language games, of course, does not necessarily lead to a manifold of incommensurable, mutually foreclosed linguistic universes. The detranscendentalized conception of a world-generating spontaneity is at least compatible with the expectation that we discover *universally occurring* transcendental features of how sociocultural forms of life *überhaupt* are constituted. Thus the medium that gives the lifeworld its structure—propositionally differentiated language—represents an empirically universal form of communication for which there is no alternative in any known form of life. Propositional contents can be used in reference to, yet independently of, particular contexts in a variety of illocutionary acts.[28] Much the same holds for epistemically relevant rules of success-controlled action. In the course of dealing with problematic situations, they disclose the world as a totality of objects that can be judged in terms of the various possibilities for manipulating or appropriating them for one's own purposes.

But even if we could empirically discover the *universality* of recurring forms of symbolic expression and practice, we would not be able to bestow *necessity* on a world that appears to be objective to all sociocultural forms of life. Only such necessity, however, could eradicate the suspicion of anthropocentrically generalizing from species-specific experiences. Structures of the mind that are deeply anchored in epistemological anthropology may determine the same mode of experience for all subjects capable of speech and action. But they cannot dispel skeptical doubt that the world as it is *in itself* partially eludes the horizon of "our" possible experience.

(2) The second issue concerns the peculiar status of rules that are supposed to retain the power of spontaneously generating the world even though they can no longer be said to be without origin. They are supposed to enable us to have access to the objective world, yet

they are not themselves supposed to have dropped down from the heavens but to have standing in the world. This kind of entity obviously eludes the transcendental distinction between the world and what is innerworldly that corresponds to the methodological dualism of understanding and observation. Pragmatism (Mead and Dewey), philosophical anthropology (Plessner and Gehlen), and even developmental cognitive psychology (Piaget) rely on a naturalistic explanation of instrumental practices, language use, and communicative action.[29] They link the hermeneutic access to structures of the mind that are embodied in the lifeworld with a biological explanation of their genesis. On the one hand, they analyze the knowhow of competently judging, speaking, and acting subjects. This reconstruction of the fundamental features of "our" forms of life then provides them with a perspective for deciphering type-specific environments at less complex "levels of the organic." On the other hand, this "top-down" hermeneutic of natural history has its complement in evolutionary theory, which gives a causal explanation of the genesis of the endowments and specific competencies of human organisms. However, these complementary approaches yield competing descriptions that cannot be seamlessly integrated into one another.

The description of epistemically relevant systems of rules is derived from the conceptual explication of intuitively mastered practices from the participant perspective. Even prior to the constitution of scientific object domains[30] these (weakly) transcendental rules determine how experiences in our practical engagement with things and events in the world are possible at all. This renders the task of giving an empirical explanation of how these intersubjective conditions of possible experience are established all the more paradoxical. The explanans for how the transcendental conditions are generated would itself already have to be subject to the conditions named in the explanandum. If we conceive of structures of the lifeworld, which make it possible for us to know anything in the objective world, as themselves occurring in the world, we become ensnared in the familiar aporias concerning the "thing-in-itself." Certainly, the constitution of a "nature-in-itself," on which Marx bases his reflections on the epistemic role of social labor, is no less paradoxical than that of a "thing-in-itself" (which even Kant treats as though it were something in the world when he asserts that it "affects" our senses).[31]

Marx's first step is to give the transcendental concept of cognition a materialist turn.[32] The world of the natural environment is constituted as nature that is objective "for us" by means of the same forms of social labor whereby the physical "material transformation" between society and its material substrate is accomplished. The next step is to interpret this materialist connection between knowledge and labor[33] naturalistically. At the level of sociocultural development, natural evolution is supposed simultaneously to produce "subjective nature," that is, the organic endowment of *Homo sapiens,* and the conditions under which he has cognitive access to what is to him "objective nature." In short, "nature in itself," along with "subjective nature," creates the conditions for the appearance of an "objective nature." However, if there is a rigid, that is, inescapable, correlation between objective nature and the possible forms of coping with nature that are determined by subjective nature, then the constitution of a "nature in itself" can only be the result of a metaphysical glimpse behind the stage set by the human mind.

The aporias we face as a result of detranscendentalization seem to show that the transcendental formulation of the problem cannot be separated unscathed from the assumptions of transcendental idealism. However, the paradoxical consequences result not so much from a pragmatist transformation of the transcendental approach as from the representational model of knowledge to which Kant himself subscribed. A *nonclassical* form of epistemological realism, which must be accepted in the wake of the linguistic turn, can be combined with a "weak" naturalism without relinquishing the transcendental-pragmatic approach.

V   Weak Naturalism—After Kant and Darwin

Today, the opposition between Quine's strong naturalism and Heidegger's idealism of the history of Being shows up in a variety of forms. By addressing these two predominant theoretical strategies, I would like to introduce the option of a weak naturalism that both sides ignore.

(1) The heirs of Hume are less affected than the heirs of Kant by the two problems to which the detranscendentalizing move gives rise. The unsettling questions regarding the objectivity of knowledge and the difference between the world and what is innerworldly do not even arise unless we start with the assumptions of the transcendental approach in the first place. Strong naturalism, whose paradigmatic representative has been W. V. O. Quine, allies itself with a scientific understanding of our cognitive abilities. All cognition is ultimately to be reducible to empirical processes. The transcendental architectonic drops out, as does the difference between the conditions of how the world is constituted (or of world disclosure), which call for conceptual analysis, on the one hand, and states of affairs and events in the world, which can be explained causally, on the other.[34] If we repudiate the transcendental difference between the world and what is innerworldly, then we also get rid of the assumption that is necessary for generating skepticism about a "world of appearances," which might represent a partial segment or a perspectivally distorted view of a "world in itself." And as the methodological dualism of an interpretive reconstruction of our lifeworld, on the one hand, and the explanation of processes in the objective world, on the other, dissipates, so does the paradoxical task of somehow reconciling the "internal perspective" of transcendentally conceived practices of the lifeworld with the "external perspective" of their causal genesis.

Yet the naturalist continuation of the empiricist tradition comes at a price. It requires an objectivist assimilation of our normative practices to observable events in the world. For a philosophy that relies exclusively on the means of conceptual analysis, this approach gives rise to the problem of translating the intuitive knowledge of subjects capable of speech and action into an idiom that is continuous with the theoretical idiom of the nomological empirical sciences. Quine's solution to this problem accounts for his worldwide success. After the logical positivists of the Vienna Circle had already discarded the Kantian assumption of synthetic a priori judgments, Quine went on to reject the analytic–synthetic distinction, which Carnap had retained. Together with the thesis of the indeterminacy of translation, this move leads to an epistemological holism that not only overcomes the last remnants of Fregean meaning Platonism, but also guts the very idea of meaning. Quine's critique is directed not only at the Platonist objectification of "thoughts," which Wittgenstein had already criticized by other means. Rather, the replacement of the hermeneutic notion of linguistic meaning by the behaviorist concept of stimulus meaning eliminates *all* normative connotations from the notions of language and linguistic understanding.

Wittgenstein used the concept of rule-following in order to reconstruct the normative self-understanding of competent speakers. This self-understanding now is transposed into a theoretical idiom that comprehends "radical" translation, for instance, as a processing of sense data geared toward hypothesis-formation and undertaken with an objectifying attitude. The point of this theoretical strategy is to pave the way for a strictly naturalistic understanding of one's own linguistic behavior *from within the participant perspective*. Yet the very alienating scientization of intuitive knowledge that accounts for the success of this strategy simultaneously gives rise to the Achilles' heel of strong naturalism. Subjects who are capable of speech and action and engaged in communicative practices cannot but orient their thinking and doing by norms and be affected by reasons. They cannot recognize themselves in Quinean objectifying descriptions. Strong naturalism runs aground on the cognitive dissonance between the self-understanding of competent speakers, which is easy to corroborate, and a counterintuitive, ruthlessly revisionist self-description. The latter, by denying speaker intuitions, robs philosophy of language of its only reliable evidential base.

(2) It seems that in order to do justice to the normative self-understanding of participants and to maintain a transcendental approach without retracting our move toward detranscendentalization, we cannot avoid the aporetic consequences of the latter. No doubt Heidegger's concept of the history of Being can be understood as an attempt to resolve the paradox of a world-constituting spontaneity that is itself situated in the world.

Heidegger takes the linguistic turn by reinterpreting the transcendental spontaneity constituting a world of objects of possible experience as the world-disclosing power of language.[35] Every natural language projects a categorial semantic horizon that articulates a historical linguistic community's cultural form of life and preunderstanding of the world as a whole. Hence Heidegger conceives the transcendental difference between the world and what is innerworldly as an ontological difference between Being and beings and makes the prevailing understanding of Being dependent on the a priori meaning of a given form of linguistic world disclosure. The invariant consciousness of transcendental subjects thereby is reduced to the historical transformation of "ontologies" that are grammatically inscribed in the prevailing languages at any given time. From the model of innerworldly history, the notion of the history of Being takes on the characteristics of a contingent course of events or "happening" [Geschehen] in which subjects capable of speech and action are embroiled. But it situates the "events" [Ereignisse] of epochal interpretations of the world at the transcendental level of an a priori constitution of meaning that those living in that epoch cannot escape. Subjects capable of speech and action are thus fatalistically at the mercy of the history of Being.

This concept allows Heidegger to take account of the detranscendentalization of a world-constituting spontaneity by historicizing the a priori meaning without paying the price of aporetic consequences. On the one hand, he manages to maintain the methodological distinction between ontological and ontic investigations by means of the transcendental difference between world and what is innerworldly. Thus the movement of metahistorical destinies is not at the same level as the succession of innerworldly contingencies. On the other hand, Heidegger also has an argument ready for the objectivity of knowledge. Because it is *Being itself* that metahistorically projects itself, what is revealed to subjects in the light of Being cannot come under suspicion of being a *merely subjective* segment of the Being of the whole. Whatever beings are concealed or revealed by the world-disclosure of Being are beings in themselves.

However, the price that yes- and no-saying subjects must pay for this fatalism of Being is obvious. The esoteric "remembrance" [Andenken] knows that, in the light of an "unforethinkable" destiny, it is free from the justificatory burdens of rational speech and discursive thought, and it claims to have privileged access to the truth. For the self-understanding of autonomous beings, who can be made to take rationally motivated positions, this presumption is no easier to make good on than the naturalistic leveling of our normative self-understanding.

The problems arising from a detranscendentalizing pragmatism can be unraveled in a rather different way if we disentangle the amalgam of naturalism and scientism. If we do so, it is imperative to draw the right conclusions from the rejection of the representationalist model of knowledge.

(3) For pragmatists, cognition is a process of intelligent, problemsolving behavior that makes learning processes possible, corrects errors, and defuses objections. Only if it is severed from the context of experiences connected to actions and of discursive justifications does the representational function of language suggest the misleading picture of thought representing objects or states of affairs. The "mirror of nature"—the one-to-one representation of reality—is the wrong model of knowledge[36] because the two-place relation between picture and pictured and the static relation between a proposition and a state of affairs obscures the dynamics of knowledge accumulation through problem solving and justification.

In the spatial dimension, knowledge is the result of working through experiences of frustration by coping intelligently with a risk-filled environment. In the social dimension, it is the result of justifying one's ways of solving problems against the objections of other participants in argumentation. And in the temporal dimension, it is the result of learning processes fed by the revision of one's own mistakes. If knowledge is regarded as the *function* of such a complex structure, it becomes clear how the passive moment of experiencing practical failure or success is intertwined with the *active* [*konstruktiver*] moment of projecting, interpreting, and justifying. Empirical judgments are *formed* in learning processes and *emerge from* how problems are solved. It is therefore pointless to gauge the idea of the validity of judgments by the difference between reality and appearance, between what is "in itself" and what is given "for us"—as though knowledge of something that is presumed to be immediate had to be purified of any subjective contribution and intersubjective mediation. Rather, knowledge results from the cognitive function of these contributions and mediations. From a pragmatist perspective, reality is not something to be copied; we take note of it performatively—as the totality of resistances that are processed and are to be anticipated—and it makes itself known to us solely in the constraints to which our problem-solving activities and learning processes are subject.

The representational model of knowledge, which conceives "*Darstellung*" as the representation [*Vorstellung*] of objects or the replication [*Abbildung*] of facts and "truth" as correspondence between representation and object or between proposition and fact, misses the cognitive-operational significance of "overcoming" problems and of the "success" of learning processes. What we learn from reality by actively coping with it and from objections by exchanging them in discourse precipitates into justified interpretations. To be sure, everything that is the case and can be represented in true propositions is real. But in our daily coping as well as in experiments, we rub up against constraints. Their facticity drives home the fact that objects offer resistance, which is why we presuppose the objective world as a system of possible referents—as a totality of objects, not of facts.

If we presuppose this pragmatic concept of knowledge, we can opt for a naturalism that preserves the transcendental difference between the world and what is innerworldly, in spite of detranscendentalization. This conception is based on a single metatheoretical assumption: that "our" learning processes, that are possible within the framework of sociocultural forms of life, are in a sense simply the continuation of prior "evolutionary learning processes" that in turn gave rise to our forms of life. For then the structures that form the transcendental conditions of possibility for our kinds of learning processes themselves turn out to be the result of less complex, natural learning processes—*and thereby themselves acquire a cognitive content.* The "continuation" of learning processes at a higher level, however, must be understood in the sense of a "weak" naturalism that makes no reductionistic claims. A "strongly" naturalistic explanatory strategy aims to *replace* the conceptual analysis of practices of the lifeworld with a scientific neurological or biogenetic explanation of the achievements of the human brain. In contrast, weak naturalism contents itself with the basic background assumption that the biological endowment and the cultural way of life of *Homo sapiens* have a "natural" origin and can in principle be explained in terms of evolutionary theory.

This blanket assumption of an evolutionary continuity that permeates culture, as it were, refrains from making any philosophical assumptions about the relationship of mind and body (in the sense of eliminative or reductive materialism, for example); on the contrary, it keeps us from reifying a difference between methodological approaches that are themselves ontologically neutral. As long as we cast the issue in transcendental terms, we have to distinguish sharply between the hermeneutic approach of a rational reconstruction of the structures of the lifeworld, which we undertake from the perspective of participants, and the observation-based causal analysis of how these structures naturally evolve. Only the idealistic fallacy of inferring an ontological difference between mind and body (or Being and beings) from a methodological distinction misleads us into locating the transcendental conditions of objective experience in a transmundane realm of the intelligible—or of the history of Being. Conversely, the naturalistic fallacy is but the other side of the same coin; it simply assimilates transcendental conditions to empirical conditions, without considering the aporia of self-referentiality, and projects them onto a scientifically objectified realm.

Weak naturalism neither incorporates nor subordinates the "internal perspective" of the lifeworld to the "external perspective" of the objective world. Rather, it keeps these theoretical perspectives separate, connecting them at the metatheoretical level by assuming a continuity between nature and culture. To the extent that the natural evolution of species can be conceived as the result of "problem solving"—*by analogy* to our own learning processes that are possible at the level of sociocultural development—this background assumption becomes more specific. Problem solving has led to increasingly complex stages of development with correspondingly higher levels of learning. How precisely this "analogy" is to be understood and how far this initially metaphorical phrase of "evolutionary learning" gets us are questions that cannot be decided within the framework of either of the two theories—especially since their connection is established by means of this very analogy. The vocabulary of learning, the precise meaning of which is initially determined from "our" participant perspective (and on which the concepts of learning employed in developmental psychology, for instance, are based) must not be simply reinterpreted in neo-Darwinist terms, or else weak naturalism loses its point. The interpolation of different "stages" of learning processes at different levels explains only why we can preserve the distinction between the world and what is innerworldly without having to project the contingency of what is "necessary for us" in the here-and-now of empirical processes onto the beyond of events in the history of Being. For the conception of natural evolution as a process *analogous to learning* ensures that structures that have evolved naturally and make our learning processes possible *themselves* have cognitive content. This in turn explains why the contingent circumstances of its genesis need not detract from the universality and necessity of "our" view of the objective world.[37]

If natural evolution is viewed in terms of increasing problem-solving capacities, emergent properties acquire a cognitive value that from "our" point of view is represented as an accrual of knowledge. This is also true for emergent properties that characterize sociocultural forms of life as such. Even the transcendental structures that make possible everyday experiences with and statements about what is—for us—an objective world can then be understood as the result of cognitively significant developmental processes. In accordance with our naturalistic background assumption, whatever in "our" epistemic situation proves to be an unavoidable presupposition such that any attempt to disprove or revise it seems meaningless is taken to have been generated by contingent circumstances. But if such transcendental conditions (in the weak sense) arose from cognitively significant processes of adaptation, constitution, and selection (or may be thought to have thus arisen), then the contingency of our epistemic horizon, which is necessary or, in any event, inescapable "for us," is no longer connected to the modality of a contingent process that would be cognitively neutral. The learning analogy, which we apply to developments that are governed by mutation, selection, and stabilization, portrays the endowment of the human mind as the intelligent solution to problems that itself developed under the constraints of reality. This perspective pulls the rug out from under the very idea that worldviews are species-relative.

VI Realism without Representation

(1) Kantian pragmatism is the response to an epistemologically troubling implication of the linguistic turn. Contrary to the assumptions of mentalism, our cognitive ability can no longer be analyzed independently of our linguistic ability and our ability to act, because as knowing subjects we are always already within the horizon of the practices of our lifeworld. For us, language and reality inextricably permeate one another. All experience is linguistically saturated such that no grasp of reality is possible that is not filtered through language. This insight constitutes a strong motivation for attributing the kind of transcendental role to the intersubjective conditions of linguistic interpretation and communication that Kant reserved for the necessary subjective conditions of objective experience. In place of the transcendental subjectivity of consciousness we now find the detranscendentalized intersubjectivity of the lifeworld.

Thus far, the order of explanation of transcendental philosophy beginning with reflection on one's own achievements is unaffected by the linguistic turn. Wittgenstein's pluralism of language games even suggests a transcendental-idealist reading.[38] But once we combine transcendental pragmatism with weak naturalism, the genetic primacy of nature over culture calls for the adoption of epistemic realism. Only the realist presupposition of an intersubjectively accessible objective world can reconcile the *epistemic* priority of the linguistically articulated horizon of the lifeworld, which we cannot transcend, with the *ontological* priority of a language-independent reality, which imposes constraints on our practices. The presupposition of a "mind-independent" world that is "older" than human beings can of course be interpreted in different ways.

The medieval debate about the problem of universals, which was still very much on Peirce's mind,[39] also left its mark on competing understandings of the concept of the world after the linguistic turn. If the "world" that is presupposed according to formal pragmatics is all that is the case—"the totality of facts, not of things"[40]—then abstract entities such as propositional contents or propositions must also be taken to be "something in the world." Contrary to this conceptual-realist assumption of a world that is "in itself" propositionally structured, nominalism conceives the world as the totality of spatiotemporally individuated "objects" about which we can state facts. *Prima facie* the nominalist conception is supported by the grammatical evidence that we cannot locate facts, in contrast to things and events, as something existing or occurring in the world.[41] Caesar's murder is a datable *event* in the world. We can make the statement that Caesar was murdered more complete by adding the date in question, but the circumstance thus described is, if the statement is true, a *fact* that does not as such occur in the world. Whether we conceive the world as consisting of things or of propositions is a fundamental conceptual decision that has significant implications for ontology, epistemology, and the corresponding concepts of truth and reference. Here I shall confine myself to two remarks.

(a) From an ontological point of view, nominalism is metaphysically less suspect than conceptual realism. A sufficiently abstract conception of objects as well as of what we mean by their *extralinguistic* existence can be explicated in terms of how singular terms (and existential quantifiers) are used. In contrast, the obtaining of states of affairs can be explicated only in terms of the assertoric mode of declarative sentences, that is, by appealing to the truth of sentences that must be established or challenged *intralinguistically*, as it were, by means of other sentences. In referring to objects, the "obtaining" of facts certainly points beyond the language of statements of fact. Yet if facts have but a "veritative being,"[42] which is to be distinguished from the "existence" of objects, then they do not obtain independently of the language in which the propositions in question are stated. For the critique of metaphysics, the very assumption that the world is propositionally articulated hence triggers the suspicion that conceptual realism transgresses the bounds of what the philosophy of language is able to establish.

We always already know how to behave in accordance with rules, and this practice bespeaks a familiarity with the "existing universalities" of a lifeworld that is normatively structured by rules from the outset. To that extent, participation in these practices easily gives rise to a conceptual-realist view. However, this conceptual realism takes the form of Platonism only if it is projected beyond the horizon of the linguistically structured lifeworld onto the constitution of the objective world itself.

(b) The extension of *linguistic* conceptual realism to the world itself also brings back—albeit in a postmentalist Fregean version—the mirror-model of knowledge that pragmatism rejected for good reasons. From an epistemological point of view, the assumption of a world whose structure is homologous with the propositional structure of language has implications for the concept and function of experience. For it means that experience functions as the medium for a kind of transformative osmosis of existing states of affairs into the propositional contents that correspond to them. Conceptual realism imposes on experience the function of taking in facts and making them present to the senses—or intellectually intuiting them.[43] However, this contemplative notion of experience eliminates any room for sociated subjects to contribute *constitutively* to successful problem solving and learning from within their lifeworld by coping intelligently with a risk-filled and frustrating reality. If experience is a medium through which existing states of affairs are replicated, then the objectivity of knowledge requires the traceless elimination of all active constituting elements. However, it is only the interpenetration of constituting activity and experience that can make sense of our fallibilism. Only the constitutive contribution of our faculties to knowledge accounts for why the increasing flood of knowledge must be channeled through the floodgates of the continual revision of existing knowledge and why even well-grounded beliefs can be false. Against the background of expectations about how we act, sensory contact with objects in the world provides *stimulating* points of reference for interpolating facts. We must not confuse the information we acquire through this contact with the world, and which takes linguistic form, with its source, that is, with what we experience.

The two arguments presented in (a) and (b) suggest an "ontological division of labor." The basic concepts of realism and nominalism reflect the methodological difference between a participant's hermeneutic access to the intersubjectively shared lifeworld, on the one hand, and the objectivating attitude of a hypothesis-testing observer interacting with what she encounters in the world, on the other. Linguistic conceptual realism is tailored to a lifeworld in the practices of which we participate and the horizon of which we cannot transgress. By contrast, the nominalist conception of the world takes account of the insight that we must not reify the structure of propositions we use to describe something in the world into the structure of what there is. At the same time, conceptualizing the world as a "totality of things, not of facts" explains the connection between language and world. The concept of "reference" must clarify how the ontological primacy of a nominalistically conceived objective world can be reconciled with the epistemic primacy of a linguistically articulated lifeworld. For the epistemic primacy must not consume the ontological, if we are to comprehend the transcendental fact of learning in realist terms.

(2) On the one hand, linguistic practice itself must make it possible to refer to language-independent objects about which we assert something. On the other hand, the pragmatic presupposition of an objective world must be but a *formal anticipation* if it is to ensure that any subject whatever—rather than just a given community of speakers at a given time—be able to refer to a common system of possible referents and to identify independently existing objects in space and time. Hilary Putnam has dealt with the question of how it is possible for learning processes to traverse the bounds of different time periods and forms of life specifically in terms of the sameness of objective reference—a notion that is no less important in science than in everyday usage.[44] If an interpretation that was rationally acceptable under certain epistemic conditions is to be recognizable as an error in a different epistemic context, then the phenomenon to be explained must be preserved in switching from one interpretation to the other. Reference to the *same* object must remain constant even under *different* descriptions.

In everyday communication, laypersons and experts are able to communicate effortlessly about the same objects despite their very different theoretical backgrounds. Within a heterogeneously constituted community where knowledge is unequally distributed among laypersons and experts, there is a "linguistic division of labor" at work that belies the incommensurability of their more or less perspicacious background understanding.[45] In scientific practice, the problem of reference becomes acute when we ask how epistemic progress is possible across theoretical paradigm shifts, for this requires that basic concepts of one theory must be reinterpreted at a deeper level, as it were, within the framework of the other theory, while preserving sameness of reference. In keeping with "pragmatic realism," Putnam develops a solution that fits well with some of my own reflections here.[46]

He, too, takes as his starting point the idea that the gaps between different paradigms or frameworks are bridged by a shared pragmatic presupposition. The presupposition of a world of objects that exist independently of our descriptions and are nomologically connected plays the role of a synthetic a priori for inductive scientific practice and indeed for any empirical theorizing. Given this premise, an interaction can emerge between world-disclosing basic theoretical concepts, on the one hand, and learning processes within a thus preinterpreted world, on the other. This interaction is circular, yet nonetheless advances our knowledge. The theoretical paradigm has a transcendental function inasmuch as it is what makes it possible for learning processes to take a particular direction. On the other hand, it remains fundamentally fallible inasmuch as the revisionary power of learning processes can retroactively necessitate a reinterpretation of the basic concepts. Putnam shows how this is possible with his analysis of natural kind terms like "gold," "water," and "heat," whose everyday use anticipates their scientific conceptualization.

Such expressions have multiple connotations or meaning stereotypes that, in any given context, selectively though by no means exhaustively serve to identify what we have before us as gold, water, or heat. Any current reference stands under the proviso that the same mapping could be undertaken in a different epistemic situation, under the guidance of a different stereotype, and using a different procedure. The presence of alternative possibilities expresses the realist intuition that we refer *provisionally* to the extension of a concept and that this extension is supposed to be language-independent.[47] The extension of the concept, which guides the reference, is assumed to be invariant. At no time must this extension be reduced to a set of criteria that determine reference if an empirically grounded reinterpretation of natural kind terms, whose reference remains constant, is to be possible. Putnam explains how this is possible in terms of the dual descriptive-referential role of indexicals. For even though they may initially have been used as denotations, the same stereotypes can in other epistemic contexts be used predicatively as *descriptions* of the same, but differently identified, objects in order to test the adequacy of the conceptual determination and, if necessary, to revise it.

This grammatical role switch of course is viciously circular and fails to lead to an expansion of knowledge if the indexical use of the denoting phrase is already *fully* determined a priori by the sense [*Sinn*] of the corresponding description. To avoid this, the various ways of referring to the same objects from different perspectives and by different procedures must have a common source in practice. As we have seen, linguistic communication and purposive activity are linked in that both formally presuppose an objective world. Speakers and actors communicate with one another and intervene in the same objective world. Speakers *qua* actors are always already in contact with objects they encounter in their everyday practice. The semantic relations that participants in communication explicitly establish in making their assertions are rooted in practices. They are secured performatively even if the semantic content of denotations that have worked up until now becomes problematic. This primacy of performatively securing semantic relations remains intact even if everyday practice differentiates increasingly demanding or specialized measurement procedures or mapping rules.

Putnam's theory of reference explains how we can *improve* the conceptual determination of an object while keeping reference constant. Here linguistic knowledge, which allows us to see the world in a certain way, changes in response to increased empirical knowledge. This can happen only if it is possible to refer to the same object under different theoretical descriptions. However, even if competing statements preserve reference across theories, this does not yet explain which of these statements is true. The truth of descriptive statements can be justified only by means of other statements, the truth of empirical beliefs only by means of other beliefs. "Satisfaction" of the truth conditions of an empirical proposition cannot be reduced to "satisfaction" of conditions of successful reference. Independently of the question of preserving reference, we thus face the further problem of how we can preserve a nonepistemic conception of truth even though we have epistemic access only to the truth conditions of propositions—an access mediated by reasons.

VII Truth and Justification

The reality facing our propositions is not "naked," but is itself already permeated by language. The experience against which we check our assumptions is linguistically structured and embedded in contexts of action. As soon as we reflect on a loss of naive certainties, we no longer face a set of basic propositions that are "self-legitimating." That is, there are no indubitable "starting points" beyond the bounds of language, no experiences that can be taken for granted within the bounds of reasons. The semantic-deductive concept of justification does not extend far enough; the chains of justifications lead us back to the contexts from which they originate. It seems that the truth of one proposition can be warranted only by its coherence with other, already accepted propositions. Yet neither the assumption of epistemological realism, nor the power of learning processes to revise from within the context in which they arise, nor the universalist import of context-transcendent claims to truth can be reconciled with a thoroughgoing contextualism.[48]

The attempt to combine the language-transcendent understanding of reference with a language-immanent understanding of truth as ideal assertibility promised a way out of this dilemma. On this view, a statement is true if and only if, under the rigorous pragmatic presuppositions of rational discourse, it is able to withstand *all* efforts to invalidate it, that is, if and only if it can be justified in an ideal epistemic situation. Inspired by C. S. Peirce's famous suggestion, K.-O. Apel, H. Putnam, and I have all at one time or another defended some version of such a discursive concept of truth.[49]

For my part, I initially determined the meaning of truth procedurally, that is, as confirmation under the normatively rigorous conditions of the practice of argumentation. This practice is based on the idealizing presuppositions (a) of public debate and complete inclusion of all those affected; (b) of equal distribution of the right to communicate; (c) of a nonviolent context in which only the unforced force of the better argument holds sway; and (d) of the sincerity of how all those affected express themselves. The discursive concept of truth was on the one hand supposed to take account of the fact that a statement's truth—absent the possibility of direct access to uninterpreted truth conditions—cannot be assessed in terms of "decisive evidence," but only in terms of justificatory, albeit never definitively "compelling," reasons.[50] On the other hand, the idealization of certain features of the form and process of the practice of argumentation was to characterize a procedure that would do justice to the context-transcendence of the truth claim raised by a speaker in a statement by rationally taking into account *all* relevant voices, topics, and contributions.

The epistemic conception of truth transforms the (two-place) validity [*Gültigkeit*] of the proposition p into the (three-place) validity [*Geltung*] "for us" or acceptance "by us"—the ideal audience (Perelmann) that must be able to justify the claim to truth raised on behalf of p if indeed this claim is justified. Only the ideal extension of the circle of addressees can counteract the particularism inherent in the reference to the first-person plural. What is at issue here is not expanding the audience of possible participants in argumentation in the social dimension, but an idealization of its achievements in time and space. For the conceptual connection between validity [*Gültigkeit*] and the proven or acknowledged validity of p (its social force [*Geltung*] "for us") points to "us" as potential participants in ideal processes of justification.[51]

The procedural conception of truth as discursive redemption of truth claims is counterintuitive to the extent that truth is obviously no "success concept." To be sure, for us there is an unavoidable epistemological connection between truth and justification as long as we are at the level of discourse. But I have in the meantime become convinced (among other things, by discussions with Albrecht Wellmer and Cristina Lafont) that this does not amount to a conceptual connection between truth and rational assertibility under ideal conditions. Otherwise we could not take truth to be a property of propositions that they "cannot lose." Even the arguments that here and now irresistibly convince us of the truth of p can turn out to be false in a different epistemic context. Pragmatically "irresistible" reasons are not "compelling" reasons in the sense of logical validity. The *cautionary use* of the truth predicate—no matter how well justified p may be, it could nonetheless turn out to be false—can be understood as the grammatical expression of a fallibility that we often experience ourselves while arguing and observe in others when looking back at the course of past arguments in history.

Either the normative content of the pragmatic presuppositions of rational discourse is insufficient to rule out the fallibility of a consensus discursively attained under approximately ideal conditions. Or the ideal conditions of rational assertibility that are sufficient for this lose the power of regulative ideals to guide behavior because they cannot even approximately be met by subjects capable of speech and action as we know them.[52] These objections have prompted me to revise the discursive conception of rational acceptability by *relating* it to a pragmatically conceived, nonepistemic concept of truth, but without thereby assimilating "truth" to "ideal assertibility."

Despite this revision, the concept of rational discourse retains its status as a privileged form of communication that forces those participating in it to continue decentering their cognitive perspectives. The normatively exacting and unavoidable communicative presuppositions of the practice of argumentation now as then imply that impartial judgment formation is structurally necessary. Argumentation remains the only *available* medium of ascertaining truth since truth claims that have been problematized cannot be tested in any other way. There is no unmediated, discursively unfiltered access to the truth conditions of empirical beliefs. After all, only the truth of unsettled beliefs is subject to question—beliefs that have been roused from the unquestioned mode of functioning practical certainties. Although we cannot sever the connection of truth and justification, this *epistemically unavoidable* connection must not be turned into a *conceptually inseparable* connection in the form of an epistemic concept of truth.

The practices of the lifeworld are supported by a consciousness of certainty that in the course of action leaves no room for doubts about truth. Problem-solving behavior processes frustrations that occur against the background of stable expectations, that is, in the context of a huge body of beliefs that are naively taken to be true. Actors rely on certainties of action in their practical dealings with an objective world, which they presuppose to be independent and the same for everyone. And these certainties in turn imply that beliefs that guide actions are taken to be true absolutely. We don't walk onto any bridge whose stability we doubt. To the realism of everyday practice, there corresponds a concept of unconditional truth, of truth that is not epistemically indexed—though of course this concept is but implicit in practice. In general, the reliability of expectations that are subjectively immune to frustration must not be consciously placed under some kind of fallibilist proviso in the course of action. From the perspective of the routines of the lifeworld, the truth of propositions becomes a topic of discussion only when practices fail and contradictions arise. As a result, what has hitherto been taken for granted and thus accepted as valid comes to be seen as merely "presumed truths," that is, as fundamentally problematic truth *claims*. As such, they become thematized if a proponent wagers against an opponent, as it were, that she can justify a proposition that is presented as hypothetically valid. Only once they make the transition from action to discourse do participants take a reflective attitude and dispute the now thematized truth of controversial propositions in the light of reasons for and against it.

The stratification of the lifeworld into action and discourse sheds light on the different roles played by the concept of truth in the two domains. Beliefs that are implicitly held to be true in success-controlled action and truth claims implicitly made in communicative action correspond to the presupposition of an objective world of things that are dealt with and judged. Facts are asserted of objects *themselves*. This nonepistemic concept of truth, which manifests itself only operatively, that is, unthematically, in action, provides a justification-transcendent point of reference for discursively thematized truth claims. It is the goal of justifications to discover a truth that exceeds all justifications. This transcending relation guarantees the difference between truth and rational acceptability, but puts the participants in discourse in a paradoxical position. On the one hand, they are able to vindicate controversial truth claims only thanks to the convincing power of good reasons. On the other hand, even the best reasons are under the proviso of fallibility so that precisely at the point where the truth and falsity of propositions is the only issue, the gap between rational acceptability and truth cannot be bridged.

Yet this raises the question why a discursively reached agreement among participants in argumentation should authorize one to accept the convincingly *justified* claim that p is true instead of the *truth* of p in the first place. The pragmatist response I have developed in the course of my debate with Richard Rorty takes as its starting point the idea that discourses *remain* embedded in the context of lifeworld practices because it is their function to reestablish a partially disrupted background understanding. In a sense, the function of argumentation is to dispose of failing practices and unsettled practical certainties. This is how I wanted to explain why it is not reasonable for participants in argumentation to continue to maintain the reflective attitude they adopt temporarily *in their role as actors* once all objections have been exhausted and they have convinced themselves that a truth claim is justified. Instead, they ought to take the successful deproblematization of questions of truth as a license for returning to their naive coping with the world.

However, this is a functional explanation that presupposes what needs to be explained, namely, the rational basis for switching from the perspective of discourse to that of action. But for a good justification of p to be sufficient for accepting p as true, even though "truth" must not be identified with "rational acceptability," the kinds of reasons that authorize such a transition must *already* make sense *to the participants in discourse themselves.* They must not merely bring to light a latent motive that can be attributed to actors because they are always already under pressure to act. It is not that those involved, as participants in argumentation, that is, in a discursive context, could regain this consciousness of infallibility that supports the routine practices of the lifeworld. But they are all the better able to convince themselves of the truth of empirical beliefs the more clearly the reasons establish an internal connection between having acceptable beliefs and rationally acquiring these beliefs. This idea has been developed by L. Wingert in connection with E. Gettier's analysis of knowledge.[53]

Traditionally, there are three conditions that must be met for attributing to S the knowledge that p: p must be true; S must believe that p; and S must be able to justify her belief that p. These are necessary but not sufficient conditions. Ad hoc reasons whereby S may be able to explain why she believes that p will not do for showing the presumed true belief to be knowledge. Only reasons whereby S *learned* that p create an *evident genealogical* connection between S's knowledge and the rational acquisition of this knowledge. Only reasons *based on which S* could *recognize* that p are an indication of S's having learned from the world. Wingert calls a justification *constructive* if it operates with the sorts of reasons that can prove a knowledge claim to be the result of a learning process, no matter how fallible that process may be. Reasons based on which S claims to know that p draw their special authority from the fact that they can be understood as reasons that have involved a learning subject "in the world itself."

Wingert's argument is persuasive and helps to bridge, albeit not close, the gap between truth and justification by examining processes of justification. For the concept of learning produces the legitimating connection between knowledge and rational knowledge acquisition for participants in argumentation. But it does not endow their discursively justified beliefs with the infallibility of certainties of action. Insofar as knowledge is justified based on a learning process that overcomes previous errors but does not protect from future ones, any current state of knowledge remains relative to the best possible epistemic situation at the time. Even the agreement reached by way of a "constructive" justification that convincingly terminates a discourse for the time being yields knowledge that is fallible and subject to improvement. At least those involved are in a position to know this to be the case *in their role as participants in discourse*. Actors capable of dealing with the world feed on their certainties of action. But for subjects who reflectively ascertain their

knowledge in the context of discourses, a proposition's being true
and its fallibility are two sides of the same coin.

VIII Progress in Legal Discourse

The epistemic concept of truth uncoupled the validity of descriptive
statements from the notion of a correspondence between proposition and fact. This was a profitable move for the cognitive conception of morality inasmuch as talk of "moral truth" no longer had to
be saddled with the problem of how to represent moral facts. If the
illocutionary meaning of affirming propositions is no longer connected with the ontological meaning of the existence of facts, moral
cognitivism no longer needs to pay the counterintuitive price of
moral realism, which turns attractive values and binding norms into
knowable facts. But now the question arises whether the reasons that
make us give up the epistemic concept of truth also have implications for the concept of normative rightness.

In the present context I need not enter into issues concerning the
foundation of discourse ethics. What is of interest here is solely that
a cognitivist but nonrealist conception of morality still requires an
epistemic concept of "moral truth" or rightness. The validity of a
norm *consists* in its discursively demonstrable worthiness of recognition. A valid norm deserves to be recognized because and insofar as
it would be accepted, that is, recognized as valid under (approximately) ideal conditions of justification. The revised concept of
truth leaves intact the rationalizing power of a public, inclusive, nonviolent, and decentralizing form of argumentation among equals.
But it connects the result of a successful justification with something
in the objective world. The rightness of moral judgments and norms
lacks such a justification-transcendent point of reference. The concept of "normative rightness" can be reduced without remainder to
rational justification under ideal conditions. It lacks the ontological
connotation of reference to things about which we state facts.

Instead of the resistance of objects, which we run up against in the
lifeworld, here we have the opposition of other social actors whose
value orientations conflict with ours. This objectivity of other minds
is in a sense made of softer stuff than the objectivity of a world that

can sometimes take us by surprise. If moral claims to validity nonetheless owe their binding force to something unconditional and *analogous to truth,* then the orientation toward ever increasing inclusiveness of other claims and persons must somehow compensate for the missing reference to the objective world. We project this ideal, expanded social world of legitimately regulated interpersonal relationships from a moral point of view. In fact, this point of view can function as the equivalent of the assumption of an objective world because it is rooted in pragmatic presuppositions of argumentative practice that are equally not up to us.[54]

Using the nonepistemic concept of truth as a foil, the epistemic concept of rightness puts the constructivist move of discourse ethics in the right light. Subjects capable of speech and action judge the actions and conflicts in question with regard to a universe of well-ordered interpersonal relationships that is to be realized and that they themselves *project.* To be sure, they engage in argument from a moral point of view that is not at their disposal *qua* participants in discourse, and which to that extent *constrains* their justificatory practices. It is not up to them how they construe "the kingdom of ends," but they project it as a universe the realization of which is up to them. The meaning of normative rightness has no ontological connotations because moral judgments are to accord with a social world that is, although not freely chosen, nonetheless ideally projected. Without the contribution of morally acting subjects, it cannot become actual.

Certainly after the detranscendentalization of the free will of rational beings, this constructivism is connected with the problems of self-referential moral action developed by Hegel in *The Phenomenology of Spirit* in his discussion of the French Revolution. Hegel, who attributes the actualization of reason to Absolute Spirit, pursues the aporias of revolutionaries who, like Robespierre, acted with moral intent.[55] I shall have to return to this issue since the deflationist conception of the relationship between theory and practice that I present in the final essay[56] will otherwise remain unintelligible.

Deontology inverts the order of explanation we find in emotivism, virtue ethics, or utilitarianism. It does not appeal to the subjective standpoint of the agent—neither to feelings of empathy or

sympathy, nor to the guidance of one's conception of the Good, nor
to the calculus of anticipated utility or harm. Rather, it accounts for
moral action from the objective standpoint of binding norms that affect the rational will of free subjects via good reasons and constrain
it in reasonable fashion. Kant's profound notion of autonomy connects moral insight into what is good for all, so to speak, with a notion of freedom that expresses itself in one's obedience to
self-imposed laws alone. This does not yet make the eternally valid
moral laws the result of a legislation that could be represented as a
process in time. In the atemporal noumenal "kingdom of ends," the
prevailing order of the law coincides with rational acts of legislation.
The empirical self needs only to make sure which laws it has given
itself *qua* rational self.

Only by being detranscendentalized does the metaphor of "legislation" take on something of the original political meaning of the
process of legislation—of the construction of a legal order extending
through time. Even given an unchangeable moral point of view, this
means that when new issues arise, new norms must be developed and
justified in light of new challenges of history. This is illustrated today
in the area of bioethics, for example. This variability is handled in part
by distinguishing questions of justification from questions of application,[57] in part by forcing the resumption of discourses of justification if
the problems of application prove to be recalcitrant. However, this
does not affect the deontological account, according to which moral
action is justified based on objectively valid norms rather than on
subjective practical orientations. Only constructivism introduces
a teleology that is not straightforwardly compatible with a deontological conception of morality. Constructivism results from the
discourse-ethical shift from the rational activity of an isolated subject
to participation in an intersubjective discursive practice.

As long as a person who is acting morally and making moral judgments understands herself to be a member of a transparent kingdom
of rational beings, she need look neither left nor right. But once transcendental necessitation enters the communicative infrastructure of
concrete forms of life, we are no longer dealing with pure rational
beings, but with people made of flesh and blood interacting with
one another. As soon as free will loses its purely rational character,

sociated individuals encounter one another in social space and historical time. They have to reach an understanding with one another about what they are morally obligated to do, and they have to obey intersubjectively recognized norms together. In the imperfect conditions of the real world, however, they cannot be sure (a) that the pragmatic presuppositions of rational discourse, which are necessary for reaching an understanding, are always met, and (b) that all participants, even when they agree, actually comply with the norms recognized to be valid.

First, there is the question of whether discourses are *accessible*. Unfavorable circumstances, missing motives, insufficient competencies all impede participation in practical discourses deserving of the name, especially in conflicts most in need of nonviolent resolution. To be sure, there is rarely serious disagreement about the core of moral edicts; but the more complex societies become, the more often there are unusual issues and unsurveyable situations that require new regulations or raise difficult problems of application. In societies where there is a moral division of labor, it is by no means clear how concrete duties are to be distributed (to what extent and to whom). But even in modern societies, inclusive, uncoerced and rational forms of deliberation, where the demand for moral clarification can be taken care of discursively, are unlikely. Second, there is the question of whether the moral demands that are made are *reasonable*. Even on the assumption that rational judgment-formation leads to broad cognitive consensus, it remains an open question whether cultural traditions and processes of socialization, habits and institutions, that is, whether "the mores" [*die Sitten*] provide the required motivations. Unless valid norms are turned into a universal practice, an essential condition for justifying them as morally binding remains unfulfilled. This does not undermine their validity, but it does mean that there are then normative grounds on which failure to obey them can be excused.

These two difficulties that arise in the wake of detranscendentalizing the kingdom of ends can be met by complementing morality with the force of the rule of law. In functionally significant domains, discourses of justification and application require binding institutionalization no less than compliance with warranted norms itself

does. Because positive law presents itself as the appropriate medium
for such an institutionalization in modern societies, the democratic
state today provides the legal-political framework for the core of rational morality—a core that can and needs to be institutionalized.
Karl-Otto Apel also takes it that "the demand to solve all morally significant conflicts of interest by means of practical discourses about
validity claims, in which violent strategic practices are neutralized,
can be realized approximately only if a constitutional state is established that has a monopoly on violence and can thus effectively relieve its citizens from the burden of having to fight for their justified
interests on their own."[58]

This move brings us to the genuinely troubling problem of
morally self-regarding action, a problem that goes to the very heart
of deontology. What are the moral standards for a practice whose
goal is the legal institutionalization of the presuppositions of moral
action that can be reasonably expected of agents? Is there something like a metamorality of action whose goal it is to fulfill the necessary institutional conditions for moral judgment formation and
moral action? Apel argues for extending the discourse principle
along the lines of an "ethics of responsibility." Here, the term does
not refer to taking into account the consequences of one's actions.
The latter would be deontologically beyond reproach; as I have suggested, it is already built into the formulation of the principle of universalization[59] and plays an important role in the application of
norms.[60] Rather, Apel has in mind the process of *establishing* conditions that make it possible to enter into practical discourses and
make it reasonable to act morally. Apel introduces a basic norm of
co-responsibility that makes it a duty *for every political actor* to act so as
to promote progressive institutionalization of "the nonviolent practice of moral rationality," all the while taking into consideration
what is reasonable given legitimate interests in self-determination.

Apel himself recognizes that the "moral responsibility for institution-
alizing law and morality" privileges a certain goal and cannot itself be
justified as a universal norm or in light of norms already recognized
to be valid. "Complementing" the principle of universalization in
the way he suggests is a teleological move and thus a breach of
the bounds of deontology. Action the goal of which is to realize

conditions under which morally justified action would be universally possible and reasonable cannot itself be fully subject to the standards of this morality. If there are standards for this, they would have to be antecedent to a deontologically conceived morality because they are supposed to legitimize prudential compromises between the moral end and the strategic choice of means. Such standards can at best be justified by appeal to figures in the history of philosophy who transfer the responsibility for the consequences of actions from political actors to world history. Yet Apel rejects this kind of maneuver to ease his burden of argument.

With or without the sanction of the history of philosophy, every morally self-regarding action ensnares those involved in aporias. Either the moral end sanctifies morally dubious means, or the legitimate weighing of moral demands against strategic considerations cannot appeal to any supermoral standards for justifying exceptions from morality. This dilemma led Hegel to the conclusion that abstract morality must not have the last word.[61] However, unless we believe in the progress of Absolute Spirit, we cannot rely on the concrete ethical life of existing institutions and prevailing traditions, either.

Constructivism replaces the static eternal validity of natural law with a dynamic, prudential, and, at the same time, morally insightful process of legislation. Taking this into account gives rise to a different picture that at least defuses the aporias. Obeying justified moral norms that are applied in particular contexts is the wrong model for analyzing political action within the framework of constitutional democracies. Although such action takes place in *existing* institutions, it can be understood as an element of a long-term constitutional process. Unlike morality, the law has to bridge the gap between norm and reality normatively by means of legislation. This holds not only for the legal enforcement of valid norms, but also for the very process whereby norms are produced. The egalitarian universalism of the law of a democratic constitutional state gives rise to a "dialectic between equality in law and in fact" (Robert Alexy). This dialectic does not allow the legal system to come to rest and destroys any appearance of staticity.[62]

A formally equal distribution of rights alone cannot guarantee equal private and public autonomy for all citizens. Materially conceived "equal rights"—equality in terms of the content of rights—requires that everyone in fact has equal opportunity to exercise their equally distributed rights. Equal rights must have "equal value" for legal persons finding themselves in quite different situations through no merit or fault of their own. In this connection, John Rawls talks about the "*fair value* of equal rights." However, the distribution of situations and opportunities in life (within a population as well as across generations) usually changes as a result of structural transformations in society for which individuals are not responsible. If only for this reason, citizens of constitutional democracies have to understand their constitution as a constitutional *project* that requires a continuing realization. The dialectic between equality in both law and fact accounts for the "principle of exhaustion" according to which the existing constitution of a democratic state simultaneously implies the injunction to keep exhausting the normative content of its principles under changing historical conditions.

However, since this goal of constitutional politics is legitimated by the basic norms of the constitution itself, such a long-term reformist practice fits well with a deontological conception of the law and the constitution. The political realization of a system of rights is a practice that is undertaken in accordance with and along the lines of already existing systems of rights. Constitutional norms themselves determine the procedure according to which they become "concrete" in light of changing circumstances. This proceduralist understanding of the constitution allows for a conception of the troublesome business of how norms are "realized" as simply a "concretization." Seen as input to the dynamic of constitutionally institutionalized, constitutional processes, the ends of a practice aimed at the "actualization of reason" no longer float about in a moral-legal vacuum. In its reformist-domesticated form, teleology is internalized into the process of realizing the constitutional state and is thus *subordinated* to the normativity of the constitution.

This subordination of teleology of course does not entirely solve the problem of morally self-regarding action but pushes it off to the gray areas of those national and international systems that are democratically constituted pretty much only on paper. Though even undeniably democratic states are involved in the continuing process of realizing the fundamental principles of their constitutions, this does not convey legitimacy on regimes that obviously only pay lip service to human rights. Only regimes that, by means of appropriate policies, clearly aim at reducing the gap between purported constitutional norms and a constitutional reality that falls short of these norms can demand loyalty from their citizens. Since the end of World War II, we have been in a chronic state of an underinstitutionalized cosmopolitan global order at the international level. The transition from classic national law [*Völkerrecht*] to establishing a cosmopolitan law creates the kinds of gray areas of legitimacy that embarrass even learned legal experts—no less, incidentally, in cases of humanitarian nonintervention than in cases where carrying out such intervention is highly problematic.

Hegel's problem is defused only to the extent that political actors already find themselves in a cycle of realizing "existing" norms or of pursuing a "universally recognized" project. In any given case, it is hard to tell what is going on and when—against one's will—natural self-determination has the last word. That these problems are no longer the sole purview of purported experts, but are transmitted into worldwide controversies about legitimacy, is a first step in the right direction. In addition, participants must know that this kind of public controversy has to be carried out in the light of publicly acceptable reasons, independently of any philosophy of history or *Weltanschauung*.

1

Hermeneutic and Analytic Philosophy: Two Complementary Versions of the Linguistic Turn

In a series of lectures on German philosophy "since Kant," the names of Fichte, Schelling, and Hegel and their critical references to Kant are, of course, a must.[1] No less a must, though, would seem to be Wilhelm von Humboldt, the philosopher and linguist who, together with Herder and Hamann, forms the alliterative triumvirate of a romanticist critique of Kant.[2] In contrast to the idealist mainstream, this response to transcendental philosophy in terms of a philosophy of language was long in coming but, in the end, rich in consequences within the discipline. It was Heidegger who, looking back at Humboldt, and informed by the Humboldtian tradition of linguistics,[3] first recognized the paradigmatic character of hermeneutics as developed by Droysen and Dilthey. At about the same time, Wittgenstein, in turn, discovered a new philosophical paradigm in Gottlob Frege's logical semantics. There is thus both a hermeneutic and an analytic version of what would later be dubbed the "linguistic turn."

My interest here is in seeing how these two versions relate to each other. I will do so, however, from the autobiographical perspective of my own generation. The tension between critical rationalism and critical theory that was unleashed in the early 1960s in the polemics between Popper and Adorno concealed another opposition with political as well as philosophical connotations. After the end of World War II, hermeneutics, having been continued without interruption during Nazism, was confronted with the currents of an analytical philosophy of science and a critical social theory, both returning from exile. This tension was on the minds of a generation who had taken up their studies after the war under the unbroken influence of Dilthey, Husserl, and Heidegger, and then faced the powerful continuation of this tradition by Gadamer and other students of Heidegger. In any case, it is the constellation defined by Gadamer, Adorno, and Popper that explains the two thrusts of an immanent critique of hermeneutics, which I will outline with reference to the work of my colleague and friend, Karl-Otto Apel. The self-critical development of the hermeneutic approach into a transcendental or, as I prefer to say, formal pragmatics would not have been possible without responding to the stimulating suggestions and insights of the analytic tradition. In my view, the traditions of hermeneutics and analytic philosophy today are complementary rather than competing.

First, I will elucidate the philosophical significance of Humboldt's theory of language (I). This will be the background against which we will see where the two versions of the linguistic turn as carried out, respectively, by Wittgenstein and Heidegger coincide. As it is, the paradigm shift from the philosophy of consciousness to the philosophy of language, which took place in two very different ways, surprisingly results in the same privileging of an "*a priori* of meaning" [*Sinnapriori*] over the representation of facts (II). It is in response to this devaluation of the cognitive dimension of language that in my generation the attempt was made to reestablish the universalist tendencies of Humboldt's philosophy of language.[4] In opposition to Wittgenstein's contextualism of language games, Heidegger's idealism of linguistic world disclosure, and Gadamer's rehabilitation of prejudice, and based on Humboldt's critique of Kant, Apel presents us in turn with a pragmatically transformed Kant (III).[5]

I

Humboldt distinguishes three functions of language: the cognitive function of forming thoughts and representing facts; the expressive function of manifesting emotions and arousing feelings; and finally, the communicative function of talking, of raising objections or coming to an agreement. The interplay between these functions presents itself differently depending on whether it is seen from the semantic point of view of how linguistic content is organized, or from the pragmatic point of view of how speakers communicate with one another. While semantic analysis focuses on the *linguistic worldview,* pragmatic analysis foregrounds the process of *dialogue.* On the one hand, Humboldt explores the cognitive function of language in connection with the expressive features of a people's mentality and form of life while, on the other hand, he analyzes the same function in the context of discourses in which interlocutors can ask questions, give answers, and raise objections. The tension between the particularism of world disclosure and the universalism of fact-stating discourse pervades the hermeneutic tradition as a whole. Because both Heidegger and Gadamer opted for a one-sided resolution to this tension, it became a challenge for the generation that followed them. But let us first turn to Humboldt's transcendental conception of language.

(1) The romantic concept of a "nation" is the point of reference for the world-making character of language: "Man thinks, feels, lives in language alone, and has to be formed by it in the first place."[6] Humboldt conceives languages as "organs of the peculiar ways of thinking and feeling of nations."[7] The lexicon and syntax of a language structure the totality of fundamental concepts and ways of understanding that articulates a preunderstanding of everything the members of the linguistic community may encounter in the world. For the nation it has shaped, every language articulates a particular "view" of the world as a whole.

Between the "construction" and "inner form" of a language and a particular "picture" of the world, Humboldt establishes an "inseparable connection." The horizon of meanings projected a priori by a language "[is] equal to the circumference of the world": "Every language draws a circle around the nation to which it belongs, stepping outside of which is possible only to the extent of simultaneously entering into the circle of another language."[8] Thus, the formula of language being the "formative organ of thought" must be understood in the transcendental sense of spontaneous world-constitution. Through the semantics of the worldview, a language simultaneously structures the form of life of the linguistic community; in any case, one is reflected in the other. This transcendental conception of language—which encompasses both culture and cognition—is at odds with the four fundamental premises of the dominant philosophy of language from Plato to Locke and Condillac.

First, a holistic conception of language is incompatible with a theory according to which the meaning [*Sinn*] of complex sentences is composed of the meanings [*Bedeutungen*][9] of their parts, that is, of individual words or elementary sentences. According to Humboldt, individual words acquire their meanings from the context of the sentences they help construct; sentences, from the coherence of the texts they help form; and kinds of text, from the organization or segmentation of a language's entire vocabulary. Second, the idea of a linguistically articulated worldview structuring a community's form of life is at odds with the traditional privileging of the cognitive function of language. Language is no longer primarily seen as a means of representing objects or facts, but as the medium of expressing a people's spirit. Third, a transcendental concept of language is incompatible with the dominant instrumentalist view of language and communication according to which signs are used to label, so to speak, prelinguistically formed ideas, concepts, and judgments in order to facilitate cognitive operations and to communicate beliefs or intentions to others. Finally, this priority of meaning over intention corresponds to the priority of the social character of language over the idiolects of individual speakers. A language is never the private property of an individual speaker, but generates an intersubjectively shared web of meaning, embodied in cultural expressions and social practices: "Phenomenologically, every language evolves as something social only, and human beings understand themselves only by testing the understandability of their words on others."[10]

(2) As a medium of objective spirit, language transcends the subjective mind, enjoying a peculiar autonomy from it. Humboldt elucidates this objectivity not only of linguistic expression, but of every symbolic expression, in terms of how we are shaped by the developmental process [*Bildungsprozess*] that we undergo in learning a language. The power of tradition, of "what is brought to us *en masse* by

means of entire epochs and nations," has an objective effect on later generations.[11] On the other hand, Humboldt develops an expressivist model of language use. There is an interplay between the objectivity of the rules governing a language, and the subjectivity speakers manifest in their performance: "It is in its being subjectively effected and dependent that language is objectively effecting and independent. For nowhere, not even in writing, has it a fixed abode. Its dead part, so to speak, must again and again be reproduced in thought, as living in speech or understanding."[12] This circular process of language, which is both *ergon* and *energia* at once, illustrates "a power man has over language that is like the power we have shown it to have over him."[13] Thus not only the subjects' sensibility and temperament come into play, but also their experiences in the world, in confrontation with reality: The objectivity of the world, however, is made of different stuff from that of the "objectivity" of linguistic forms "which undeniably give the mind a certain direction and impose upon it certain constraints."[14] Different languages may produce different worldviews, but the world itself appears as one and the same to all speakers.

The idea, however, of the "objective world" "appearing" as the same world to members of different linguistic communities presents certain difficulties. Though language as such is suited for the "production of objective thought" and fulfills the cognitive function of the representation of facts, these facts can be described only within the horizon of a specific linguistic worldview. For what is expressed in the grammatically fixed "modes of denotation" [*Bezeichnungsarten*] for objects is the specific "view" of "multifaceted objects" and, to that extent, something subjective, the temperament and particular character of a linguistic community. The cognitive and the expressive functions of language can be fulfilled only simultaneously.[15] How, then, is it possible that despite the differences of collectively shared linguistic perspectives members of different linguistic communities look at the same world or, in any case, at a world that appears to them as objective? This question of the commensurability of linguistic worldviews was already being discussed in the early nineteenth century.

If we conceive the world-making character of a natural language in a strictly transcendental sense, that is, as constituting the world of possible objects of experience, the worldviews inscribed in different languages must claim a validity that, for the linguistic communities concerned, is a priori necessary.[16] But this premise would mean, as Hamann already pointed out in his metacritique of Kant's *Critique of Pure Reason,* that the a priori of meaning inherent in linguistic worldviews, being plural, must lose the universal validity of a transcendental a priori. Rather, the preunderstanding of the world as a whole, as structured by an individual language, is "a priori contingent and indifferent, but a posteriori necessary and indispensable."[17] Humboldt evidently means to forego this obvious consequence. Notwithstanding certain misleading phrasing,[18] he does not see the linguistic worldview as a semantically closed universe from which speakers might escape only in order to be converted to another worldview.

(3) In this respect, Humboldt is no more troubled by the particularism of the linguistically disclosed world of a nation than by the peculiar character of its form of life, because he does not examine the cognitive function of language only from a semantic point of view. He relies on a division of labor between the semantics of linguistic worldviews and the formal pragmatics of dialogue—"of a dialogue where there is true exchange of ideas and feelings." It is the role of pragmatics to work out the universalist aspects of the process of communication. Semantics, it is true, discovers language as the formative organ of thought: the interpenetration of language and reality is such as to preclude any immediate access to an uninterpreted reality for the knowing subject. Reality—the totality of objects of possible descriptions—is always already "absorbed" into a specific horizon of meanings and, in Humboldt's words, "assimilated to" one's own language. But from the pragmatic point of view of the "living use of speech," a countertendency to semantic particularism becomes apparent. In dialogue, which "can be seen as the focal point of language,"[19] interlocutors want to *understand* each other and, at the same time, to reach a mutual understanding about something, that is, to come to an agreement. And this also holds for communication across the boundaries of different linguistic communities.

Humboldt addresses translation as the limit case that illuminates normal instances of interpretation. In doing so, he places equal emphasis on both of its aspects: the resistance that linguistic differences present for attempts to translate the utterances of one language into another, and the fact that this resistance can be overcome: "the experience of translating from highly different languages . . . shows that any series of ideas can be expressed, albeit with widely differing degrees of success, in any one of them."[20] Indeed, the hermeneutic tradition has never really doubted the possibility of translating the utterances of one language into all other languages; the only question was how to explain the almost transcendental fact that any semantic distance can be bridged: "Lucid recognition of difference requires (from the interpreter) a *tertium quid*, namely, unimpaired and simultaneous consciousness of the structures of one's own and of the foreign language."

Humboldt postulates a "superior point of view" from which the interpreter "assimilates what is foreign to himself, and himself to it."[21] Thus, the encounter of strangers learning to *understand* each other across linguistic gaps takes place, from the outset, in formal anticipation of such a "third" point of view. They must take up this point of view, however, with regard to the same objects about which they want to reach mutual understanding.[22] Communicative language use and the cognitive function of language interlock insofar as both sides must, from their own perspective, share the assumption of, and refer to, the convergence point of an objective world. To the extent that strangers can argue about "the same" state of affairs (or, if need be, know how to explain why reasonable disagreements can be expected to persist), they will find a common language and learn to understand each other. Linguistic expressions can be understood only by knowing the conditions under which they could be used to reach mutual understanding about something in the world. A shared view of reality as a "territory halfway between" the "worldviews" of different languages is a necessary presupposition of meaningful dialogue *überhaupt*. For the interlocutors, the concept of reality is connected with the regulative idea of a "sum total of all that is knowable."

This internal relation between linguistic competence and the possibility of reaching mutual understanding about something in the world explains why Humboldt attaches a cognitive promise to the communicative function of language. In discourse a worldview is supposed to prove itself against the opposition of others in such a way that, with the progressive decentering of individual perspectives, the meaning horizons of all participants expand—and increasingly come to overlap. This expectation, however, is warranted only if the form of dialogue and the pragmatic presuppositions of discourse can be shown to include a critical potential capable of affecting and shifting the horizon of a linguistically disclosed world itself.

Humboldt tries to prove this by analyzing the system of personal pronouns present in all languages. He distinguishes between the Ego-Id relation of the observer and the interpersonal I-Thou relation that is constitutive of a speaker's attitude in performing a speech act. Everyone can decide for herself whether to choose the expressive attitude of a first person revealing her subjective experiences or ideas, or the objectivating attitude of a third person perceiving and describing her environment. But the attitude of a speaker toward a second person to whom she is addressing her utterance is dependent on a complementary attitude of another who is supposed—but cannot be made—to do the same. By conceding the role of the speaker to the first person, the addressee must consent to being himself addressed in the attitude of the second person. In dialogue, both sides can enter this relationship only on a mutual basis. One person concedes the performative role of the speaker to another only with the proviso that roles be exchanged, thus ensuring the communicative freedom to reply for both.

In the use of personal pronouns, Humboldt detects an "unalterable dualism" grounded in the speech situation itself: "All speech is tuned to address and response."[23] This dialectical structure creates a public space, giving actual "social existence" to the intersubjectively shared lifeworld. This intersubjectivity of communication, generated by dialogue, is at the same time a necessary condition for the objectivity of thought: "Even thought is essentially accompanied by a propensity to social existence, man yearns . . . even for the sole purpose of thinking, for an Alter, a Thou corresponding to the Ego or I; a concept seems to him to attain its definiteness and certainty only by its being reflected in the faculty of thought of another." The objectivity of one's own judgment is established only when "the representing subject really sees the thought outside of himself, which is possible only in another representing and thinking being. But between one faculty of thought and another, there is no mediation but language."[24] The second person's reply to a speaker's utterance not only can facilitate, in the case of an affirmative response, social integration, but also implies, in view of possible objections, the critical power of confirmation and refutation. We learn from the world by learning from *each other*.

Humboldt, of course, does not pursue his study of the pragmatic interplay of the cognitive and the communicative functions of language along the lines of a theory of argumentation focusing on discourse about truth claims. Choosing instead the hermeneutic theme of "mutual understanding of alien speech," he turns to the moral implications of an exchange between competing worldviews and cultures. As the horizon of one's own understanding of the world is expanded, one's value orientations, too, are subject to relativization: "If there is one idea that can be found throughout history to enjoy an ever wider acceptance . . . it is the idea of humanity, the endeavor of bringing down the frontiers which all kinds of prejudice and biased views erect between people, and of treating all of humanity, regardless of religion, nationality, and color, as one big tribe of closely related brothers."[25] Humboldt not only establishes an internal relation between understanding and communication. More generally, he sees a cognitive dynamic at work in the practice of reaching mutual understanding. Even when dealing with purely descriptive questions, this dynamic contributes to the decentering of the linguistic worldview and, indirectly, through the expansion of horizons, fosters universalist perspectives in questions of morality as well. This humanistic nexus of hermeneutic open-mindedness and egalitarian morality is lost in Dilthey's and Heidegger's historicism. It will take a critique of twentieth-century philosophical hermeneutics to bring it back.

II

We find in Humboldt the outlines of an architectonic of philosophy of language that has to this day remained the standard frame of reference for a pragmatic transformation of Kantian philosophy.

From a semantic point of view, Humboldt has developed the transcendental concept of the "world-making" spontaneity of language in two respects. Language is constitutive both on the level of the cultural patterns of interpretation of a linguistic community and on the level of its social practices. For cognition, language matters in that it articulates a preunderstanding of the world as a whole, which is intersubjectively shared by the linguistic community. This worldview serves as a resource of shared patterns of interpretation. Inconspicuously pointing out relevant perspectives and shaping prejudices, it creates the unproblematical background, or framework, for possible interpretations of what happens in the world. At the same time, for social practice, language matters in that it shapes the character and form of life of a nation. This linguistically structured lifeworld forms the background for everyday communication and marks the points of contact between philosophy of language and social theory.[26] The achievements of language as the formative organ of thought will later be analyzed by Heidegger as linguistic "world-disclosure"; the latter, however, must be distinguished from the "constitution" of lifeworld contexts for situations of action and communicative processes.

From a pragmatic point of view, Humboldt deals with the general structures of discourse. The formal features of dialogue shed light on the interlocutors' roles, attitudes, and interpersonal relations. Interlocutors address their utterances to second persons, expecting to be understood and to get a reply. The content of discourse is differentiated in terms of whether the participants want to communicate about events in the objective world or about normative claims and value orientations of social and cultural life. Humboldt obviously takes rational discourse in which claims and reasons are exchanged to have the power of transcending the limits of particular worldviews. To explain how this is supposed to be possible, however, he merely gestures in the direction of intercultural communication.

The mutual understanding of other cultures and forms of life and reciprocal learning among strangers serve to correct and overcome prejudices. For Humboldt, the decentering of one's horizon of meaning is more generally bound up with the advancement of universalistic value orientations. But the fact that different interpretive perspectives come closer to one another horizontally, as it were, does not yet explain how we can grasp facts in the vertical dimension of reference to the objective world, and how controversy about statements of fact can yield knowledge. The absence of a convincing analysis of the representational function of language, that is, of the conditions of reference and propositional truth, continues to be the Archilles' heel of the entire hermeneutic tradition.

This deficiency reflects an estrangement of rhetoric and grammar from logic that set in with Renaissance humanism. Humboldt shares the justified distrust of the way in which logic abstracts propositions from speech acts and discursive contexts: "As long as logical analysis is concerned with thought only, instead of the grammatical analysis of speech, there is no need for the second person. . . . What is representing, then, has only to be distinguished from what is represented, not from what is receiving and reacting."[27]

This is exactly what formal semantics does in focusing on the representational function of language. This research tradition was initiated by the mathematician and logician Gottlob Frege, who was in no way connected to the tradition of Humboldt, Schleiermacher, Droysen, and Dilthey. In spite of his interesting observations on the illocutionary force that only the act of assertion confers on propositions, Frege essentially confined himself to the logical analysis of simple propositions. In formal semantics, the communicative dimension of language that, for Humboldt, was the locus of communicative rationality, is exempted from logical analysis and left to empirical approaches. This neglect of a formal pragmatics the outlines of which are discernible in Humboldt, however, applies to Heidegger as much as to Frege. Heidegger took up but one of the lines of argument in Humboldt's philosophy of language, the semantic one. Unlike Frege, he starts out from the world-disclosing function of language, rather than from its representational function, and focuses on the semantic analysis of basic conceptual and semantic structures inherent in the form of language as such, that is, in what Humboldt called *innere Sprachform.*

Thus, both analytic and hermeneutic philosophy, while approaching language from opposite starting points, confine themselves to its semantic aspects: to the relation of sentence and fact, on the one hand, and to the conceptual articulation of the world inscribed in language as a whole, on the other. The two sides use different means: the tools of logic, on the one hand, and the methods of content-oriented linguistics, on the other. Still, the abstraction is the same in both, the holistic approach of content semantics and the elementaristic approach of formal semantics. Both treat the pragmatics of speech as derivative; they certainly do not expect the structural features of speech to make an essential contribution to the rationality of communication.

Humboldt, by contrast, had elaborated a categorial framework providing for three levels of analysis. The first level is concerned with the world-making character of language, the second with the pragmatic structure of speech and communication, and the third with the representation of facts. Hermeneutic and analytic approaches are located on the first and on the third level of analysis, respectively. Both are committed, in their own way, to the primacy of semantics over pragmatics. Hence they face the same problem of how to reverse the initial abstraction without undertaking any undue reductions. Let me briefly account for the gains and losses on the part of Frege and Heidegger relative to Humboldt.

(1) Humboldt was aware of the fact that we understand a linguistic expression if we know under what conditions we can use it in order to reach an understanding about something in the world. It was Frege, though, who explained this internal relation of meaning and validity at the level of simple assertoric sentences. He starts out from sentences as the smallest linguistic units capable of being true or false. Thus, "truth" can serve as the basic semantic concept for explaining the meaning of linguistic expressions. The meaning of a sentence is determined precisely by the conditions under which the sentence is true (or that "make it true"). Wittgenstein, like Frege, conceives the sentence or proposition as an expression of its

truth conditions: "To understand a proposition means to know what is the case if it is true."[28] This opening move has a number of interesting implications.

If only sentences have a determinate meaning [*Sinn*] because they are the only form in which a state of affairs or a complete thought can be expressed, the meaning [*Bedeutung*] of individual words must be assessed in terms of their contribution to the construction of true sentences. But since the same words may serve as building blocks for quite different sentences, this "context principle" seems to suggest that all the expressions of language are interconnected by a complex web of semantic threads. Such a holistic conception of language, however, would jeopardize the semantic determinacy of individual sentences. Frege, therefore, at the same time defends a "principle of compositionality" according to which the meaning of a complex expression is composed of the meanings of its parts. The corresponding idea in Wittgenstein's *Tractatus* is that a logically transparent language fulfilling the exclusive function of representing facts must be constructed truth-functionally out of atomic propositions.

Another consequence that follows from the primacy of sentence over word (or of judgment over concept) is the rejection of the traditional view that linguistic symbols are essentially names for objects. Frege analyzes simple propositions on the model of mathematical functions that can be fulfilled with different values. This enables him to explain the interplay of two different acts: predication of properties, on the one hand, and reference to objects to which these properties are attributed, on the other. And just as predication must not be assimilated to reference, so predicates or concepts must not be assimilated to names. "Sense" [*Sinn*] must not be confused with "reference" [*Referenz*], nor propositional content with the act of referring [*Bezuguahme*] to the object about which something is being said. Only on this condition is it possible for us to make different, perhaps contradictory assertions about the same object and to compare them with one another. If we were not capable of recognizing the identity of the same object under different descriptions, there could be neither cognitive advances nor revisions of languages and the "worlds" they semantically "disclose."

Frege's concepts of "sense," "reference," and "truth" are generally acknowledged to define the range of a multifaceted ongoing discussion of the representational function of language and its relation to the objective world. As can be seen from the highly problematic construction of his doctrine of an independent realm of "thoughts," however, the later Frege found it difficult to situate language within the coordinates of facts, thoughts, and the formation of judgments in the human mind. At the same time as Husserl, he had advanced a convincing critique of contemporary psychologism; but not until Wittgenstein's turn to a transcendental conception of language is the symbolic embodiment of "thoughts expelled from consciousness" in the medium of language taken seriously.[29] Wittgenstein ascribes to the universal, logically transparent, fact-stating language a world-making character. The limits of language "are the limits of my world," while the propositions of logical semantics show us the "scaffolding of the world." The categories of the understanding, which for Kant constitute the objects of possible experience, are replaced in Wittgenstein by the logical form of the elementary proposition: "To give the essence of a proposition means to give the essence of all description, and thus the essence of the world."[30] It is with this step that Wittgenstein ratifies the linguistic turn initiated by Frege.

The logical analysis of language acquires its philosophical significance by replacing the paradigm of consciousness with the paradigm of language, thus revolutionizing mentalist foundations. For Russell or Carnap, the method of explaining forms of thought by way of a logical analysis of linguistic forms is still bound up with traditional empiricist epistemology. This methodologically limited understanding of the linguistic turn[31] is as yet far from a challenge to the mentalist paradigm as such. Not until Wittgenstein's thesis that the form of the assertoric proposition determines the structure of what can possibly be a fact do we get at the very premises of the philosophy of consciousness. He later, and for good reason, abandoned this conception of a universal, fact-stating language. The world-constituting nature of language, however, is retained even as its transcendental spontaneity is transposed from the dimension of representation to the dimension of linguistic practice.

Wittgenstein undertakes a detailed critique of mentalism only after replacing the linguistic forms of an unreflective, rationalist thought that he had investigated in the *Tractatus* with a plurality of grammars for language games that are constitutive of as many forms of life. It is through Wittgenstein, therefore, that Frege's intuitive distinction between "thoughts" [*Gedanken*] and "ideas" [*Vorstellungen*] is given an unequivocal interpretation. We cannot "experience" the meaning of a sentence because understanding is not a mental event but depends on rule-following: "Compare: 'When did your pain stop?' and 'When did you stop understanding the word?'"[32] Knowing how to use a criterion is a practical skill—just as one "knows how" to play chess—but it is neither a mental state nor a psychological property.

(2) Heidegger takes a different route, but arrives at a similar critique of the philosophy of consciousness. Without so much as a glance at the philosophy of language, he first elaborates an "existential analytic" of human *Dasein*, while taking up and integrating the ways in which he was influenced by both Dilthey and Husserl. These influences explain why his investigation, which starts from an entirely different angle, ends up converging with Humboldt's view that "there is world only where there is language."

According to Dilthey, the historical human sciences of the nineteenth century were supposed to differ from the natural sciences in virtue of developing the traditional art of textual interpretation into a method of understanding meaning [*Sinnverstehen*]. Their goal is not the nomological explanation of empirical events but the understanding of meaning embodied in all kinds of symbolic expressions, cultural traditions, and social institutions. Heidegger takes this allegedly scientific operation of *Verstehen*, or understanding, out of its methodological context and radicalizes it to constitute a fundamental feature of human existence. The original task of human beings is to understand their world, and themselves in this world: "In every understanding of world, existence is understood with it, and vice versa."[33] *Being and Time* is supposed to conceptualize the structure of this a priori understanding of self and of being.

Heidegger replaces the phenomenological model of describing perceptions of objects by the hermeneutic model of interpreting

texts, but retains the basic outline of Husserl's "transcendental phenomenology": "the meaning of phenomenological description as
method lies in interpretation."[34] The perspective of the observer perceiving objects is replaced by the perspective of an interpreter trying
to make sense of what people's utterances and their forms of life
mean. Such a phenomenology with a hermeneutic twist is, however,
not primarily concerned with the manifest content of an utterance,
but with the tacit contextual features of its performance. Already
Husserl had analyzed the pre-predicative stratum of the concomitant horizons of perceived objects as "an associatively structured
field of passive and antecedent givens," characterizing the world of
subjective experience as the "universal ground of belief for experience."[35] Heidegger takes advantage of the differentiated phenomenological descriptions of such background phenomena in his
analysis of the referential totalities [Verweisungszusammenhänge] that
are disclosed to human actors in their practical dealings with things
and events of their familiar environment. He investigates the linguistic
articulation of the preunderstanding of the world as mirrored in the
everyday projects, expectations, and anticipations only within the
horizon of which something becomes intelligible to us as something.
The phenomenon of this "fore-structure of understanding" is
Heidegger's point of convergence with Humboldt's transcendental
conception of language.[36] At the same time, he derives a conclusion
of considerable philosophical import from the semantic a priori of
the linguistic worldview.

For instance, by ascribing the property "blue" to the car in which
the expected guests at last arrive, we determine this car "as" blue. This
"predicative as" is distinguished, by Heidegger, from a "hermeneutic
as," which depends on categories of a prior, but implicit, conception
of the world as a whole. In certain practical respects, our world is
grammatically articulated into different types of processes and objects, of animate and inanimate objects, of objects that we find or
that we produce, of bodies that move and can be moved, into which
we knock, which appear in a different light by night or by day, and
so on. The strategic move, then, that allows Heidegger to prejudge
all the rest is the subordination of the "predicative as" to the

"hermeneutic as," which is rooted in the basic conceptual articulation of beings as a whole. It follows that we can ascribe or deny particular properties to particular objects only after they have been made accessible to us within the conceptual coordinates of a linguistically disclosed world—that is, after they have been "given" to us as objects that are already implicitly interpreted and, in key respects, categorized. With this a priori classification of types of objects, language per se preempts any specific inquiry as to which properties may be here and now predicated of which entities. All the speaker herself may "discover" within this inescapable semantic web is which of the linguistically projected possibilities of truth is realized in any given case.

For Heidegger, the fact that a predicate fits an object, as well as the truth of the corresponding predicative sentence, is a derivative phenomenon that depends on an "enabling of truth" in the sense of a prior world-disclosure as a linguistic "happening of truth." With this latter notion, however, the universalist meaning of truth is relinquished. An ontological "truth" that changes with the mode of world disclosure no longer appears in the singular of "the one and indivisible truth." Rather, the "undisclosedness" of particular types of objects is determined by a transcendental "event" of linguistic world-disclosure, which in itself is neither true nor false, but rather just "happens."

This primacy of the "hermeneutic as" over the "predicative as" marks the crucial difference from a truth-conditional semantics. The latter also, to be sure, holds that the meaning of linguistic expressions determines the truth conditions of the sentences they form. But this is not tantamount to claiming that it is irrevocably predetermined on the semantic level which properties might in the long run be ascribed to which categories of objects. As long as we separate the predication of properties from the reference to objects, and as long as we are able to recognize objects as the same under different descriptions, there is the possibility of learning—of increasing our knowledge of the world in such a way that it may lead to a revision of our linguistic knowledge.

Philosophical hermeneutics fails to appreciate the cognitive function of language in its own right and the specific significance of the propositional structure of declarative sentences. As a result, Heidegger rules out any interaction between linguistic knowledge [*Sprachwissen*] and empirical knowledge [*Weltwissen*]. He does not even consider the possibility that what words in a language mean, on the one hand, and the results of learning processes within the world, on the other, can mutually affect one another, because he gives unlimited primacy to the semantics of linguistic worldviews over the pragmatics of communication. In contrast to Humboldt, he transfers the locus of control from the *achievements* of the participants in discourse to the higher-order *events* of linguistic world-disclosure. Speakers are prisoners in the house of their language, and it is language that speaks through their mouths.[37] *Authentic* discourse is nothing but an announcement of being; that is also why listening takes precedence over speaking: "Speaking is of itself a listening. Speaking is listening to the language that we speak. . . . We do not merely speak the language—we speak by way of it."[38]

Wittgenstein came to a similar conclusion, though by a less mystifying route. The pragmatic turn from truth-conditional semantics to the use theory of meaning—and from one universal fact-stating language to the many grammars of language games—signifies not only a detranscendentalization of language. Wittgenstein's descriptive approach to actual language use simultaneously levels off the cognitive dimension of language. Once the truth conditions that one has to know in order to use assertoric sentences correctly are read off from habitual linguistic practice, there is no longer a clear-cut difference between the validity [*Gültigkeit*] of an utterance and its social acceptance [*Geltung*]—what we are entitled to is assimilated to what we are merely accustomed to. By transferring the world-constituting spontaneity to the diversity of historically given language games and forms of life, Wittgenstein confirms the primacy of the a priori of meaning over the determination of facts: "All testing, all confirmation and disconfirmation of a hypothesis takes place already within a system. And this system is not a more or less arbitrary and doubtful point of departure from all our arguments: no, it belongs to the essence of what we call an argument."[39] Just like Heidegger, Wittgenstein relies on the background of an understanding of the world that, in itself, is not capable of being true or false, but determines a priori the standards for the truth and falsity of propositions.

III

The history of theoretical philosophy in the second half of our century can very roughly be said to be characterized by two major currents. On the one hand, there is a synopsis of the two protagonists, Wittgenstein and Heidegger. The higher-level historicism of language games and epochal world disclosures is the common source of inspiration for a postempiricist philosophy of science, a neopragmatist philosophy of language, and the poststructuralist critique of reason.[40] On the other hand, there continues from Russell and Carnap onward an empiricist analysis of language with a merely methodological understanding of the linguistic turn, a strand that has gained worldwide acceptance through the work of Quine and Davidson. From the outset, Davidson assimilates an interlocutor's understanding of a linguistic expression to an observer's interpretation of data[41] and ends up with a nominalist conception of language that accords primacy to the passing idiolects of individual speakers over the social realm of linguistically embodied and intersubjectively shared meaning.[42] With this move language loses the status of social fact, which Humboldt had attributed to it by subsuming it under the concept of objective spirit.

In the present context, however, I am interested in a third current represented by philosophers as diverse as Putnam, Dummett, and Apel. What these authors have in common is that they take seriously the linguistic turn in the sense of a paradigm shift, without paying the price of the culturalist assimilation of being true to taking to be true. It is characteristic of these thinkers that they fight on two fronts: against the half-hearted linguistic analysis that merely tackles the old problems of Kant and Hume by new means,[43] on the one hand; and, on the other hand, against a semantic particularism that is hostile to the enlightenment and ignores the rational self-understanding of language users as creatures for whom reasons are binding.[44]

This twofold thrust already characterizes Karl-Otto Apel's *Habilita-tionsschrift* dating from the late 1950s. Objecting to an intentionalist conception of linguistic meaning as well as to an instrumentalist con-ception of linguistic communication, he calls to mind Humboldt's in-sight "that every understanding of the world also [!] presupposes a synthetic a priori of meaning (not necessarily in the form of complete sentences, but certainly in the form of sentence structures, categories, concepts, even of word meanings . . .)."[45] On the other hand, Apel is wary of isolating the function of linguistic world-disclosure from the cognitive function of the representation of facts. He postulates, instead, a "relation of mutual presupposition" and "interpenetration" between a particularist "projection of meaning" [*Bedeutsamkeitsentwurf*] and "universalist thinking [*Denkansatz*]." He takes his cue from Kant's architectonic of reason and understanding. What corresponds to "reason" as the faculty of world-constituting ideas is the semantic a priori of a linguistic worldview. However, only through the understanding, that is, only by being incorporated in successfully functioning practices, does this a priori take hold in the life of a society. Whereas a "poietically" projected meaning deter-mines particular forms of apprehension, this projection, conversely, depends on corroboration by successful "practice."[46] Thus, the prob-lem of a "mediation" between meaning and practice is clearly stated; what remains unclear is how such a mediation is supposed to work.

The same problem presents itself to Michael Dummett, albeit against a completely different background—without any reference to the Humboldtian tradition. Dummett follows Wittgenstein in ad-mitting that language games project intersubjectively shared hori-zons of meaning and shape cultural forms of life. Languages, being public institutions, dovetail with the prevailing practices of a linguis-tic community. But in opposition to Wittgenstein's use theory of meaning, which takes the critical edge off truth conditions and thus denies the cognitive dimension of language any authority of its own, Dummett gives truth-conditional semantics an epistemic turn. If a sentence is an expression of its truth conditions, then, in order to understand it, we must be able to *know* the conditions under which the sentence *is* true. Knowing the observable circumstances indicative of the speakers' habit of taking it to be true is not enough.

Knowledge of truth conditions is based on knowledge of the reasons that explain why they obtain if they do. Because of this internal relation between a proposition's truth conditions and the kinds of reasons that might justify a corresponding truth claim, the practice of justification, that is, the game of argumentation, acquires a particular significance also for Dummett.

The language game of asserting involves not only making and rejecting assertions, but also justifying or refuting them: "Accepting or rejecting a statement made by another, checking whether it was warranted, and evaluating circumstances as warranting or not warranting an assertion made at once or subsequently—all these are activities which demand to be described in any full account of the practice of using language: they are all components of that practice. A statement's satisfying the condition for it to be true, is certainly not in itself a feature of its use. The question at issue is whether there is nevertheless a need to appeal to it in a characterization of linguistic practice."[47] For Dummett, too, the formal pragmatics of the language game of giving and asking for reasons is the basis of a theory of meaning as opposed to the ad hoc character of a merely descriptive linguistic phenomenology. Karl-Otto Apel's idea of a transcendental pragmatics stems from the same intent.

(1) The state of argumentation in Germany after World War II was special inasmuch as the analytic tradition, having been interrupted by the war, had to be reappropriated.[48] In the course of this enterprise, Apel was one of the first to discover, from a hermeneutic point of view, the convergences between Heidegger and Wittgenstein.[49] Any metacritical response to Heidegger's critique of reason, however, also (if not primarily) had to engage with philosophical hermeneutics as Hans-Georg Gadamer had just cast it in *Truth and Method,* published in 1960.

Unlike Heidegger, Gadamer does not approach the analysis of understanding meaning semantically in terms of linguistic world-disclosure, but pragmatically in terms of communication between author and interpreter. He examines the practice of interpreting canonical texts along the lines of a conversational logic of question and answer in a way reminiscent of Collingwood. "Dialogue" is seen as the model for an exchange between interlocutors reaching mutual understanding about something in the world. In dialogue, the intersubjectivity of a shared lifeworld, rooted in the reciprocity and interchangeability of the perspectives of first and second persons, is interconnected with reference to something in the objective world that is being talked about. As Humboldt had already realized, there is a dimension of referential relation [*Sachbezug*] inherent in communication. And this relation establishes an internal relation between the meaning of what is said and its possible truth. Otherwise Humboldt would not have been able to link the hermeneutic expansion of the horizon of mutual understanding [*Verstehen*] immediately with the hope of *reaching* universal agreement [*Verständigung*].

At first glance, it would seem that Gadamer rehabilitates, along with the communicative dimension of language, the universalist promise of reason. He too claims that attempting to understand one another tends to result in an expansion and, eventually, in a "fusion" of initially divergent horizons of understanding. And, as Gadamer is well aware, this dynamic of mutual understanding follows the logic of a progressive process of communication about the matter at hand. Gadamer's conclusions are nevertheless quite different from Humboldt's. As for Heidegger, the referential relation that guides the process of communication is supposed to be possible only against the background of a preestablished consensus within shared traditions. One can see why even this pragmatically oriented hermeneutics must ultimately take an "ontological turn"[50] by looking at the motives underlying the whole enterprise.

Gadamer develops his hermeneutics in response to the "problem of historicism" that had occupied his contemporaries since Nietzsche's *Second Untimely Meditations*. Gadamer means to stand up against objectivism in the humanities, which, it seems to him, isolate the great historical traditions from their context, confine them to the museum, deprive them of their intrinsic potential for stimulation, and thus neutralize them as "formative powers." His orientation, therefore, is to the example of the hermeneutic appropriation of classical works—literary, artistic, religious, and, more generally, all works coming out of dogmatic traditions such as legal documents. With regard to the lasting impact of classical works, reflecting on an interpreter's initial situation can bring to light the insight that is crucial for Gadamer. The preunderstanding that an interpreter brings to a text is already pervaded and shaped by the effective history of the text itself, whether the interpreter likes it or not.

This explains, first, why the process of interpretation—that is, revision of the preunderstanding through confrontation with the text, and progressive specification of it in a virtual dialogue with the author—is possible only on the basis of a shared context of tradition that always already encompasses both sides. Second, since the interpreter is thus placed in the context of the events of the tradition, interpreting a paradigmatic text consists in applying superior knowledge to the situation at hand. Hermeneutic work may thus carry on a tradition without immobilizing it through reflection or impairing its binding character. The essentially conservative task of hermeneutics thus consists in promoting the ethical self-understanding of an inherited community. Third, therefore, the methodological effort of the humanities or indeed any attempt to assimilate interpretations to scientific propositions is based on a misconception. Any hermeneutic ascertainment of the living core of a tradition depends on an unproblematic a priori background consensus. And what is articulated in it in turn is the pregiven understanding of self and world of one's linguistic community. Hence, the contrast between "truth" and "method." Any methodological procedure that is meant to warrant the truth of propositions would only distort the revelatory truth of tradition.

Gadamer reduces the ancient hermeneutic principle of understanding an author better than he understands himself to understanding him in ever new and *different* ways. Apel, in contrast, stresses that hermeneutics, as a scientific discipline, must not relinquish the goal and standard of a "better understanding." Conditions necessary for understanding cannot even be explicated without, at the same time, raising "the methodologically pertinent question of the validity of competing interpretations." If the normative concept of truth is not to be revoked in favor of a de facto epochal transformation of world disclosure, "all interpretation must remain bound to reflection on its validity."[51] Apel proposes to explain the commensurability of different linguistic worldviews in terms of pragmatic universals. He is guided by a simple idea: the very practices that are made possible by our linguistic knowledge, together with our cognitive coping with the world, in turn test that linguistic knowledge, if only indirectly. "The possibility of shaping the subjective understanding of meaning a priori implies the converse possibility of restructuring the semantic component of "living" languages by means of a *pragmatically* successful communication about meaning at the level of language use."[52]

(2) The intellectual constellation of the late 1950s and early '60s made it plausible to discuss the cognitive dimension of language in terms of both scientific knowledge and of *enlightenment*. Enlightenment differs from science in its reflexive reference to the knowing subject; it "is not primarily progress of knowledge, but loss of naiveté."[53] Against an antiscientistic Gadamer, one could, with Popper, call on the testimony of the learning processes of empirical science: Wasn't there a cumulative growth of knowledge after all? And against the traditionalistic Gadamer, one could, with Adorno, proceed along the lines of a critique of ideology: Did not a de facto victorious power of repression, which destroyed the very conditions of uncoerced communication, impose itself along with the effective history of a prevailing tradition? Moreover, since Gadamer had developed his ideas in the context of the methodology of the human sciences, it made sense to cast the critique of *Truth and Method* in terms of a controversy about "explanation and understanding."[54] The two lines of argumentation of the critique of science, on the one hand, and the critique of ideology, on the other, subsequently converged in a theory of knowledge and human interests, which in the meantime, however, has been passed over by mainstream philosophical discussion.[55]

In the present context, this attempt is of interest only inasmuch as it sketches the outlines of a transcendental hermeneutics or formal pragmatics.[56] Two distinctions were important for countering the pluralism of allegedly incommensurable worldviews. Apel first distinguishes the constitution of the object domains of the natural and human sciences from the semantic a priori of different languages and linguistic worldviews. The former is interlinked with universal structures of purposive-rational action and social interaction.

A domain of observable states and events is structured by necessary conditions for instrumental interventions, while the domain of symbolic objects and meaningful expressions immediately mirrors the infrastructure of communication and interaction. Thus, general structures of action take the role of a pragmatic a priori for "objects of possible experience," whether they are accessible to perception or interpretation. This pragmatic a priori determines the objects of possible experience as well as the categorial meaning of statements, both about things and events and about persons and their utterances and contexts. Second, Apel distinguishes between this a priori of experience and an a priori of argumentation in the form of the general pragmatic presuppositions of rational discourse in which truth claims are verified. In contrast to Kant, Apel thus separates the *constitution of objects* from the *reflection on validity* by distinguishing between the pragmatic conditions for the objectivity of possible experiences and the communicative conditions for the discursive redemption of truth claims.[57]

In giving a pragmatic interpretation of how we reflect on validity, Apel discovers the general pragmatic presuppositions of any cooperative search for truth. He is inspired by Peirce's model of an unlimited communication community where investigators justify their fallible assumptions to one another with the aim of reaching an agreement (which is always in principle open to revision) by discursive means, that is, by diffusing counterarguments (which may be raised at any time). This idea not only provides the impetus for a discursive conception of truth,[58] but also marks the point of departure for a discourse ethics that develops an intersubjectivist reading of Kant's categorical imperative. While Gadamer basically has an Aristotelian conception of hermeneutic understanding, that is, as the promotion of an ethical self-understanding of a community constituted by shared traditions, Apel puts forward a Kantian conception of morality oriented toward questions of justice. For Apel, language takes the systematic place of a (pragmatically transformed) "consciousness in general" and becomes the necessary condition "of the possibility as well as the validity of mutual- and self-understanding and hence, simultaneously, of conceptual thought, the cognition of objects, and meaningful action."[59]

(3) To be sure, this comprehensive program is inspired by a hermeneutic concept of language; but, except for its incorporation of a Peircean semiotics, it lacks the very core of a theory of language—a "theory of meaning," to use the expression in the sense of the analytic tradition. The fact that Apel takes a methodological dispute over the role and scope of the workings of the understanding as his starting point explains why he initially developed his program in terms of epistemology and then continued in the direction of moral theory.[60] But in the context of a social theory based on the complementary concepts of communicative action and lifeworld,[61] this lack of a theory of language in the narrower analytical sense became obvious.[62] Two basic preliminary decisions for developing such a theory of meaning, however, had already been made: the uncoupling of the formal pragmatics of communication from the particularist implications of the semantics of linguistic world-disclosure, on the one hand; and the differentiation between the levels of rational discourses and of action, as well as a further distinction between truth and moral rightness, on the other. I want to conclude by at least mentioning the most salient basic assumptions of this formal pragmatic theory of meaning, in order to show how significant results of analytic philosophy can be incorporated into and elaborated from a hermeneutic point of view.

(a) Speech act theory as developed by Austin and Searle[63] provides a suitable framework for situating the fundamental insight of Dummett's theory of meaning[64] within a theory of communicative action.[65] First, a remark on the internal relation of *meaning* and validity is in order. Dummett's semantic thesis is that we understand a sentence if we know both how to warrant its truth and what the consequences of our accepting it as true are for our actions.[66] This conception is already tailored to the fact that, in performing a speech act and claiming that its propositional content is valid, a speaker expects a hearer to take a critical stance. The hearer understands the expression if she knows, on the one hand, the kinds of reasons in light of which this validity claim deserves intersubjective recognition and, on the other hand, the consequences for how to act that follow from accepting the validity claim.[67] The internal connection between the meaning of an expression and the conditions of its rational acceptability follows from a pragmatic conception of understanding and communication according to which the illocutionary success of a speech act is assessed in terms of the conditions for the yes/no positions taken toward criticizable validity claims.

(b) Communication aimed at reaching mutual understanding is inherently discursive; at the same time, we can differentiate between the levels of discourse and action. In communicative action, validity claims are raised naively and more or less taken for granted in the context of a shared lifeworld. As soon as they are problematized and made the object of a justified controversy, interlocutors switch (in however rudimentary a fashion) from communicative action to another form of communication, namely, a practice of argumentation, willing to convince one another of their views as well as to learn from one another. Under the changed communicative presuppositions of such a rational discourse,[68] beliefs that up to this point were part of an unproblematic background are examined as to their validity. In the process, descriptive statements about something in the objective world are differentiated from normative statements about legitimate expectations within the social world.

(c) More or less behind the backs of the participants, the linguistically structured lifeworld shapes the context of dialogue and provides a source of communicative content. This *lifeworld* has to be distinguished from the formal presuppositions of an *objective* as well as a *social* world, which speakers and actors make when linguistically referring to the world or when practically coping with the world more generally. What from an epistemological point of view used to be conceived as the constitution of two object domains has now been sublimated, in formal pragmatics, into a presupposition of purely formal systems of reference, or "worlds." The "objective" and the shared "social" world constitute the grammatical system of reference for everything that speaker and actor can ever encounter in the world. These frameworks lack any content beyond the conditions necessary for reference either to possible objects or to possible interpersonal relations and norms—objects about which we state facts in an objectifying attitude, or relations and norms that we claim to be binding in a performative attitude.

(d) The question remains how the pragmatic universals that are constitutive for communicative action, for rational discourse, and for how propositions latch on to the world [*Weltbezüge der Aussagen*] can break through the ethnocentrism of linguistic worldviews and linguistically structured lifeworlds. As we have seen with Gadamer, the communicative dimension of language per se does not possess a universalist potential. As learning processes always start within a particular horizon of meaning, their results can alter the limits of this linguistically disclosed world only if empirical knowledge is not merely made possible by linguistic knowledge, but actually can have the power to revise it in turn. This power of revision is explained by the discursive processing of action-related experiences. We have such experiences either in pragmatically coping with an objective world, which we presuppose as the same for and independent of all of us, or in our interactive coping with members of a social world that we presuppose to be shared.[69] Experiences that indicate the collapse of routine practices can initiate a revision of assumptions and normative expectations and, ultimately, even affect linguistic knowledge itself.

(e) This performative failure to cope with the world—be it because of the recalcitrance of the objective world that refuses to play along, or because of a conflict with an alien, and normatively dissonant, form of life—is hard to deny. In this regard, the difference between discourse and action comes to the fore in a different way, that is, not as an intralinguistic difference between levels of communication, but as a difference between language and nonlinguistic (yet propositionally structured) action. Once validity claims are routed out of the contexts of goal-oriented coping with reality or norm-governed social interactions, they are thematized, verified and, if need be, revised in discourse. In order to learn *from the world* and to correct prior empirical beliefs, the hypothetical attitude of participants in discourse requires the complement of abductive imagination, whereas the context-transcending dynamics built into the very form of rational discourse has an immediate significance for learning from one another. It is to be expected that discourse leads to a decentering of lifeworld perspectives. In cases of conflicts of interaction that have to do with morality, this decentering fosters the mutual expansion of each participant's horizon of value orientations. This is necessary if they are to arrive at mutually recognized norms by way of generalizing their values.

(f) This formal-pragmatic approach develops the concept of language on the basis of a notion of discourse where interlocutors raise criticizable validity claims in their utterances. Validity claims that can be backed by reasons are of two kinds: we claim truth for propositions about things and events in the objective world, and rightness for propositions about normative expectations and interpersonal relations that, at eye level, so to speak, are part of a social world that is accessible in a performative attitude only. The cognitive function of language attains a relative independence from the function of world-disclosure both in the domain of sociomoral learning and in the (more narrowly "cognitive") domain of coping with external reality. That is why a theory of communicative action grounded in this conception of language is able to link up with a materialist theory of society.

(4) I have not yet mentioned the most salient and striking difference between the hermeneutic and the analytic tradition. Since analytic philosophy of language more or less confines itself to issues it has inherited from the epistemological tradition, it lacks a certain sensibility for as well as the tools for dealing with the looser and larger issues of a diagnostics of an era. Since Hegel, the philosophical discourse of modernity has, therefore, been the domain of so-called continental philosophy. In this regard, the opposition between analytic and continental currents, which has otherwise become obsolete, still somewhat makes sense.[70] Even Wittgenstein's reflections on the *Zeitgeist*—his antiscientistic frame of mind, his critique of science and technology, his skepticism about progress, his loathing of sociology, the contrast of "culture" and "civilization," the devaluation of "talent" and cleverness in contrast to "genius," in short: the ready-mades of a "German ideology" that set him apart, unfavorably, from his teacher, Bertrand Russell[71]—still are of a rather private and ornamental nature and, in any case, do not affect the structure of his inimitable philosophical work.

For Heidegger, in contrast, cultural criticism is a pervasive feature of his entire philosophy. The author of *Being and Time* already brings together Aristotle and Kierkegaard, pre-Kantian metaphysics and post-Kantian ethics in the grand posture of a critic of his time. After the *Kehre*, the widely influential critique of science and technology and of the totalitarian features of the age as a whole is inspired by a convincing deconstruction of Cartesianism and an engagement with Nietzsche. Heidegger thus takes up issues that had already been discussed, in a similarly critical vein though in a different manner, by Max Weber and George Lukács. His using the critique of metaphysics in order to carry out his analysis of the present provides the idealist counterpart to the materialist critique of objectification. In the present context, though, I am mainly interested in the homogenizing and at the same time fateful character of Heidegger's diagnosis of the destiny of modernity. This diagnosis itself—a self-empowering subjectivity practicing an all-around objectification—is not novel. It is the mirror image of the "dialectic of enlightenment." Heidegger's specific contribution is that he figures the phenomena of self-preservation running wild as the doomed eruption of a fateful power into history. For he conceives them as the fateful symptoms of an understanding of self and world that, having taken hold of modernity, levels and overpowers all differences.

"Technology" takes on features of a "*Seinsgeschick*" because the critique of metaphysics by means of which Heidegger wants to oppose the prevailing philosophy of the subject is grounded in the conception of linguistic world-disclosure. A more differentiated view of modernity emerges if we steer clear of this hypostatization of the world-disclosing function of language. Indeed, as soon as we admit that there is a dialectics of world-disclosure and learning processes within the world, the monolithic and fateful character of a worldview prejudicing all and everything falls apart. At the same time, the diagnosis itself is deprived of its idealist character, since the pathologies of modernity can then no longer be attributed to the semantics of an ineluctably distorting preunderstanding of the world. This is what a final look back on Humboldt may teach us.

Humboldt himself, to be sure, did not make any significant contribution to a critique of modernity. What he saw, though, were the dysfunctional consequences of blocking the ability of linguistic communication to function as a mechanism of social integration.

Communicative action fosters individuation and social integration at the same time.[72] Language "unites through individuation, "thus saving the communicatively sociated subjects "from degeneration through isolation."[73] From this point of view, characteristic social pathologies can be explained as disturbances of a communicatively mediated social integration. Since the issue, then, is the analysis of patterns of systematically distorted communication, philosophy can no longer solve the problem on its own. Whereas Heidegger carries out his diagnoses of his time single-handedly, Humboldt's philosophy of language suggests a division of labor with social theory. Although a lifeworld that is reproduced though communicative action provides a resource of social solidarity, this solidarity is at the same time always in danger of being overpowered and even destroyed by two further mechanisms of social integration in modern societies, namely, markets and bureaucracies.[74] From this perspective, modernity is threatened not by a monotonous and inescapable *Seinsgeschick,* which is as vague as it is sinister, but by systemic and above all economic imperatives consuming the lifeworld resources of social solidarity.

2

From Kant's "Ideas" of Pure Reason to the "Idealizing" Presuppositions of Communicative Action: Reflections on the Detranscendentalized "Use of Reason"

For my friend, Thomas McCarthy, at 60

In his preface to *Ideals and Illusions,* Thomas McCarthy characterizes the two directions that critics of Kantian conceptions of reason have taken since Hegel: "on one side are those who, in the wakes of Nietzsche and Heidegger, attack Kantian conceptions of reason and the rational subject at their very roots; on the other side are those who, in the wakes of Hegel and Marx, recast them in sociohistorical molds."[1] Even in their desublimated pragmatic forms, the Kantian "ideas" retain their original dual role. They are used to guide critique and, at the same time, are exposed as the fertile ground of a transcendental illusion: ideals and illusions. McCarthy opposes not only an iconoclastic deconstructionism that throws out the baby with the bathwater, but also an overly normative reading of Kant that leaves the illusion of pure reason intact. Even after the pragmatic turn, he keeps both functions of reason in view: the norm-setting function that enables critique and the concealing function that calls for self-criticism: "If we take a pragmatic turn, we can appreciate both aspects of the social-practical ideas of reason: their irreplaceable function in cooperative interaction and their potential for misuse."[2]

Elsewhere, McCarthy speaks of the "social-practical *analogues* of Kant's ideas of reason."[3] He is referring specifically to three formal-pragmatic presuppositions of communicative action, namely, the common supposition of an objective world, the rationality that acting subjects mutually attribute to one another, and the unconditional validity they claim for their statements with speech acts. These presuppositions refer to one another and form aspects of a desublimated reason embodied in everyday communicative practice: "the idealizations of rational accountability and real world objectivity both figure in our idealized notion of truth, for objectivity is the other side of the intersubjective validity of certain types of truth claims."[4] Thus the transcendental tension between the ideal and the real, between the realm of the intelligible and the realm of appearances, enters into the social reality of situated interactions and institutions. It is this transformation of "pure" into "situated" reason that McCarthy masterfully brings to bear against the critiques that liquidate reason through its abstract negation, such as Foucault's objectivating analysis or Derrida's use of paradox. Yet he does so without ignoring the insights gained by deconstructing those illusions of reason that seep into the very capillaries of everyday discourses.

Both the historicist tradition from Dilthey to Heidegger and the pragmatist tradition from Peirce to Dewey (and, in a sense, Wittgenstein) understand the task of "situating reason" as one of detranscendentalizing the knowing subject. The finite subject is to be situated "in the world" without entirely losing its "world-constituting" spontaneity. To that extent, the encounter between McCarthy and the followers of Heidegger, Dewey, and Wittgenstein is a domestic dispute over which side accomplishes the detranscendentalization in the right way: whether the traces of a transcending reason vanish in the sand of historicism and contextualism or whether a reason embodied in historical contexts preserves the power for immanent transcendence.[5] If cooperating subjects cope intelligently with what they encounter in the world, do their learning processes empower them to make rationally motivated revisions in their preunderstanding of the world as a whole? Is reason simply at the mercy of the "world-disclosive" happening of language, or is it also a "world-transforming" power?

In the debate with the deconstructionists, at least the *issue itself* is not under dispute. However, for the heirs of Hume—and thus for a large segment of analytic philosophy—the question of the dialectic between world-disclosing language and innerworldly learning processes barely makes any sense at all. Unless one subscribes to Kant's idea of a "world-formative" reason and the conception of an understanding that "constitutes" the objects of possible experience, there can be no grounds for detranscendentalizing the "consciousness" of knowing and acting subjects, let alone for a controversy regarding the problems that arise from such a corrective. McCarthy defends a pragmatic explication of the "situatedness of reason" against *deconstructionist objections.* I shall try to address the *lack of understanding* on the part of analytic philosophy for the very question of the detranscendentalized use of reason.

I do not, however, wish to lobby directly for a formal-pragmatic theory of meaning and repeat the familiar arguments.[6] The difficulty in understanding lies not in the details but in the point of departure. Truth-conditional semantics has also established an internal relation between meaning and the validity conditions of sentences and has thus paved the way for various conceptions of a linguistically or even communicatively embodied rationality (Davidson, Dummett, Brandom). But along the course set by Hume and Kant for or against a nominalist conception of how the human mind works, structurally similar thoughts today continue to be directed onto different tracks and in different directions.

Unless I am mistaken, the transformation of Kant's "ideas" of pure reason into "idealizing" presuppositions of communicative action raises difficulties especially for understanding the *factual* role of performatively presupposed *counterfactual* assumptions. For they are actually effective in structuring processes of mutual understanding and in organizing contexts of interaction: "This (move) has the effect of relocating the Kantian opposition between the real and the ideal *within* the domain of social practice. Cooperative interaction is seen to be structured around ideas of reason which are neither fully constitutive in the Platonic sense nor merely regulative in the Kantian sense. As *idealizing suppositions* we cannot avoid making while engaged in processes of mutual understanding, they are *actually effective* in ways that point beyond the limits of actual situations. As a result, social-practical ideas of reason are both 'immanent' and 'transcendent' to practices constitutive of forms of life."[7]

In accordance with formal pragmatics, the rational structure of action oriented toward reaching understanding is reflected in the presuppositions that actors *must* make if they are to engage in this practice at all. The necessity of this "must" has a Wittgensteinian rather than a Kantian sense. That is, it does not have the transcendental sense of universal, necessary, and noumenal [*intelligiblen*] conditions of possible experience, but has the grammatical sense of an "inevitability" stemming from the conceptual connections of a system of learned—but for us inescapable—rule-governed behavior. After the pragmatic deflation of the Kantian approach, "transcendental analysis" means the search for presumably universal, but only de facto inescapable conditions that must be met for certain fundamental practices or achievements. All practices for which we cannot imagine functional equivalents in our sociocultural forms of life are "fundamental" in this sense. One natural language can be replaced by another. But propositionally differentiated language as such (as a "species endowment") has no imaginable replacement that could fulfill the same functions. I want to clarify this basic idea genealogically, by tracing it back to Kant.

For present purposes, I am not concerned with the systematic task of explicating the concept of "communicative reason,"[8] but with the genealogical examination of the context in which this conception originated. I shall focus on the idealizing performative presuppositions of communicative action: the shared presupposition of a world of independently existing objects, the reciprocal presupposition of rationality or "accountability," the unconditionality of context-transcending validity claims such as truth and moral rightness, and the exacting presuppositions of argumentation that force participants to decenter their own interpretative perspectives. I speak of "presuppositions" because these are conditions that must be fulfilled so that what is conditioned can take on one of two values: Acts of referring can neither succeed nor fail unless there is a referential system; participants in communication can neither understand nor misunderstand one another unless there is a presupposition of rationality; truth claims can be called into question in any given context only if the corresponding propositions that are "true" in one context cannot lose that property in another; and finally, arguments neither pro nor con can have any weight unless there are communicative situations that can bring out the unforced force of the better argument. The respects in which these presuppositions have an "ideal" content shall occupy us yet.

Certainly there is a family resemblance between these presuppositions and Kantian concepts. One may presume there are genealogical connections

(1) between the "cosmological idea" of the unity of the world (or the totality of conditions in the sensory world) and the pragmatic presupposition of a common objective world;

(2) between the "idea of freedom" as a postulate of practical reason and the pragmatic presupposition of the rationality of accountable agents;

(3) between the totalizing movement of reason that, as a "faculty of ideas," transcends all that is conditioned toward an unconditioned and the unconditionality of the validity claims raised in communicative action; and

(4) finally, between reason as the "faculty of principles," which takes on the role of the "highest court of appeal for all rights and claims," and rational discourse as the unavoidable forum of possible justification.

In the first part of this essay, I shall lay out these four genealogical connections in sequence (sections 1–4). To be sure, the ideas of pure reason cannot be translated seamlessly from the idiom of transcendental philosophy into that of formal pragmatics. Establishing "analogies" is not the end of the matter. In the course of their transformation, the sharp clarity of Kant's oppositions (constitutive vs. regulative, transcendental vs. empirical, immanent vs. transcendent, etc.) diminishes because detranscendentalization signifies a profoundly invasive intervention into his basic architectonic. In light of these genealogical connections, we further discover the cross-roads where analytic philosophy of language turns away from its heritage of Kantian ideas of reason. Nevertheless, as I will show in the second part of the paper, philosophy of language arrives at normative descriptions of linguistic practice that are akin to those of a formal pragmatics more closely tied to Kant. Starting with Frege's critique of psychologism (5), I take up the discussion on the analytic side by following the strands of Davidson's principle of charity (6), Dummett's critique of Wittgenstein (7), and Brandom's conception of communication as discursive exchange of reasons (8).

I

(1) *The common objective world.* In addition to the idea of the unity of the thinking subject and the idea of God as the unitary origin of the conditions of all objects of thought, Kant includes the cosmological *idea of a unitary world* among the ideas of theoretical reason. In speaking of a "hypothetical" use of reason, Kant has in view the heuristic function of this idea for the progress of empirical research. The totalizing anticipation of the entirety of the objects of possible experience does not make cognition possible but rather guides it. Whereas empirical cognition is "the touchstone of truth," the cosmological idea plays the role of a methodological principle of completeness; it points to the goal of a systematic unity of all knowledge.[9] In contrast to the constitutive categories of the understanding and the forms of intuition, the "unity of the world" is a regulative idea.

Metaphysical thinking falls victim to the dialectical illusion of hypostatized world order because it uses this regulative idea constitutively. The reifying use of theoretical reason confuses the constructive projection of a *focus imaginarius* for ongoing research with the constitution of an object that is accessible to experience. This "apodictic"—hence excessive—use of reason corresponds to the "transcendent" use of the categories of the understanding beyond the realm of possible experience. Transgressing this boundary results in an undue assimilation of the concept of the "world"—as the entirety of all objects that can be experienced—to the concept of an object writ large that represents the world as such. The differentiation between the world and the innerworldly that Kant defends must be preserved even if the transcendental subject loses its position outside time and space and is transformed into a multitude of subjects capable of speech and action.

Detranscendentalization leads, on the one hand, to the embedding of knowing subjects into the socializing context of a lifeworld and, on the other hand, to the entwinement of cognition with speech and action. The concept of the "world" is altered along with the theoretical architectonic. I first explain what I mean by the "formal-pragmatic presupposition of the world" (a), in order to draw attention to its important consequences, namely: the replacement of transcendental idealism by internal realism (b), the regulative function of the concept of truth (c), and the embeddedness of references [*Weltbezüge*] in contexts of the lifeworld (d).

(a) As subjects capable of speech and action, language users must be able to "refer" [*sich beziehen*] "to something" in the objective world from within the horizon of their shared lifeworld if they are to reach an understanding "about something" in communicating with one another or if they are to succeed "with something" in their practical dealings. Whether in communicating about states of affairs or in practical dealings with people and things, subjects can refer to something only if they start—each on her own, yet in agreement with everyone else—with a pragmatic presupposition. They presuppose "the world" as the totality of independently existing objects that can be judged or dealt with. All objects about which it is possible to state facts can be "judged." But only spatiotemporally identifiable objects can be "dealt with" in the sense of being purposefully manipulated.

To say that the world is "objective" means that it is "given" to us as "the same for everyone." It is linguistic practice—especially the use of singular terms—that forces us to pragmatically presuppose such a world shared by all. The referential system built into natural languages ensures that any given speaker can formally anticipate possible objects of reference. Through this formal presupposition of the world, communication about something in the world is intertwined with practical interventions in the world. Speakers and actors reach an understanding about and intervene in one and the same objective world. To achieve secure semantic references, it is important that speakers are, as agents, in contact with the objects of everyday life and that they can put themselves in contact with them repeatedly.[10]

Like Kant's cosmological idea of reason, the conception of a presupposed world rests on the transcendental difference between the world and the innerworldly, which reappears in Heidegger as the ontological difference between "Being" and "beings." According to this supposition, the objective world that we posit is not the same kind of thing as what can occur in it as object (i.e., state of affairs, thing, event). But otherwise this conception no longer fits within the Kantian framework of oppositions. Once the a priori categories of the understanding and forms of intuition have been detranscendentalized and thus disarmed, the classic distinction between reason and understanding is blurred. Obviously, the pragmatic presupposition of the world is not a regulative idea, but it is "constitutive" for referring to anything about which it is possible to establish facts. At the same time, the concept of the world remains formal in such a way that the system of possible references does not fix in advance any specific properties of objects in general. All attempts to reconstruct a material a priori of meaning [*Sinn-Apriori*] for possible objects of reference—that is, to predetermine the descriptions under which it is possible to refer to objects—have failed.[11]

(b) From this perspective, the distinction between appearance and "thing-in-itself" also becomes meaningless. Experiences and judgments are now coupled with a practice that copes with reality. They remain in contact with a surprising reality through problem-solving activities that are evaluated by their success. This reality either resists our grasp, or it "plays along." Viewed ontologically, transcendental idealism, which conceives the totality of objects of possible experience as a world "for us," as a world of appearances, is replaced by an internal realism. Accordingly, everything is "real" that can be represented in true statements, although facts are interpreted in a language that is always "ours." The world itself does not impose "its" language on us; it does not itself speak; and it "responds" only in a figurative sense.[12] In asserting a state of affairs, we say it "obtains." However, this "veridical Being" of facts is mistakenly assimilated to the "existence" of objects once we conceive of the representation of facts as a kind of picturing of reality.

What we state as facts results from learning processes and remains embedded in the semantic network of possible justifications. It is therefore advisable to distinguish, with C. S. Peirce, between a "reality" that can be represented in true statements and the "world" of objects these statements are about—between "what is the case" and the "existing constraints" of what we "come up against" and have to "cope with" in our practical dealings. The "accommodation" or "resistance" of the objects being talked about is already assimilated in true statements. To that extent, the "being the case" or obtaining [*Bestehen*] of states of affairs indirectly expresses the "existence" [*Existenz*] of recalcitrant objects (or the facticity of constraining circumstances). The "world" that we presuppose as the totality of objects, not of facts, must not be confused with the "reality" that consists of facts, that is everything that can be represented in true statements.

(c) Both concepts, "world" and "reality," express totalities, but only the concept of reality can, in virtue of its internal connection with the concept of truth, be placed alongside the regulative ideas of reason. The Peircean concept of reality (as the totality of statable facts) is a regulative idea in Kant's sense because it commits the practice of fact-stating to an orientation toward truth, which in turn has a regulative function. For Kant, "truth" is not an idea, nor is it connected with the ideas of reason since the transcendental conditions of objective experience are also supposed to explain the truth of judgments of experience: "For Kant, the question . . . of the conditions of possibility of constituting objects, i.e., of constituting the meaning of objectivity, was the same as the question . . . of the conditions of possibility of the intersubjective validity of true knowledge."[13] Contrary to this, Karl-Otto Apel defends the distinction between the pragmatically interpreted a priori of experience [*Erfahrungsapriori*], which determines the meaning of the objects of possible experience, and the conditions of the argumentative justification of statements about such objects.

Peirce wanted to explain "truth" itself epistemically, in terms of progress toward truth. He defined the meaning of truth by anticipating a consensus that all participants in a self-correcting process of inquiry under ideal epistemic conditions would have to attain.[14] The unlimited ideal "community of investigators" constitutes the forum for the "highest court" of reason. There are good reasons against epistemologizing the concept of truth in this way, which assimilates "truth" to "idealized justification" or "ideal warranted assertibility."[15] Nonetheless, the *orientation* toward truth—as a property that a proposition "cannot lose"—acquires an indispensable regulative function for fallible processes of justification precisely if such processes can at best lead to decisions about the rational acceptability of propositions and not their truth.[16]

Even after objective knowledge is detranscendentalized and tied to discursive justification as the "touchstone of truth," the point of Kant's injunction against the apodictic use of reason and the transcendent use of the understanding is preserved. Only now the boundary separating the transcendental from the transcendent use of our cognitive capacity is not defined by sensibility and understanding, but by the forum of rational discourse in which the convincing power of good reasons must flourish.

(d) In a certain way, the distinction between truth and rational acceptability replaces the difference between "things-in-themselves" and appearances. Kant was not able to bridge this transcendental–empirical gap even by means of the regulative idea of the unity of the world. The reason is that the heuristic of completing all conditioned cognitions does not lead the understanding *beyond* the realm of phenomena. Even after the knowing subject is detranscendentalized, there remains a gap between what is true and what is warranted or rationally acceptable to us. Although this gap cannot be closed definitively within discourse, it can be closed pragmatically by a rationally motivated transition from discourse to action. Because discourses *remain* rooted in the lifeworld, there is an internal connection between the two roles taken on by the idea of an orientation toward truth—in the form of practical certainties in action on the one hand and as hypothetical validity claims in discourse on the other.[17]

The regulative function of the orientation toward truth, supported by the supposition of an objective world, directs processes of justification toward a goal that mobilizes the highest court of reason. That is, in the course of detranscendentalization, the theoretical ideas of reason step out of the static "intelligible world" and unleash their dynamics *within* the lifeworld. Kant says that we have only an "idea" but no "knowledge" of the intelligible realm. After the cosmological idea has been transformed into the presupposition of a shared objective world, however, the orientation to unconditional validity claims makes the resources of Kant's intelligible world available for the acquisition of empirical knowledge. Giving up the background assumptions of Kant's transcendental philosophy turns ideas of reason into idealizations that orient subjects capable of speech and action. The rigid "ideal" that was elevated to an otherworldly realm is set aflow in this-worldly operations; it is transposed from a transcendent state into a process of "immanent transcendence." For in the discursive struggle over the correct interpretation of what we encounter in the world, lifeworld contexts that are drifting apart must be transcended "from within."

Language users can direct themselves *toward* something inner-worldly only *from within* the horizon of their lifeworld. There are no strictly context-independent references to something in the world [*Weltbezüge*]. Heidegger and Wittgenstein each in his own way showed that Kant's transcendental consciousness of objects feeds on false abstractions.[18] The lifeworld contexts and the linguistic practices in which socialized subjects "always already" find themselves disclose the world from the perspective of traditions and habits that generate meaning. Everything that members of a local linguistic community encounter in the world they experience not as neutral objects, but in the light of an inhabited and habituated "grammatical" preunderstanding. The linguistic mediation of our relations to the world [*Weltbezuges*] explains why the objectivity of the world that we presuppose in acting and speaking refers back to a communicative intersubjectivity among interlocutors. A fact about some object must be *stated* and, if necessary, *justified* before others who can object to my assertion. The particular demand for interpretation arises because even when we use language descriptively, we cannot disregard its world-disclosive character.

These translation problems shed light on the thicket of lifeworld contexts, but they are not grounds for subscribing to any incommensurability thesis.[19] Interlocutors can reach mutual understanding across the boundaries of diverging lifeworlds because in presupposing a shared objective world, they orient themselves toward the claim to truth, that is, to the unconditional validity they claim when they make a statement. I shall return to this orientation to truth below.

(2) *The accountability of subjects.* The cosmological idea of the unity of the world branches into the pragmatic presupposition of an objective world as the totality of objects, on the one hand, and the

orientation toward a reality conceived as the totality of facts, on the other. We encounter a different kind of idealization in the interpersonal relationships of language users who take one another "at their word" and hold one another to "be answerable." In their cooperative dealings with one another, they must mutually expect one another to be rational, at least provisionally. In certain circumstances, it may *turn out* that such a presupposition was unwarranted. Contrary to expectations, it might *happen* that the other person cannot account for her actions and utterances and that we cannot see how she could justify her behavior. In contexts of action oriented toward reaching understanding, this kind of frustration can occur only against the background supposition of rationality that anyone engaged in communicative action must assume. This supposition purports that a subject who is acting intentionally is capable, in the right circumstances, of providing a more or less plausible reason for *why* she did or did not behave or express herself one way rather than another. Unintelligible and odd, bizarre and enigmatic expressions prompt follow-up questions because they implicitly contradict an unavoidable presupposition of communication and therefore trigger puzzled or irritated reactions.

Someone who cannot account for her actions and utterances to others becomes suspect of not having acted reasonably or "accountably" [*zurechnungsfähig*]. Even a criminal judge must first determine whether the accused could be held responsible for her alleged crime. Furthermore, the judge examines whether there are exculpatory grounds. In order to judge an offense fairly, we have to know whether the perpetrator was accountable and whether the offense should be attributed more to the circumstances or to the agent herself. Exculpatory grounds confirm the supposition of rationality that we make about other agents not only in judicial proceedings, but also in everyday life. But the example of legal discourse is a good one for comparing the pragmatic presupposition of accountability with Kant's idea of freedom.

Until now, we have considered reason "in its theoretical use" as "the capacity to judge according to principles." Reason becomes "practical" insofar as it determines will and action according to principles. Through the moral law expressed in the categorical imperative, the idea of freedom acquires its own "special kind of causality," namely, the rationally motivating force of good reasons.[20] Unlike the ideas of theoretical reason, which merely regulate the use of the understanding, freedom is constitutive for action because it is an irrefutable demand of practical reason. Of course we can always consider actions under the description of observable behavior as processes determined by natural laws. However, from a practical point of view, we have to relate actions to reasons for why a rational subject might have done them. The "practical point of view" signifies a shift in perspective to the kind of normative judgment in which we also engage when acting communicatively by presupposing rationality.

Of course the reasons that are relevant to "freedom" (in the Kantian sense) form but a fraction of the spectrum of reasons for assessing the accountability of subjects acting communicatively. Kant characterizes freedom in general as an agent's capacity to subordinate her will to maxims, that is, to orient her actions by rules whose concept she has mastered. Thus freedom of choice [*Willkürfreiheit*] enables one to adopt rules of prudence or skill depending on one's inclinations and subjectively selected ends, whereas "free will" [*freie Wille*] obeys universally valid laws that it has imposed on itself from a moral point of view. Freedom of choice precedes free will, but the former remains subordinate to the latter when it comes to the moral evaluation of ends. Kant thus confines himself to technical-practical and moral-practical reasons. Communicative action draws on a broader spectrum of reasons: epistemic reasons for the truth of statements, ethical orientations and modes of action as indicators for the authenticity of life choices or the sincerity of confessions, and, depending on the issue, aesthetic experiences, narrative declarations, cultural standards of value, legal claims, conventions, and so on. Accountability is not assessed simply by the standards of morality and purposive rationality—indeed, it involves more than just practical reason. Accountability consists, rather, in an agent's *general* ability to orient her action by validity claims.[21]

According to Kant, among the practical ideas of reason freedom is the only one whose possible realization we can conceive [*einsehen*] a priori. Hence this idea acquires legislative force for every rational being. It receives concrete expression in the ideal of a "kingdom of ends" in which all rational beings join together under common laws so that they never treat one another merely as means, but as ends in themselves. Every member of this kingdom "legislates universal laws, while also being himself subject to these laws."[22] We have an a priori understanding [*Einsicht*] of this model of self-legislation, which signifies two things. On the one hand, it has the categorical sense of an obligation (namely of realizing the kingdom of ends by one's own actions and omissions). On the other hand, it has the transcendental sense of a certainty (that this kingdom *can* be advanced by our moral actions and omissions). We can know a priori that it *is possible* to actualize this practical idea.

Considered under the first aspect, the comparison of the idea of freedom with the supposition of rationality in communicative action is not very fruitful. Rationality is not an obligation. Even with regard to moral or legal behavior, the attribution of rationality does not mean that one's alter feels obligated to obey norms; she is merely imputed to have knowledge of what it means to act autonomously. The second aspect is more promising: The idea of freedom provides the certainty that autonomous action (and the realization of the kingdom of ends) *is possible*—and not merely counterfactually demanded of us. According to Kant, rational beings think of themselves as agents acting on the basis of good reasons. With regard to moral action, they have an a priori knowledge of the possibility of actualizing the idea of freedom. In communicative action we also tacitly start with the assumption that all participants *are* accountable agents. It is simply part of the self-understanding of subjects acting communicatively that they take rationally motivated positions on claims to validity; agents mutually presuppose that they *indeed do* act based on rationally warrantable reasons.

Of course we need not wait for social-scientific or psychological studies of behavior to show us that this performative "knowledge" is problematic. In everyday practice we are both participant and observer, and we discover that many expressions are motivated by things other than good reasons. From this empirical point of view, the accountability of communicative actors is no less a counterfactual presupposition than Kant's idea of freedom. Yet oddly enough, for the acting subjects *themselves* this empirical knowledge loses its contradictory character as they carry out their actions. The contrast between the objective knowledge of an observer and the performatively engaged knowledge of an actor is of no consequence *in actu*. First-year sociology students learn that all norms are valid counterfactually, even if they are obeyed on average: For the sociologist-observer, statistically likely cases of deviant behavior go hand in hand with any prevailing norm.[23] Knowing this, however, will generally not prevent addressees from accepting as binding any norm that the community recognizes.

Someone who is acting morally does not credit herself with "more or less" autonomy; and participants in communicative action do not attribute sometimes "a little more" and sometimes "a little less" rationality to one another. From the perspective of the participants, these concepts are binarily coded. As soon as we/act out of "respect for the law" or "with an orientation to reaching mutual understanding," we cannot at the same time act from the objectivating perspective of an observer. While carrying out our actions, we bracket empirical self-descriptions in favor of the agents' rational self-understanding. Nevertheless, the supposition of rationality is a *defeasible* assumption and not a priori knowledge. It "functions" as a multiply corroborated pragmatic presupposition that is constitutive of communicative action. But in any given instance, it can be falsified. This difference in the status of practical knowledge cannot be explained solely in terms of the detranscendentalization of the acting subject who has been dislodged from the kingdom of intelligible beings into the linguistically articulated lifeworld of socialized subjects. This paradigm shift alters the whole outlook of the analysis.

Within a mentalistic conceptual framework, Kant conceives of an agent's rational self-understanding as a person's knowledge of herself, and he abstractly opposes this first-person knowledge to an observer's third-person knowledge. The transcendental gap between these two forms of knowledge is such that the self-understanding of subjects as members of the intelligible realm cannot be corrected in principle by empirical knowledge. As speakers and addressees, however, communicatively acting subjects encounter one another literally at eye level by taking on first- and *second-person* roles. By reaching an understanding about something in the objective world and adopting the same relation to the world, they enter into an interpersonal relationship. In this performative attitude *toward* one another, they share communicative experiences *with* one another against the background of an intersubjectively shared—that is, sufficiently overlapping—lifeworld. Each can understand what the other says or means. They learn from the information and objections that their interlocutor conveys and draw their own conclusions from irony, silence, paradoxical expressions, allusions, and so on. Cases in which opaque behavior becomes unintelligible or communication breaks down represent a reflective mode of communicative experience. At this level, the presupposition of rationality cannot be refuted as such, but it is indirectly defeasible.

This kind of defeasibility does not seem to apply to idealizations in the domain of cognition, even if they also take the form of pragmatic presuppositions. The supposition of a shared objective world projects a system of possible references to the world and hence makes interventions in the world and interpretations of something in the world possible in the first place. The supposition of a shared objective world is "transcendentally" necessary in the sense that it cannot be corrected by experiences that would not be possible without it. The content of our descriptions is of course subject to revision, but the formal projection [*Entwurf*] of the totality of identifiable objects in general is not—at least not as long as our form of life is characterized by natural languages that have the kind of propositional structure with which we are familiar. At best, we may find out a posteriori that the projection was insufficiently formal. But "unavoidable" presuppositions are apparently "constitutive" for *practices* in a different sense than they are for *object domains*.

For rule-governed behavior, constitutive rules always open up the possibility of following or violating them. Beyond that, there is the possibility in principle of being able to do something and not being able to do it. Someone who has not mastered the rules of a game and is not even capable of making mistakes is not a player. This becomes clear in the course of the practice. Thus only during communicative action does it become clear who is frustrating the pragmatic presupposition of accountability and is not even "in the game." Whereas the supposition of a shared objective world is not subject to being checked against the kinds of experiences that it makes possible, the necessary supposition of rationality in communicative action holds only provisionally. The latter is open to being contradicted by experiences that participants have precisely through engaging in this practice.

(3) *The unconditionality of validity claims.* Until now, we have examined the detranscendentalized use of reason in terms of the supposition of a shared objective world and the mutual supposition of rationality that agents must make when they engage in communicative action. We have touched in a preliminary way on another sense of "idealization," which appears in the regulative function of the orientation to truth that complements reference to the world. The practice of action oriented to mutual understanding forces on its participants certain totalizing anticipations, abstractions, and transgressions of boundaries. Certainly the genealogical connection with Kant's "ideas" suggests the term "idealization" in these cases. But what do the various kinds of idealizations really have in common?

Language users must rely on a shared system of independently existing objects of reference about which they can form beliefs and which they can intentionally influence. The formal-pragmatic supposition of the world creates place-holders for objects to which speaking and acting subjects can refer. However, grammar cannot "impose" any laws on nature. A "transcendental projection" in the weak sense depends on nature "meeting us halfway." Thus in the "vertical" dimension of relating to the world, idealization consists in the anticipation of the totality of possible references. In the horizontal dimension of intersubjective relationships, the mutual supposition of rationality indicates what subjects in principle expect of one another. If reaching understanding, and thereby coordinating action, is to be possible at all, then agents must be capable of taking a warranted stance on criticizable validity claims and of orienting themselves by such claims in their own actions.

Here idealization consists in the preliminary abstraction from deviations, individual differences, and limiting contexts. Communicative disturbances and, in extreme cases, breakdowns of communication occur only when these deviations exceed the limits of tolerance. In contrast to the Kantian projection of totalities, there is a Platonic sense of idealization that makes itself felt here. As long as they maintain a performative attitude, actors are immune to acknowledging empirically observable imperfections until these reach a threshold at which the discrepancy between the ideal and its incomplete realization in a given instance becomes intolerable. The totalizing anticipation is not what is decisive in this dimension. Decisive rather is the neutralization *in actu* of negligible deviations from the ideal, toward which even objectively deviant action is oriented.

Finally, the orientation toward truth in the critical testing of unconditional claims to validity mobilizes still another kind of idealization. This kind seems excessive, for it combines the Kantian and the Platonic senses of "idealization" into an apparent hybrid. Because our contact with the world is linguistically mediated, the world eludes the direct grasp of the senses and immediate constitution through the forms of intuition and the concepts of the understanding. The presupposed objectivity of the world is so deeply entwined with the intersubjectivity of reaching an understanding about something in the world that we cannot transcend this connection and escape the linguistically disclosed horizon of our intersubjectively shared lifeworld. This of course does not rule out communication across the boundaries of particular lifeworlds. We are able reflectively to transcend whatever our given initial hermeneutic situations are and attain intersubjectively shared views on disputed matters. Gadamer describes this as a "fusion of horizons."[24]

The supposition of a common world of independently existing objects about which we can state facts is complemented by the idea of truth as a property that assertoric sentences cannot "lose." However, if fallible sentences cannot immediately confront the world, but can be justified or denied only by means of further propositions, and if there is no basis of self-warranting, self-evident propositions, then claims to truth can be tested only discursively. Thus the two-place relation of the validity [*Gültigkeit*] of propositions is extended into the three-place relation of a validity [*Geltung*] that valid propositions have "for us." Their truth must be recognizable to an audience. But then claims to *unconditional* truth unleash, under the prevailing epistemic *conditions* for their possible justification, an explosive power *within* the existing communicative relationships. The epistemic reflection of unconditionality is the ideal inflation of the critical audience into a "final" court of appeal. Peirce uses the image of the socially and historically unlimited ideal community of inquirers that continues to pursue the process of inquiry—until they reach the ideal limit of a "final opinion."

This image is misleading in two respects: To begin with, it suggests that truth can be conceived as idealized warranted assertibility, which in turn is assessed in terms of a consensus attained under ideal conditions. But a proposition is agreed to by all rational subjects because it is true; it is not true because it could be the content of a consensus attained under ideal conditions. Moreover, Peirce's image does not direct our attention to the *process* of justification in the course of which true propositions have to stand up to objections, but to the *final state* of an agreement not subject to revision. This is contrary to a fallibilist self-understanding that expresses itself in the "cautionary use" of the truth predicate. As finite minds, we have no way of foreseeing changes in epistemic conditions; hence we cannot rule out that a proposition, no matter how ideally justified, will turn out to be false.[25] Despite these objections to an epistemic conception of truth and even after abandoning foundationalist justifications, the idea of a process of argumentation that is as inclusive as possible and that can be continued at any time has an important role in explaining "rational acceptability," if not "truth." As fallible, situated beings, we have no other way to *ascertain* truth than through discourses that are both rational and open-ended.

No matter how misleading the image of an ideally extended communication community (Apel) that reaches a warranted consensus under ideal epistemic conditions (Putnam), before an ideal audience (Perelman), or in an ideal speech situation (Habermas), we can in no way forgo making some such idealizations. For the wound opened up in everyday practice by a truth claim that has become problematic must be healed in a discourse that cannot be terminated "once and for all," either by "decisive" evidence or by "compelling" arguments. Though truth claims cannot be definitely redeemed in discourses, it is through arguments alone that we let ourselves be *convinced* of the truth of problematic propositions. What is convincing is what we can accept as rational. Rational acceptability depends on a procedure that does not shield "our" arguments from anyone or anything. The process of argumentation as such must remain open to any relevant objections and any improvements of our epistemic condition. This kind of argumentative practice that is as inclusive and continuous as possible is subsumed by the idea of continually going beyond the limitations of current forms of communication with respect to social spaces, historical times, and substantive competencies. The discursive process thereby increases the responsive potential by which rationally accepted claims to validity prove their worth.

With their intuitive understanding of the meaning of argumentation in general, proponents and opponents force one another into decentering their interpretive perspectives. Thus Kant's idealizing anticipation of the whole is carried over from the *objective* to the *social* world. In the performative attitude of participants in argumentation, this "totalization" is connected with a "neutralization": they prescind from the obvious gap between, on the one hand, the ideal model of an "endless conversation" that is completely inclusive both socially and thematically and, on the other hand, the finite, spatiotemporally limited discourses that we actually engage in. Because the participants are oriented toward truth, the concept of an absolutely valid truth is reflected at the level of the discursive ascertainment of truth in performative idealizations that make this argumentative practice so demanding. Before I can enter into the details of these pragmatic presuppositions of rational discourse, I must briefly sketch the spectrum of validity claims beyond "truth." According to the Kantian concept of practical reason, we claim unconditional validity not only for true assertoric propositions but also for correct moral—and with some reservations, legal—propositions.

(4) *Discourse as the forum of justification.* Until now, whenever I have spoken about communicatively acting subjects reaching an understanding about something in "the" world, I had in mind the reference to a common objective world. The claims to truth raised for assertoric sentences have served as the paradigm for claims to validity in general. In regulative speech acts such as recommendations, requests, and commands, agents refer to actions that (they believe) their interlocutors are obliged to perform. As members of a social group, they share certain practices and value orientations, they jointly recognize certain norms, are used to certain conventions, and so forth. In the regulative use of language, speakers rely on an intersubjectively recognized or habituated constellation of habits, institutions, or rules that regulate interpersonal relations in the group so that its members know what kind of behavior they may legitimately expect of one another. (With commissive speech acts, a speaker produces a legitimate relationship by entering into an obligation; in doing so, participants assume that communicatively acting subjects bind their will to maxims and are able to take responsibility for what they promise to do.)

In such normative language games, agents also refer to something in the objective world via the propositional contents of their utterances, but they do so only incidentally. They mention the circumstances and success conditions of the actions they demand, request, recommend, accuse someone of, excuse, promise, and so on. But they refer directly to actions and norms as "something in the social world." Of course they do not conceive of norm-governed actions as social facts that form a segment of the objective world, as it were. To be sure, from the objectifying point of view of the sociologist-observer there "are" normative expectations, practices, habits, institutions, and regulations of all sorts "in the world" in addition to physical things and mental states. However, agents who are immediately involved have a different attitude toward the network of their normatively regulated interactions, namely, the performative attitude of actors who can "violate" norms only because they recognize them to be binding. They use a reference system that complements that of the objective world from the point of view of a second person whose "good will" is subject to normative expectations. This reference system lifts the relevant segment for their norm-governed action out of the encompassing context of their lifeworld for purposes of thematization. Thus members comprehend their "social world" as the totality of possible legitimately regulated interpersonal relationships. Like the "objective world," this system of reference is also a necessary supposition that is grammatically coupled to regulative (as opposed to constative) language use.

(The expressive use of first-person sentences completes this architechtonic of "worlds." Based on a speaker's epistemic authority
for sincerely expressing her own "experiences," we delimit an "inner
world" from the objective and social worlds. The discussion of first-
person perceptual and experiential reports, which arose in connection with Wittgenstein's private language argument and Wilfrid
Sellars's critique of mentalism, shows that the totality of experiences
to which a subject has privileged access cannot simply be understood as one more system of reference analogous to the objective
and social worlds. "My" experiences are subjectively certain; unlike
objective data or normative expectations, they do not have to be
identified, nor can they be. Rather, the subjective "world" is determined negatively as the totality of that which neither occurs in the
objective world nor is taken to be valid or intersubjectively recognized in the social world. The subjective world complements these
two publicly accessible worlds by encompassing all experiences that
a speaker can turn into the content of first-person sentences when
she wants to reveal something about herself to an audience in the
expressive mode of self-presentation.)

The claim to rightness of normative statements relies on the presumed validity of an underlying norm. Unlike the truth of descriptive statements, the validity domain of a rightness claim varies
according to the legitimating background, that is, according to the
boundaries of a social world in general. Only *moral* imperatives (and
legal norms such as human rights that can only be justified morally)
claim absolute validity, that is, universal recognition, in the way that
assertions do. This explains Kant's demand that valid moral laws
must be "universalizable." Moral norms must be able to command
the rationally motivated recognition of *all* subjects capable of speech
and action, beyond the historical and cultural confines of any particular social world. Thus, the idea of a thoroughly morally ordered
community implies the counterfactual extension of the social world
in which we find ourselves to a completely inclusive world of well-
ordered interpersonal relationships: *All* human beings become
brothers and sisters.

Of course it would equally be a mistake to hypostatize such a universal community of persons capable of moral judgment and action

in the sense of a spatiotemporally unlimited community. The image of the self-determined "kingdom of ends" suggests the existence of a republic of rational beings, although it is a construct that, as Kant notes, "does not exist but can be made actual by our conduct."[26] It ought to and can be brought about in accordance with the practical idea of freedom. The kingdom of ends "exists" in a certain sense, yet it is more a task we are charged with [*aufgegeben*] than something that is given to us [*gegeben*]: a mandate, not a given. This ambiguity was not the least of Kant's motives for dividing human practices into the intelligible realm and the realm of appearances. As soon as we no longer subscribe to this transcendental bipartition, we have to bring out the *constructive meaning* of morality in some other way.

We can represent moral learning processes as an intelligent expansion and reciprocal interpenetration of social worlds that in a given case of conflict do not yet sufficiently overlap. The disputing parties learn to *include* one another in a world they construct together so as to be able to judge and consensually resolve controversial actions in the light of matching standards of evaluation. G. H. Mead described this as the expansion of a reversible exchange of interpretive perspectives. At first rooted in their own particular life-worlds, the participants' perspectives become increasingly "decentered" (as Piaget puts it) as the mutual process of perspectival interpenetration approaches the ideal limit of complete inclusiveness. Interestingly, this is precisely what the practice of argumentation aims at by its very structure. Rational discourse is a process that ensures the inclusion of all those affected and the equal consideration of all the interests at play. Thus, in view of the idea that only those norms equally good for all merit recognition from the moral point of view, such discourse presents itself as the appropriate method of conflict resolution.

"Impartiality" in the sense of justice converges with "impartiality" in the sense of the discursive ascertainment of cognitive claims to validity.[27] This convergence makes sense if we compare the orientation of moral learning processes with the conditions for participating in argumentation at all. Conflicts are triggered by contradictions among social opponents with dissonant value orientations. Moral learning processes resolve such conflicts through each participant's reciprocal inclusion of the other(s). As it turns out, however, argumentation as a form of communication is already tailored to such an interpenetration of perspectives and enriching expansion of world horizons. Lest the discussion of disputed validity claims forfeit its cognitive purpose, participants in argumentation must subscribe to an egalitarian universalism that is structurally mandated and that at first has only a formal-pragmatic, rather than a moral, meaning.

The cooperative nature of the competition for better arguments is explained by the goal or function constitutive for the language game of argumentation: participants want to convince one another. In continuing everyday communicative action at the reflective level of thematized claims to validity, they are still guided by the goal of mutual understanding inasmuch as a proponent can win the game only if she *convinces* her opponents that her validity claim is warranted. The rational acceptability of the corresponding statement is based on the convincing force of the better arguments. Which argument does convince is not decided by private insight, but by the stances that, bundled together in a rationally motivated agreement, are adopted by everyone who participates in the public practice of exchanging reasons.

Now, standards for whether something counts as a good or a bad argument may themselves become controversial. Anything can come under the pressure of contrary reasons. Hence the rational acceptability of validity claims is *ultimately* based only on reasons that stand up to objections under certain exacting conditions of communication. If the process of argumentation is to live up to its meaning, communication in the form of rational discourse must, if possible, allow all relevant information and explanations to be brought up and weighed so that the stance participants take can be intrinsically motivated solely by the revisionary power of free-floating reasons. However, if this is the intuitive meaning that we associate with argumentation in general, then we also know that a practice may not seriously count as argumentation unless it meets certain pragmatic presuppositions.[28]

The four most important presuppositions are (a) publicity and inclusiveness: no one who could make a relevant contribution with regard to a controversial validity claim must be excluded; (b) equal rights to engage in communication: everyone must have the same opportunity to speak to the matter at hand; (c) exclusion of deception and illusion: participants have to mean what they say; and (d) absence of coercion: communication must be free of restrictions that prevent the better argument from being raised or from determining the outcome of the discussion. Presuppositions (a), (b), and (d) subject one's behavior in argumentation to the rules of an egalitarian universalism. *With regard to moral-practical issues*, it follows from these rules that the interests and value orientations of every affected person are equally taken into consideration. And since the participants in practical discourses are simultaneously the ones who are affected, presupposition (c)—which *in theoretical-empirical disputes* requires only a sincere and unconstrained weighing of the arguments—takes on the further significance that one remain critically alert to self-deception as well as hermeneutically open and sensitive to how others understand themselves and the world.

These argumentative presuppositions obviously contain such strong idealizations that they raise the suspicion of a rather tendentious description of argumentation. How should it be at all possible for participants in argumentation performatively to proceed from such obviously counterfactual assumptions? After all, people engaged in discourse are aware, for example, that the circle of participants is highly selective, that one side of their communicative space is privileged over the other, that one person or another remains caught in prejudices about this topic or that, that many people sometimes behave strategically, or that yes- and no-positions are often determined by motives other than a better understanding of the issue. To be sure, an observer analyzing a discourse could more accurately spot such deviations from an ideal "speech situation" than could the engaged participants, who presume they have approximated the ideal. But even when taking a performative attitude, participants do not allow themselves to be fully consumed lock, stock, and barrel by their engagement to the point of not being aware—at least intuitively—of much that they could know thematically by taking an observer's objectivating attitude.

At the same time, these unavoidable presuppositions of argumentative practice, no matter how counterfactual, are by no means mere constructs. Rather they are *operatively effective* in the behavior of the participants themselves. Someone who seriously takes part in an argument de facto proceeds from such presuppositions. This is evident from the inferences participants will draw, if necessary, from perceived inconsistencies. The process of argumentation is self-correcting in the sense that in the course of an unsatisfactory discussion, for example, reasons spontaneously arise for an "overdue" liberalization of the order of business and discussion, for changing an insufficiently representative circle of participants, for expanding the agenda or improving the information base. One *can tell* when new arguments have to be taken into account or when marginalized voices have to be taken seriously. On the other hand, perceived inconsistencies are not *in every case* the motive for such or similar repairs. This is explained by the fact that participants in argumentation are convinced by the substance of the reasons rather than by the communicative design for exchanging reasons. The procedural properties of the process of argumentation warrant the rational expectation that the relevant information and reasons get "put on the table" and bring their influence to bear on the outcome. As long as participants in argumentation proceed from the assumption that this is the case, they have no reason to be worried about inadequate procedural properties of the process of communication.

The formal properties of argumentation bear on the difference between rational assertibility and truth. Because no evidence is decisive and no arguments are compelling "in the final instance," because no assertions however well justified are infallible, it is only the quality of the discursive truth-seeking procedure that warrants the reasonable expectation that the best attainable information and reasons are indeed available and do "count" in the end. Perceived inconsistencies that provoke doubts about the genuineness of an argumentative exchange do not arise until obviously *relevant participants* are excluded, *relevant contributions* suppressed, and yes/no stances are manipulated or conditioned by other kinds of influences.

The idealizing anticipation associated with argumentative presuppositions displays its operative efficacy in its critical function: An absolute claim to validity has to be justifiable in ever wider forums, before an ever more competent and larger audience, against ever new objections. This intrinsic dynamic of argumentation, the progressive decentering of one's own interpretive perspective, in particular drives practical discourses, which aim not to assess truth claims but insightfully to construct and apply moral (and legal) norms.[29]

The validity of such norms consists [*besteht*][30] in the universal recognition that they merit. Because moral claims to validity lack the ontological connotations that are characteristic of claims to truth, reference to the objective world is replaced by an orientation toward an expansion of the social world, that is, toward the progressive inclusion of strangers and their claims. The validity of a moral statement has the epistemic significance that it would be accepted under ideal conditions of justification. However, if the meaning of "moral rightness," unlike that of "truth," is *exhausted* by rational acceptability, then our moral convictions must ultimately rely on the critical potential of self-transcendence and decentering that—as the "restlessness" of idealizing anticipations—is built into the practice of argumentation and the self-understanding of its participants.

II

(5) *The critique of psychologism.* In Kant's paradigm, language does not play a constitutive role for either theory or practice. Mentalism projects the image of a more or less active or passive mind whose contact with the world is mediated by the senses. The mind produces representations of objects and intentionally acts on these objects, but in performing these operations, the mind remains essentially unaffected by language or linguistic structures. As long as language does not beguile the mind with its idols, with merely traditional images and ideals, the mind can see through the transparent medium of language as through a clear pane of glass. In looking back at the genealogy of the mentalist origins of the detranscendentalized use of reason, we thus do not yet encounter language as a medium that gives structure to the mind and situates transcendental consciousness in the historical and social contexts of the lifeworld.

Reason comes into its own for Kant in the practical domain: After all, reason is constitutive only for moral action. This is why I have sought to identify traces of detranscendentalized reason in communicative *action*. The expression "communicative action" designates social interactions where language use aimed at reaching mutual understanding plays the role of action coordination. Through linguistic communication, idealizing presuppositions enter into action oriented toward reaching mutual understanding. Hence a philosophy of language, and particularly a semantics, that gives an account of the meaning of linguistic expressions in terms of the conditions under which speakers and hearers understand a language is the place where a Kantian formal pragmatics can come into contact with analytic approaches. Indeed, with Frege, the starting point of the analytic tradition is a fundamental idealizing presupposition that was recognized as such only after the linguistic turn. If the structures of the mind are shaped by the grammar of language, the question arises how sentences and predicate expressions in their many different contexts of use can retain the very universality and sameness of meaning [*Bedeutung*][31] that seem to be inherent in judgments and concepts.

Frege suggests that we distinguish between the semantic concept of a "thought" and the psychological concept of an "idea." To be able to communicate thoughts at all, they must cross the bounds of an individual consciousness unaltered. In contrast, ideas always belong to an individual subject in space and time. Propositions have the same conceptual content even if they are expressed as sentences or grasped by different subjects in different contexts. This leads Frege to attribute to thoughts and conceptual contents an ideal status outside of space and time. He accounts for the peculiar difference in status between thoughts and ideas in terms of the grammatical form of their expression. Unlike Husserl, Frege examines the structure of judgment or thought by examining the structure of an assertoric sentence composed of words, which is the smallest grammatical unit that can be true or false. We can see how the content of thoughts differs from the objects of ideational thinking by looking at how propositions are structured and how reference and predication dovetail with one another.[32]

For linguistic expressions to have the same meaning for different people and in different contexts, thoughts must transcend the bounds of a spatiotemporally individuated consciousness and the ideal content of thought must be independent of the stream of consciousness experienced by the thinking subject. Already on the basic level of the substrate of signs, speakers and hearers must be able to recognize the same type of sign in the manifold of corresponding signifying events. This corresponds to the presupposition of invariant meanings at the semantic level. Members of a linguistic community, in any case, must in practice start from the assumption that the grammatically correct expressions they utter have a universal meaning that is the *same* for all interlocutors in a multitude of contexts of use. Only given this premise can it turn out that utterances are occasionally incomprehensible. Of course the necessary presupposition *in actu* that expressions of a shared language are being used with the same meaning does not rule out the linguistic division of labor or meaning change over time. Changes in empirical knowledge induce changes in linguistic knowledge, and epistemic progress precipitates changes in the meaning of basic theoretical concepts.[33]

In the case of the ideal universality of meaning [*Bedeutungsallgemeinheit*] of grammatical expressions, too, we are dealing with an idealizing presupposition. This is a presupposition that, from the perspective of the observer, often—and under the microscope of the ethnomethodologist, even always—turns out to be mistaken. But as a counterfactual presupposition, it is indispensable for language use oriented toward reaching mutual understanding. Following his warranted critique of psychologism, Frege, of course, allowed himself to be seduced by meaning Platonism—which, incidentally, was one of the premises Husserl shared with Frege. The later Frege thought that the mentalist architechtonic of two realms, according to which a subjective world of ideas faces the objective world of things, had to be supplemented by a third realm, namely the ideal realm of propositions. This unfortunate move puts him in a difficult position. If the meanings of sentences are hypostatized to have an ideal being-as-such, it remains a mystery how these lofty entities of the "third realm"[34] are to interact with physical objects in the objective world, on the one hand, and subjects having ideas, on the other. The relation of the conceptual *representation* [*"Darstellung"*] of entities becomes independent of a subjective mind. And we do not know in turn how this mind is able to "grasp" and to "judge" propositions.

The ambiguous, indeed, incomprehensible, life of "thoughts banned from consciousness" (Dummett) is one of the problems Frege bequeathed to his heirs. The other is the flip side of the groundbreaking idea of introducing "truth" as the basic semantic concept for explicating the meaning of linguistic expressions. In order to understand a sentence, one has to know the conditions under which it is true, that is, to know, as Wittgenstein was to say later, "what is the case if it is true." This raises the problem of explicating the meaning of truth—the satisfaction of truth conditions. Frege's suggestion to take the truth value of a sentence to be its reference [*Bezugsgegenstand*] is obviously unsatisfactory. His own analysis of propositional structure shows that truth cannot be assimilated to reference. Thus the tradition of truth-conditional semantics since its beginnings was weighed down by two recalcitrant problems.

Removed from the stream of experiences, propositional contents had to be incorporated as meanings into the medium of linguistic expressions in such a way that the ghostly twilight zone of free-floating propositions dissolved. But a truth-conditional account of the meaning of sentences can succeed in doing this only if the basic explanatory concept of "truth" is no longer obscure. The two questions of what we are to do with propositions and how we are to understand the truth predicate can both be understood as leans against a repressed mentalistic conception of reason. From a linguistic point of view, there are two possible responses. Either, in abandoning the mentalist paradigm, we get rid of the concept of reason itself; or we remove this concept from its mentalist frame of reference and transpose it into the concept of communicative reason. Donald Davidson pursues the first strategy. By appealing to empiricist premises, he seeks to defuse the specific normativity of language that is reflected in the relation of language users to the world as well as in their interpersonal relationships to one another (6). Michael Dummett and Robert Brandom tend in the opposite direction and endeavor a step-by-step reconstruction of the normativity of communicative practice (7 and 8).

(6) *The objectification of language.* Davidson objectifies the phenomenon that has to be explained, namely, what it means to understand a

linguistic expression. By relieving the philosopher of language of his role as reader or hearer trying to understand what an author or speaker says, he makes a significant methodological decision that alters the role of the philosopher of language. Instead, he assigns the interpreter the role of a theoretician proceeding empirically. Such an interpreter observes the behavior of a foreign culture and—unlike Wittgenstein's ethnographer—looks for a nomological explanation of the as yet unintelligible linguistic behavior of the natives. Thus the communicative behavior of subjects capable of speech and action is entirely objectified; it becomes an observable with no internal link to the subject. Corresponding to this vigorous assimilation of intelligible symbolic expressions to the category of observable natural phenomena, is the assimilation of understanding meaning [*Sinnverstehen*] to explanations for which an empirical theory is required. Davidson develops such a theory by using Tarski's Convention T as the *undefined* basic concept for generating semantic equivalences.[35]

By making this move, Davidson is able to de-dramatize the problem of how to deal with the idea of truth and the ideal content of truth claims raised in communication. To solve the other problem having to do with using grammatical expressions with the same meaning, namely the problem of avoiding the Platonist duplication of sentence meanings and propositions, he suggests eliminating the concept of meaning.

Davidson takes it to be one of the advantages of his objectifying approach that he need not appeal to "meanings as entities": "no objects are introduced to correspond to predicates or sentences."[36] However, the problem does not go away entirely; it returns at the methodological level when the question arises of how the interpreter is supposed to map the evidence she has collected in the field—that is, the linguistic behavior and attitudinal features of the alien speakers—onto the theoretically generated T-sentences. In order for the interpreter to read a logical structure into the observed stream of data, she first has to divide these sequences of behavior into sentence-like units that can be mapped onto the biconditionals of the Tarskian theory. Even if such a segmentation is successful, however, the observed covariance of individual utterances with the conditions under which they typically occur is not yet sufficient for an unequivocal mapping.

In general, a competent speaker utters a perceptual sentence [*Wahrnehmungssatz*] on the basis of knowing the *lexical meaning* of the expression used only in connection with what he believes to perceive in a given situation, that is, what he takes to be true. Because word meaning and belief can vary independently of one another, the observed data—that is, an alien speaker's behavior and the conditions under which the behavior occurs—can tell the interpreter what an utterance to be interpreted means only if the alien speaker says what he takes to be true. An observer has to know whether an alien speaker believes what he says in order to determine the meaning of what is said. In order to neutralize the unwelcome interdependence of meaning and belief, the interpreter has to hold belief (i.e., what the speaker takes to be true) constant. Only the *attribution of holding true* makes it the case that the observed covariance of utterance and context of utterance counts as sufficient evidence for the theoretically informed choice of the correct interpretation. For this reason, Davdison introduces as a methodological principle the *assumption* that, as a rule, all speakers observed in the field *behave rationally* (although of course any given speaker may behave irrationally and hence unintelligibly in any given instance). This means that they in general believe what they say and do not contradict themselves as a result of what they say. Given this premise, the interpreter may presume that the observed speakers have the same perceptions and beliefs in most situations so that both parties agree on a massive set of beliefs. This does not rule out discrepancies in any given case, but the principle enjoins the interpreter to "maximize agreement."

It is important to note here that the methodological principle of charity requires an interpreter to attribute "rationality" as a behavioral disposition to a foreign speaker from an *observer's perspective.* This attribution must not be confused with the *performative* presupposition of rationality undertaken by interlocutors. In the one case, the concept of rationality is employed descriptively, and in the other normatively. In both cases, we are dealing with a fallible presupposition: "The methodological advice to interpret in a way that optimizes agreement should not be conceived as resting on a charitable assumption about human intelligence. . . . If we cannot find a way to interpret the utterances and other behavior of a creature as revealing a set of beliefs largely consistent and true by our own standards, we have no reason to count that creature as rational, as having beliefs, or as saying anything."[37]

This formulation (which reappears in Davidson's argument against the scheme–content distinction) indicates that the methodological principle has a transcendental status.[38] The attribution of rationality is a necessary presupposition not only for radical interpretation, but also for everyday communication among members of the same speech community.[39] Without the mutual presupposition of rationality, we could not have a sufficiently shared basis for communicating given our different theories of interpretation (or idiolects).[40] Within the framework of a unified theory of language and action "holding true" is then once more reconnected with a general "preference" for true sentences ("preferring one sentence true to another").[41]

The rationality of action is assessed in terms of the usual standards: logical consistency, general principles of success-oriented action, and consideration of empirical evidence. In his reply to a paper by Richard Rorty, Davidson has recently formulated the principle of charity as follows: "Charity is a matter of finding enough rationality in those we would understand to make sense of what they say and do, for unless we succeed in this, we cannot identify the contents of their words and thoughts. Seeing rationality in others is a matter of recognizing our own norms of rationality in their speech and behavior. These norms include the norms of logical consistency, of action in reasonable accord with essential or basic interests of the agent, and the acceptance of views that are sensible in the light of evidence."[42]

Interestingly, the normativity of human behavior that the attribution of rationality aims at also serves as Davidson's criterion for delimiting the language of physics from the language of the mental: "There are several reasons for the irreducibility of the mental to the physical. One reason . . . is the normative element in interpretation introduced by the necessity[!] of appealing to charity in matching the sentences of others to our own."[43] Against the monistic point of view of a scientistic natrualism, Davidson wishes to maintain at least a thin line demarcating mind and nature. Richard Rorty is able to raise strong arguments against this heroic effort because in doing so, he is simply radicalizing Davidson's own strategy of deactivating the rational potential inherent in linguistic communication.[44] After all, it is by no means obvious how Davidson is able to maintain a perspectival mind–body dualism once he has completely objectified rational behavior and reduced understanding linguistic expressions to the *theoretical* explanations on the part of an interpreter taking an *objectifying* attitude. For the linguistic understanding and the standards of rationality that Davidson at first assumes the radical interpreter to have did not come from nowhere. They require further explanation.

Radical interpretation does not suffice for making sense, within the chosen empiricist framework, of how the interpreter herself was able to learn how to speak, of how language could have emerged in the first place. If language users are "rational [*geistige*] beings" because they can take intentional attitudes to logically connected propositional contents, and if it is the intentional structure of their speech acts and their actions that requires the interpreter to attribute rationality to them and to employ mental concepts, the question of how something like intentionality itself could emerge remains open. Davidson's answer, as we know, is the model of a "triangular" learning situation where two organisms simultaneously respond to "the world" and to one another. His analysis is a kind of logical genesis of the acquisition of elementary linguistic expressions. Davidson wants to show how from "our" point of view, but given naturalistic premises, two highly developed and intelligent, but still prelinguistic beings belonging to the same species might have learned to take the kind of distance that we call "intentional" from their natural environment that provides them with sensory stimulation by using symbols that have the same meaning for them.

The assumption of an objective world of things to which we can *refer* is constitutive for the intentional constitution of the mind. This reference to the world [*Weltbezug*] is the presupposition for making statements about objects and taking different attitudes toward propositional contents. On this description, intentional consciousness emerges at the same time as a propositionally differentiated language. Now, the genesis of this consciousness is to be thought of as having originated in a kind of interaction with the world for which the reference to a world that is supposed to be objective is not yet constitutive. The world is only causally connected to language. This naturalistic premise fits with one of the theses of what is called "externalism," namely that language is "anchored in the world" by means of a basic perceptual vocabulary and owes its semantic content to an intelligent processing of causal sensory stimulations: "[I]n the simplest and most basic cases, words and sentences derive their meaning from the objects and circumstances in whose presence they were learned. A sentence which one has been conditioned by the learning process to be caused to hold true by the presence of fire will . . . be true when there is a fire present."[45]

This account reduces the *meaning* of an expression and the *truth* of a sentence to the *causal* circumstances in which they are learned. Yet the process that is described as a conditioning in the causal language game stands in counterintuitive tension with our self-understanding as rational beings. Hence Davidson wants to explain how the *intentional distance to and from the world* might have been produced *by* the world itself in terms of a stimulus-response model. Belonging to the same species, two organisms are disposed to respond similarly to a stimulus that initially has a direct conditioning effect. When these two organisms interact with one another, they acquire the specifically intentional distance to this stimulus by not merely perceiving it themselves, but by simultaneously perceiving through mutual observation that the other is responding to the same stimulus in the same way: "Enough features are in place to give meaning to the idea that the stimulus has an objective location in a common space; it's a matter of two private perspectives converging to mark a position in intersubjective space. So far, however, nothing in this picture shows that either we, the observer, or our subjects . . . have a concept of the objective."[46]

Of course it is still not clear how one is supposed to know that the other is responding to *the same* object as oneself. Both subjects have to find out whether they have the same object in mind. And that requires communication. Yet they can enter into the relevant kind of communication only if they use the response pattern that they perceive to be similar (or part thereof) as a symbolic expression at the same time and direct it as a message to the other. They have to communicate with one another *about what exactly* stimulated their respective response: "For two people to know of each other that they are so related, that their thoughts are so related, requires that they be in communication. Each of the two has to speak to the other and be understood by the other."[47] A stimulus that produces a similar reaction in the two parties involved is transformed "for them" into an object, that is, a thing in a shared objective world, if they communicate "about it" by means of their behavioral response that they now symbolically address to one another. This communication goes beyond the mutual observation of a similarity in response and turns the triggering stimulus into an object. Only as a result of such communicative use does the pattern of the two similar behavioral responses simultaneously take on the same meaning for both parties.

The intuition Davidson is expressing with the image of triangulation is clear: References and intentional attitudes to something in the objective world are possible only from the perspective of an interlocutor. And based on communicatively established intersubjective relations, this perspective is coordinated with the perspective of at least one other speaker. Objectivity emerges with the taking of an intentional distance to the world. Interlocutors can acquire such a distance only by learning to communicate with one another about *the same thing.* However, it is hard to see how Davidson could account for this interlocking of objectivity with an equiprimordial intersubjectivity by appealing to a fictitious learning situation. The problem is not the basic epistemological premise of externalism, but the methodological solipsism of the solitary observer.

These two organisms find themselves in the same environment and mutually observe each other having similar responses to some *one* stimulus in their environment. But how are they supposed to be able to communicate to one another that they have in view the *same* stimulus—unless they already have the corresponding concept available to them? Yet they acquire this concept only by means of a criterion they apply in the same way—that is, by means of a symbol that has the same meaning for them both. Only then are they able to communicate about objectively present similarities. Certainly, if someone, a teacher, say, could take on the role of radical interpreter relative to a child, she would find out whether she and the child "mean the same thing," in order to correct the child's mistakes if necessary. But this instance of triangulation would at best explain how children acquire basic components of perceptual vocabulary as they grow up in an existing linguistic community. It says nothing about the possibility of the *origin* of intentionality in the mutual observation of organisms whose responses to certain parts of their environment are similar though not yet intentional.

The mutual perception of objectively *similar* responses can give rise to the mutual attribution of the *same* response pattern only once the participants apply the *same* criterion. For different subjects can determine objective similarities only in certain, intersubjectively established respects. As Wittgenstein puts it, they have to be able to follow a rule. It is not enough that similar responses occur from the point of view of a nonparticipant observer; the participants themselves must *notice* a similarity in response with regard to the same stimulus or object.[48] This presupposes what is supposed to be explained: "all awareness of sorts, resemblances, facts, etc. . . . . is a linguistic affair."[49] Davidson does emphasize the social core of the normativity of mind, one of the features of which is intentionality, the relation to a *shared* objective world. Yet he does not conceive this social nature in terms of the perspective of a member of a form of life that she "finds herself" sharing with others. The latter would mean that a member of this form of life would not only as a matter of fact have similar behavioral dispositions as others but would also be at least intuitively conscious of this agreement.

"Belonging" or "membership" means sharing with one's fellows a prior understanding of what makes one's own way of life a common way of life. The choice of an objectivist approach that assimilates the understanding of meaning to explanation guided by theory indicates that one has opted for methodological solipsism. The latter forces one to reduce every communicative consensus to the constructive result of coordinating and overlapping interpretive accomplishments that everyone undertakes individually from his own observer perspective without being able to draw on a wealth of existing, objectively regulated yet at the same time subjectively present commonalities. Otherwise, Davidson might have introduced triangulation in the spirit of G. H. Mead as a mechanism that explains how two members of the same species interacting with one another can become aware, through mutual perspective-taking, of what their shared patterns of response mean and how this meaning thus becomes available *qua* symbol to both parties.[50]

(7) *Language as rule-governed practice.* Philosophical hermeneutics takes the opposite position to objectivist approaches. On this view, the preunderstanding that guides the process of interpretation is not checked against observations of another's behavior like an empirical hypothesis. Rather, it is explicated and corrected as it would be in a dialogue by means of questions and answers. Even if they first have to develop a shared language, interlocutors move within a horizon of a background understanding they already share. This procedure is circular inasmuch as whatever an interpreter learns to understand is the fallible result of explicating a preunderstanding, no matter how vague it may be. As Gadamer, in agreement with Davidson, emphasizes, the interpreter here starts from the pragmatic presupposition that the text to be interpreted can have a clear meaning only if it is taken to be the expression of a rational author. Only against the foil of such a "fore-conception of completeness" can texts turn out to be unintelligible, utterances opaque. "This is obviously a formal condition of all understanding. It states that only what really constitutes a unity of meaning is intelligible."[51]

The hermeneutic presupposition of rationality evinces an astonishing family resemblance to Davidson's principle of charity. This resemblance goes even further. Just as the "radical interpreter" has to pay attention to the circumstances under which an alien speaker utters something she presumably holds true, Gadamer's interpreter has to pay attention simultaneously to the text *and* to its subject matter. First one has to "understand the content of what is said" before one can "isolate and understand another's meaning as such".[52] This is the hermeneutic version of the basic premise of formal semantics, according to which the meaning of a sentence is determined by its truth conditions. In another respect, however, there is a significant difference. Whereas Davidson's interpreter attributes to the native the disposition to follow the norms of rationality she follows *herself* from an observer's point of view, Gadamer's interpreter presupposes from a participant's point of view that his interlocutor expresses herself rationally in accordance to *shared* standards of rationality. The performative presupposition of rationality, unlike the objectifying attribution of rationality, starts from a shared rather than a merely objectively matching understanding of rationality.

However, the global model of a conversation, which feeds on vital traditions, lays claim to a large number of unelucidated presuppositions. To make it accessible to a more precise analysis, formal pragmatics shrinks the totality of this hermeneutic scenario down to the skeleton of a basic exchange of speech acts oriented toward reaching mutual understanding. The rational potential operating at the macrolevel of communicative action is once more subject to Wittgenstein's microlevel investigations of rule-governed behavior. As a result of this move, Wittgenstein serves as the inspiration for the nonempiricist branch of the Frege tradition all the way to Dummett and Brandom. In contrast to the Carnap–Quine–Davidson tradition, these authors start from normatively regulated practices in which we engage together and which give rise to an intersubjectively shared context of meaning. Methodologically, they are attuned to the perspective of co-participants who make explicit the know-how of competent speakers.

What looks like a web of idealizing presuppositions to a "top-down" formal pragmatic analysis is discovered "bottom-up," as it were, by the analytic approach that runs counter to detranscendentalization. For it turns out that from this side, too, the presupposition that words have the same meanings points to the more complex presuppositions that we share an objective world, that language users are rational, and that truth claims are unconditional. The lowest level of idealization cannot be thought of independently of these further idealizations. Wittgenstein repudiates Frege's meaning Platonism without giving up the insight that it is possible to communicate universal and identical meanings publicly. Dummett maintains that the representational function of language and thus reference to the objective world have a certain independence relative to the intersubjectively shared form of life and the background consensus of the linguistic community. Brandom, finally, provides a detailed account, within the framework of a formal pragmatics, of rationality and of the accountability that participants in discourse mutually attribute to one another. Of course I am calling to mind these way stations along an extremely dense history of argumentation only in broad brush strokes in order to make the web of idealizing presuppositions visible from this perspective as well.

The meaning of a symbolic expression exceeds the particular circumstances of its instantiation. Wittgenstein analyzes this Platonic moment of the universality of meaning that is connected with every predicate or concept in terms of "rule-following." Whereas from an observer's point of view, "regular" behavior merely accords with a rule, "rule-governed" behavior requires that the acting subject itself have a concept of the rule it is following. This is reminiscent of Kant's distinction between "acting in accordance with the law" and acting "out of respect for the law." However, Wittgenstein does not yet have complex norms of action in mind but rules generating simple operations: rules of arithmetic, logic, or grammar that he investigates on the model of rules for games. In this way he analyzes the lowest level of normativity characteristic of mental activity. Rules must be mastered practically because, as Aristotle was already aware, they cannot govern their own application without implicating actors in an infinite regress. The implicit knowledge of how to follow a rule precedes the explicit knowledge of what rule one is following. One must "know how" to engage in a rule-governed practice before one can make this know-how explicit and formulate the rules one knows intuitively as such. From the fact that knowledge of rules is grounded in skills, Wittgenstein infers that anyone trying to understand her practical knowledge is already a participant in a practice, as it were.[53]

This analysis of the particular normativity of this kind of basic rule-governed behavior further shows that we are trained in these practices together; they are inherently social. Rules are "normative" in the weak sense of being as yet untouched by any connotations of binding or *obligating* practical norms. Rules bind a subject's free will by "directing" her intentions in a particular direction:

• Rules "bind" the will in such a way that acting subjects seek to avoid possible rule violations; following a rule means refraining from "acting against" the rule.

• If someone is following a rule, she can make mistakes and is subject to being criticized for making mistakes; unlike knowing how to follow a rule in practice, judging whether a given form of behavior is correct requires an explicit knowledge of rules.

• Someone who is following a rule must in principle be able to justify her actions to a critic; hence the virtual division of labor between the role and knowledge of a critic and the practitioner is part of the concept of rule-following itself.

• Therefore, no one can follow a rule solipsistically, on her own; the practical mastery of a rule signifies the ability to take part in a social, habituated practice; as soon as subjects reflectively ascertain their intuitive knowledge in order to justify themselves to one another, they are already engaged in this practice.

Wittgenstein accounts for Frege's ideal universality of meaning in terms of an already existing or given "agreement" among participants in a shared practice. This agreement is an expression of the intersubjective recognition of rules that are tacitly followed. Against such a background, participants can "take" a certain behavior as exemplifying a rule or understand it as "complying with" a rule. Because it is in principle possible for disagreements to arise about whether a given behavior is correct, the implicitly concurrent "yes" or "no" on the part of a potential critic is part of the meaning of the normative validity of a rule. The binary coding of rule-governed behavior as "right" or "wrong" simultaneously functions as a built-in self-corrective mechanism.

Of course it remains unclear at first what the *ultimate* standard of public criticism is. It seems that criticism cannot extend to the underlying intuitive rules themselves since they are constitutive for the practice in question, say, the game of chess. Since Wittgenstein analyzes the grammar of language games on the model of parlor games, he regards (on a not entirely uncontroversial reading) a linguistic community's de facto habitual agreement as an irrevocable authority for judging what is right and wrong—as the kind of certainty where "the spade is turned." At least this is how we can make sense of the later Wittgenstein's shift from truth-conditional semantics to the use theory of meaning. Frege had determined the meaning of a sentence in terms of truth conditions that establish the correct use of a sentence. If now we can read truth conditions off of the local background consensus that has become routine by convention among members of a linguistic community, it is easier to do without the troublesome concept of sentences being true or false and to describe prevailing language use directly: "The meaning of a statement or form of statement is therefore not to be explained by stating the condition for it to *be* true, but by describing its use."[54]

The argument loses its plausibility though if we recall Frege's context principle according to which the meaning of individual words is a function of their potential contribution to the meaning of true sentences. Accordingly the meaning of individual predicates or concepts can be derived not immediately from the conditions of use of individual words, but from the context of the sentences in which they are used correctly *if the sentences are true.* The meaning of these sentences on the whole is determined by the conditions under which they can be used truthfully [*wahrheitsgemäss*]. Whether someone is using the predicate "red" correctly, that is, whether she has mastery of the corresponding rule of predication, is assessed in terms of the sample sentences that must be true if they are to express successful test results—say, a sequence of references to red objects.

Similarly, the practical mastery of the rules of mathematics or logic is confirmed by the correctness of the relevant propositions. Insofar as we are dealing with operational rules that have a cognitive function, their "validity" does not seem to be explicable by appealing to existing conventions—unlike game rules that have been explicitly agreed on and are not rooted in some prior practical knowledge. Instead, they can be explained in terms of how performing these operations in accordance with rules contributes to the formation of true statements. In the domain of simple cognitive operations, rule-governed behavior bespeaks a normativity that already *refers* to the truth and rational acceptability of statements in a natural language. A Wittgensteinian teacher checks what a pupil does in applying rules. The teacher's elementary "yes" or "no" unfolds—reveals itself in the full sense of its validity—only at the more complex level of discourse where discursive partners take yes- or no-positions on truth claims with empirical content.

Dummett brings to bear Frege's original insight against the later Wittgenstein in a similar fashion. His objection is essentially based on the fact that the assessment of a statement's truth depends on whether it represents a fact and not on whether the speaker conforms to how it is used in his surroundings. The epistemic authority of warranted assertibility is not exhausted by the social authority of the linguistic community. In the wake of the linguistic turn, to be sure, it is clear that the representation of states of affairs is dependent on the medium of language, for every clear thought can find expression only in the propositional form of a corresponding assertoric sentence. Thinking is coupled to the representational function of language. Yet a correctly expressed proposition is true not because the rules governing its use reflect the consensus or worldview of a given linguistic community, but because, applied correctly, these rules warrant the rational acceptability of the sentence. The rules geared to the representational function of language make it possible to refer to objects and states of affairs whose existence or obtaining is not decided by local habits, but by the world presupposed to be objective itself. Speakers cannot communicate about something in the world unless the very world they suppose to be objective "communicates" with them.

Wittgenstein uses the expression "grammar of a language" in the broad sense of a "grammar of a form of life" because every natural language is "interwoven," through its communicative function, with the basic conceptual articulation of the worldview and the social structure of a given linguistic community. Nonetheless, linguistic rules must not be assimilated to mere custom because every language enjoys a certain autonomy vis-à-vis the linguistic community's cultural background and social practices. This autonomy is due to the interplay between linguistic and empirical knowledge. Linguistic world-disclosure makes innerworldly learning processes that feed empirical knowledge possible in the first place. But empirical knowledge of the world retains a revisionary power over linguistic knowledge because the representational function of language cannot be reduced to its communicative use: "A statement's satisfying the condition for it to *be* true is certainly not in itself a feature of its use. . . . Statements do not in general acquire authority from the frequency with which they are made. We need, rather, to distinguish what is merely customarily said from what the principles governing our use of language and determinative of the meanings of our utterances *require* or *entitle* us to say."[55] This peculiarity of the representational function of language is reminiscent of the shared presupposition of an objective world that participants in communication must undertake in order to be able to make assertions about something in the world.

(8) *Communication as discursive exchange of reasons.* On the other hand, Dummett, contrary to Frege, sticks to Wittgenstein's insight that language is rooted in communicative action and that its structure can be made transparent only by means of explicating the know-how of competent speakers. He does, however, emphasize one particular practice above all other complex contexts of use, namely the language game of asserting, objecting, and justifying, where semantically warranted "commitments" and "entitlements" ("what the principles of language *require* and *entitle* us to say") are the explicit topic. The privileged position of rational discourse can be accounted for by the epistemic turn Dummett gives to truth-conditional semantics. Since there is no linguistically unmediated access to truth conditions, it is possible to understand a sentence only by knowing how to recognize that its truth conditions are satisfied. The conditions that make a sentence true are known only by way of the reasons, or the right kind of reasons, that a speaker could cite in asserting the sentence to be true: "Identifying someone's taking a sentence to be true with his willingness to assert it, we distinguished two criteria of correctness: how the speakers establish or come to recognize sentences as true; and how so recognizing them affects their subsequent course of action."[56]

Of course this closed discursive structure of communication becomes visible only if there is cause to doubt the intelligibility or validity of a speech act. Communicative exchange, however, practically always takes place against an implicitly concurrent discursive shadow theater because an utterance is intelligible only to someone who knows the reasons (or kinds of reasons) that make it acceptable. According to this model, speakers *implicitly* present one another with reasons for accepting each other's utterances even in ordinary everyday communication; they demand such reasons from each other and mutually evaluate the status of their utterances. One decides whether she takes the argumentative commitment [*Verpflichtung*] the other has undertaken to be warranted or not.

Robert Brandom makes this model the starting point of a formal pragmatics that brings together Wilfrid Sellars's inferential semantics with an impressive logical investigation of the practice of "giving and asking for reasons." He replaces the basic semantic question of the theory of meaning, namely what it means to understand a sentence, with the pragmatic question of what an interpreter is doing when she appropriately "takes and treats" a speaker as someone who has raised a truth claim in uttering *p*. The interpreter attributes to the speaker a commitment to justify *p* if necessary and herself takes a stance toward this claim [*Wahrheitsanspruch*] by according or denying the speaker the entitlement to assert *p*. I have discussed this theory elsewhere.[57] Here I am interested in the necessary presupposition of rationality that is undertaken in such discourses. Brandom does start from the premise that speaker and hearer treat one another as rational beings for whom reasons "count." Through argument, speakers and hearers can become committed or entitled to recognize validity claims that are in principle criticizable. However, what is missing in Brandom is the intersubjective interpretation of objective validity according to which the practice of argumentation is linked to a strong idealizing anticipation.

Brandom situates the normativity of language capable of "binding" rational subjects in the unforced force of the better argument. This force develops by way of a discursive practice where participants rationally justify their utterances to one another: "This force is a species of normative force, a rational 'ought.' Being rational is being bound or constrained by these norms, being subject to the authority of reasons. Saying 'we' in this sense is placing ourselves and each other in the space of reasons, by giving and asking for reasons for our attitudes and performances."[58] This kind of rational responsibility is constitutive of our self-understanding as language users. At the same time, this rational self-understanding provides the standard for the inclusive "We"-perspective from which each person qualifies as "one of us."

Interestingly, Brandom begins his book, very much in the tradition of Peirce, Royce, and Mead, with an intersubjectivist conception of a universalist concept of reason. These pragmatists basically conceive universalism as the avoidance of exclusion. The We-perspective that allows rational beings to distinguish themselves from other organisms as "sapient rather than sentient" forbids all particularism, but not pluralism: "The most cosmopolitan approach begins with a pluralist insight. When we ask, Who are we? or What sort of thing are we? the answers can vary without competing. Each one defines a different way of saying 'we'; each kind of 'we'-saying defines a different community. It points to the one great Community comprising members of all particular communities—the Community of those who say 'we' with and to someone, whether the members of those different communities recognize each other or not."[59] This capital "C" could designate the ideal point of reference for the rational acceptability of those unconditional, that is, context-transcendent, validity claims that we have to be able to justify before an "ever wider" audience. There is no pragmatic equivalent for this idea in Brandom—say, in the form of discursive presuppositions that maintain the dynamics of a progressive decentering of pluralist interpretations. To see why, I want to highlight and critique one aspect of what is overall an impressive work.

Like the analytic tradition in general, Brandom neglects the cognitive significance of the role of the second person. He gives no weight to a speaker's performative attitude to her addressee—an attitude that is constitutive for any conversation—and does not really conceive the pragmatic relation of question and answer as dialogical exchange. This objectivism shows up, for example, in dealing with the problem of how to preserve the methodological "primacy of the social" without, in questions of epistemic validity, giving the last word to the consensus of the linguistic community. Brandom opposes the collectivist image of a linguistic community commanding authority with the individualistic image of isolated relationships of pairs of speakers. Two individual subjects mutually attribute commitments and grant or deny entitlements to one another. Each side forms its judgment monologically so that neither has to "meet with" the other in the intersubjective recognition of a validity claim. Although Brandom talks about "*I-Thou*" relations, he in fact construes these as relations between a first person committed to the truth of a statement and a third person attributing—by her own lights—a truth claim to the first. The act of attribution, which is fundamental for the entire discursive practice, objictifies the second person into a third person being observed.

It is no accident that Brandom prefers to equate the interpreter with an audience that evaluates the utterances of a speaker it *observes*—rather than an addressee from whom the speaker expects to get an answer. Because he does not even consider the possibility of taking a dialogical attitude toward second persons, Brandom is forced in the end to undo the internal connection between objectivity and intersubjectivity in favor of a "primacy of the objective." The individual seems unable to secure the epistemic independence from the collective authority of a given linguistic community except by taking a monological distance. Such an individualistic description misses the point of linguistic communication.

Everyday communication is supported by the context of shared background assumptions so that the need to communicate arises especially when the beliefs and intentions of subjects making independent judgments and decisions have to be brought into unison. The practical need to coordinate plans of action is what brings into relief the interlocutors' expectation that their addressees undertake a commitment regarding their own validity claims. They expect an affirmative or negative response that counts as an answer. For only the intersubjective recognition of criticizable validity claims can generate the kind of commonality on the basis of which bonds can be established on which both sides can rely and which shape subsequent interactions.

The practice of argumentation merely continues, albeit at a reflective level, where communicative action leaves off. Hence individual participants in argumentation who maintain their orientation toward reaching mutual understanding on the one hand are enveloped in a shared practice; on the other hand, they have to take a warranted stance on thematized validity claims, that is, they are under the gentle pressure to evaluate these claims autonomously, on their own. There is no collective authority to constrain the range of their individual evaluations or to mediate any individual's competence to make judgments. The peculiar Janus-face of unconditional claims to validity fits with these two aspects. As *claims,* they aim at intersubjective recognition; the public authority of a consensus that has been achieved under conditions where it could have been challenged can ultimately have no substitute in the private insight of some individual who knows better. As claims to *unconditional* validity, however, they go beyond any de facto established agreement. What is rationally accepted here and now can turn out to be false under better epistemic conditions, before a different audience, and in the face of future objections.

A discussion can do justice to this Janus-face of unconditional validity claims only on the idealizing assumption that all relevant reasons and information to which there is access are brought to bear. By making this strong idealization, our finite mind anticipates the transcendental insight into the ineluctable grounding of objectivity in linguistic intersubjectivity.

3

From Kant to Hegel: On Robert Brandom's Pragmatic Philosophy of Language

Robert Brandom's *Making It Explicit* is a milestone in theoretical philosophy just as Rawls's *A Theory of Justice* was a milestone in practical philosophy in the early 1970s. Displaying a sovereign command of the intricate discussion in analytic philosophy of language, Brandom manages successfully to carry out a program within philosophy of language that has already been sketched by others,[1] without losing sight of the vision inspiring the enterprise in the important details of his investigation. The work owes its exceptional rank to its rare combination of speculative impulse and staying power. It painstakingly works out an innovative connection of formal pragmatics with inferential semantics, articulating a self-understanding that was already available as a tradition but was in need of renewal. Using the tools of a complex theory of language Brandom succeeds in describing convincingly the practices in which the reason and autonomy of subjects capable of speech and action are expressed.

Brandom develops a new pragmatic vocabulary for the Kantian perspective of a finite mind that uses concepts and operates rationally within the constraints of an independently existing world, and autonomously within the limits of a social environment: "Picking us out by our capacity for reason and understanding expresses a commitment to take *sapience,* rather than *sentience* as the constellation of characteristics that distinguishes us. Sentience is what we share with nonverbal animals such as cats—the capacity to be *aware* in the sense of being *awake.* . . . Sapience concerns understanding or intelligence, rather than irritability or arousal."[2] We are the beings whose essence it is to participate in the practice of "giving and asking for reasons." In calling one another to account, we accept responsibility before one another for everything we do. We allow ourselves to be affected by reasons, that is, to be enlisted by the binding "force of the better argument." Whenever we apply concepts and whenever we obey the semantic rules and the norms of inferential thought we move in the "space of reasons"—in the sphere where reasons count.[3]

I begin the first part of the essay by characterizing Brandom's approach as a whole and by dealing with his innovative combination of formal pragmatics and inferential semantics (I). I then set out the question that Brandom himself considers to be central, of why we may lay claim to objective validity for the contents of our utterances (II). In section III, I sketch Brandom's answer to this. These first three sections serve to reconstruct critically a train of thought that ultimately leads beyond what can be discerned by taking the perspective of the participants in discourse themselves. In the second part of the essay (IV–VI), I engage with the consequences of the conceptual realism that Brandom, in his pursuit of the question of objectivity, considers himself compelled to adopt.

I

(1) Brandom focuses on the role of speech acts in discourse, thereby setting the course for a pragmatic analysis of language. Assertoric speech acts, which are seen as fundamental, serve both as vehicles for and as reasons for and against truth claims ("claims"). What counts as a good reason depends on logical and conceptual-semantic rules that are followed intersubjectively. These can be read off the practices of a linguistic community.[4] Ultimately decisive for this analysis are the yes/no positions with which participants respond to each other's validity claims.[5] Thus Brandom analyzes language in terms of discursive practice, which he conceives as an exchange of acts of communication regulated by means of mutual "scorekeeping." Every participant assesses the validity claims of the others by comparing them with his own and keeps track of how

many points everyone has scored. This pragmatic approach follows Wittgenstein's insights that the practical and nonpropositional know-how is prior to explicitly thematized knowledge (a) just as the social practices of a linguistic community are prior to the private intentions of individual speakers (b).

(a) Brandom takes as his starting point norms of speaking and acting that guide behavior by way of implicit knowledge. A holistically constituted language structures the pre-predicatively known lifeworld of speakers who know how to make and understand utterances; for this they do not need any explicit knowledge of rules or principles. However, in acquiring their natural language, participants have at the same time acquired the competence to render explicit this concomitant, merely habitual "knowing-how" and to transform it into a thematic "knowing-that." Subjects capable of speech and action are in principle able to retrieve reflexively and express explicitly what they know how to do in practice.[6] Brandom talks about the "expressive power" to be able to *say* how one does something. What serves this purpose is our logical vocabulary. We employ logical expressions to make explicit the intuitive knowledge of how to use our semantic vocabulary correctly in accordance with rules: "In a weak sense, any being that engages in linguistic practices, and hence applies concepts, is a *rational* being; in the strong sense, rational beings are not only linguistic beings but, at least potentially, also *logical* beings. This is how we should understand ourselves: as beings that meet this dual expressive condition" (p. xxi).

Brandom's own theory methodologically exploits this tendency toward self-retrieval and reflexive upgrading of itself that is built into language. Just as logic articulates intuitively mastered logical rules, formal pragmatics (as the title of the book indicates) is supposed to reconstruct our knowledge of how to use language: "A theory of expression . . . is to explain how what is *explicit* arises out of what is *implicit*. In the first instance, it must explain how propositional content (the form of the explicit) is conferred by norms that are implicit in discursive practice—that is, what proprieties of use having such a content consist in. Then it must show how these same implicit, content-conferring norms can themselves be made explicit in the form of rules or principles" (p. 77).

(b) With the linguistic turn, epistemic authority passes over from the private experiences of a subject to the public practices of a linguistic community. Of course, when understanding the propositional content that is being communicated takes the place of "representing objects," what happens is not simply a turning away from the representational model of knowledge. The transition to a communicative model of reaching understanding [*Verständigung*] puts the seal on the priority of the social also in the sense that the members of a linguistic community mutually recognize one another as responsible subjects. By way of a communicative socialization they become involved in a web of intersubjective relations in which they are responsible to one another. Because this responsibility must be redeemed in the coin of reasons, the discursive practice of giving and asking for reasons constitutes the infrastructure of everyday communication as well.

The priority of the social is, furthermore, bound up with the methodological decision that the theoretician adopt the attitude of a second person and analyze the utterances of a speaker from the perspective of *an interlocutor*. Here Brandom is following a pragmatist tradition that escapes the snares of an objectifying mentalism by analyzing the relevant phenomena from the point of view of an agent performing an action. Thus, for instance, the descriptive question of what "truth" is or means is replaced by the performative question of what we are doing when we take something to be "true"—for example, when we underscore that we are adopting true statements, or recommending their adoption to others, or generally finding them useful, and so on. Brandom employs this anti-objectivist strategy for examining discursive practices in general: "The basic explanatory challenge faced by the model is to say what structure a set of social practices must exhibit in order properly to be understood as including practical attitudes of *taking or treating* performances as having the significance of claims or assertions" (p. 141). As we shall see, however, the theorist must not only take up the perspective of a hearer seeking to *understand* the content of an utterance; she has to adopt the performative attitude of a participant in interaction who "takes or treats" the speech act of an interlocutor as a claim [*Wahrheitsanspruch*][7] in order to *find out* whether she herself can accept it.

(2) The methodological decision to consider the utterances of a speaker from the recipient's perspective of a participant who takes a position on a claim has important consequences. The basic question of the theory of meaning—what does it mean to understand an assertion or a proposition?—is replaced by the question: what is an interpreter doing when she "appropriately takes or treats" a speaker as someone who raises a truth claim in his speech act? Two steps must be distinguished here. First, the interpreter attributes to the speaker a speech act wherein he raises the claim that *p* is true, thereby committing himself to *p*. The attributed act ("undertaking") is understood by the interpreter as binding on the speaker ("commitment"). In choosing the assertoric mode the speaker feels bound to provide reasons, if necessary, for why he holds *p* to be true. However, reasons cannot be understood unless their "weight" is estimated at the same time. This explains, second, why the interpreter in turn takes a stance [or undertakes a commitment—Trans.] with regard to the validity claim she attributed to the speaker. She evaluates whether *p* obtains also from her own point of view; if so, she acknowledges the speaker's entitlement to claim *p*. (Naturally, this is a matter of taking a stance even if the interpreter does not come to any conclusive assessment and abstains for the time being from agreeing with or rejecting the claim.)

Thus Brandom describes an assertion as a speaker's utterance that allows any interpreter whatsoever to deem it appropriate to attribute a truth claim and corresponding commitment to the speaker. The status of the proposition *p*, which determines whether the speaker is entitled to assert *p*, depends on how the interpreter assesses the truth claim raised by the speaker—on whether or not she adopts the validity claim attributed to him. The analysis thus starts from the practical attitudes of an interpreter, in particular with her "yes" or "no" responses to truth claims. What is decisive is how a speech act *appears* to the interpreter—what she takes it to be.

It is this decision in favor of an analysis of speech acts as they are "taken to be" that explains the priority of the attitudes of the interlocutors over the status of their utterances. This priority also motivates the imagery of "scorekeeping," and indeed, the overall comparison of a conversation with a baseball game. In the paradigmatic case, discursive practice consists in an exchange of assertions, questions, and answers that the interlocutors mutually attribute to one another and assess with regard to possible reasons; here, everyone keeps track from her own point of view of who was entitled to which speech acts, who accepted which assertions in good faith—and, finally, who overdrew the generally approved account of credibility by not vindicating their validity claims discursively, thereby discrediting themselves in the eyes of the other players. Every participant who "scores points" with her contributions simultaneously calculates the "score" others attain with theirs.

(3) Brandom's originality resides less in this particular conception of formal pragmatics than in his next ingenious move: Brandom links up the description of discursive practices with a semantic theory in such a way that the two interlock like cog wheels. To this end, he appropriates Dummett's epistemic explication of meaning: we understand an assertoric sentence if we know both the conditions under which it may be asserted and the consequences that would follow for the participants from accepting the assertion. This epistemic conception of linguistic understanding is tailored to the perspective of a second person who can ask for reasons for the satisfaction of the assertibility conditions and who can make inferences from the accepted assertion.[8] Furthermore, Brandom follows Sellars in assuming that such justifications, which refer to the circumstances and the consequences of the possible application of an expression, are supported by "material" inferential relations built into the semantic content of a linguistic expression.[9] An inferential semantics, according to which the conceptual content of a linguistic expression may be analyzed with the help of the roles that this expression can play in material inferences, matches—as its mirror image—a conception of discourse, defined by Brandom as the "production and consumption of reasons." Participants in discourse understand an expression in light of the reasons that make it acceptable with respect to the conditions and consequences of its correct application. To be sure, Brandom dissociates himself from an overburdened inferentialism by also admitting empirical reasons with which a chain of justification can break off—perceptions that count as reasons without requiring further justification in turn.

It is not, however, empirical knowledge but linguistic knowledge that equips the interpreter with the knowledge of the rules that establish the conditions and consequences of the correct use of linguistic expressions. At any rate, this is how the relationship between semantics and pragmatics appears from the point of view of semantics: discursive practice, as it were, puts into operation the network of inferential relations built into the vocabulary of a language. The positions taken by the participants in discourse to the mutually attributed validity claims run along tracks that are marked out by the semantic implications of the content of a given utterance. The concepts that unfold discursively are made available in advance by semantics. On the other hand, Brandom is too much of a pragmatist to be convinced by a picture of language as the "house" of discourse. At any rate he counters the idealism of a linguistic world-disclosure from which there is no escape for the members of a given linguistic community with an alternative conception: he conceives of discursive practice not as a hostage to a knowledge of meanings inherited a priori but rather as a generator of concepts.

The conceptual norms that, from a semantic point of view, are given along with linguistic knowledge can, from a pragmatic perspective, be regarded as a result. With this, however, the relationship of the semantic reservoir of potential meanings to the inferential practice is reversed:

Expressions *come* to mean [my emphasis] what they mean by being used as they are in practice, and intentional states and attitudes have the contents they do in virtue of the role they play in the behavioral economy of those to whom they are attributed. Content is understood in terms of proprieties of inference, and those are understood in terms of the norm-instituting attitudes of taking or treating moves as appropriate or inappropriate in practice. A theoretical route is accordingly made available from what people do to what people *mean*, from their *practice* to the *contents* of their states and expressions. In this way a suitable pragmatic theory can ground [!] an inferentialist semantic theory; its explanations of what it is in practice to treat inferences as correct are what ultimately license appeal to material proprieties of inference, which can then function as semantic primitives. (p. 134)

But what does "in practice" mean? Although this corroborative authority is elucidated through reference to the "behavioral economy"

of the participants and the "norm-instituting" force of their attitudes, it is never really explained. If the practice of mutually attributing and assessing truth claims cannot already be guaranteed through
the semantic establishing of materially valid inferences, then of what
kind are the constraints on truth? Something or other has to corroborate the correctness of the application of concepts—"the assessment of truth."

A few pages after the practical attitudes of the participants in discourse have been accorded priority vis-à-vis semantic rules, we read
the following:

> A semantically adequate notion of correct inference must generate an ac-
> ceptable notion of conceptual content. But such a notion must fund the
> idea of *objective* truth conditions and so of *objectively* correct inferences. Such
> proprieties of judgment and inference outrun actual attitudes of taking or
> treating judgments and inferences as correct. They are determined by how
> things actually are, independently of how they are taken to be. Our cogni-
> tive attitudes must ultimately answer to these attitude-transcendent facts.
> (p. 137)

This "realist" objection, which Brandom seems to raise against himself, is hardly consistent with a "phenomenalist" stance. The latter
language-immanent way of proceeding obliges the theorist to speak
not of truth and reference but of how truth and reference *appear*
to an interpreter attributing truth claims and references to other
players.[10] Brandom will in fact take *this* path in his attempt to satisfy
the demands of realist intuitions. Before we follow him there, however, I would like to set out the question of objectivity on its own
terms.

II

So long as explanation is supposed to proceed from the "attitudes"
of the participants in discourse via the "status" of their utterances to
the "objectivity" of their content, the acts of attributing and assessing
validity claims have to shoulder the burden of explaining the objective content [*Wahrheitsgehalt*] of what is communicated. As indicated,
these practical attitudes serve Brandom as a key for the normative
features of the discursive logic of scorekeeping. In a certain sense,

the participants in discourse confer normative status on their utterances. By attributing an assertion to another and acknowledging it as correct, one interlocutor as it were endows this utterance with a (putatively objective) content and institutes for it the status of a true assertion. This procedure of "instituting" a normative status is conceived by Brandom according to the contractualist model of establishing positive rights: "Our activity *institutes* norms. . . . A normative significance is imposed on a nonnormative world, like a cloak thrown over its nakedness, by agents forming preferences, issuing orders, entering into agreements, praising and blaming, esteeming and assessing" (p. 48).

Norms are not intrinsically part of nature; they are imposed on natural dispositions and modes of behavior by the will of intelligent beings. Norm-governed behavior is distinguished from merely regular behavior in that the acting subjects know what is expected of them and follow the *concept* of a norm against which they can infringe. Brandom explains the genesis of such norms by the fact that a community recognizes and sanctions certain modes of behavior as correct or deviant. The legislator undertakes a binary coding of behavior as, respectively, desirable or undesirable and imposes rewards and punishments on the corresponding normative behavioral expectations. However, this empiricist explanation does not as yet do justice to the nature of beings who allow themselves to be guided by rational motives.[11] The legislation itself has to comply with rational standards: "Our dignity as rational beings consists precisely in being bound only by rules we endorse, rules we have freely chosen (like Odysseus facing the Sirens) to bind ourselves with" (p. 50).

Brandom adopts Kant's conception of autonomy in order to distinguish rational legislation from acts of pure free choice [*Willkür*]. The legislator acts autonomously when he binds himself by precisely those norms that he chooses on the basis of *insight*. The free will is the rational will that allows itself to be determined by good reasons: "Kant's reconciliation of us as free in virtue of being rational, with us as bound by norms in virtue of being rational—and so of freedom as constraint by a special kind of norm, the norms of rationality— accordingly involves treating the normative status of moral obligation as instituted by normative attitudes" (p. 51). However, this very observation shows that comparisons drawn from moral and legal philosophy are not sufficient to make plausible the priority of the "normative attitudes" of the participants over the normative status of their utterances. For the model of self-legislation (in the sense of Kant and Rousseau) already presupposes that the legislator is guided by the very norms of rationality that supposedly first have to be "instituted"—what is at issue, after all, is the "instituting" of these conceptual norms. Norms have to be established "rationally" in accordance with norms of reason, and this process therefore cannot itself provide the model for an explanation of normativity. Before the participants in discourse appear as "legislators" of norms of action, they "always already" feed on the conceptual normativity internal to the structure of speech.

Brandom misunderstands himself to a certain extent because he makes use of an overly inclusive conception of normativity and assimilates norms of rationality in the broadest sense—logical, conceptual, and semantic rules as well as pragmatic ones—to norms of action.[12] Naturally, the practice of argumentation lends itself particularly well to a description in terms of rights and obligations. The proponent of a truth claim is obliged to provide justifications while the opponent has the right to object. Both sides are bound by presuppositions of communication and rules of argumentation that define "the space of reason." In this "space" reasons can float freely and unfold their rationally motivating power unimpeded so as to affect the mind—the "practical attitudes" of the participants in discourse—in the right way. It is part of the meaning of the rights and obligations within argumentation that they bring into play the curiously unforced force of the better argument. Being affected by reasons is, however, quite a different matter than being obliged by norms. Whereas norms of action *bind* the will of agents, norms of rationality *direct* their minds.

That Brandom tends to assimilate rational norms to practical norms may be connected with the origins of his conception of practice. One source is Wittgenstein, who conceives of the grammar of language games as the infrastructure of forms of life. In doing so he reduces logical, mathematical, and grammatical rules, along with cultural patterns and norms of action, to a common denominator.

His conception encompasses cognitive and sociocultural rules without distinction. No less than to his reading of Wittgenstein, however, Brandom's conception of "discursive practices" is indebted to an unconventional interpretation of the first division of *Being and Time*.

The famous analysis of equipment [*Zeuganalyse*] betrays Heidegger's unacknowledged proximity to pragmatism. Prior to all discursive processes of reaching understanding being-in-the-world is defined according to "contexts of involvement" [*Bewandtniszusammenhänge*] that we disclose in our practice of coping with things. In an early essay on Heidegger, Brandom proposes an interpretation of this division of *Being and Time* that is close to what we might call transcendental sociology.[13] How one typically reacts to things in performing actions and what a community recognizes as suitable and appropriate reactions in any given case determines the meaning of the "equipment." Its meaning consists in that *as* which one takes it. In contrast to Heidegger himself, however, Brandom starts from the priority of the social. On this reading, the functional interconnections of a social practice determine how a linguistic community interprets the world, that is, the hermeneutic "as" of their coping with the world. In the case of individuals this pre-predicative understanding of the world finds expression in dispositions to "respond" to similar stimuli in the same manner as others do. The members of a linguistic community thus "institute" meanings through mutually recognizing their typified answers as "suitable and appropriate." In doing so, the epistemic authority of the members joins forces with the social authority of the community.

What is important for our present purposes is Brandom's argument that discursive practice first emerges from this amalgam of a pre-predicative interpretation of the world. With the "assertion as new social mode of response," what up to now was merely "ready-to-hand" is transformed into something "present-at-hand": "Asserting and the practices of giving and asking for reasons which make it possible are themselves a special sort of practical activity. Responding to something by making an assertion about it is treating it *as* present-at-hand."[14] This background enables us to understand why Brandom grants priority to the practical attitudes of the participants in discourse over the normative status that they mutually confer on their statements. It also allows us to understand why he tends in addition to assimilate rational validity to social validity. On the other hand, the final part of his essay—which, though more vulnerable to criticism on philological grounds, is philosophically more interesting—also shows why Brandom does not endorse the consequences suggested by the later Wittgenstein and the later Heidegger. He keeps his distance from the contextualism of language games just as much as from the idealism of linguistic world-disclosure.

For Heidegger, the category of the present-at-hand always carried the pejorative connotation of an "objectification" arising with statements about something present-at-hand. Against this kind of reading that is critical of objectivism, Brandom elaborates the independent cognitive function that grounds the superiority of propositionally differentiated speech and discursive practices over pre-predicative coping with things that are merely ready-to-hand. One might say that he liberates Heidegger's analysis of equipment from the *schmalz* of cultural criticism. Constative speech takes things that are ready-to-hand out of contexts of interests guiding practical projects and brings them into the discursive context of inferential thought as objects about which we can state facts:

When the property of heaviness is discerned in the present-at-hand object which was ready-to-hand as a hammer, a claim is made whose appropriateness is not a matter of serviceability for or obstruction of any particular practical ends or projects. . . . [I]n the game of . . . giving and asking for reasons authority over the appropriateness of claims has been socially withdrawn from the sphere of usefulness for practical ends.[15]

There is a direct route from here to the important qualification that Brandom has made with regard to the "priority of the social." In questions of epistemic validity the consensus of a given linguistic community does not have the last word. As far as the truth of statements is concerned, every individual has to clarify the matter for himself in the knowledge that everyone can make mistakes. Interestingly, the Heidegger essay makes plausible *both* his tendency to assimilate norms of rationality to norms of action *and* his confidence in the rationality of the practice of communication [*Verständigung*]. For Brandom's assertion of a fallibility proviso that holds even for the collectivity as a whole gives rise to the following question: how can an utterance, whose status depends on how an interpreter assesses the commitments and entitlements she attributes to the speaker, come to have an objective content that may well extend beyond what interpreters can know and do in the given context?

The question of the truth of utterances—and of the objectivity of their content—goes against the grain of an explanatory strategy that progresses from pragmatics to semantics:

[I]f actual practical attitudes of taking or treating as correct institute the normative statuses of materially correct inferences, and [if] these material proprieties of inference in turn confer conceptual content—that content nonetheless involves objective proprieties *to which the practical attitudes* underlying the meanings *themselves answer*. How is it possible for our use of an expression to confer on it a content that settles that *we might all be wrong* about how it is *correctly* used, at least in some cases? How can normative attitudes of taking or treating applications of concepts as correct or incorrect institute normative statuses that *transcend those attitudes* in the sense that the instituting attitudes can be assessed according to those instituted norms and found wanting? (p. 137, my emphasis)

Despite his phenomenalist approach, Brandom evidently wants to satisfy realist intuitions.

Such a constellation of arguments is not atypical for approaches that draw the conclusion from the linguistic turn that language and reality are for us inextricably entwined. We can explain what is real only through recourse to what is true. And because the truth of beliefs and sentences can be justified or repudiated only by means of other beliefs and sentences, we cannot step out of the magic circle of our language. Pragmatism makes a virtue out of this necessity by bidding farewell to notions of correspondence and by analyzing "what is true" in terms of the performative attitude of someone who "treats (something) as true." Of course, pragmatism comes in various versions today. These versions may be differentiated, on the one hand, according to whether they regard realist intuitions as compelling or proffer revisionist descriptions for them, and on the other, according to whether they conceive of the contact between our practices and the world as a direct confrontation in action or as mediated through opposition in discourse. In the first respect Brandom's position differs from Richard Rorty's neopragmatism, in the second respect from Hilary Putnam's internal realism.

Each of the two basic realist intuitions may be formulated as mirror images of one another with regard to the truth of statements and to our contact with the world (reference to objects).[16] Concerning the first, the "cautionary use" of the truth predicate implies that no matter how well justified statements may be they can turn out to be false in light of new evidence. What corresponds to this difference between truth and justification, when it comes to reference, is the supposition that a world that is not of our making imposes contingent constraints on us that we "rub up against" when they frustrate our expectations. Concerning the second intuition, the use of the truth predicate in the sense of unconditional validity implies that true statements deserve to be accepted as valid by everyone everywhere. What corresponds to this universality of truth is, with regard to reference, the supposition that the world is one and the same for everyone no matter from which perspective we refer to something in it. We thus presuppose both the existence of possible objects, about which we can state facts, and the commensurability of our systems of reference, which permits us to recognize the same objects under different descriptions.

Against this background we can situate Brandom's view between Rorty's position and Putnam's. Richard Rorty wants to satisfy the first of the two intuitions mentioned above while subjecting the second to revision; he disputes the putative context-independence of truth claims and reckons with the incommensurability of different interpretations of the world. Brandom, by contrast, wants to take account both of truth's claim to universality and of the supposition of one and the same world. On the other hand, he does not conceive of our contact with the world as one that surprises us in the sense of constraining our attempts to cope with reality. In other words, Brandom wants to avoid Rorty's contextualism without including in his pragmatics a Putnamian analysis of how we learn from confrontations with the world.

I shall continue by first of all taking up the two strands of the argument with which Brandom explains the objective content of utterances from a phenomenalist point of view (III). These attempts at explanation propel him in the end toward a linguistic variation on an objective idealism that does not sit well with the picture of a pragmatist transformation of Kantianism presented hitherto (IV). This path from Kant to Hegel explains the objectivist conception of communication that fails to do justice to the role of the second person to which Brandom himself lays claim (V). Furthermore, the methodological privileging of assertoric speech acts also leads to unfortunate consequences in moral theory (VI).

III

Brandom tells two different stories in order to explain the objective, "attitude-transcendent" content of those semantic and conceptual norms that guide participants in discourse: ". . . the objectivity of conceptual norms . . . consists in maintaining the distinction between the normative *statuses* they incorporate and the normative *attitudes* even of the whole community—while nonetheless understanding those statuses as instituted by the practical normative attitudes and assessments of community members" (p. 55). The main weight of the book lies in the original story that is told in chapters 5–8; this places the burden of explanation on a particular anaphoric way of speaking (1). The other story, told in chapter 4, treats perceptions and actions as entries into and exits from discursive practice (2). We shall subsequently look at how the two stories are supposed to fit with and to complement one another.

(1) Brandom starts with an attempt at a kind of transcendental "derivation" of the two-part structure of simple predicative sentences. This is supposed to answer the question of why we use singular terms at all, thereby presupposing the existence of objects to which we attribute or deny properties. This complex set of reflections relies on the logical role accorded to the substitution of equivalent expressions in preserving [*Übertragung*] inferential relations. However, the substitutibility of an expression becomes important for the question of objectivity especially in connection with the anaphoric recurrence to something that has been said. For Brandom understands the two semantic expressions "refers to" and "is true," which

are essential for the representing of states of affairs, not as a relational expression and a predicate but as operators for forming anaphorically dependent expressions (indirect descriptions and "prosentences"). He develops his argument in three steps.

(a) Drawing on Frege's analysis of "recognition judgments," Brandom investigates the role of singular terms, which in language reflect the act of reference to something in the world by marking what is being talked "of" or "about." For, with the help of singular terms, we have to refer to objects in such a way that we can recognize them again even under *different* descriptions: "Taking it that an expression is being used to pick out an object is taking it that the *same* object could be picked out in some *other* way—that some commitment-preserving substitutions involving that expression are in order" (p. 430). Brandom explains this specific achievement, without which we could not get beyond the boundaries of a signal language limited to the situation in which it originates,[17] in terms of the capacity to construct anaphoric chains and thus to guarantee coreference of recurrent tokens.

The deictic use of demonstrative pronouns would play no significant cognitive role if it could not be picked up anaphorically through recurrent tokenings and descriptions. Brandom understands anaphora as the linguistic mechanism by means of which a connection is established between general, that is, reproducible contents and unrepeatable deictic acts: "Deixis presupposes anaphora. No tokens can have the significance of demonstratives unless others have the significance of anaphoric dependents; to use an expression as a demonstrative is to use it as a special kind of anaphoric initiator" (p. 462). Only the intralinguistic reference to antecedent parts of the sentence makes it possible to refer to objects that, going beyond individual deictic acts, we have to be able hold onto as reidentifiable objects. "Without the possibility of anaphoric extension and connection through recurrence to other tokenings, deictic tokenings can play no significant semantic role, not even a deictic one" (p. 465).

(b) The relation between language and world is not, of course, exhausted by the reference of singular terms to objects; it must also include the representation of facts a speaker may assert about objects. This aspect of the language-world relation is expressed in the propositional attitudes the speaker has to states of affairs. These attitudes in turn become a topic for debate when an interpreter refers de dicto to an utterance in order to say that the state of affairs described de re looks *different* from her perspective than it does from the point of view of the speaker—and moreover, explains why it does so. However, such differences of opinion between speaker and interpreter can be expressed only if the two refer to the *same* state of affairs in such a way that each of them uses the operator ". . . is true/untrue" as a proform in order to link up with what the other speaker has said [*Aussage*]. Here, too, anaphora plays an important role; this time, however, in the *interpersonal* use of language. An interpreter has to refer to another's contributions to discourse in such a way that she can substitute the assertion she attributes to him— and she herself challenges—with a counter assertion that refers to the same object or to the same subject matter: "Interpersonal anaphora achieve just the effect that matters for securing communication in the face of differences in collateral commitments" (p. 486). For the interpreter, the difference between the truth claim ascribed de dicto and her own truth claim raised de re makes visible the objectivating attitude that the speaker adopts with regard to the state of affairs he asserts and—from the point of view of the interpreter, wrongly—holds to be true.

(c) Finally, interpersonal anaphora, in connection with the difference in perspectives articulated by the distinction between de dicto and de re descriptions, is the right tool for analyzing the objective content of a subjectively attributed and assessed utterance. For with the concept of "objectivity" Brandom wants to mark the difference between what the participants think they know and what they actually do know. Interpersonal anaphora explains how an interpreter deals with this "Platonist" distinction. By ascribing a truth claim p to a speaker, an interpreter herself is implicitly claiming that the assertion that the speaker has undertaken a commitment to p is true. At the same time, Brandom distinguishes between attributing a truth claim in the form of a de dicto ascription and acknowledging this truth claim that the interpreter thereby adopts as her own in the form of a de re ascription.

If the interpreter now starts from different background assumptions and considers the same objects or states of affairs from a different perspective than the speaker, she may well arrive at a different assessment of what has been said because the speaker—from the interpreter's point of view—is wrong about the *actual consequences* of what he has said. The interpreter assesses the putative assertion of fact *in light of those of its consequences that are unnoticed by the speaker himself* in a different way than the speaker. This means, however, that the interpreter rejects the attributed truth claim because she can draw on a reservoir of potential inferences that, without being fully exploited by the speaker himself, is contained within the utterance: "In this way, every scorekeeping perspective maintains a distinction in practice between normative status and (immediate) normative attitude—between what is objectively correct and what is merely *taken* to be correct" (p. 597). Consistent with Frege's critique of psychologism, Brandom assumes that a statement that a speaker claims to be true contains a reservoir of potential inferences that extends far beyond its manifest content and can *steer* the critical positions of an opponent. The propositional content of a statement can have implications that per se determine how the statement *ought* to be assessed by an interpreter, which may deviate from the speaker's own assessment.

(2) However, this argument, which is based on how we treat the difference in perspectives between speaker and interpreter, does not as yet provide a satisfactory explanation of the problem of objectivity. The question remains open to what or to whom the stated contents owe those "objective properties" to which the differential positions of the interpreter "answer."[18] The interpreter's claim to "know better" can, of course, be just as wrong as the claim of the speaker being interpreted; indeed, *everyone* could be mistaken. There is no perspective, not even that of the community as a whole, that guarantees privileged access to truth. If, however, everyone has the same fallible access to truth, then even the anaphorically expressed difference in perspectives between speaker and interpreter provides no answer to the question "How is it possible for our use of an expression to confer on it a content that settles that we might all be

wrong about how it is correctly used, at least in some cases?" (p. 137). With regard to this phenomenon, still awaiting clarification, one might perhaps think of "natural kind" terms such as "gold" (or, trivially, "whales") that Hilary Putnam uses to illustrate how we have *revised* our use of language as a result of new knowledge about the *correct* extension of these terms.[19] Does Brandom provide an answer to this question in his chapter on "Perception and Action"? Is this *second story* supposed to provide an answer to the still open question of the objectivity of propositional contents at all?

On the one hand, perceptions and actions, through the grammatical form of judgments and intentions, are propositionally—that is, linguistically—structured. On the other hand, they mark the entry into and exit from the discursive practices in which, even from the internal perspective of the participants in communication, language comes into contact and is interlocked with the world. Insofar as this is the case, sensation and successful action count as the two routes by which the constraints of an objective world presumed to be independent of and identical for "us," are imposed on "us"—even after the linguistic turn. It is true that Brandom opposes (in my view with good reason) the externalist thesis according to which perceptual judgments owe their epistemic authority exclusively to the causal chain that extends from the perceived situation itself to the perception of the situation (pp. 209ff.). Naturally, however, he accepts perceptions as the empirical foundation of "immediate judgments." He even goes so far as to hold that perceptions function in discourses as reasons that do not for their part require any further justification: "Non-inferential reports can function as unjustified justifiers. . . . So observation provides regress-stoppers, and in this sense a foundation for empirical knowledge" (p. 222). Brandom explains this position—which sounds somewhat empiricist and, at any rate, deviates from Peirce—in terms of dispositions acquired through learning. "Reliable observers" are trained to react in a sufficiently differentiated way to stimuli in their environment: "The basis of observational knowledge, then, is that it should be possible to train individuals reliably to respond differentially to features of their environment by acknowledging doxastic commitments" (p. 224).

In this way a picture of language arises according to which the network of semantic threads among an infinite number of potential sentences is, as it were, anchored in reality at the nodes of deducible observational sentences. Is this kind of anchoring in itself sufficient, however, to satisfy the realist intuition of an independent world that can challenge even our best description? In the background is Wittgenstein's model of learning a language. Adults teach their children the vocabulary for colors through use of examples, by showing them various red things in their surroundings for the predicate "red" and various blue things for the predicate "blue." This training in the "correct" use of language operates on the tacit assumption that the accompanying sentences "This is a red object" or "This is a blue object" are *true* within the framework of established linguistic practices. In cases of doubt, therefore, the perception of objects (and the truth of the corresponding observational sentences) can serve as a control mechanism for the correct application of the predicates: "Look, if you compare this jacket with the red one here and the yellow one over there, you can see that it is more orange than red." This, roughly speaking, is how parents correct the linguistic knowledge of their children by using examples taken from experience. But does experience have the power over and above this to correct the intersubjectively habitualized language use of the competent adults themselves? So long as it is merely a matter of learning a language, what is correct is determined according to what the community of those who have command of the language take to be correct.

Perceptions certainly mark a point of intersection between language and the world. However, this does not as yet say anything about the extent of the veto power that an objective world can exert vis-à-vis unsuitable semantic rules. We may learn through experience about linguistic inconsistencies by learning, for example, that peanuts are legumes.[20] But can we "learn" through our dealings with reality that, according to our present empirical standards, what we once had correctly called "gold" in accordance with what was established semantically in our language, is no longer "gold"? Clearly, Heidegger and (in a different way) Wittgenstein did not credit experience with such a far-reaching revisionary power.

On their view, a linguistic community's horizon of experience is, through the grammar of a language or a language game, categorially interpreted and conceptually articulated "preontologically"—that is, *always already*—in such a way that intraworldly experiences lack the power to repudiate what language itself, structuring the world a priori, has already disclosed about the world in advance. Having transferred the spontaneity of world-constitution from the transcendental subject to language, Heidegger and Wittgenstein had to give up the realist premise of a world independent of "our" constitutive accomplishments. And because natural languages always occur in the plural, this led to the problem of the translatability or commensurability of different linguistic world-projects—a problem that also called into question the other premise of a world that is the same for everyone.

Brandom, who is evidently not prepared to tolerate antirealist consequences, cannot accept a transcendental *linguistic* approach, whether this be given a culturalist turn (MacIntyre), an onto-historical one (Derrida), or a pragmatist one (Rorty). He is confident that the power of experience to contradict our beliefs can initiate learning processes that affect linguistic knowledge itself:

[T]he inferences from circumstances to consequences of application (which are implicit in conceptual contents) are subject to empirical criticism in virtue of inferential connections among the contents of commitments that can be acquired noninferentially. So it may happen that one uses the term "acid" in such a way that a substance's tasting sour is a sufficient condition for applying it, and that it will turn litmus paper red is a necessary consequence of applying it. Finding a substance that both tastes sour and turns litmus paper blue shows that such a concept is inadequate. (p. 225)

If one argues in this way, of course, one must also confront the question of how such learning processes that result from intraworldly stimuli can intervene in a world-disclosing semantics and in the basic conceptual articulation of semantic contents themselves.

Curiously, Brandom is content merely to *mention* the above example. One searches in vain for an analysis of empirically driven learning processes that not only compel individual members of a linguistic community to correct their flawed linguistic knowledge but force the community as a whole to revise habitualized semantic or conceptual rules. The weight Brandom places on experience in the development of objective concepts and corresponding semantic rules results from the way in which he connects the two stories he tells. The very order of the chapters raises doubt as to whether the analysis of perception and action is supposed to answer the question left open by the penetrating reflections on the central role of anaphora.

IV

How is it possible to conceive of the sedimentation of empirical knowledge about the world in linguistic knowledge as a check on linguistic knowledge by empirical knowledge? Semantically relevant learning processes would have to explain how empirical contact with things and events can trigger a revision of the antecedently given ("world-disclosing") linguistic categories and conceptual norms. Brandom rejects a naturalist explanation. However, as I show in (1), a pragmatist explanation, which would fit with the structure of his theory, cannot be developed solely from the phenomenalist viewpoint of an interpreter understanding a language. For this reason, as I show in (2), Brandom sees himself compelled to adopt a conceptual realism that, by making claims about the structure of the world "in itself," undermines his discourse-theoretic analysis of reality as "appearing" in language.

(1) Like Putnam, Brandom is convinced that "reason can't be naturalized." For this reason, the philosopher of language retains the internal perspective of the participants themselves and distinguishes the social world of utterances, interactions, and attitudes that are accessible through understanding meaning (or through translation) from the objective world of observed states and events that can be explained causally: "The critical classification of things into objective and social is itself a social, rather than objective or ontological categorization of things according to whether we treat them as subject to the authority of a community or not."[21] A naturalistic explanatory strategy guarantees causally explicable states and events an ontological

priority over social practices, which are described in normative terms. These social practices are supposed to be traced back to causally explicable processes. This means that the categorial components of a linguistically structured lifeworld have to be reformulated in a nominalist language referring to observable states and events. The content and form of grammatical utterances are described, for example, in the functions and characteristics of datable speech events[22] or (as happens today in the cognitive sciences) are translated into the neuronal processes of the brain. The more radical the translation, however, the less the intuitively known phenomena are recognizable as the same phenomena under their new, objectivist description.[23]

To be sure, the nonnaturalist explanatory strategy preferred by Brandom runs up against the converse problem: how can the states and events that we perceive and describe in nominalist terms find an entry point into the space of reasons? We have already encountered this problem in connection with the relationship between deixis and anaphora. The intralinguistic recurrence to singular deictic acts replaced by demonstrative pronouns was supposed to explain how unrepeatable "tokens"—coupled with perceived events—can be brought into the discursive chain of repeatable "types," thereby being made recursively accessible. Here, admittedly, Brandom treated deixis itself, the act of direct reference, as only a reflection of anaphora, that is, as a derivative phenomenon that did not appear to require further explanation. For our present purposes we can leave aside the question of whether this proposal suppresses rather than clarifies the problem of reference. At any rate, the question under consideration of how linguistic and empirical knowledge interact seems to call for an investigative perspective broader than a language-immanent one.

Brandom's own example—of how observing a piece of litmus paper unexpectedly turning blue provides a reason for correcting the hitherto established rules of application for the concept "acid"— points in this direction. Here, perception is generated through an experimental action. Such an experiment, however, merely exploits the internal connection between perception and action that already exists in everyday practices and that makes possible ordinary "learning from experience." We check whether an action is successful by observing whether the consequences it might be expected to have do in fact occur. If they do not, we know that we have to revise the assumptions underlying the plan of action. Ever since Peirce's "doubtbelief" model, in his middle period, pragmatism has regarded the successful carrying out of an action as the most important criterion for corroborating empirical beliefs. Habitualized practices are corroborated by their continued functioning, that is, in the very fact of their being carried out unimpeded. In our practical "coping" with reality, certain perceptions acquire a pronounced revisionary power as control mechanisms that inform us about failures—about the nonoccurrence of the expected consequences of our actions. Here, generalized behavioral certainties—beliefs that have congealed into behavioral habits—form the background that, as it were, hones dissonant perceptions into negations of expectations, thereby according them the sense of a repudiation experienced in practice, of a necessity to revise existing beliefs. In perceiving an unsuccessful action, the actor "rubs up" against a frustrating reality that terminates its hitherto attested willingness to play along, as it were, in an actioncontext that is no longer functioning.

The objective world can register this "resistance" only performatively by refusing to "go along with" *targeted interventions* in a world of causally interpreted sequences of events. In this way it registers an objection only in the operational sphere of instrumental action. This explains why Brandom, who has committed himself to a phenomenalist analysis of language, does not take into consideration the pragmatist explanation of semantically relevant learning processes.[24] Naturally, what agents experience when their actions fail in confrontation with reality is itself linguistically structured, but this is not an experience *with* language or within the horizon of linguistic communication. A perception that is contrary to our beliefs destabilizes our certainties about how to act. Only if agents distance themselves from their practical coping with the world and enter into rational discourse, objectifying the situation that was originally "ready-tohand" in order to reach understanding with one another about something in the world, can such a perception become a discursively mobilized "reason." It then enters as criticism into the *conceptual* economy and the semantic inferential resources attached to existing views, setting in motion revisions, if necessary.

The dynamics of success-controlled action that, as in the case of the litmus test mentioned above, provides the impetus for a revision of concepts and of the semantic resources does not even begin to come into view so long as the investigation remains confined to the attitudes, interactions, and utterances of participants in discourse. Perceptual judgments play a different role in engaged coping with reality than in the communicative horizon of attributing, justifying and acknowledging truth claims. For Brandom, however, actions or acts remain essentially speech acts. What interests him principally about the intentional actions with which we intervene causally in the world are the justificatory reasons. I shall come back to this presently. To the extent that the acts that can in principle be justified actually do require justification, they are incorporated into discursive practice *as* speech acts. Thus Brandom's investigation can proceed unwaveringly straight from perception to action without taking notice of how perceptions are embedded in contexts of action and without paying attention to the revisionary power that accrues to perceptions only through their feedback relation to "coping"—to the success-controlled practice of dealing with problems.

The practice of giving and asking for reasons can make good on its promise to help the better arguments be heard in any given case only if the semantic and conceptual norms that determine contents and guide the yes/no positions of participants guarantee an objective content. However, Brandom's analysis of perceptions and actions is evidently not intended for purposes of developing a notion of *learning from experience* that could explain the truth and the "objective" content of utterances.

(2) Brandom does not rescue the realist intuitions by recourse to the contingent constraints of a world that is presupposed to exist independently and to be the same for everyone. On such a view, interlocutors process these constraints by bringing their constructive interpretations of states of affairs and events into harmony with the contingencies they experience in practice in their frustrating encounters with the world. He does not conceive of the world we encounter in any way nominalistically but rather—incidentally, like

the later Peirce[25]—"realistically," if, in contrast to modern epistemological realism, one uses this term in the sense of a metaphysical conceptual realism. For Brandom sees the objectivity of our concepts and material rules of inference as anchored in a world that *is in itself conceptually structured.* The conceptual relationships of the world, it appears, merely unfold discursively in our argumentations, thus finding expression in the conceptual structures of our knowledge of language and of the world: "The conception of concepts as inferentially articulated permits a picture of thought and of the world that thought is about as equally, and in the favored cases *identically,* conceptually articulated" (p. 622).

This "realist" understanding of the world, according to which both our discursively acquired thoughts and the world captured in thoughts are inherently of a conceptual nature—that is, are made of the same stuff—grants to experience no more than a *passively mediating* role. From this point of view, sensation does not provide the negative stimuli or prompts to which the imaginative power of a mind that operates constructively responds with interpretations; it does not mediate the encounters with the world against which a fallible mind tests and corrects its interpretations. Rather, experience is demoted to the medium by way of which concepts—which exist in themselves—are impressed on the receptive human mind.[26] A conceptually structured world gets the human mind involved in conceptual articulation. Brandom makes no secret of his basic assumption that knowledge in this sense is ontologically grounded:

Facts are just true claims. . . . It is these facts and the propertied and related objects they involve that are cited as stimuli by interpreters who are specifying the reliable differential responsive dispositions in which the contents of empirical contents originate. These noninferential dispositions (the locus of our empirical receptivity) accordingly do not constitute the interface between what is conceptually articulated and what is not, but merely one of the necessary conditions for a conceptually articulated grasp of a conceptually articulated world. . . . (p. 622)

Thus abandoning a nominalist conception of objectivity has an effect not only on the naturalism that predominates in the empiricist American tradition up to Quine, Davidson, and Rorty. It also turns the architectonics of post-Hegelian, postmetaphysical thinking in general on its head.[27] Kant had distinguished between noumena and phenomena, between the intelligible realm of freedom, which is directly accessible to transcendental reflection, and the world of intrinsically unorganized phenomena on which the human mind imposes its categories. In neo-Kantianism and in Dilthey's writings, this dualism had taken the shape of a dualist theory of the natural sciences and the humanities, before reappearing in Heidegger as ontological difference—as the difference between the hermeneutically disclosed world that we ourselves are, and the entities that we encounter in the world and with which we have to cope. In "understanding" [*Verstehen*], that is, in the basic hermeneutic operation of the humanities, Heidegger recognizes the basic feature of human existence itself. As the entity that "has to be its own Being," the human being has an in-built disposition toward articulating her understanding of the world and of herself. As a result, the structure of the world in which she finds herself is by its very nature accessible to her, whereas all entities within the world appear in the horizon of her linguistic world-projections—and can be interpreted and dealt with only in terms of this categorial interpretation.

With this hermeneutic turn the classical definition of the relationship between nature and history was reversed. A nominalistically disqualified nature can respond only to *our* questions, and in our language, we are intuitively familiar—from within, as it were—with the symbolic forms of historical life in which all human existence [*Dasein*] is effected. It is true that the hermeneutic understanding of the meaning of historical constructs no longer shares the foundationalist claim of the metaphysical knowledge of essences; nonetheless, it continues to share the mode of intellectual intuition of universals—whereby, of course, the essences, ideas, or concepts have retreated from the nature of things into the rules of language.[28] In a sense, the notion of a linguistically constituted lifeworld, accessible and intelligible in its general structures from within, that is, from the participant's perspective, takes over the legacy of a metaphysically understood realism, whereas everything within the world in the sense of a modern, epistemologically understood realism is conceived as the manifold of causally explicable yet contingent states and events.

By and large pragmatism has shared this conceptual shift with hermeneutics. Because Peirce, Mead, James, and Dewey take not the understanding of texts but rather problem-solving behavior in practical coping with a contingent reality as the starting point for their analyses, they are immune to the temptation to transfigure the world-disclosing power of language as the poetic force of the extraordinary. They are not tempted to reintroduce metaphysics by the back door. For the pragmatists, the intersubjectively shared lifeworld is rather the site of a cooperative and communicative everyday practice in which, as in the case of Piaget, the innovative-experimental and the discursive features of fallible learning processes or, as in the case of the later Wittgenstein, the interactive features of grammatically regulated language games stand out. However, for Dewey as for Wittgenstein or Heidegger—and this is the tradition out of which Brandom develops his normative pragmatics—what is concealed behind objectivity is nothing but the challenge of "intraworldly" contingencies that "we" have articulated in "our" concepts and deal with constructively. Here, too, the transcendental architectonic of a "phenonomenal" world that holds sway from Kant to Husserl remains to a certain extent intact: a nominalistically conceived objective world makes itself known to the active intelligence solely in the horizon of a lifeworld in which we "always already" find ourselves as the members of a linguistic and cooperative community.

Like McDowell, Brandom intervenes in this architectonic of the interlocking of the intersubjective lifeworld and objective world by conceiving of the objectivity of "our" concepts as an articulated mirroring of the objective content of a world that is in itself conceptually structured: "Concepts conceived as inferential roles of expressions do not serve as epistemological intermediaries, standing between us and what is conceptualized by them. This is not because there is no causal order consisting of particulars, interaction with which supplies the material for thought. It is rather because all of these elements *are themselves conceived as thoroughly conceptual, not as contrasting with the conceptual*" (p. 622, my emphasis).

With this, the insight that once stood at the beginning of linguistic philosophy is given what one might call an objectivist reading.[29] Together with the Wittgenstein of the *Tractatus* Brandom conceives

of the world as the totality of facts: "the world consisting of everything that is the case, all the facts, and the objects they are about."
Facts are just what can be stated in true sentences: "facts are just true
claims." In contrast to Wittgenstein, however, Brandom does not understand this formulation in the sense of a transcendental linguistic
idealism according to which the limits of our language are the limits
of our world. He finds an *objective* linguistic idealism more congenial:
because facts, in which the world consists, *are* essentially what can be
stated in true sentences, the world itself is of this kind, namely, of a
conceptual nature. For this reason the objectivity of the world is not attested to by contingencies that we experience through sensation and
in our practical coping with the world but only through the discursive resistance of persistent objections.[30]

V

Brandom's normative pragmatics seems initially to express a pragmatist self-understanding on the part of rational organisms along
Kantian lines. As the analysis progresses, however, this picture
changes. Let us recapitulate. As a result of a plausible methodological decision, Brandom examines discursive practices from the point
of view of a second person attributing and assessing truth claims.
This, however, gives rise to the question of how, from the indirect
viewpoint of a fallible interpreter, it is possible to distinguish merely
taking a claim to be true from being entitled to do so. Brandom
gives not just one but several answers to this question regarding the
truth and objective content of utterances, whose status is supposed
to depend on the discursively achieved "yes" or "no" of interlocutors. Yet, these partial answers prove to be merely steps along a path
that leads resolutely beyond the Kantian starting point of the enterprise. I have described this path as leading from Kant to Hegel. This
in itself is not as yet an objection. It was certainly not without good
reason that Frege, Dilthey, and Peirce introduced the linguistic,
hermeneutic, and pragmatic turns. Moreover, the turning away
from Hegel on the part of Feuerbach, Marx, and Kierkegaard was
equally well grounded. A *tacit* return to objective idealism can
scarcely be possible anymore. I would like therefore (1) to recall the

post-Hegelian situation in which we still find ourselves before (2) problematizing Brandom's metaphysical realism with reference to one of its consequences, namely, his surprisingly objectivist understanding of discursive behavior.

(1) The critique that guides postmetaphysical thinking is simple enough: we would have to adopt a standpoint outside of our language, practices, and forms of life in order to be able to know in any given case that the structures of our understanding of the world reflect structures of the world that are made *of the same stuff* as our concepts. A "God's-eye view" is denied us. For idealism, of course, there is another way to ascertain "existing concepts"; for it cannot be ruled out from the outset that the basic assumption of conceptual realism could be grounded through reflection on the evolution of one's own state of consciousness. In this vein, Romantic philosophy of nature was a hermeneutic attempt to bring the processes of a nature that had been objectified—and, accordingly, alienated—by the natural sciences back into the progressively expanded perspective of our linguistically structured lifeworld, thereby making nature *intelligible.*

Naturally, this project of decoding nature "from above" is guided by the interest of subjects capable of speech and action in recognizing their *own* genesis in natural history:[31]

Anything can be treated as subject to the norms inherent in social practices, with a greater or lesser degree of strain. Thus a tree or a rock can become subject to norms insofar as we consider it as engaging in social practices. We can do this either by giving it a social role, for instance, that of an oracle, or simply by translating its performances as utterances. . . . Of course, in such cases we must allow that the item in question is only a member of our community in a derivative or second-class fashion, for it is not capable of engaging in very many of our practices, or even of engaging in those very well. This is the strain involved in translating ordinary occurrences rather than simply explaining them. . . .[32]

Someone who wants to read the Book of Nature assumes that nature will open its eyes and provide answers as soon as we regard it as our alter ego. This hermeneutic anticipation reveals asymmetries between our world and the worlds of less highly organized organisms. A resocialized nature has to be divested of the—comparatively— overly complex features of a linguistically structured lifeworld.

Against this backdrop, however, the discursively constituted world of
rational organisms can appear as a segment of a more comprehensive picture. As, for instance, when Brandom uses the concept of "intentionality" as a guiding thread in order to hint at the categorial
stratification of the world as a whole. Whereas the lower strata lack
all signs of intentionality, we may ascribe simple intentionality to
more highly organized organisms and "original intentionality" to
ourselves, who *mutually* attribute intentionality to one another.[33]

Of course, fleeting associations of this sort do not as yet suffice to
make the old kind of realism plausible. A carefully worked-out philosophy of language can retreat from speculative topics and demand
that it be criticized in its own terms. Large-scale reservations about the
architectonics of the theory as a whole have to be cashed out in the
coin of specific objections if they are not to run into the sand. It is
therefore useful to keep in mind one of the consequences that follows from thus altering the architectonics of the theory.

To a certain extent the supposition of a world that is entirely conceptually structured relieves the finite and fallible human mind of
the burden of the *constructive* endeavor to develop its *own* concepts
in terms of which it can interpret what happens in the world. Objective idealism shifts the burden of explanation from the cooperative
efforts within an intersubjectively constituted lifeworld onto the constitution of what there is [*des Seienden*] as a whole. According to
Brandom, the objective content of the preexisting conceptual relationships needs only to be unfolded in discourses. The "effort of the
concept," which otherwise would be a matter of cooperative learning by way of the constructive interpretations of a communication
community, is replaced by a "movement of the concept," which proceeds through discourse and experience but over the heads of most
of the participants. Objective idealism divests them of the epistemic
authority (and also of the moral autonomy) they have to assert so
long as they do not have the option of direct access to a supposed
conceptual structure of the universe. This may explain why Brandom
uses a conception of communication that does not really do justice
to the position of the specific role of the second person.

(2) With good reason, Brandom denies the actually prevailing consensus of the linguistic community an ultimate epistemic authority.

A definitive privileging of the linguistic community vis-à-vis its individual members would blur the distinction between the rational acceptability and the mere acceptance of a truth claim. Individual interpreters decide in any given case whether a validity claim is justified, but all participants, the interpreter as much as the speaker, can be mistaken. There is no bird's-eye view from which we can know definitively who is right. The "scorekeeping responsibilities," and hence also the responsibility for yes/no positions to which one is entitled, lie with the individual participant in discourse: "There is only the actual practice of sorting out who has the better reason in particular cases" (p. 601). Brandom wants to grant priority to symmetric "*I-thou* relations" between first and second persons over asymmetric "*I-we* relations" in which the individual is, so to speak, overpowered by the collectivity. But does he make good on this claim?

Brandom contrasts the collectivist picture of a linguistic community that commands ultimate authority with the individualist picture of isolated pairs of interpersonal relationships, but he does not take into account the horizon of meaning of a linguistically disclosed world that is shared intersubjectively by all members. He analyzes the attribution of validity claims, and their evaluation, without taking into consideration the complex interconnections of the first-, second-, and third-person perspectives. He actually construes what he calls the "I-thou relation" as the relation between a first person who raises validity claims and a third person who attributes validity claims to the first. Up to now I have followed Brandom's own wording of his account. On closer examination, however, it turns out that the act of attributing, which is of fundamental importance for discursive practice, is not really carried out by a *second* person. There can be no second person at all without the attitude of a first person to a second person. This condition is not satisfied in Brandom's model. It is no accident that Brandom prefers to identify the interpreter with a spectator who assesses the utterance of a speaker and not with an addressee who is expected to *reply to the speaker*. Every round of a new discourse opens with an ascription that the interpreter undertakes from the observer's perspective of a *third* person.

This is confirmed by Brandom's examples. If, during a court case (p. 505), the prosecutor asserts that the defense attorney has brought in a pathological liar as a (supposedly) trustworthy witness, and the defense attorney replies that the man he has just called to the witness stand is in fact a trustworthy person, then the communicative exchange is played out on two different levels: on one level, both the prosecutor and the defense attorney are speaking to one another in that, by means of de re and de dicto descriptions, they reciprocally dispute the correctness of each other's utterance. At the same time, of course, they are aware of the presence of the judges, the jurors, and the spectators who, on a second level of communication, are following their exchange and silently assessing it. Interestingly, Brandom singles out the indirect communication of the speakers with the spectators who are listening to them—rather than the communication of those directly involved—as the paradigmatic case.

Certainly, in the courtroom the judges hearing the case and the jury listening to it are the ones who are keeping score, as it were, of how the discussion is progressing and are forming a judgment as to who is scoring points in order to be able to say in the end, for example, how the statement of the controversial witness is to be assessed. *During* the dispute, however, a reaction is required not from the listeners but from the parties directly involved who address their utterances *to one another* and who expect each other to *take positions.* Listeners have a different role than hearers. The listeners take on the role of third persons waiting to see what happens, while those directly involved adopt a performative attitude and, in thus taking toward each other the attitude of a first person toward a second, expect a response from each other—regardless of whether this be a positive or negative assessment or an abstention. The mere attribution of a validity claim—and its assessment undertaken *in foro interno*—does not as yet constitute a reply. A research strategy that confuses the first level of communication with the second ignores, in overlooking this important distinction, the grammatical role of the second person.

Brandom does not, it is true, share Davidson's naturalism, but he does share with him a certain theoreticism in that he conceives understanding an expression as a mapping operation—rather than as the hermeneutic interpretation of a text. In attributing validity claims and entitlements to a speaker, the interpreter maps her own descriptions and assessments onto the observed speech acts of another. Evidently Brandom assumes that the result of communication consists in the simplest case in an epistemic relation—a relation between what the speaker says about something in the world and the attribution of what is said undertaken by the interpreter. However, this objectivist description misses the point of linguistic communication [*Verständigung*].

The intention that a speaker connects with an utterance amounts to more than just the intention that an interpreter attribute to him the right belief without his being interested in the interpreter's stance regarding this belief. Rather, as an interlocutor, the speaker uses his assertion to make a demand on an addressee to say "yes" or "no" publicly; at any rate he expects some kind of reaction from her that can count as an answer and that can produce obligations relevant to subsequent interactions *for both parties*. Only an "answer" can confirm or revise views on which (and on whose implications) both parties have to be able to rely in the further course of their interaction. Everyday communicative exchanges are "carried" by the context of shared background assumptions. Moreover, as the beliefs and opinions of subjects who make independent decisions are relevant for coordinating their actions, the need for communication arises in turn from the necessity of keeping these beliefs and opinions consonant with one another. Communication is not some self-sufficient game in which the interlocutors reciprocally *inform* each other about their beliefs and intentions. It is only the imperative of social integration—the need to coordinate the action-plans of independently deciding participants in action—that explains the point of linguistic communication.

The transmission of information from sender to receiver is the wrong model because it fails to take account of the structural interpenetration of first- and second-person perspectives.[34] By raising a truth claim for a proposition in a speech act—and, if necessary, being prepared to provide reasons for it, a speaker does not merely "make (the interpreter) understand"—in a Gricean sense—that he holds p to be true. He not only wants to be understood correctly, he also wants to *reach an understanding* [*sich verständigen*] with someone about p. If possible, the addressee is supposed to accept the truth claim. For what is said can enter into their subsequent interactions as a premise only if both *share* the belief that *p*. Truth claims have a built-in orientation toward *intersubjective* recognition, and it is only such recognition that can place the seal on an agreement reached between participants in communication about something in the world.

If one understands the goal of communication [*Verständigung*] in this normative sense as rationally motivated agreement, the basic question of a theory of meaning can be answered easily. We understand a speech act when we know the conditions and consequences of the rationally motivated agreement that a speaker could attain with this speech act. In short, to understand an expression is to know how to use it in order to reach understanding with someone about something.[35]

Certainly, Brandom, too, replaces the information-transmission model with another model of communication: his mutual "scorekeeping" is taken from baseball. However, a strategic team game such as baseball is about a calculated adjustment to the reactions of others and not about a consensual cooperation that can meet the demands of social integration. A different—but just as deficient—model is ballroom dancing: "I have in mind thinking of conversation as somewhat like Fred Astaire and Ginger Rogers dancing: they are doing very different things—at least moving in different ways—but are coordinating, adjusting, and making up one dance. The dance is all they share, and it is not independent of or antecedent to what they are doing."[36] This comparison confirms that Brandom is opting for methodological individualism. According to the latter, discursive practice emerges from inferences that each individual participant draws for herself based on mutual observation. This picture rules out the possibility for the participants to *converge* in their intersubjective recognition of the same validity claim and can *share* knowledge in the strict sense of the term.

The objectivist conception of the process of communication becomes fully intelligible only against the background of conceptual realism. At any rate, such a conception explains why a discursive practice that is comprised of the—in each case, individual—contributions of the participants and is not the result of a cooperative accomplishment nonetheless grounds the presumption of objectivity. Distinguishing between truth and "taking-true" can remain up to each individual participant in discourse. It does not require a "community of justification" to direct itself toward the goal of a discursively achieved agreement because (everyone assumes that) the objectivity of propositional contents is guaranteed by the conceptual structure of the world, which is merely unfolded and articulated in discourse. Only an objectively embodied reason, as it were, that has shifted from the life-world into the objective world can relieve intersubjective justificatory practices of the burden of collectively *assuming the warrant* for truth and objectivity. Thus, an objectivist conception of communication, which misses an essential dimension of linguistic communication— that of the intersubjective relation to second persons, whose recognition validity claims aim to elicit—also casts a problematic light on the conceptual realist picture of the universe in which this conception has its roots.

VI

The objectivism that results from the background assumption of conceptual realism has implications for our understanding of morality similar to those it has for the concept of communication. If the practice of giving and asking for reasons merely articulates preexisting conceptual relations, discursive practices essentially serve epistemic purposes in a narrow sense. Discursive practice then operates in the mode of making statements or giving descriptions—"in the fact-stating line of business." Assertoric speech acts become the model for speech acts in general. I shall show that (1) the Hegelian continuum of concepts that extends through our discourses makes Kantian differentiations within the category of reason more difficult, in particular the distinction between theoretical and practical reason. Furthermore, (2) the assimilation of norms to facts has undesirable consequences, leading to, among other things, a moral realism that is not likely to be defensible.

(1) It is true that the privileging of assertions is in keeping with a "privileging of logos in human language" characteristic of the

philosophical tradition as a whole.[37] But the very figures who play godparent to Brandom's normative pragmatics—Peirce and Dewey, Heidegger and Wittgenstein—are the ones who have broken with the prejudices of ontology, epistemology, and formal semantics. Without joining in Ludwig Klages's lament about Western "logocentrism,"[38] they have all fought against the classical view that grasping essences or representing objects or asserting facts enjoy priority over practical coping with the world. Continuing a transcendental line of inquiry, they were interested in the constitutive accomplishments of the social, linguistically structured lifeworld and made us aware of the multiplicity of the types of speech acts, validity claims, and practices in which our cognitive coping with the world is embedded. Brandom, too, takes up his investigation from precisely this perspective; as shown, however, he sees himself compelled by the problem of objectivity to make a certain about-face. From the phenomenalist perspective, which he retains, he arrives at the conclusion that the presumptively conceptual structures of the universe impress themselves on our discursive practices.

Given an exclusively cognitive relation to the world, however, constative speech in general moves to the forefront. All communicative practices—even those that, like expressive, aesthetic, ethical, moral, or legal discourses, do not involve fact-stating—are supposed to be analyzable on the basis of assertions. The unity of the world, which is conceptually structured through and through, and which takes on a reflexive shape in the lifeworld of rational beings, also levels the distinction between norms and facts that is of concern to us here: "Concepts are rules, and concepts express natural necessity as well as moral necessity" (p. 624).

Brandom himself makes use of the vocabulary by means of which we, in the horizon of our world, distinguish between facts and norms, events and actions. However, he conceives of everything we do in applying concepts as action in a broader sense. Unlike Kant, Brandom reduces practical and theoretical reason to the common denominator of rational activity. According to this view, judgments and beliefs are just as much norm-governed as are intentions to act, with the result that they cannot be differentiated in terms of whether they refer descriptively to facts or prescriptively to actions.

Thus Brandom includes *all* utterances that can be criticized and justified in the realm of the normative in general; on the other hand, it is supposed to be *only facts* in light of which actions as well as linguistic utterances can be criticized and justified. The realm of freedom is intrinsically entwined with the realm of necessity: "Fact-stating talk is explained in normative terms, and normative facts emerge as one kind of fact among others. The common deontic scorekeeping vocabulary in which both are specified and explained ensures that the distinction between normative and nonnormative facts neither evanesces nor threatens to assume the proportions of an ultimately unintelligible dualism" (pp. 625ff.). For our present purposes what is most interesting about this assimilation of norms to facts is the implication that true normative sentences represent facts in the same way as descriptive sentences—in this case, as simply normative facts.

This conclusion already follows from the privileged position of assertoric speech acts, which serve as a model for practical commitments. On the one hand, Brandom relativizes the metatheoretical distinction between facts and norms with respect to the normative language within which this distinction has to be made. On the other hand, he treats normative states of affairs as facts on the assumption that we always have to use a normative idiom when making statements. Here Brandom is thinking of his own enterprise: his normative pragmatics ultimately aims to give true descriptions of discursive practices in normative terms. However, Brandom elides the significant fact that, in everyday practices, the normative vocabulary above all serves purposes of guiding our actions and not cognitive purposes of logical explication. He annexes everything about which we make statements in any kind of evaluative or prescriptive language whatsoever to the realm of normative facts: "Corresponding to the distinction between normative and nonnormative vocabulary is a distinction between normative and nonnormative facts. . . . In this way the normative is picked out as a subregion of the factual" (p. 625).

(2) As the enterprise develops, however, it becomes clear that assertoric speech acts—given their ontological connotations of truth and existence—provide too narrow a basis for an adequate examination of regulative language use. Brandom proceeds in three steps: he first compares the argumentative duties [*Rechtfertigungspflichten*] that we tacitly assume in our intentional actions with the justificatory duties [*Begründungspflichten*] that are attached to assertoric speech acts (a). He then explicates how actions can be justified in the form of practical inferences (b). This is supposed to lead us to the following point: that despite some asymmetries all actions can be justified [*rechtfertigen*] in the same way as assertions of facts (c).

(a) Like assertions, actions belong to the category of rational expressions because subjects capable of speech and action bear responsibility for their intentions to act as much as for their judgments. In both cases reasons can be given and asked for. The raising, attribution, and acknowledgment of doxastic commitments [*epistemische Ansprüche*] have a counterpart with respect to practical commitments [*praktische Vorhaben*]. Just as, by making an assertion, a speaker undertakes a commitment to the judgment that *p*, so too the intentionally acting subject makes known her intention to make *p* true. Because in both cases "commitment" implies readiness, if necessary, to supply reasons for the belief expressed in the speech act or for the intention expressed in the action, the analysis of attributing "commitments" and acknowledging "entitlements" can be applied in the same way to practical projects [*praktische Vorhaben*] as to truth claims. From the perspective of an interpreter the agent is entitled to do what he intends if he acts with (or even explicitly on the basis of) good reasons. Brandom does not, however, raise the question of whether the "responsibility" that the agent bears for his action is *exhausted* by the epistemic justificatory responsibility, which, of course, is all that can be at issue in the case of assertions.

(b) Like Kant, Brandom explains rational action as the capacity to act according to maxims, that is, in accordance with the concept of a rule. Every project presupposes free choice [*Willkür*], that is, the capacity to bind one's own will to the idea of a rule, in other words to commit oneself to following such a rule. For this reason practical inferences refer to maxims or rules of action such as (to stick with Brandom's examples) "Bank employees are obliged to wear neckties" or "One ought not harm anyone to no purpose." Of course, expressions such as "are obliged to" or "ought" occur only in explicit rules of action; they articulate a deontological meaning that generally remains hidden. Normally, material inferences suffice, for example: "I am a bank employee going to work, so I shall wear a necktie" or "Repeating the gossip would harm someone, to no purpose, so I shall not repeat the gossip."

Depending on the *underlying* norms, there are various types of reasons for action that bind the will of the agent in various ways: prudential reasons, for example, that I had better open my umbrella in order to keep dry, conventional reasons, such as dress codes for bank employees, or moral reasons such as the injunction not to harm anyone to no purpose. So far so good. What do we justify with, however, when we justify these various types of actions? Do we justify norms essentially in light of facts?

(c) As a result of his background assumption of conceptual realism, Brandom tends toward a monism that levels the distinction between facts and norms. Within the framework of a discursive practice that privileges truth claims and assertoric speech acts, the justification of propositions, be they of a normative or descriptive kind, can be understood only as justification by (or with the help of) facts: "Practical commitments . . . are unintelligible apart from all reference to the overt undertaking of commitments by speech acts; that is why they are an essentially linguistic phenomenon. But . . . the only sort of speech act they presuppose is assertion, the acknowledgment not of practical but of doxastic commitments" (p. 266). Although norms of action can be described as facts from the observer's perspective, they can be justified only from the participant's perspective. This is evident from the very *form* of practical inferences, which refers to an "I." From this perspective, however, assertoric speech acts and facts play no *essential* role in the justification of norms.

Brandom himself points to an asymmetry between justified commitments and justified doxastic commitments. If a speaker's claim that *p* is true is valid, everyone should be able to regard it as justified. Clearly, the same does not hold for a practical commitment such as opening an umbrella when it rains. In a given situation it is rational only for a particular agent to open her umbrella in order to stay dry. At any rate, the motive for acting in this way is agent-relative. Because the preferences that motivate the choice of prudential reasons are something merely subjective, Kant calls such actions guided by preference "heteronomous."

This asymmetry affects the binding power and the scope though not, as yet, the epistemic quality of the reasons. Prudential reasons are *supported* by considerations of expediency that are justified by facts. Thus the implicitly observed rule about opening an umbrella in order to stay dry has an empirical content and to this extent can be justified or criticized independently of the agent. In the case of a purposive-rational choice of means, the rules adopted by the agent establish the connection between a subjective reason for acting and an instrumentally employed factual knowledge. As I have said, factual reasons for the fitness of the means determine the will of the agent only insofar as she has already committed herself to certain ends, in which case the preferences themselves do not require any further justification.

From a Kantian point of view, the more the agent's will is determined by rational considerations, the more rational the practical commitment. An agent acts autonomously to the extent that he frees himself from contingent determinations, that is, from mere preferences or from conventional considerations of status and tradition. Even status-dependent or traditional behavior is less heteronomous than prudential or purposive-rational action because institutional or cultural reasons, irrespective of the preferences of the individual members of a corresponding collectivity, demand recognition from all members. Only moral reasons, however, bind the wills of agents *unconditionally,* that is, independently of a given individual's preferences even of the value-orientations of a given community. Kant speaks here of autonomy because the morally good will allows itself to be guided *exclusively* by good reasons. Whereas prudential and conventional reasons bind free choice only relative to given interests and existing social values, moral reasons claim to penetrate the will completely, that is, to determine it absolutely. Brandom takes account of this.

Prudential reasons lay claim to being valid for (at least) one person: the agent herself; conventional or ethical reasons for several: the members of a collectivity or a culture. Moral reasons, however, demand recognition and respect on the part of all rational subjects—all who take part in discourses and can allow themselves to be affected by reasons are members of the spatially and temporally unbounded moral community. In the case of moral reasons, the asymmetry between the justification of doxastic and practical commitments dissolves: for moral actions, as for assertions, we claim universal validity. However, this similarity in the *scope* of their validity should not be allowed to conceal the contrast between the *bases* for their validity. The reasons with which moral actions can be justified have a different epistemic status than factual reasons. It is precisely in practical inferences of a moral—but also of an ethical or a conventional—sort that an asymmetry in the category of reasons becomes evident: for the justification of these practical commitments, facts do not constitute a sufficient, indeed not even a necessary basis.

It makes sense to think that, from an epistemic point of view, agents undertake practical commitments requiring justification by performing intentional actions in a manner similar to that in which interlocutors undertake doxastic commitments requiring justification by making assertions. However, it does not follow from this, as Brandom believes, that the justification of intentions to act may be understood in terms of the model of the vindication [*Begründung*] of assertoric speech acts:

Explicitly normative vocabulary can be used to make claims (for example "Bank employees are obliged to wear neckties" or "One ought not to torture helpless strangers"). Those claims can be taken-true, can be put forward as, or purport to be, true. Since facts are just true claims . . ., this means that norm-explicating vocabulary is in the fact-stating line of business. . . . In this way the normative is picked out as a subregion of the factual. (p. 625)

A justification of the normative expectation that bank employees ought to wear neckties will rely (if, indeed, there is any plausible justification at all) less on factual arguments than on "strong evaluations," for example, on the connection between certain dress regulations and those value-orientations that the members of a bourgeois culture, from their perspective, connect with the trustworthy handling of financial business. The justification of a moral principle such as "*Neminem Laedere!*" will appeal to a certain conception of justice or to the universalizability of corresponding interests, thus once again not essentially to facts but to normative standpoints or to procedures with normative implications.

The deontological understanding of morality, which Brandom himself also favors, does not fit the conceptual-realist understanding of the moral vocabulary he proposes in order to anchor the objective content of our concepts (of all concepts, including evaluative and moral ones) in the conceptual structures of the universe. In other words, a Kantian conception of autonomy does not sit well with a picture that smooths over the discontinuity between facts and norms. Rather, such a conception comprises the expectation that subjects capable of speech and action meet the challenge of constructive accomplishments. Certainly, rational beings who find themselves in an intersubjectively shared lifeworld have also to assume discursive responsibility before one another for how they cope with a contingent reality. However, their practical responsibility for what they ought to do is not exhausted by their epistemic (or doxastic) responsibility for what they may assert about what happens in the world. Under the contingent constraints of an objective world that gives them no normative guidance for coping with one another, they have to come to a mutual understanding *together* regarding which norms they want to regulate their coexistence legitimately.

4

From Kant to Hegel and Back Again: The Move toward Detranscendentalization

One could describe the history of the most interesting currents of post-Hegelian philosophy as a movement toward detranscendentaliz-ing the knowing subject, in one version or another. But one would not include Hegel in that movement in spite of the fact that nobody did more to set the stage for it. Hegel was the first to put the transcendental subject back into context and to situate reason in social space and historical time. Humboldt, Peirce, Dilthey, Dewey, Cassirer, and Heidegger are among those post-Kantian philosophers who were, or, if we think of Wittgenstein, could have been influenced by Hegel in their attempts to treat language, practice, and historical forms of life as dimensions of the symbolic embodiment of reason. In his Jena period, Hegel did in fact introduce language, labor, and symbolic inter-action as media through which the human mind is formed and transformed. Considering Hegel's intersubjective notion of spirit it is difficult to understand why we are hesitant to describe Hegel as a pro-tagonist of detranscendentalization. At first glance, one might per-haps suppose that his rationalism separates him from subsequent generations. But although philosophy of language, pragmatism, and historicism undermined the status of a noumenal subject beyond space and time, they do not necessarily lead to the kind of contextual-ism that has given rise to the familiar debates concerning the ethno-centricity or incommensurability of standards of rationality.[1]

There are, of course, many points of view from which we might draw a line between the "last metaphysician," or the speculative, idealist and monist thinker, on one side, and those who came after and who could no longer make sense of the conception of an absolute spirit, on the other. But we might equally stress the many affinities that run across "the Revolutionary Break in 19th Century Philosophical Thought."[2] From this point of view, it is mentalism that stands out as the real watershed separating Kant and Fichte from Hegel and those who followed in his footsteps of detranscendentalization. I would like to take up once again[3] Hegel's attempt to criticize and transcend the mentalist framework. I would also like to consider why he gambled away what, from hindsight at least, appear to be his original gains. In doing so I shall focus on what Michael Theunissen has aptly called the "repressed intersubjectivity" in Hegel,[4] but this time from an epistemological angle.[5]

A rough sketch of what I understand by mentalism and its transcendental turn will first (I) allow us to distinguish between the problematic meaning of self-reflection, which is constitutive for the mentalist paradigm as such, and three inconspicuous modes of self-reflection that are independent of the conceptual framework of mentalism. The rational reconstruction of necessary subjective conditions of experience, the critical dissolution of illusions about oneself, and the decentering of one's own perspectives for the sake of moral self-determination are such paradigm-neutral types of self-reflection. The second part (II) deals with what Hegel regards as the misleading dualisms of the "philosophy of reflection" and why he thinks there is no need to bridge any gap between the mental and the physical, the sphere of our consciousness and the sphere of what we are conscious of. In his accounts the knowing subject "always already" finds itself "with its other." In his postmentalist conception of subject-object relations, Hegel is also motivated by the key idea in the rising *Geisteswissenschaften*—the idea of *Geist* or spirit. It is this concept that underlies the contemporary articulations of the historicity of the human mind, the objectivity of its manifestations, and the individual features of actors and their contexts. The third and main part of the essay (III) is devoted to the "media" of language, labor, and interaction that Hegel introduces during the Jena period. They are supposed to anticipate and structure all actual relations that the knowing, acting, or interacting subject can ever enter into with its other. The love relationship provides the first pattern of mutual recognition and is moreover an important exemplification of the interpenetration of the universal, the particular, and the individual, that is, of what becomes the logical form of any totality, the "concrete universal." In the following section (IV) I will treat the dialectics between master and slave (in the *Phenomenology*) as an introduction to the intersubjective constitution of objectivity. Our knowledge of the objective world has a social nature. Hegel counters the resultant temptations of historicism, however, by attempting to justify the modern form of thought as resulting from a history of rationality. Finally (V) I will turn to the question of why Hegel opted for objective idealism rather than for the alternative strategy that was now open to him. On the basis of what later became a pragmatist and intersubjectivist model of self-consciousness, Hegel could have advanced a postmentalist conception of the self-justifying culture of the enlightenment.[6] But he conceived the modern self-critical and self-determining spirit, which he so powerfully described as rejecting everything not authorized by its own standards, merely as a stage on the way from objective to absolute spirit. And this led him to fall back on the mentalist conception of self-reflection that he had so harshly criticized earlier. The knowing subject, assuming now the shape of "absolute spirit" that allows nothing external to itself to exist, internalizes what previously had been external differences between subject and object, mediated by language, labor, and mutual recognition.

I

(1) The simple term "mentalism" conceals an incredibly complex history of thought that stretches at least from Descartes to Kant, and from Fichte via Sartre to contemporaries like Roderick Chisholm and Dieter Henrich.[7] Without entering at all into this discourse, I want only to recall in broad brush-strokes the constitutive elements of the conceptual framework that Kant inherited and transformed.[8]

(a) The epistemological turn that we associate with Descartes starts with the question of how we can ascertain that we are at all capable of achieving knowledge. This leads to a new conceptualization of knowledge in terms of a subject's possession of "ideas" of objects. The innovation is indicated by the third term, "idea" or "representation," that now mediates between the knowing subject and the world. While the subject has ideas of objects, the world consists of everything that can be represented by a subject.

(b) The knowing subject is identified with a self or an ego. This conception of self-reference allows for an answer to the epistemological question of how we can acquire second-order knowledge of how we acquire first-order knowledge of objects. This is possible in virtue of *self-consciousness*, of reflection on myself as a subject capable of having ideas or representations of objects. In representing my representings, I disclose an internal space, called "subjectivity." Thus, the sphere of consciousness, the realm of ideas, is from the outset intertwined with self-consciousness. Moreover, self-reflection means *apperception*, that is, the consciousness that I am conscious of something.

(c) Self-reflection or apperception is at first taken to be an inconspicuous act that could give a clear epistemic meaning to the ancient ethical imperative "know thyself." This new epistemological notion of self-reflection suggests a dualist paradigm of subject-object-relations that can be spelled out in three basic assumptions:

• Via *introspection*, the knowing subject has privileged access to its own more or less transparent and indefeasible ideas that are given in the mode of self-evident immediate experience.

• This self-reflexive awareness of our own representings opens the way to a genetic account of the roots of how we acquire knowledge of objects via the medium of experience.

• Since introspection is the route to subjectivity and since ascertaining the objectivity of knowledge is a matter of getting to its subjective roots, the validity of epistemological statements is assessed directly—and that of all other statements indirectly—in terms of *truth* as subjective evidence or *certainty*.

(d) These basic assumptions—the myth of the given, the grounding of knowledge in its subjective origins, and the idea of truth as certainty—articulate the conception of "the mental" as distinguished from "the physical." There are three intuitive dualisms underlying this distinction. The mental is circumscribed by a boundary, drawn from the first-person perspective, between what is "inside" and what is "outside" of my consciousness, or between ego and nonego. This coincides with two further delimitations: the boundary between what is immediately given and what is given in an indirect way, the private and the public realm; and the boundary between what is certain and what is uncertain, the indefeasibly true and the fallible.

Of course, this separation of the knowing subject from the sphere of its objects raises questions about their interaction, in particular the classical epistemological questions about the origin of knowledge and the direction of fit and causal influence. Empiricism and rationalism answered the question of origin in favor of knowledge a posteriori and knowledge a priori, respectively; while the answers to the questions of causal direction, developed in the realist and idealist traditions, opted in favor, respectively, of the receptivity and the spontaneity of the human mind.

(2) This is the baseline for a brief characterization of the transcendental turn in epistemology that challenged Hegel to move in the opposite direction of detranscendentalizing the knowing subject. To put it briefly: Kant started with the idea that the knowing subject determines the conditions under which it can be affected by sensory input. The world of objects of possible experience is the product of the world-making spontaneity of a subject who is neither passively exposed to causal stimulation by a contingent environment nor capable of producing a world of its own just by fiat. The knowing subject is conceived as an operating subject that frames "with perfect spontaneity an order of its own according to ideas, to which it adapts the empirical conditions" (A 548ff.).

The activity of projecting or of "constituting" a world of possible objects evinces aspects of both dependence and freedom—the freedom for cognitive legislation of a finite mind that must respond to the contingent constraints of reality. Guided by world-constituting ideas, the correct representation of objects of experience results from an interplay between understanding and sensibility.[9] Kant gives a genetic account of how the transcendental subject determines the conditions of what for it can appear as something in the objective world. The spontaneous mind is said to process the content it has received via sensory experience by conceptually forming the sensory raw material, thereby bringing unity and universality to the manifold of disordered particulars. The interaction of the knowing subject and the world is thus again explained in terms of oppositions: spontaneity versus receptivity; form versus matter; the universal and synthesized versus the particular and manifold.

These dualisms indicate how Kant wishes to solve a problem that he inherits from the mentalist paradigm, one that establishes the contrast between a representing subject and a world of objects offered for representation. At the same time, he also inherits those unanalyzed notions of subjectivity and self-reflection that are constitutive for the mentalist framework. The conception of transcendental apperception—the "I think" that must accompany all my representations—still relies on the same intuition that Leibniz had connected with the term "apperception." It is not until Fichte's *Wissenschaftslehre* that the confusing implications of this notion come to the fore. If the representation of an object is the only mode in which we can gain knowledge, a self-reflection that operates as a representation of my own representings could not but turn the transcendental spontaneity that escapes all objectification into an object.

(3) However, we must carefully distinguish this paradigm-specific notion of self-reflection from other, paradigm-neutral types of self-reflection. In Kant, we find at least three such types that are independent of the mentalist framework:

• In the "Transcendental Analytic" of the first *Critique* Kant is mainly engaged in making explicit those rules in accordance with which the knowing subject determines the objectivity of what it takes to be an experience. This kind of transcendental reflection is what we might call a rational reconstruction of the necessary presuppositions of observational judgments. (In the context of developmental epistemology, Jean Piaget even conceives this type self-reflection as a learning mechanism; he attributes the operation of what he calls "reflecting abstraction" to the mind of the developing child itself.)

• In the "Transcendental Dialectic" Kant makes a different use of self-reflection. Here his aim is to make us aware of unconscious reifications that result from an unchecked application of the categories of the understanding beyond the limits of experience. Kant generally understands the dissolution of an illusory understanding of self and world as a process of *enlightenment* that leads to a loss of naiveté, rather than to progress in knowledge. He further stresses the internal relation between this type of critical self-reflection and emancipation. (In a clinical context, Sigmund Freud places this critical analysis of what remains unconscious for us in the service of therapeutic ends.)

• The concept of autonomy reveals yet another relation between self-reflection and freedom. The categorical imperative enjoins us to reflect on our choice of maxims in the light of an impartial consideration of the compatibility of our decisions with what everyone could will. This requires decentering one's understanding of oneself and of the world by considering everyone else's perspectives. While rational reconstruction serves an epistemic purpose and while critique in the sense of overcoming illusions about oneself fosters ethical self-awareness, this moral demand on self-reflection lies at the core of practical reason.

II

(1) Hegel is convinced that the classical epistemological questions of the origins of knowledge and about direction of fit as well as Kant's dualist responses to them arise only from mentalist premises that are mistaken to begin with. To displace them, he analyzes the problem of the "thing-in-itself" that stems from Kant's specific view of the interaction between understanding and sensibility (a) and then attacks the underlying opposition between subject and object that forms the core of mentalism (b).

(a) The assumption that objective experience and true judgment result from two independent sources, spontaneous understanding (guided by ideas) and receptive sensibility, leads Kant to the distinction between appearances and "things-in-themselves." In the course of his career, Hegel refers again and again to an obvious problem widely debated at the time: How can we know and conceptualize a reality that is supposed to be prior to any experience and to escape all our concepts? How can Kant say of such an inaccessible reality that it "affects" our senses, if the concept of causal influence—like all concepts of the interaction, cooperation, or combination of spontaneity and receptivity—belongs only to one of the two sides, namely to the categorizing activity of understanding? The paradox of conceiving the inconceivable applies to the related dualisms of form and matter (or scheme and content) and of the universal and particular (or the one and the many).[10] It is only in such polar opposites that the given material not yet structured, the unrepeatable token not yet integrated in an ordered system, or the multiplicity lacking any order and unity is conceived as something prior to any conceptualization. What is said to be given and found, or to be particular and manifold, is as much a conceptual matter as what is made, generalized, and synthesized in accordance with a rule. Hegel's response is to develop the notion of "media" that structure the possible relations between subject and object in advance.

(b) The mentalist concept of a bounded, self-contained subjectivity is the main target of Hegel's attacks in his Jena lectures. It is the conception from which all the oppositions I have mentioned derive: inside versus outside, private versus public, immediate versus mediated, and self-evident versus fallible. Hegel's aim is to set aside these contrasts and to free the essentially practical spontaneity of the transcendental subject from the prison of self-enclosed inferiority of an ego narcissistically aware of its own operations. Hegel instead describes the subject as involved in processes and embedded in contexts that anticipate the possibilities of, and provide the links for, any actual subject-object-relation. The subject finds itself already connected with an environment and functioning as a part of it. Hegel flatly denies that the knowing, speaking, or acting subject has to bridge an original gap between itself and the "other." A subject that is always already linked to the world does not need to be compensated for an original lack of connection. Speakers and actors find themselves in the course of established performances and practices, while their perceptions and judgments are shaped by conceptual networks in advance. A subject cannot be with itself before being with an other, so that self-awareness only emerges from encounters with others.

This crucial experience is not only an epistemological insight; it is also the key to Hegel's normative concepts of love—*Bei-sich-selbst-sein im Anderen*—and freedom—*Im Anderen bei-sich-selbst-sein*.[11] The core intuition is, however, developed in an epistemological context in connection with the critique of the mentalist conception of a representing consciousness cut off from, and opposed to, the world of representable objects. Against the mentalist conception of subject-object relations, Hegel maintains:

It is entirely misleading in the case of empirical intuition, as in the case of memory or conceptualization, to regard these moments of consciousness as composed of the two sides of the opposition, each contributing a part of the resulting unity, and to ask what is the active element in each part of the compound.[12]

Regarding the controversy between realist and idealist interpretations, Hegel adds that this misleading discussion should rather be focused on those "media" that structure the coordination of subject and object prior to the actual relations they enter into. Subject and object are relata that exist only with and in their relations, so that their mediation or intermediary can no longer be conceived in mentalist terms. He nevertheless uses the general term "spirit" for the media of language, labor, and mutual recognition, which he selects for closer analysis between 1803 and 1805. "We should really speak neither of such subjects, nor of such objects, but of *Geist*."[13]

(2) The choice of the term *Geist* recalls the origin and rise of the *Geisteswissenschaften* after 1800. Though the great works of the founding fathers—of Leopold Ranke, Jakob and Wilhelm Grimm, Carl von Savigny, and others[14]—had not yet been published, a new historical consciousness and a philosophy of historicism already formed a background for the emerging disciplines that would revolutionize the classical concept of the humanities in the course of Hegel's lifetime. They were already manifest in the earlier works of Justus Möser, Gottfried Herder, Johann Georg Hamann, Friedrich Schleiermacher, Wilhelm v. Humboldt, and Friedrich Schlegel.[15] With this historical mode of thought, three dimensions gained philosophical significance for the first time: the historicity of the human mind (a), the objectivity of symbolic forms (b), and the individuality of actors and their historical contexts (c). This shift was relevant to Hegel's concept of "objective spirit," which pointed the way out of the mentalist cul-de-sac.

(a) The new historical consciousness[16] soon reached philosophy and took hold of its self-understanding. Philosophy had to face the problem of a two-sided finitude of the human mind, which now appeared as determined not only by its confrontation with the contingent stimuli of nature but also by the contingencies and selective forces of a historical tradition. The noumenal status of a transcendental subject beyond space and time is now challenged by influences that affect our view of the world and our self-understanding not only from without, through sensory channels, but intrinsically through the communication of meanings that indirectly shape the mind. With this shift, the classical epistemological question is transformed into the problem of historicism that has been with us ever since. A philosophy that becomes aware of its own place in history encounters a different sort of skepticism. That is why Hegel feels the need to come to grips with an unsettling modernity and to "capture his time in thought." Once we recognize the historical origin and cultural background of our standards of rationality, the question arises whether the standards that are valid *for us* may also claim to be valid *in and for themselves.* This leads Hegel to a genetic account, tracing the path of consciousness through history. In the light of such a history of rationality, we must convince ourselves that we came to accept our present standards as a consequence of learning how to correct past mistaken views. The genetic justification takes the form of a reconstruction of a learning process that remains skeptical even relative to skeptical objections that have roused us from our naively accepted beliefs in the first place.

(b) The most significant feature of the historical world is the symbolic structure of what actors intersubjectively share: worldviews, mentalities and traditions, values, norms and institutions, social practices, and so forth. These phenomena make up the object-domain of the *Geisteswissenschaften.* They also highlight the media through which a sociocultural lifeworld is reproduced—language and communication, purposive action and cooperation. It is to Hegel's credit that he discovered the epistemological relevance of language and labor. He uncovered in them the "spirit" that a priori unites the knowing subject with its objects in ways that undercut any dualist description. Language and labor provide media in which the internal and external aspects, sundered by the mentalist approach, now merge. This also sheds new light on the inherently practical nature of the transcendental subject. The synthesizing activity that was supposed to operate within the boundaries of subjectivity is now unbound and spills over into public space:

> The speaking mouth, the laboring hand, even the legs, if you will, are the actualizing and accomplishing organs which embody the act as act, or what is inward, in themselves. The externality which the act acquires through them makes it a reality separated from the individual. Language and labor are forms of expression in which the individual no longer contains and possesses himself within himself, but allows the inward to become completely external, and surrenders it to the other.[17]

The internal is externalized in a symbolic medium that stretches beyond the boundaries of subjectivity. In the spoken word and in the performed action there remains no opposition between inside and outside. Compared to mental episodes and observable events, these objectifications are the persisting elements that, in virtue of their symbolic medium, gain independence even from the intentions of speakers and actors and from their incidental manifestations.

(c) In addition to the historicity and the peculiar objectivity of symbolic forms there is one additional feature of cultural phenomena that—notwithstanding Leibniz's *Monadology*—was never previously captured by philosophy: individuality. This feature distinguishes human beings even from higher animals that reproduce their lives only as exemplars of a species:

> What the individual does for himself immediately becomes something done for the whole species . . . and in the same way the being and activity of the whole species becomes the being and activity of the individual. Animal selfishness is immediately unselfish, and selflessness, the cancellation of the particularity of the individual, immediately benefits the individual.[18]

Animals lack an awareness of themselves as individuals, while humans gain the specific self-understanding of persons who relate to each other as ego and alter, and who form communities while retaining a consciousness of absolute individuality. With this "emergence of the animal's essence from its singularity," nature becomes history, and spirit, which had at first been externalized in nature, returns to itself. Once history—the sphere in which subjects encounter one other—advances to philosophical relevance, philosophy faces the task of differentiating carefully between particularity and individuality.

Observers identify particular entities, of certain kinds, under specifying descriptions, and thus distinguish them from other particulars. But the identity of persons also depends on their self-descriptions. Persons distinguish themselves from all other persons through the self-attribution of a unique life-history. They can present themselves with reference to a life-project of their own, and can raise the claim to be recognized by others—as this individual. The individual character of communicating and interacting persons is, moreover, mirrored in the specific features of the social practices and cultural forms they share with others. Hegel was the first philosopher to be acutely aware of the challenge posed by this fact. All historical phenomena participate more or less in the dialectical structure of those networks of mutual recognition, within which persons become individuated through socialization.[19] Since Hegel recognizes intersubjectivity as the core of subjectivity, he also realizes the subversive implications of the mentalist move to identify the knowing subject with an ego.

"I" understand myself simultaneously as "a person" [*Person überhaupt*] and as an "unmistakeably unique individual" [*unverwechselbares Individuum*]. I am a person in general, sharing personhood—the constitutive features of knowing, speaking, and acting subjects—with everyone else, but I am also an unmistakably unique individual who is shaped by, responsible for, and irreplaceable in a unique life-history. At the same time I have come to understand myself as being both person and individual only by growing up in a particular community. And communities essentially exist in the form of networks of mutual recognition among members. Members recognize each other in their roles as persons and individuals as well as members. It is this intersubjective structure of communities that informs Hegel's logical conception of totality as a "concrete universal."

With genus, species, and *ens singularis,* traditional logic provided a division of terms that raises "particularity" above the bottom level of concrete entities to a somewhat higher level of abstraction and thus located the "particular" between the "universal" and the "individual." In some contexts the particular then gained the connotation of the typical. But before Hegel, the term "individual" was never endowed with the strong meaning of a fully individuated human being. He correlates those logical categories with the three dimensions of the social infrastructure of mutual recognition, by which members recognize each other as members of a particular group, as persons sharing their personhood, and as individuals deserving to be treated as distinct from all other individuals. Particularistic relations among members of a specific community interpenetrate with universalistic relations among individual persons who owe each other equal respect and concern in view of both the common humanity shared by all and the absolute difference of each from everyone else.[20]

III

(1) The cultural and academic background of the Jena period helps us to understand how Hegel's general concept of spirit springs from the idea of an "objective" spirit that reaches beyond the minds of single subjects, while connecting and encompassing them. It is between 1803 and 1805 that Hegel brings this concept to bear on the epistemological questions of how spirit anticipates and structures relations between the knowing subject and its objects. In his Jena lectures that pave the way for a transition to *The Phenomenology of Spirit* (1807), the concept of spirit is explained in terms of the mediating functions of language, labor, and mutual recognition. Although the conscious subject and the object that subject is conscious of are still distinct from each other, they are brought together by, or within, "third" or "middle" elements, while at the same time contributing to the reproduction of these "media": "their unity appears as a middle between them, as the work of both, as the third element to which they are related and in which they are one."[21] It is in the manifestations of language and work that a consciousness comes to exist: "That first bound existence of consciousness as middle is its being as language and as tool. . . . "[22] Hegel pursues the formation of the single mind in its encounter with nature before he deals with family,

society, and state, or more abstractly with the intersubjectivity of social interaction as the proper sphere of objective spirit. Language is
presented as the medium through which theoretical consciousness
develops (a), and labor as the medium through which practical intelligence develops (b). The results of these developments—descriptions
of nature and tools as efficient means for mastering it—can persist,
however, only in the horizon of an intersubjectively shared world.
They then form parts of the culture of a community or of the material infrastructure of a society (c).

(a) The role of what Hegel calls in these Jena lectures "the
media" is best illustrated by language, "the first creative energy of
spirit."[23] Focusing on the cognitive function of representation,
Hegel first analyzes language from a semantic point of view. It is in
the form of language that sensations assume the conceptual structure of perceptions, memories, and judgments: "Consciousness (organizes itself) in language as the entire domain of the ideal."[24]
Through the medium of language the mind is internally connected
with what it conceives as something beyond or outside itself. The distinction between the representing subject and the object of representation is "superseded" insofar as the subject's activity lives from
the "name-giving" or conceptualizing force of language, while the
represented object is singled out and taken up by the name and concept given to it. The knowing subject moves from the start within a
horizon of possible experience that is disclosed for it by language.
There is no base of brute sensory input prior to, and devoid of, symbolic mediation.

Hegel destroys the myth of the given through an analysis of the
material implications of words and sentences. The particular item of
a concrete experience, say, "something blue," is implicitly related to
the abstract notion of color and located somewhere on the color
scale. I know that the blue object I see over there is a colored thing
that is neither green nor red nor yellow, that is lighter than violet
and darker than orange.[25] Because my linguistic knowledge organizes
my actual perception, I cannot perceive anything without integrating it in a conceptual network. This is why Hegel connects language with memory as he will connect labor with tools. The animal's

consciousness of fleeting images is transformed into the fixed order of names, so that the human mind must learn to remember names: "The exercise of memory is therefore the first activity of the awakened mind."[26] We will see below that only the collective memory of a people, in the form of shared traditions, keeps and transmits the knowledge and the view of the world gathered by individual minds.

(b) What language in its cognitive function provides for the knowing subject, labor provides for the actor. Hegel conceives of labor as purposive intervention in the world by which actors realize their ends and satisfy their needs. Practical intelligence becomes manifest in and gains existence through labor. As in the case of language, "mediation" is again meant to set aside the mentalist suggestion of a gap to be bridged. A subject engaged in working does not first gaze at an object with which she then has to get into contact. An actor who wishes to cope with reality assumes a performative attitude toward what happens to her in the world. Work is conceived as a performance. And in view of the performative aspect of practice, the problem of how the actor establishes contact with an object—call this the problem of reference—cannot arise at all. Labor is a complex process into which reality enters in an indirect way. As long as an established practice works, reality "goes along" with it. If it fails, a resisting reality "objects to" expectations from within our practice on conditions settled by our own engagement. An actor is always already with its other.

What the worker has learned in the process of coping with reality congeals in the tools he invents for extending his control over nature. The tool is what survives the vanishing moments of actual intervention and satisfaction: "The tool is the existing, rational middle. . . . It is that in which labor acquires permanence, that which alone remains of the worker and what was worked on, and in which their contingency is externalized."[27] The semantic content of words and sentences enjoys a peculiar independence from the actual utterances of individual speakers. This objectivity of linguistic meaning finds its counterpart in the objectivity of a technology that accumulates the experience and knowledge of previous generations. With a view to the mechanical loom of his time, Hegel even anticipates the automation of industrial work: "Here the drive withdraws entirely from labor; it allows nature to work against itself, looks calmly on, and controls the whole process with little effort—artfulness."[28]

(c) The mediating role of language and labor undermines the mentalist conception of subject-object-relations. However, as long as the analysis focuses on the theoretical and practical consciousness of a single subject in confronting nature, the specific meaning of "objectivity"—of the superindividual status that language and labor, memory and tool occupy—still remains unclear. Language can assume communicative functions and carry on traditions only within a community of speakers. And only within a cooperating society that allows for a social division of labor can technology assume its proper role. In virtue of their contributions to a shared view of the world and a common form of life, both become parts of what Hegel calls objective spirit or *Volksgeist*.[29] The collective spirit embodied in a community is as much "objective" as it is intersubjectively shared by members who live from the same traditions and participate in the same practices. What is in need of explanation is, therefore, this sense of "sharing" or "having in common." What does it mean to say that members of a collective share a worldview or a form of life, or engage in a common practice, or carry on in the same tradition?

Hegel's preferred mode of explanation refers to various forms of mutual recognition. From early on, he chooses "being in love with and being loved by somebody" as a key to analyzing the modern version of the classical Aristotelian notion of ethical life. In a love relationship, the object of recognition is the character and natural individuality of an entire, sexually attractive person. The passionate relation itself is described as "being for the other" [*Sein für Anderes*], which gives the lover in turn "the satisfaction of having one's own essence in the other."[30] In a symmetrical relation the point of mutual recognition is that the two persons involved seem to sacrifice their independence; but in fact each gains a new kind of independence by coming to recognize, in the mirror of the eyes of the other person, who he or she is. Both become for themselves the kind of characters they mutually attribute to each other. Both gain awareness of their individuality by seeing their own images reflected in the dense and deep exchange of an intimate interpersonal relation.

The general structure of mutual recognition can be read off from this modern, obviously romantic model. The two lovers encounter each other simultaneously as same and different. Only as persons different from each other do they attract one another; but they become united as equals in their love: "(In love) each is like the other in the very same respect in which each is opposed to the other. In differentiating himself from the other each also equates himself with the other."[31] While recognizing their different characters, they also recognize each other as equal persons, each with a will of his or her own. But one aspect is still missing. The fleeting relation in which the lovers recognize each other as equal and different can be maintained only within a broader and stabilizing context of reciprocal normative expectations. This means that the two must also recognize each other as members of a community—at first of a family, in which rights and duties crystallize around socialization and material reproduction, the education of the child, and property or income.

Relations that are constitutive for the intersubjectivity of sharing a worldview and having a form of life in common thus develop in three dimensions of mutual recognition, namely, the particular, the universal, and the individual. They obtain among members who know themselves as members but accept each other also as persons who are equal and different at the same time. I will leave aside the details of the two additional patterns that Hegel takes from modern private and public law, contractual relations between legal persons and self-legislation among citizens of a constitutional state.[32] The recognitive structure remains the same, while the self-understanding and the meaning of freedom that the parties gain by their mutual attributions and confirmations undergo change. Under private law persons mutually recognize their legally constructed liberties; whereas citizens, under a constitutional regime, recognize each other as authors and members of a self-determining political community, which realizes the spirit of a particular people in the ethical form of civic solidarity. For Hegel, the *Geist eines Volkes* means "universality in the complete freedom and independence of the individual."[33]

(2) One can well understand why the structure of mutual recognition offers itself as an explanation of what it means to share a view or to participate in a common practice. A successful analysis of the constituent features of the intersubjectivity of possible encounters among speaking and acting subjects would clarify the pragmatic framework for the communicative use of language and for any social practice. But it is far from clear what it might contribute to a revision of mentalist epistemology. We can draw different epistemological conclusions from what we have discussed so far.

One side might argue as follows. "Language" and "labor" are understood as manifestations of spirit. The unifying achievements of "spirit" are best analyzed in terms of structures of mutual recognition. How language and labor mediate between the knowing and acting subject and its objects should, therefore, be interpreted in terms of "sharing" traditions and forms of life and "participating" in shared practices. That would require an explanation of the "objectivity" of spirit in terms of the "intersubjectivity" of a shared social world. The epistemological problem of overcoming the mentalist dualism would then be solved by an assimilation of subject–object relations to intersubjective relations. The contextualized and performative familiarity of "being with the other" that precedes any distancing from nature of the language user or worker is understood as being similar to the intimacy created by a close and symmetric interpersonal relation, where each reaches an awareness of himself only by being with, in, and for the other.

The other side might propose the weaker interpretation I tend to favor. For the assimilation of our relation to the world to the ego–alter relation seems to go too far. We realize why "language" and "labor" can do the job of mediation between subject and object, if we keep in mind that the model of a single subject confronting the objective world abstracts from a background that is only subsequently made explicit. Hegel at first attributes theoretical and practical consciousness to a single subject, while ignoring the fact that this subject must have been socialized in the communicative and cooperative practices of a community. In virtue of this implicit context, the actual perception of anything ("that blue there") is already made to fit in the categorial network of a linguistically disclosed world, so that oppositions between the general and the particular or between the one and the many can figure only as contrasts within, and not as Kantian dualisms reaching beyond, the available conceptual space. Similarly, a worker facing a constraining reality within an established form of social practice benefits from a preestablished contact with that reality, so that the oppositions between spontaneity and receptivity, form and matter appear as intrinsically related performative aspects of an integrated enterprise, and not as puzzling dualisms. These aspects cannot appear as opposites while one is engaged in a practice if reality is already an integrated, concurrent component of that practice.

However, this reading works only on the premise that the structure of mutual recognition fulfills a specific epistemic role. For a language to be shared and a social practice to be joined one condition must be met: Participants who find themselves related to one another in an intersubjectively shared lifeworld must at the same time presuppose—and assume that everybody else presupposes—an independent world of objects that is the same for all of them. A view cannot be shared if it is not a view of or about something obtaining in "the" world, and a practice cannot be performed in common if it is not situated in what obtains in "the" world, meaning that it is one and the same world for everybody. The structure of mutual recognition that is constitutive for the intersubjectivity of shared traditions and forms of life must therefore also provide the basis for the formal presupposition of an objective world.

IV

(1) An intersubjective constitution of the objective world looks like the reversal of a problem that Husserl failed to solve in his fifth "Cartesian Meditation"—the monadological constitution of intersubjectivity by the transcendental ego.[34] Husserl faced this problem because the move from the primordial to the objective world requires the intersubjective interpenetration of the perspectives of two different subjects. Instead of starting from the premise of transcendental subjectivity, Hegel starts from the pure intersubjectivity of the relationship of recognition. In his analysis of love as the first model of mutual recognition, Hegel did not yet have to worry about the intersubjective constitution of the world. Love is a worldless passion

absorbed in Being-with-the-Other. There is no need to explain why for both partners a world that they perceive from different perspectives appears as the same world. However, once the actors have gained their independence and turn against one other, the issue of the controversial objectivity of the world comes up for the subjects themselves. When he arrives at this point in his Jena lectures, Hegel presents the "struggle for recognition" as an equivalent of Hobbes's state of nature. The same struggle for recognition appears at a somewhat different place in the *Phenomenology of Spirit*. There it marks the first transition from "consciousness" (of the single mind) to the intersubjective constitution of "self-consciousness": "Self-consciousness is in and for itself in so far as, and by virtue of the fact that it is for another which is in and for itself; that is, it exists only as something recognized."[35] In the course of a complex struggle for recognition, participants are supposed finally to become aware of the mutuality of each's recognition of the other as a self-conscious being: "They recognize each other as mutually recognizing one another."[36]

The explicit topic here is the struggle for a new stage of independence, provoked by the first encounter of one conscious being with another. The moment independent subjects face one another, they discover the strange fact of a plurality of viewpoints from which people perceive the world differently and pursue various projects of their own. Suddenly each party realizes the monadological past of his own view of the world and now feels the pressure for extending his own perspective so as to incorporate the fact that his opponent acts from a different point of view. What first appears as the practical matter of a power struggle for self-assertion in the face of an other will turn out to have cognitive relevance. For each party, the struggle aims at confirming those standards by which self-conscious persons, with beliefs and projects of their own, take things to be reasonable, or efficient, or with which they criticize others for doing so in one way and not another. Terry Pinkard captures the point well:

The activity of making knowledge-claims is part of our overall practice of dealing with the world. . . . Since two points of view can clash, there will be problems of conciliating one individual's claims with the conflicting claims of others. But a genuine conciliation could come about only . . . if they could judge their own claims not completely internally to their own point of view and experience but could judge them in terms of something that would transcend that subjective experience. . . . Since the objective, impersonal point of view cannot be discovered . . . the agents themselves must construct a social point of view.[37]

Rather than a power struggle for the end of repression, for emancipation, a struggle of life and death, the dialectic of recognition between master and slave reflects the social construction of what claims to be an impartial view on "the" world. This perspective is what makes it possible to refer to the objective world and to form intersubjectively binding judgments.

The main argument of this section is to prove that this impartial view is a necessary cognitive condition for the social constitution of a truly independent self-consciousness. Being forced to work for the master, the socially dependent slave finally succeeds in turning the tables, thanks to the cognitive independence he acquires in virtue of what he learns from the work with which he extends his control over nature. The master's satisfaction of his desires is mediated by his "having the slave work over the things of the world for him. The slave, however, . . . comes to see his own point of view embodied in the artifacts of his work."[38] Although the slave first makes the master's view his own, the master, in the course of his interaction with the slave, comes in turn to recognize and acknowledge the elaborations and extensions of their common perspective that, step by step, result from the slave's intelligent interaction with the world.

We must keep in mind here one implication of that close-knit relation in which one gives the commands while the other must follow them. In the master–slave relation the doings of one side are the doings of the other—*das Tun des einen ist das Tun des anderen*. This interlocking is crucial for the dialectical development of perspectives:

The master must now learn to coordinate his own views with those of the slave and understand that his mastery over the slave is only a contingency and not . . . a mirror of some metaphysical truth "out there." . . . The dialectic of master and slave was initiated by each identifying his own projects as authoritative for what counts as good reasons for belief and action, but each has now found that he cannot identify what is his own without reference to the other's point of view—that is, reference to the sociality common to both.[39]

This social dependence explains why the world is the *same* for both of them; the learning that takes place in the course of laboring away at the world explains why it is the *objective* world.

(2) The section on the master and the slave does not quite lead to the anticipated end of a reflexive and mutually symmetrical coordination of subjective perspectives in an impartial point of view. But the intersubjective constitution of self-consciousness provides a particular experience for both parties: They become aware of the social nature of what they take to be objective experience and knowledge. That is to say, a subject cannot achieve self-consciousness without realizing the "sociality of reason" (Terry Pinkard). What counts as knowledge depends on standards that are not just "mine" or "yours," but that deserve to be recognized by everyone. Despite the remaining difference between subjective standpoints, only such intersubjectively binding standards can enable us to develop, from a presumably impartial point of view, the same beliefs about the same things we encounter in "the" world.

This result has three important implications. Hegel discusses the first under the title of "unhappy consciousness." As soon as we become aware of the social construction of objectivity, skepticism breaks into the confines of the naive, self-centered consciousness. A spiral of self-reflection is set in motion, which terminates in the disquieting to-and-fro between our quest for, and our doubt concerning the possibility of, objective knowledge. Though it remains a pervasive feature of modernity, the skepsis in skepticism finally gives way to the assumption of a common human reason that can justify, by its own devices, both an objectifying science of nature and an enlightened mode of ordering social life.

Under the title of "observing reason," Hegel, next discusses the method and limits of an objectifying science of nature. The essence of man escapes any "scientific image of man," as Sellars was to call it. If science is understood, however, as a historical project, and if the type of rationality expressed in science and enlightenment is seen as part of a historical formation of consciousness, we face the third and most important implication, namely, the problem of how we are to justify our own standards. Hegel's critique, after all, must be based on a genuine self-understanding of the human condition and the human world.

Hegel speaks from within an intellectual culture that thinks itself capable of establishing its own foundation. Unless this position is to become one among many historically relativized points of view, the genesis of "our" standards must be presented as the result of a learning process that has been completed, at least for the time being. This is the project Hegel is engaged in in *The Phenomenology of Perception,* and it signals a turn from naturalism, from transcendental philosophy, but also from historicism. Reason is not an appropriate object either for a science based on observation; it is not made of the kind of stuff that would allow for a naturalistic explanation. No more can it be equated with the self-reflection of an invariant subjectivity beyond space and time. The embodiments and manifestations of reason that transcendental analysis ignores are part of reason itself. Nor does a situated reason that tries to understand its own historical genesis lend itself to a simple historical narrative.

We fail to understand the strategy Hegel pursues in his *Phenomenology of Spirit* unless we understand the kind of self-reflection he actually practices. He employs ethical self-understanding, an Aristotelian type of self-reflection that is as independent of the mentalist paradigm as is the rational reconstruction of necessary epistemic presuppositions or the critique of unconscious objectifications, or the decentering of one's own perspectives (a). He counters the temptations of historicism with a genetic account of reason that presents the history of reason as a learning process (b). Following this path, however, he is led to reconceptualize the subject of this process in a way that amounts to a relapse into mentalism (c).

(a) In his Jena lectures Hegel shed new light on the practical nature of theoretical reason. Practical intelligence reaches beyond its transcendental confines not only through language and labor; the human mind reveals its practical nature by manifesting itself "publicly" in a social space established by mutual recognition. Spirit is at home in what the members of communities share—the views and practices of their lifeworld. Intersubjectively shared forms of life are reflected in mentalities and traditions, in the kind of historical formations that Hegel analyzes, for instance, under the titles of stoicism, skepticism, enlightenment, and so on. In virtue of such historical and symbolic objectifications, spirit is essentially "objective" spirit. In any case, the subjective mind is led to recognize itself as an abstraction from spirit—from the spirit of a people. Hegel recapitulates this itinerary of self-reflection in the first parts of the *Phenomenology*. Like a biographer, he describes for us, the readers, those shifts in consciousness that are revealed to and suffered by a remembering subject once she becomes involved in autobiographical self-reflection. The author wants to have his readers learn, through analyzing the memories of the remembering subject, how this subject came, stage by stage, to be convinced of what she now accepts as the valid standards of her understanding of self and world. And since this understanding is shared by us, the author thereby guides his readers to pursue the genesis of what, once enlightenment is complete, they, too take to be binding standards of rationality.

The expressivist notion of "spirit"[40] introduces intersubjectively shared forms of life, mentalities, and traditions as points of reference for a self-reflection that follows the pattern of ethical self-understanding by individuals and communities. This type of first-person (singular or plural) reflection on one's own formation process is meant to clarify questions of identity. The self-critical remembrance of how we came to accept ourselves and to want to be recognized by others as the kind of person or community we are—this ethical self-understanding is to reassure us of our own identity. This self-reflective process requires a unique combination of descriptive and evaluative operations. First introduced by Aristotle under the title of "phronesis," the most sophisticated analysis is presently offered by philosophical hermeneutics.[41] However, for the purposes of giving an account of the history of reason, the hermeneutical appropriation of a classical tradition in which we recognize a spirit of our own provides but an incomplete model. Hegel had to extend the model of ethical self-understanding by replacing the "self" with something as impersonal as reason. "Phenomenological" self-reflection comprises a rather complex form of analysis that integrates elements of rational reconstruction of presuppositions and of the critical dissolution of illusionary self-images with the hermeneutical clarification of modern identity, that is with a self-awareness of standards appropriate for justifying a shared view of the world and a common form of life.

(b) This detranscendentalizing move toward a retrospective comprehension of how we came to accept those standards by which we presently justify our collective understanding of ourselves and the world is deeply ambivalent. Granted that there is no transcendental consciousness that can self-reflectively, through awareness of its own operations, reveal invariant patterns of reason, we must nevertheless admit a disquieting fact: Our standards of rationality, which require us not to accept anything as true or binding, efficient or valuable unless it is justified by our own lights, are certainly part of our modern forms of life and internally liked to them. If they were, however, just part of a particular form of life, no genetic account of how people like us, having been socialized in certain ways, came to affirm the prevailing standards, nor any hermeneutic reassurance of our modern identity, could save our claims to validity from the suspicion of being as context-dependent as those superseded standards.

Therefore, Hegel must understand phenomenological reflection differently from sheer ethical self-understanding. He must prove that our standards of rationality, and the modern forms of life they are part of, result from what we, from our point of view, can recognize as a process of learning. Hegel conceives of the process by which "we" have come to accept the standards we now regard as binding and to use the categories we now regard as the right ones as a curriculum for a transformation of consciousness that spirit has had to undergo. The necessity of this process is of a logical sort since, in developing its self-understanding, consciousness follows a particular schema or pattern. At every level, it resolves cognitive dissonance by making explicit what were hitherto implicit presuppositions of a worldview that has become problematic. Thus it takes an emancipating attitude that allows it to remove existing conflicts and contradictions.

Even among those who are prepared to follow Hegel's strategy up to this point, the next question divides Hegelians from post-Hegelians: Who is the "we" that is supposed to learn, and whose is the "spirit" the conceptual genesis of which we are supposed to comprehend self-referentially? Are "we" the members of Western culture and of everybody who joins us in an intercultural discourse on the standards of rationality that have come to prevail today on a global scale? This interpretation would allow for a strictly intersubjectivist approach that recognizes the spirit of modernity in the proceduralism of reflective perspectives. Or must we reckon with a spirit that surpasses the modern forms of life in which it first manifests itself? That spirit is not "ours" because it is not entirely absorbed in the present set of rational procedures. We, the sons and daughters of modernity, would have to think of ourselves as players in a larger process.

The mere expectations that we, who still hold fast to *our* practice of "giving and asking for reasons" (Brandom), could be caught up in the wave of a *further* change of consciousness, would already trigger a transformation of the spirit of modernity. The modern culture of self-critical enlightenment would then appear as a transitory stage in a process the subject of which knows more, even has access to a different *kind* of knowledge than is available to the reflective capacity of present generations. Hegel, however, is not Heidegger. He does not romanticize what is completely other. He trusts philosophers, or anyone who has "ever felt the internal need to grasp something," to be able to transcend the horizon of a limited, intersubjectively constituted spirit. Whereas "our" spirit remains tied to the reasonable "yes" and "no" of our peers, those who transcend it can "stand on the side of subjective freedom not in the particular and contingent, but in that which exists in and for itself."[42]

(c) Among Hegel scholars in the United States today there is a certain inclination to give the notion of "absolute spirit" an intersubjectivist reading and to treat it in a deflationist manner. On this reading, absolute spirit is taken to comply with the postmetaphysical insight "that it is only the community's linguistic and cultural practices and the socially instituted structures of mutual recognition that provide the grounds for determining who one is."[43] The absolute is supposed to differ from the objective spirit not in virtue of the intersubjectivity of worldwide religious and philosophical discourse, but solely in virtue of the removal of all social boundaries, that is, the full inclusion of all with a human face. On this reading, absolute spirit is something like a source of inspiration for an expanded and secularized communal religion.

Religion is a form of institutionalized social practice in which a community reflects on what it takes to be the "ground" of everything else that is basic to its beliefs and practice; it is the communal relfection on what for a community on Hegel's terms counts as "existing in and for itself."[44]

Once the religious stage of absolute spirit has assimilated the form of objective spirit into a shared form of life and its content has been determined to be the epistemic role of justifying beliefs, it is easy to divest the idea of the absolute of all its excesses. It then signifies "that the human community comes to an awareness that it is in working out the internal requirements of its own reason-giving activity that it sets for itself what is to count for it as absolute principles."[45]

This might be a good strategy for exhausting as much of the substance of Hegel's reasoning as we inhabitants of a disenchanted world might be prepared to buy. Moreover, we can thus connect Hegel also with post-Hegelian strands like pragmatism and hermeneutics, philosophy of language, and philosophical anthropology.

An intersubjectivist reading of "spirit" remains, however, deficient by Hegel's own standards, in at least two important and interrelated respects. From the viewpoint internal to any—even the most inclusive—community, there remains, first, an *unmediated* difference between the social world we intersubjectively share and the objective world we have to cope with; and there remains, second, an unresolved tension between our contestable view of what is rationally acceptable "for us" and the assumed impartial view of what is unconditionally valid "in and for itself." What is rationally acceptable by our lights is not necessarily what is objectively true. Even if it is guided by the idea of unconditional validity, finite spirit remains caught in its present and past and is thus ignorant of future and better knowledge.

The structural difference between intersubjectivity and objectivity cuts in both directions and hence differentiates postmetaphysical thinking from objective idealism. First, there is no reason why we, the heirs to a sweeping process of secularization, should hope for a deeper understanding of the contingencies of nature "from within"— why we should succeed in grasping nature not merely by developing hypotheses from observations but by a nonnominalist approach to a presumed essence of, or conceptual structure inherent in, nature. Second, nor can we break out of the horizon of our language and our reason-giving practices and replace the fallible impartiality, and decentered "We"-perspective of rational discourse, with the objective point of view of an ideal observer. We can certainly engage in moves toward transcending our epistemic contexts from within, but there is no context of all contexts that we would actually be able to survey. Nothing entitles us to expect to have the final word.

V

(1) Even the collective spirit of an ideally enlarged community including all human beings would be marked by the finite features and constraints of its intersubjective constitution. Hegel would never have accepted such a deflationary reading of the notion of absolute spirit. Of course, even on the objective idealist reading, transformations occur in the consciousness of individual subjects; it is socialized individuals who go through the learning process he describes phenomenologically. However, the process appears as *learning* only to the self-critical members of a modern, self-justifying Enlightenment culture. And it is specifically to this audience that Hegel, as an author, directs another of his crucial points: Through a further shift of perspective from "for itself" via "for us" to "in and for itself," his enlightened contemporaries are supposed to achieve a decisive step beyond the modern stage of consciousness. Those to whom Hegel's presentation is addressed are supposed not just to look back on a series of transformations of consciousness that already lies *behind* them; they are supposed to become aware, as if through a form of conversion, of the power of spirit. Like a kind of fate, spirit permeates the sphere of the successive spirits of peoples [*Volksgeister*], the history of intersubjective forms of life. Hegel's expectation that his readers will accept this view marks the high threshold between objective and absolute spirit, which the deflationary reading tries to level out. With this move Hegel strips from the concept of spirit the traces of origin in the intersubjective forms of objective spirit. Spirit, as it develops, defines itself essentially through

its primacy over nature, and this means ontologically: *"For us* spirit has nature as its precondition, but in fact it is the truth and the *absolute first* of nature."[46]

We have followed Hegel through his Jena period and have emphasized the antimentalistic dimension of his turn away from the philosophy of reflection. But his rejection of the notion of a subjectivity disclosing itself through introspection did not prevent him from continuing to rely on other forms of self-reflection. The rational reconstruction of the necessary preconditions of cognitive operations, the critique of unconscious hypostatizations and false self-images, the decentering of self-centered perspectives, the securing of one's own identity—all these achievements are entirely independent of self-reflection in the sense of that representation of one's own ideas which is essential to the mentalistic account of self-consciousness. But at the end of the Jena period, the "self" of an obscure self-consciousness is still the only model Hegel had available for a higher-level subjectivity to which a higher knowledge could be ascribed. Such knowledge is supposed to be categorically superior to all knowledge emerging from the cooperative quest for truth of participants in the rational discourses of a self-justifying culture.

Absolute spirit embodies and perpetuates the *Tathandlung* [primordial act] of Fichte's self-"positing" ego, since it pervades the processes of natural evolution and world history. Hegel still understands this act, which occurs continuously throughout nature and history, as self-reflection writ large. Its goal is a "self-comprehending knowledge," which in fact consists in the recollection of all the stations through which self-externalizing spirit has passed in the process of realizing itself as absolute. Hegel says of this "final shape of spirit" that "it gives itself its complete and true content also as the form of the self."[47] He employs the concept of subjectivity to conceptualize the return of spirit to itself, the move "from substance to subject." But this is the very concept that he himself had so convincingly criticized. Certainly he cannot have recourse to this model without taking account of his own earlier critique of mentalism.

Previously he had reached the view that the relations between subject and object do not begin from the knowing and acting subject itself, but arise within the prior structures of language, labor, and interaction. The inward and subjective surrendered its priority to the external and objective. Being-with-oneself is "always already" mediated by being-with-the-other. Self-consciousness is formed in relations of mutual recognition between subjects, each of whom can recognize itself only in the other. The acculturation processes though which subjects emerge have themselves no subject. Originally, the media through which the history of the detranscendentalization of the subject was played out were subjectless subjects—as yet not manifestations of a higher-order subject.

But by the end of the *Phenomenology of Spirit,* it becomes clear that Hegel was presupposing such a subject as the basis of the history of consciousness. This subject is thought of as the One and All, as the totality that "can have nothing outside itself." Therefore absolute spirit must internalize the formative processes that were anonymously guided up to that point as the history of its own development, thereby restoring the primacy of subjectivity. It can no longer tolerate "the other of itself" as the constraining opposition of a resistant reality, or as an alter ego with equal rights *external to* itself. It can accept such an other only *within itself,* downgraded to the status of raw material for its own process of development. The thorn of alterity, the tension of a distance that is both bridged and maintained, is removed from "being-with-the-other." The other is now what is in and for itself one's own, but is encountered in the recollected form of past self-alienations. Hegel identifies this "other" with what happens in time, with the working out of the movement of the Concept, whereas the absolute self is understood as the Concept that engulfs time within itself, that consumes it, as it were. But this means that the historicity of reason ceases to pose a challenge. At the least, the challenge is blunted if logic once again wins out over history in the traditional way: "Time is the concept which is there . . .; this is why spirit necessarily appears in time, [but] it [only] appears in time for as long as it has not comprehended its pure concept, in other words not *abolished* time."[48] Spirit, alienated in time, triumphs over time once more. It is the Platonic element that remains identical with itself throughout an eternal coming to be and passing away.

The media of language, labor, and mutual recognition, which once testified to an antimentalistic turn, either entirely disappear within the developed system, or assume a modest role. *Language* is assimilated to the expressivist model of a body that makes manifest psychological impulses.[49] The notion of the body as a medium of expression that reveals an inner life fits better with the mentalistic image of a subjectivity that must alienate itself before it can recognize itself in its alienated forms of expressions. *Labor* and the *tool* disappear entirely from a "phenomenology of spirit," which is reduced to a subdivision of the chapter on "subjective Spirit" (*Encyclopaedia*, §§ 413–439). These concepts now serve only to explicate the notion of purposive activity as a logical category.[50] It is true that the *struggle for recognition* appears in the *Encyclopaedia* at the appropriate place. But the intersubjective structure of reciprocal recognition is no longer relevant for the mentalistic account of self and self-reflection, given that in the *Logic* Hegel unfolds the concept in accordance with the model of the "ego," or of pure self-consciousness.[51] Intersubjectivity is repressed from subjectivity, leaving no trace in the presentation of the absolute Idea.

(2) There is an obvious explanation for this reversal. A postmentalistic conceptual framework, in which an intersubjectively constituted "objectivity" of spirit would take over the theoretical role of "subjectivity," cannot satisfy the ambitious demands Hegel had in mind from the very beginning, in his "philosophy of unification" [*Vereinigungsphilosophie*].[52] He always expected philosophy to fulfill, the task of reconciling modern human beings both with their objectified inner nature and with a subjugated outer nature, thereby overcoming the alienation of the individual from society. In what was—according to his own lights—a realistic manner, Hegel wanted to restore the fractured ethical world of modernity to the unity and spontaneity of an unimpeded and undamaged flow of life, yet without prejudicing the indispensable achievements of subjective freedom. Charles Taylor correctly ascribes this intention to Hegel.[53] This conventional explanation will not disconcert anyone who has come to terms with the constellation of postmetaphysical thinking. Even after metaphysics, the speculative interest retains its own dignity. It would be much more unsettling if Hegel had found difficulties in the intersubjective approach itself. Was there perhaps an *internal* reason that led him in the end to depart from the intersubjectivist

track he had started along in Jena? My assumption is that his critical retrospective account of the French Revolution provided a spectacular backdrop for his desire to avoid one specific consequence of detranscendentalization.

Setting aside other motivations, Hegel's skepticism about modern forms of "revolutionary praxis" (Marx) explains why he will not allow the subjectivity of socialized individuals to be exhausted by the reflexive mobility of intersubjectively shaped forms of consciousness. He wants this subjectivity to be contained in the more stable forms of an objective spirit whose rational substance can be judged only from the viewpoint of absolute spirit (a). But if this rather implausible solution is nonetheless the result of a serious diagnosis, we must pose the question that motivated Hegel's subordination of objective to absolute spirit in a different way. The excessive demands on subjects which the framework of a self-justifying culture structurally generates have preoccupied Right Hegelians right up to the present day (b).

(a) Hegel is convinced that the culture of the Enlightenment reaches its highest stage of moral consciousness in Kant's theory. Although autonomy remains the indispensable criterion of subjective freedom for Hegel, he always regarded the "moral view of the world" as encouraging the destabilization of ethical relations.[54] In the relevant passages of the *Philosophy of Right* (§§ 105–156), he shows that a universalist ethics of duty, which is guided only by the moral standpoint of the generalizability of maxims, tends to hang in midair. Of course, Hegel makes no effort to give a fair interpretation of Kant, let alone an intersubjectivist reading of the principle of universalization, one that might have suggested itself after the detranscendentalization of the noumenal "ego."[55] But three of his objections to the effort of abstraction demanded by ethical formalism still deserve consideration. First, such formalism neglects the actual motives and inclinations of morally acting persons. Moral commands do not automatically harmonize with the given preferences or the more long-term need-dispositions and value orientations that agents have developed in the course of their socialization. Second, Kant takes just as little account of the problem of the complexity and unpredictability of the consequences of actions, consequences that are sometimes attributed to actors. In confused, entangled situations good intentions often have bad outcomes. Third, formalism has no solution for the problem of how to apply general norms to concrete cases—especially when norms that seem equally appropriate at first sight clash with each other.[56]

The thrust of Hegel's arguments is that abstract morality demands too taxing a motivational and cognitive effort on the part of individuals. This shortfall has to be compensated for at the institutional level. Objective spirit must make good what subjective spirit cannot manage alone. Hegel attributes to an ethical life that has become objective "an existence which rises above the subjective opinions and preferences of individuals."[57] He perceives in the major institutions of society an actually existing form of reason that reaches beyond the limited horizons of subjective spirit. Institutions coordinate ideas with interests and functions. They harmonize the legitimating *ideas* of the ethical powers both with the *interests* of social members and the *functional imperatives* of a differentiated social system. Through the specification and imposition of concrete duties, institutions relieve the burden on the will and intelligence of overtaxed individuals. On the other hand, individuals should not have to accept anything that they cannot perceive to be justified. The modern state has "the tremendous strength and depth to allow the principle of subjectivity to reach completion in the self-sufficient extreme of personal particularity, and yet to bring it back to substantial unity."[58] This is why Hegel is willing to subordinate subjective spirit to objective ethical life only on condition that institutions have taken on a rational form, measured by the criterion of the realization of equal freedoms for all.

Hegel favors a strong institutionalism, provided the state roughly corresponds to its concept as developed by philosophy. But as a contemporary of the French Revolution, he is aware of the problem this condition immediately generates: How are we to define a praxis that does not run along the comfortable tracks laid down by an *existing* constitutional state, but which must cope with the task of bringing rational institutions into existence? In a situation where the liberal mechanisms of a republican community are lacking, effective and inclusive procedures and practices for the legitimation, approval, and application of laws first have to be established. But, on Hegel's view, this task is too much for politically acting subjects, both as individuals and as a collective. The reasons he takes this view derive from his critique of Kant's moral theory.

Without the constraining effect of rational institutions, figures such as Robespierre or Fries, the leaders of a revolution or a national movement, will relapse to the stage of abstract moral consciousness. They become entangled in the aporias of a calculated commitment to the *creation* of the conditions under which it would be reasonable to expect people to behave morally. They believe themselves entitled to act strategically, and if necessary even to accept the violation of moral norms, in order to achieve this higher moral goal. This argument is based on a convincing insight, for any such policy threatens to become repressive, to harm the interests of others. It assumes that its own *subjective* anticipation of what it takes to be the good eliminates the need for an intersubjective endorsement that is currently unavailable (and may indeed be impossible in the given circumstances). Such an endorsement, however, is the only guarantee of the equal freedom of all. In his reflections on "Virtue and the Way of the World" Hegel anticipated the debate over what was later to be called "revolutionary ethics." The fact that an ambitious praxis that aims at a general transformation of morality can flip over into the terrorism of virtue has been tragically confirmed by the totalitarian regimes of the twentieth century.

But this essentially legitimate objection acquires a different value for Hegel. If persons, even in straightforward cases of moral action, need relief from the burdens of decision, then this must apply even more in cases where self-regarding moral action is raised to the level of politics. The problem of overtaxing self-determining persons becomes more acute as the problem of overloading a culture that seeks to create a new ethical foundation for itself by means of a revolutionary transformation of state and society. Hegel responds to this problem with his conviction that history as a whole follows the path of reason. Politically acting citizens can be released from the burden of creating the morally supportive institutions of the constitutional state only by a reason that can realize itself historically through its own dynamic. But this requires the construction of a transition from objective spirit to absolute knowledge. Such a construction has to be able to reassure us that, seen from the standpoint of the philosophy of history, the ethical reality of the modern world is on the way to becoming rational, even without our cooperation. The uncoupling of absolute spirit from objective spirit simultaneously disconnects theory from practice. In this way, assessment of whether and how far the existing institutions are rational becomes a matter for speculative philosophical diagnosis, which always comes too late to teach the world how it ought to be.

(b) From a postmetaphysical point of view, however, we can no longer base our judgments on such an authority. Yet our contemporary Hegelians seem to be in the right when they regard themselves as the fortunate heirs of a historical process that has established the liberal mechanisms and procedures of a democratic regime on an almost worldwide basis. Certainly, the majority of citizens in the West can feel confident in the view that, at least in their historically favored regions of the world, constitutions have been effectively established that have made the generations alive today the clear beneficiaries of *existing* institutions and procedures. Citizens of these democratic regimes have been freed from the morally ambiguous exploits of revolutionary avant-gardism, since societies have now become too complex to be radically "overthrown." On the other hand, the only thing that has made Hegel's problem more tractable is the fact that the proceduralistic mechanisms of the constitutional state have turned the process of the *realization* of civil rights, through an institutionalized democratic practice of self-determination, into a long-term task. This is a task that, according to Hegel himself, should not even exist.[59]

A constitutional state that has become reflexive institutionalizes the constitution as a *project*. Through the medium of law it internalizes the tension between the subjective consciousness of the citizens and the objective spirit of the institutions. It is this tension that Hegel sought to relieve by subordinating both to absolute spirit. A democratic practice of self-determination does not entirely dissolve this tension, but makes it the driving force behind the dynamics of public communication structured by constitutional norms. Hegel was forced to blame the difference he perceived between the "concept" and the "existing reality" of the state—understood as the "fetter of something abstract which has not been freed into the concept"[60]—on the limited subjectivity of overburdened individuals. Nowadays the same dissonances energize the institutionalized clash of opinions and decision-making processes within the political public sphere. They are also stimuli for social movements. To the extent that a society becomes capable of acting politically and can shape itself, a democratic constitution *empowers* citizens to achieve a progressive institutionalization of equal civil rights. Of course, the procedures of the democratic constitutional state can only offer good prospects of success, rather than a guarantee, even when they are institutionalized in a favorable environment. But they still give a postmetaphysical answer to Hegel's question concerning the structural overloading of the modern subject. They make possible the radical reformism of a self-transformation of society that is normatively required by the existing constitution itself.

Of course, the conditions enabling political action must be fulfilled. And this requirement can give rise to doubts about even such a solution. Under the privileged economic and social conditions of the postwar period, the citizens of the OECD countries may in fact have had and used the opportunity to commit themselves to a project that was in *harmony* with the principles of the *existing* constitutional order. This was the project of realizing the equal value of equal liberties for everybody. But Hegel's problem returns in a different form, when we consider those societies where the immaculate wording of the constitution provides no more than a symbolic façade for a highly selectively enforced legal order.[61] In such countries social reality controverts the validity of norms that cannot be implemented for lack of the material preconditions and the necessary political will. A similar tendency toward "Brazilianization" could take hold even of the established democracies of the West. For even here the normative substance of the constitutional order could be hollowed out. This will happen if we do not produce a new balance between globalized markets and a politics that can extend beyond the limits of the nation state, and yet still retain democratic legitimacy.[62]

My unintended use of the expression "produce" reminds us once again of the Hegelian problem of excessive demands. Today this problem takes the form of a structural overloading of the democratically constituted nation-state.[63] A solution can be expected only from a constellation in which the institutionalized principles of an egalitarian universalism could acquire sufficient impetus. The motivational force of social movements would have to combine, in a favorable historical moment, with the intelligence of systems capable of developing through learning. After Hegel, even philosophical reason, now fallible, has no better answer. The rose in the cross of the present may have grown pale, but it is not yet completely faded.

5

Norms and Values: On Hilary Putnam's Kantian Pragmatism

Hilary Putnam has subjected the logical empiricism of his teachers Reichenbach and Carnap to a trenchant critique, all the while remaining faithful to its scientistic ethos and to its Kantian frame of mind. The result of this combination of critical distantiation and adherence is a pragmatism in the spirit of Kant. Putnam takes up the transcendental insight in its linguistic form and gives it a realist turn. The detranscendentalization of the knowing and acting subject affects the metaphysical background assumptions regarding the realm of things-in-themselves and the realm of appearances, but it leaves the core of Kant's philosophy untouched; what I have in mind here is the self-understanding of rational subjects as finite and autonomous beings for whom reasons "count." Following in Kant's footsteps, Putnam both recognizes the rational authority of science and counters the scientistic detachment of this authority in order to make room for practical reason. The authority of the lifeworld, that is, of common sense and morality, is also rational. However, Putnam does not reach this goal by way of delimiting practical from theoretical reason.

He does not equate the peculiar objectivity of value judgments with the validity of moral judgments, which is analogous to truth; unlike Kant, he does not derive it from an *ought*, that is, from a mode of validity that is different from the truth of empirical statements. Rather, Putnam holds that there is a continuum between judgments of fact and judgments of value. Our interests and value orientations are so deeply inscribed in our view of things that it would be a senseless undertaking to try to rid facts, which are pervaded by values, of all that is normative. If, however, empirical statements, whose truth we do not doubt, are inextricably intertwined with commitments to values, then—so the central argument goes— it is just as senseless to deny that evaluative statements that explicitly express such values can be true or false.

Because Putnam remains an epistemologist even beyond the bounds of epistemology, he tends even in practical philosophy toward a kind of internal realism. Whereas in metaphysics and epistemology he proceeds along the lines of a linguistic Kantianism, in practical philosophy, he takes a pragmatist reading of Aristotle as his point of reference. Here, *eudaimonaia*—human flourishing— has the last word. Putnam understands autonomy in the classical sense of leading a reflective life rather than in the Kantian sense of rational moral self-legislation. By putting my description of Putnam's philosophy in these terms, I am implicitly raising the question of how high the price of this split loyalty is. Would Putnam the pragmatist not be better off if he remained a Kantian all the way?

I want to get to an answer to this question indirectly, in a way appropriate to today's occasion.[1] In part I, I shall outline how Putnam incorporates the legacy of the *Critique of Pure Reason* in his epistemology and continues to search for the right way to navigate between dogmatism and skepticism (1). This road leads him to a postmetaphysical conception of realism (2) that cannot be reconciled either with a naturalistic reductionism of mind (3) or with a contextualist relativism with regard to truth (4). In part II, I shall show how, based on the pragmatist conception of reason he has introduced in the context of epistemology, Putnam deals with issues in practical philosophy (5). Against noncognitivist as well as relativist approaches, he defends the objectivity of value orientations from the Aristotelian perspective of striving to live a good life (6–7). However, it is not easy to bring a pragmatist virtue ethics into harmony with the universalist validity of an egalitarian morality and the foundations of liberal democracy (8–9).[2]

I

(1) Kant took skepticism to be a "task master" that awakens metaphysics from its "sweet dogmatic slumber" but must not remain caught in metaphysical doubt. Kant's "critique" uses the skeptical method in turn so that reason reflects on itself in order to uncover the transcendental illusion of dogmatic uses of the understanding. This same positioning of critique between dogmatism and skepticism, incidentally, is repeated in the two frontlines that early critical theory established vis-à-vis neo-Thomism, on the one hand, and neopositivism, on the other. Max Horkheimer regards the former as an attempt to "revive past theories of objective reason,"[3] and the latter as the absolutization of a scientific method that is fundamentally unenlightened. For logical empiricism, like traditionalism, has to resort to self-evident first principles in order to be able to claim that Science is the "absolute authority."[4]

Putnam shares not only Horkheimer's political intent, but also his Kantian way of delimiting "critique" in both directions. He is as much against dogmatism, which appears in the form of *metaphysical realism*, as he is against empiricist skepticism. To be sure, he criticizes the latter from a different point of view. Whereas Horkheimer still directed his critique against the Vienna Circle, Putnam sees how that earlier view evolved into the later Carnap's conventionalism. Horkheimer revealed the scientistic identification of *truth* and *science* to be a form of dogmatism; Putnam concurs with this argument, but uses it to make a different point. He no longer faces the skeptic in his classical form, but in the modern guise of the cultural relativist, and observes how analytic philosophy of science becomes inextricably caught up in relativism by trying to preserve even minimal metaphysical intuitions.

The dogmatic core of skepticism can be recognized in a relativism that is blind to the normative character of truth and justification: "Positivists attempted to sidestep the issue [of the normativity of the mind—J. H.] by saying that which definition of justification (which definition or 'degree of confirmation') one accepts is conventional or a matter of utility, or simply a matter of accepting a 'proposal.' But proposals presuppose ends or values. . . . Since there are no universally agreed upon ends or values with respect to which posi-tivist 'proposals' are *best*, it follows from the doctrine that the doc-trine itself is merely the expression of a subjective preference for certain language forms (scientific ones) or certain goals (predic-tion). We have the strange result that a completely consistent posi-tivist must end up as a total relativist."[5] The *internal realism* Putnam developed in the mid-1970s (and which he has not significantly modified since) is directed as much against relativism as the current form of skepticism as it is against metaphysical realism as a form of dogmatism.

The Kantian legacy can be discerned not only in the motivation for this delimitation; internal realism itself clearly has its origin in transcendental philosophy (2). This also explains why detranscen-dentalizing the knowing subject leads neither to Quinean natural-ism (3) nor to Rortyan contextualism (4).

(2) Putnam the epistemologist assumes that language and reality are inextricably interwoven for us. But he does not understand their interpenetration as the symptom of some *constraint* on the human mind that is imprisoned, as it were, by the structures of its language and denied reliable cognitive access to reality. Rather, language *makes possible* access to a reality that could not be conceived as inde-pendent of our representations except in linguistic forms of represen-tation. Metaphysical realism chases a fictitious view from nowhere, an external God's-eye point of view on an uninterpreted world. This is how it gives rise to the ontological picture of a "ready-made" world, the paradigm of knowledge as "representational thought," and the correspondence theory of truth. It is by engaging with these three concepts that Putnam develops his internal realism.[6]

As we cannot grasp reality except in terms of our concepts, the idea that we could somehow step in between the linguistic realm of concepts and "naked" reality, purified, as it were, of all subjective components makes no sense. In coping intelligently with what we encounter in the linguistically disclosed world, we can certainly re-vise our language. But we cannot step outside the horizon of lan-guage itself; at best, a horizon can shift or expand. This insight destroys the illusion that we might be able to compare propositions and facts in order to determine whether they correspond to or fit with one another. Hence the notion that the world causes representations in the knowing subject that represent [*abbilden*] objects in the world more or less correctly also falls apart.

Together with the correspondence theory of truth and the representational theory of knowledge, the metaphor of "the book of nature" is devalued. Nature is not waiting to be described "in its own language": "There is no such thing as the world's own language, there are only the languages that we language users invent for our various purposes."[7] Putnam is fighting against the model of the world as consisting of objects or facts that exist once and for all independently of our conceptualizations and that impose themselves on our minds so unequivocally as to allow for but one way of representing them: "We don't have notions of the 'existence' of things or the 'truth' of statements that are independent of the versions we construct and of the procedures and practices that give sense to talk of 'existence' and 'truth' within those versions."[8]

Thus we have the outlines of a conception of linguistic transcendentalism that takes account of competing descriptions of the same states of affairs, but leaves no room for Kant's skeptical idea of the *thing-in-itself*. It continues to maintain the basic realist premise that all language users refer to one and the same world: "Realism is understood simply as the idea that thought and language can represent parts of the world which are not parts of thought and language."[9] Although Putnam shirks the concept of the transcendental, we can readily see why the transcendental approach continues to appeal to him. He has learned from Kant to describe the constitution of the human mind in such a way that its finitude is a mark of excellence, not a shortcoming. The linguistically articulated world horizons in which our relation [*Bezug*] to a shared objective world is inscribed are not inserted between mind and world like filters. Conceptual systems or languages are sets of conditions of *possibility*. They do not cover reality like a veil in order to obscure the view. They focus our view of the world so that we are able to correct our beliefs in our joint coping with the world and our discursive coping with others. An altered knowledge of the world in the long run also alters the linguistic knowledge that initially has to provide us access to the world: "If the notion of an absolute point of view is unintelligible, then not being able to speak from the absolute point of view is not an incapacity."[10]

(3) Naturally, the linguistic turn also changes the transcendental perspective on the necessary conditions of objective experience and judgment. The transcendental subject forfeits its status beyond space and time and is transformed into many subjects capable of speech and action and situated in the cooperative contexts and practices of their linguistically articulated lifeworlds. *Qua* competent speakers, they are, on the one hand, social actors partaking spontaneously in linguistically interpreting the world. This process of interpretation takes the place of the transcendental constitution of objects. *Qua* rational agents having to deal with contingencies in the world, on the other hand, they retain the initiative to undertake learning processes and novel interpretations whereby prior linguistic contexts of meaning can be revised. Transcendental reason has come down from its supersensible pedestal and has sedimented itself in the pores of the practices and forms of life of actual linguistic communities. As a result of this cultural embodiment of reason, the transcendental distinctions become less clear. However, they do not disappear entirely. The distinction between the realm of reason and the realm of appearances returns in detranscendentalized form.

The threshold between the *lifeworld* and the *objective world* is not leveled. Subjects capable of speech and action find themselves in lifeworld contexts; they communicate about and intervene in the objective world. If we shift from the perspective of a participant in the practices of our lifeworld to the point of view of an observer focusing on something in the objective world, the very normativity that is characteristic of all mental activity escapes us. The special kind of intentionality of referring, or assuming an attitude, to objects and facts remains present to us only as long as we maintain a certain distance from the objective world from within the intersubjective horizon of shared practices. Other beings clearly lack this kind of distance. By switching to the observer's perspective, the semantic dimension is closed off to us and we no longer have access to the intuitive knowledge of rational beings who have been socialized in grammatical languages and normative forms of life. The inescapability of the lifeworld manifests itself in the self-referential character of ordinary language, which we cannot get around by appeal to a hierarchy of meta-languages or by strict objectification.[11] Concurring with Wittgenstein and Dummett, Putnam stresses that "[t]he use of the words in a language game cannot be described without using concepts which are related to the concepts employed *in* the game."[12] As soon as we take an objectifying attitude and look at it merely from without, language punishes us, as it were, by withdrawing its semantic dimension. This holds true for the accomplishments and forms of expression of the human mind in general. Because they are normatively structured, they can be described and made explicit only in terms of a normative vocabulary: *Reason cannot be naturalized.*

Putnam takes up the counterintuitive picture according to which language and the world are connected only causally but not semantically. His target is Quine's thesis of the indeterminacy of reference: "Stimulations of nerve endings are caused (or 'prompted') by external things, and knowledge of what those things are is not available to the organism. . . . Given the lack of any rational connection between the surface irritations and what is outside (or inside) the skin, it is not to be wondered at that language ends up without any determinate reference to reality."[13] In contrast, Putnam develops a theory of direct reference. We have to be able to recognize objects under different descriptions or, if necessary, across paradigms as *the same* objects. Otherwise we could not explain the fact that there are no a priori discernible limits to our finite mind's capacity to learn.

Putnam's metacritique of Quine's rejection of a priori analytic truth perhaps brings him closest to Kant. If all propositions were a posteriori, we would have to put logic on the same level as empirical science. Putnam uses the Fregean critique of psychologism to argue against this widely accepted view. In doing so, he uses a specifically Kantian figure of thought. He uses the principle of bivalence as an example to show that we simply have no way of understanding what it would mean to negate logical truths: "logical truths do not have negations that we (presently) understand."[14] It makes no sense to try to negate propositions whose truth cannot be further justified yet must always already be presupposed in *other* propositions. This claim has the form of a transcendental argument (in the weak sense of the term). This *indispensability argument* is "weak" insofar as it argues not that a presupposition is unrevisable or necessary, but that it is— for the time being—unavoidable, that we cannot imagine it being otherwise.

(4) The idea that something is unthinkable or meaningless "for us" presupposes as a point of reference a "we" that includes all rational beings. After the linguistic turn, we can of course no longer conceive of this inclusive we as the platform of transcendental consciousness. The role of the first-person plural can be taken on only by concrete communities who carry on existing discourses of justification and initiate new ones. Only in these forums is it possible to see which arguments are able to withstand criticism in the long run. This raises the question, however, of whether transcendental consciousness, having evolved into so many historical forms, splinters into just as many fragments of reason or whether the cultural manifold of its public employment manifests *the same* communicative reason. As a Kantian, Putnam defends a reflective universalism both at the scientific level of theory selection and at the lifeworld level of cross-cultural communication.

In discussing the incommensurability thesis, he insists that the shifts in meaning that basic concepts undergo in the transition from one theory to another do not rule out the possibility of translating one theory into another. Putnam counts on practices of justification that can transcend the bounds of particular paradigms: "It is important to recognize that rationality and justification are presupposed by the activity of criticizing and inventing paradigms and are not themselves defined by any single paradigm. . . . [And] if there is a nonparadigmatic notion of justification, then it must be possible to say certain things about theories independently of the paradigms to which they belong."[15]

Scientific discourses are embedded in contexts of the lifeworld. Since the world of science by no means imposes a single correct language, the perspectives from which we describe what happens in the world and the vocabularies we use to do so also depend on our interests and the contexts in which we live. This pragmatic grounding of theory formation once again calls for contextualism, only now with regard to the whole of a cultural form of life. Do the standards of rationality that underlie our justificatory practices merely reflect the particular character of our own culture? According to this sort of methodological ethnocentrism, we are prisoners of our cultural universe and cannot but assimilate inherently alien expressions to our own standards of rationality. Interestingly, Putnam counters this view by pointing out that the relationship between interlocutors is necessarily symmetrical.[16] No matter how alien their respective cultures, when two people enter into conversation in order to reach an understanding about something, they mutually have to take the perspectives of speaker and hearer. The system of personal pronouns builds a reciprocal exchange of perspectives between first and second persons into the communicative use of natural languages, and this reciprocity renders a solipsistically understood cultural relativism meaningless.

The pragmatic constraint of taking the perspective of the other—together with the realist supposition of an objective world and the requirement of logical consistency—forms the basis of commonality on which even interlocutors who are culturally distant from one another can mutually correct one another and develop a common language. To be sure, there is no employment of reason outside of any context whatsoever, nor any standards of rationality that do not have to be interpreted in local contexts. But in the course of critique itself reason fights against all local determinations: "Talk of what is 'right' and 'wrong' in any area only makes sense against the background of an inherited tradition; but traditions themselves can be criticized. . . . Reason is . . . both immanent (not to be found outside of concrete language games and institutions) and transcendent (a regulative idea that we use to criticize the conduct of all activities and institutions)."[17] Reason is not some free-floating process, but the tendency to transcend all particular contexts from within is inscribed in the actualization [*dem Vollzug*] of a given situated form of reason—if only so that it can immediately reappear in broadened contexts and different embodiments.

II

(5) Here the issues of practical philosophy can be seamlessly connected with the solutions provided in metaphysics and epistemology,

because Putnam—in the tradition of the pragmatist logic of inquiry—already conceives the process of inquiry itself as an instance of social collaboration. Even if the community of inquirers undertakes its cooperative search for truth under the special conditions of an experimental engagement with nature and a communicative engagement with experts, this complex undertaking embodies none other than the very type of intelligence that determines our ordinary practices and everyday communication. There is an internal connection between the practice of inquiry and the contexts of the lifeworld in which it is rooted. Putnam explicates this in terms of the reflexivity peculiar to all success-controlled action: "All cooperative activity involves a moment of inquiry, if only in the ongoing perception that the activity is going smoothly or not going smoothly. What is essential to the rational . . . conduct of (scientific) inquiry is thus, to some extent, essential to the intelligent conduct of all cooperative activity."[18] By making this move, Putnam liberates himself from a scientistically foreshortened concept of rationality according to which everything that does not fit with the logic of inquiry is taken to be irrational. Discourses that—in the narrower sense of nomological empirical science—are nonscientific are not thereby *unscientific*. Philosophy itself belongs more with the humanities than with the natural sciences.

Of course everything we learn from the sciences counts as knowledge for the time being, but the sciences do not exhaust all that we can know. The objectifying procedures of science, for instance, lack reflection on the conditions under which objective knowledge becomes possible in the first place. In arguing that scientific knowledge is incomplete, Putnam appropriates the distinction between understanding and reason that Kant uses in the *Critique of Pure Reason*. What matters to him is not only the epistemological use of reason, but the inherently practical nature of reason in general. A scientistic self-understanding of the sciences is first and foremost wrong because it fails to realize that the practice of inquiry is embedded in a horizon of value orientations: "As Kant saw, what the universe of physics leaves out is the very thing that makes that universe possible for us, or that makes it possible for us to construct that universe from our 'sensory stimulations'—the intentional, valuational, referential work of 'synthesis.' I claim, in short, that without values we would not have a *world*."[19] The point here is that a philosophical clarification of the epistemic activities of the understanding *in itself* calls for the practical justification of value orientations.

Without ethics, epistemology is incomplete because reason as such is practical. Naturally the practice of inquiry is directed toward truth and objectivity and is in that sense "value-free." But the collaborative search for truth is itself a normatively structured enterprise. Independent of the fact that problem selection trivially depends on what is taken to be relevant, that is, on extrinsic value orientations, inquiry manifests an *intrinsic* normative structure. Among other things, this is manifested in the standards according to which theories are assessed and accepted. It is well known that coherence, simplicity, and elegance determine theory selection as much as the preservation of otherwise well-confirmed theories or predictive power and instrumental potential, that is, the technical applicability of empirical knowledge. These cognitive values are "action-guiding" in a similar fashion as ethical values. Not only do they have instrumental value, they are also binding and may themselves become the object of discussion and argument.

Yet if inquiry allows itself to be guided by value orientations without thereby endangering the claim that its statements are objective, why should value judgments in other domains count as any less objective: "There are 'ought-implying facts' in the realm of belief fixation; that is an excellent reason not to accept the view that there cannot be 'ought-implying facts' anywhere."[20] This formulation already indicates the argumentative strategy Putnam uses to transplant realism from its home turf in epistemology to ethics. Putnam first defends the "objectivity" of values (6); second, he argues against the cultural relativization of their validity (7); and finally he seeks to justify his own brand of value realism within the framework of a pragmatist understanding of coping with a situation and of problem solving (8).

(6) Putnam is sympathetic to virtue ethics à la Moore, on the one hand, and à la Max Scheler or Nicolai Hartmann on the other. As we shall see, he justifies the objectivity of value judgments in a rather Wittgensteinian fashion. Yet even Putnam seems not to escape the

suggestion that all claims to validity have the assertoric force of claims to truth. He, too, seems to assume that the objectivity of value judgments can be modeled on the truth of empirical judgments. If, however, this epistemological account of the dimension of validity *qua* truth [*Wahrheitsgeltung*] is supposed to tell us something about the objectivity of judgments in general, then the ontological connotation of judgments of fact—the "obtaining" of states of affairs that is warranted by the world itself—also colors judgments of value: "a truth worthy of the name has to be world-guided."[21] True value judgments represent truth-analogous values—"ought-implying facts." However, to extend cognitive realism to values is to postulate facts that are "queer" (in Mackie's sense) inasmuch as they run counter to our grammatical intuitions. Empirical judgments say how things are in the objective world whereas evaluative judgments enjoin us to value or treat something in our lifeworld in some way or other. The problem is obvious: even if value judgments have no descriptive content [*Sinn*], they are supposed to be "true" or "false" like empirical judgments. But there are different senses in which judgments can be correct, depending on whether their content is empirical or normative.

Kant takes account of this intuition at least with regard to the narrowly circumscribed class of moral judgments by differentiating the concept of reason. He distinguishes between theoretical and practical uses of reason, depending on whether the ideas of pure reason refer to the heuristics of the activities of the understanding of *knowing* subjects or to the regulation of the will of *desiring* and *acting* subjects. Assertoric judgments that say what is the case are valid in a different sense than moral judgments that say what is categorically binding. Moral insights are "objective" in a different sense than empirical judgments. Thus "ought-statements" are stripped of the ontological connotation of natural law. Generalizable norms *deserve* recognition because they are equally in the common interest of all or are equally good for everyone. The validity of norms is assessed in terms of the anticipated relations of mutual recognition in the inclusive "kingdom of ends." Norms, unlike facts, do not fit with the objective world, that is, with the constraints to which we are subject in our problem solving and our coping with a frustrating reality.

Putnam attacks this deontological conception. Rightly, he begins by attacking the strict separation of duty and inclination, which leaves no room for the fact that values demand recognition. Because only moral values can meet the standard of universalizability, the Kantian differentiation of reason seems to require a naturalistic treatment of all nonmoral values. Putnam therefore argues not only against empiricist noncognitivism, but also against the empiricism that remains in the wake of Kantian moral theory and according to which the bulk of nonmoral value orientations are reduced to mere inclinations.[22] Not only morality, but the entire universe of preferable and desirable phenomena required for the good life are to be captured within the horizon of rational speech. Value judgments are to yield propositions that can be true or false in the sense of a pragmatically conceived realism not only within the narrow deontological sphere of questions of justice, but across the entire spectrum of questions regarding the good life.

Here, Putnam is relying on familiar arguments by Iris Murdoch. It is no accident that indicative sentences formed by using predicates like "cruel," "horrifying," "impertinent," "modest," "capricious," or "ruthless" take the grammatical form of descriptive statements. The logic of how these "thick" evaluative descriptions are used speaks against the suggestion by Hare and others to analyze value judgments in terms of a factual and an attitude component. In using sentences that represent some situation in this manner, speakers also evaluate that situation. To describe *is* to take a stance. In light of their evaluative vocabulary, speakers discover salient features of their environment, features that, say, attract or repel them, and that they would not really be able to discern unless they could simultaneously see through the spectacles of their world-disclosing language how they *ought* to respond to them.[23] As native speakers, they "know" intuitively what is creepy about a person's appearance, what is attractive or repelling about some encounter, what is irritating about some experience—indeed, why one situation is significant at all and another irrelevant. In acquiring this vocabulary, they simultaneously acquire the right words for articulating what they care about, how they plan their own life, or how the community to which they belong collectively understands itself.

Using Wittgenstein's concept of a language game, a convincing case can be made to the effect that important components of a culture's practical wisdom congeal in its evaluative vocabulary and in the rules for how to use normative sentences. To that extent, I agree with Putnam. But this does not yet tell us in what sense this evaluative wisdom or knowledge enjoys the status of *objectivity*. Of course values that are constitutive for a community's form of life are intersubjectively recognized in that community. And insofar as this recognition is based on sound reasons, the objectivity of value judgments expresses more than the social fact of the acceptance of underlying normative standards within a cultural framework. A commonsense knowledge of these kinds of intersubjectively shared value orientations would not have become habitual even in local contexts unless it had been "corroborated" in practice. This is where Putnam picks up and asks how normatively charged idioms can be corroborated if not in a way similar to empirical idioms, namely "by reality." This seems to speak against the idea that the validity of ethical knowledge is culture-specific and that such knowledge can provide no guidance outside the relevant traditions and forms of life.

(7) Putnam presents three arguments against differentiating between the modes of validity of judgments of fact and judgments of value: the "overlap" mentioned above between cognitive and noncognitive values (a); the family resemblance between a pluralism of theories and a pluralism of world views (b); and the normative assessment of alien practices and social conditions (c).

(a) As I have shown, Putnam conceives the normative basis of inquiry as convincing evidence that there is no such thing as a value-neutral determination of the facts in science any more than there is in ethics or in any other domain of knowledge. This move, of course, allows him to dedramatize the opposition between empirical and ethical knowledge only if he can establish that there is a continuum between cognitive and noncognitive value orientations. But cognitive values are characterized by the fact that they are functionally related to truth, a feature that all other values lack. Putnam responds to the objection that these kinds of values are specifically "truth-enabling" with the unpersuasive argument that truth itself is a value that "overlaps" with other values.[24] Yet it is not truth as such but the epistemic concept of ascertaining truth that is the regulative idea guiding our practices of inquiry and justification. Truth is not a good that one might possess to a greater or lesser degree but a concept of validity.

(b) Putnam deals extensively with the thesis that we count on the possibility of correspondence in the domain of empirical knowledge, which we cannot reasonably expect in the domain of ethical knowledge. Of course Putnam does not deny the pluralism of life projects and "conceptions of the good" (Rawls) that are often embedded in metaphysical or religious worldviews. He does dispute, however, that such a diversity of interpretations is characteristic only of practical and not also of empirical knowledge: "We simply do not have the evidence to justify speculation as to whether or not science is 'destined' to converge to some one definite theoretical picture."[25] This argument, too, does not go far enough. To be sure, the *pictures of the world* that the natural sciences provide do not aim at some point of convergence—if only because scientific theories do not make up some kind of unified body knowledge. At best they can be embedded in the context of such overall pictures, images, or comprehensive doctrines. But given realist premises, Putnam himself relies on intertheoretical translatability that inveighs against the incommensurability thesis. He further puts his money on the constancy of theory change that makes it possible for subsequent physical theories to include (not worldviews but) similes from prior theories as limit cases.[26]

Unlike theories, worldviews have the power to structure a whole life. They are more likely to satisfy our need for direction than our theoretical curiosity.[27] The pluralism of worldviews therefore differs from competing scientific theories in terms of the kind of dissensus that can *reasonably* be expected. We are not talking here about the usual *burdens of judgment*,[28] but about *reasonable disagreements* that render any further attempt to reach a consensus after all meaningless or even dangerous. For in practice, such an attempt can lead to the suppression of legitimate differences. Good reasons for expecting reasonable disagreements are good reasons for suspending the effort to convince others that one's own view is right.

This is not to say, however, that ethical decisions cannot be rationally justified or that ethical issues cannot be clarified through discourse. We simply have to look at them from the right perspective.[29] Ethical-existential questions—what is best for me overall? who am I and who do I want to be?—arise from the first-person perspective just as ethical-political questions about the collective identity and way of life do. Casting the issue in terms of ethics already means selecting the context of one's own life history or of our collective form of life as the point of reference for this kind of hermeneutic self-reflexion. This explains why practical wisdom is intuitive as well as context-dependent. Unlike an objectifying science, reflection on one's own practices and on the various situations in one's life does not bring any counterintuitive kind of knowledge to light. And since such reflection guides what we do or don't do within the horizon of our own lifeworld, there is no universal validity claim connected with ethical wisdom. Even if they have the same communicative infrastructure at their disposal, lifeworlds always manifest themselves in the plural.

(c) Finally, there is the thesis of strong value relativism, according to which forms of life, ethical worldviews, and cultures are essentially made up of "thick" concepts of values, so that even legitimately regulated interpersonal relationships can be evaluated only from a local perspective.[30] In contrast, Putnam rightly insists that abstract concepts like "good" and "right," "ought" and "obligation," play the same grammatical role in all evaluative idioms. This common semantic dimension makes it possible to make transcontextual value judgments about how other cultures behave.[31] Putnam is right to ask why we should refrain from making judgments about the Aztec practice of human sacrifice, for example, if we can say that their mythology is false.

However, this example points in the direction of a deontological distinction that Putnam himself rejects, namely the distinction between a universalist morality of justice and particularist ethics of the good life. We call the torture of human beings "cruel" not only here for us, but everywhere and for everyone. Yet we feel by no means justified to object against strange child-raising practices or marriage ceremonies, that is, against core components of the ethos of a foreign culture, as long as they do not contradict our *moral* standards. The latter are those central values that differ from other values in virtue of their universal claim to validity. Clinical intuitions that we allow to guide us in evaluating (of course only in extreme cases) the pathologies of entire social systems point in a similar direction.[32] What strikes us as "wrong" or "abnormal" about such conditions of alienation or abnormality is the disintegration of the "social fabric," that is, the violation of the very minimum of societal solidarity that is simply the flip side of universal standards of justice.[33] Yet Putnam is not happy with this deontological distinction between universal norms of action and particular values. For the categorical transcendent binding nature of moral injunctions (and of moral expressions like "cruel") brings into play the validity of an "ought" that cannot be reduced to the validity of truth expressed in judgments of fact.

(8) The metacritical discussion of Putnam's objections against Bernard Williams's ethical theory[34] suggests that, compared to subjective or arbitrarily postulated preferences, values have a certain objectivity, but that this objectivity cannot be understood realistically on the model of the sense in which statements of fact have empirical content. Rather, it relies on the intersubjective recognition of evaluative standards [*Wertstandards*] for which we can give good reasons by reference to a corresponding form of life. Conceived as intersubjectivity, the objectivity of value judgments is always indexed to particular communities. But in questions of posttraditional justice, evaluative standards come into play that transcend the context of *existing* communities. The objective validity of a universal morality is marked by its internal relation to an "ever wider community," as George Herbert Mead puts it. In virtue of this context transcendence, moral validity acquires a *constitutive significance,* even though it must be explicated in the same social sphere of recognition as the objectivity of nonuniversal values.

Those moral judgments that *merit* universal recognition are "right," and that means that in a rational discourse under approximately ideal conditions they could be agreed to by anyone concerned. The analogy to the claim to truth consists in the demand for rational acceptability; the truth of descriptive statements can also come out and be confirmed only in rational discourses that are as comprehensive and persistent as possible. However, there is only similarity between these two validity claims. The validity concept of moral rightness has lost the ontological connotation of the justification-transcendent concept of truth. Whereas "rightness" is an epistemic concept and *means* nothing but worthiness of universal recognition, the meaning of the truth of statements cannot be reduced to epistemic conditions of confirmation, no matter how rigorous they might be: truth goes beyond idealized justification. This difference between "truth" and "moral rightness" mirrors the distinction between theoretical and practical reason.

As a thoroughgoing realist, Putnam seeks to avoid this bifurcation of reason and a corresponding differentiation of validity [*Geltungsdimension*] (into objective validity and normative validity). To illustrate the indivisibility of validity he has on occasion used examples such as the sentence "If Peter had studied harder, he would have become a better philosopher." Indeed, logic establishes connections between all expressions, no matter to what semantic domain they belong. But, as the alleged counterexample shows, the logical connection of clauses does not indicate a leveling of illocutionary modes, because one mode always becomes primary for the speech act as a whole. As soon as a speaker asserts the above counterfactual conditional, that is, as soon as she uses it in the assertoric mode, she is thematizing and thus raising a truth claim. The evaluation of Peter's philosophical achievements that is expressed in the main clause would have to be thematized in a different grammatical form as, for example, by means of the evaluative statement, "Jane is a better philosopher than Peter." The correctness or rightness of this value judgment depends on the acceptability of the underlying standard and on whether that standard is being applied correctly. Obviously empirical, evaluative, and moral statements differ in terms of the category of reasons that are in each case appropriate for justifying the statements in question. And the type of reasons differentiates the sense of validity of the corresponding utterances, that is, their illocutionary meaning.

If we consider that mathematical statements, aesthetic evaluations, and hermeneutic interpretations in turn require *other types* of reasons, the traditional sorting under theoretical and practical reason is not specific enough. Like empirical or mathematical judgments, moral judgments differ from nonmoral value judgments in virtue of raising a universal claim to validity. They can reasonably be expected to meet with universal consent. Nonmoral value judgments about someone's "modesty" or "lovability" do not merit unqualified universal consent, but merely the recognition of those who interpret the underlying standard of value in the same way, either by habit or for good reason. The fact that the domain of validity of this kind of value judgment is culture-specific or depends on a particular form of life does not detract from its cognitive content. On the other hand, there is a link between the universal validity of moral judgments and the context-transcendence of a completely inclusive equal treatment of all persons. Together with the objectivity of value judgments, this normative validity [*Sollgeltung*] occupies the social dimension of validity that consists in worthiness of recognition. Correct moral judgments owe their universal validity not to their corroboration by the objective world like true empirical judgments, but to rationally motivated recognition. Of course they have to earn this recognition not only here "for us" but in the discursive universe of all subjects capable of speech and action. According to the constitutive meaning of normative validity, everyone is obligated to help bring about such an inclusive realm of legitimately regulated interpersonal relations. This sense of validity is related in turn to the sense of validity of mathematical propositions on an intuitionist reading. Like the rightness of moral statements, the analytic truth of mathematical propositions lacks the justification-transcendence possessed by the factual truth of empirical propositions. However, mathematical propositions refer to states of affairs like empirical propositions do and not, like moral statements, to actions that bring about intended states of affairs in the world.

Putnam of course does not claim that value judgments have the same descriptive sense as empirical judgments. Nevertheless, he wants to ensure that evaluative statements have the same realist sense of validity as true empirical statements. This has implications not only for the justificatory strategy we employ in moral theory. Here we can set aside the difficulties that moral realism faces.[35] In the present context, there is another, more important implication. The rejection of the differentiation between objective and normative validity leads to a leveling of the difference between particular values and universal, and universally binding, moral norms of action. Giving up this deontological distinction, however, threatens the very universalist conception of morality Putnam does not want to relinquish either. This is illustrated by John Dewey's pragmatist ethics, with which Putnam sympathizes.

Dewey starts with the picture of a collaborating community coping aggressively with the unexpected contingencies of its environment. This community deals with all challenging situations, whether they are a matter of theoretical or practical issues, the same way, namely through "intelligent behavior." By "intelligent behavior" Dewey understands problem-solving behavior characterized by social collaboration, creative hypothesis formation, and experimental interventions. And since human intelligence is indivisible, value orientations are no less subject to testing than empirical beliefs. Problems always arise out of some situation, that is, they are perceived and dealt with in some context of interaction. Within this global frame of reference, empirical beliefs, interests, instrumental considerations, value orientations, and broader ethical goals form a web in which beliefs can mutually correct one another: "As a means to an envisaged end a situation can be evaluated as better or worse, as more or less efficient, as having more or less other undesirable consequences. As an end in view a situation is evaluated both in terms of means necessary to its realization and in terms of its future consequences. All these evaluations are rational. . . ."[36]

This holism turns out to be fruitful for analyzing the creative generation, development, and sedimentation of values. It gives insight into the genealogy, corroboration, and stabilization of values in the practices of a community.[37] For by definition, intelligent behavior aims at improving a situation that is assessed as "better or worse." Dewey's agents are guided by their intuitive understanding of what is good for them in everything they do. If their success-controlled actions go wrong or their normatively regulated practices fail, they cannot but learn from such experiences and draw inferences about how to revise individual judgments of fact and value. This is because *in the comprehensive context of a shared life project,* experiences and empirical beliefs are logically connected to purposes, preferences, and values. And what for the individual is a particular life project, for an organized community is the idea of the commonweal.

By following Dewey in appealing to collectively shared interpretations of the good life, Putnam, too, in good Aristotelian fashion,
makes the rationality of corroborated normative beliefs [*Wertüberzeugungen*] dependent on the ethical self-understanding of a collective.
The classical notion of an examined life remains authoritative. In a
collaborative community, those value orientations are rational that
foster the common good—or what the members of the community
take to be the common good—in a given situation: "Dewey's conception of inquiry is social; the relevant question is . . . what would
happen if individuals *and communities* followed Dewey's 'scientific
method' or 'method of intelligence.' . . . Communities in which we
live are concerned with what they themselves describe as 'the common good.'"[38] This connection of the rational revision of normative
beliefs with the collective self-understanding of a given community
and its cultural form of life does not fit with a realist, let alone a universalist, understanding of values.

(9) Not even Aristotle, who was certainly no pluralist and did not
yet doubt that the polis was the sole authoritative form of life, accorded to practical wisdom objectivity in a robustly epistemic sense.
We modern pluralists must really ask how normative relations and
conflicts can be settled *among* collectives with contradictory ideals,
"ideals of human flourishing," given the premise that any rational
genealogy of values is bound to the We-perspective of a collaborative
community concerned with its own common good. Can the fundamental premises of egalitarian universalism, can human rights and
democracy, can the normative foundations of a pluralism that is sensitive to difference and that Putnam and the pragmatists defend so
strongly be at all reconciled with a pragmatist virtue ethics?[39]

People who are not joined by shared forms of life or practices encounter one another as others. Putnam expects them, too, to enter
into discourse and communicate with one another if there is a need
to resolve something: "Even if our maxims employ vocabularies as
different as can be, we can engage in discussion (in the normative
sense of 'communicative action') with the aim of coming to a common vocabulary and a common understanding of how that vocabulary
should be applied."[40] It seems difficult to meet this expectation if we
already have to presuppose the background of an intersubjectively

shared conception of the common good for people's rational normative beliefs to develop intelligently. Since those involved in this situation can take recourse to nothing but the procedures of argumentation as such, Putnam now draws on the concept of procedural rationality: "For pragmatists, our conceptions of rationality *and justice* [my emphasis] are almost 'pure procedural conceptions' even though the procedures are imperfect. . . . Truth and goodness independent of these procedures are at best regulative ideas."[41]

Intelligent behavior, which Dewey elucidates in terms of hypothesis-formation and testing, can certainly be understood as an instance of procedural rationality. But if what is at issue is the rationality of values, this intelligence has to be operating against a particular background; it has to be applied from the perspective of community members concerned with their common good. This *vertical* We-perspective, from which everyone can identify everyone else as a member of *the same* cooperative community, is missing, however, in discourses that cross communal boundaries. In practical discourses that transgress strong cultural boundaries between different collectives, the participants take on a first-person-plural perspective that is not vertically directed at all members top to bottom, but *horizontally* at the mutual inclusion of the other. From this perspective alone can they check whether a norm is in the equal interest of all those affected, regardless of whether they belong to the community or are strangers. Another pragmatist, George Herbert Mead, has given a constructivist account of this *moral point of view*: It has to be generated by all participants symmetrically and reciprocally taking on each other's perspectives.

Mead's intersubjectivist reading of the categorical imperative emphasizes the necessity of decentering one's given ego or ethnocentrically limited interpretive perspectives. Reciprocal perspective-taking makes one's own position dependent on the consideration of the polycentric structure of how all other parties understand themselves and the world. In this process, the normative validity of binding norms is understood in the sense of worthiness of universal recognition. This differentiation of the dimension of validity does not signify a validity *dualism*. For the gentle force to inclusive reciprocal perspective-taking is embedded in the pragmatic presuppositions of discursive practice, on which the justification of *all* beliefs—be they empirical or mathematical, evaluative or moral—depends. Of course the need to decentralize becomes particularly significant with regard to questions of justice. In moral discourse, interlocutors who can contradict one another encounter each other not in the role of arbitrary others, but as particular individuals. Only as irreplaceable and unmistakable persons do they belong to the moral realm.[42]

The morality of equal respect and joint responsibility for everyone can no more be justified from the ethical perspective of a single community concerned about its common good than can human rights or liberal democracy. Putnam, who would like to deal with both under the heading of cognitive realism, likes Dewey's epistemological justification of democracy: "Democracy is not just one form of social life among other workable forms of social life; it is the precondition for the full application of intelligence to the solution of social problems."[43] This argument is a double-edged sword if we consider that Dewey explains intelligent behavior in terms of the model of scientific method. Contrary to Dewey's own intention, it also allows for a reading according to which a scientific expertocracy is the superior form of social organization. If it is implemented with sufficient discursive structures, the democratic process has epistemic functions also and especially with regard to questions of justice that cannot be resolved either by merely compromising on interests or by appealing to a common ethos. But this function can be accounted for better with Kant and Mead than with Aristotle and Dewey. For given a pluralism of legitimate world views, conflicts of justice can be resolved only if the disputing parties agree to create an *inclusive* We-perspective by mutual perspective-taking.

6

Rightness versus Truth: On the Sense of Normative Validity in Moral Judgments and Norms

There is an essential connection between freedom and truth, and any misconception of truth is, at the same time, a misconception of freedom.
—*Herbert Marcuse (1939, from the* Nachlass)

From its very beginning in Plato, philosophical idealism has been of the conviction that we can "know" the Good. Almost as old is the controversy over what kind of knowledge this is. The ways in which Plato, Aristotle, and Kant answer this question depend on how the spheres of Good and Bad (or Evil) are determined: Is the Good related to Being as a whole? Does it refer only to the good life of rational beings? Or does it stem only from the good will of those acting from duty? Is the Good expressed in the cosmos, is it embodied in a community's ethos, or does it consist in the moral character of a rational ego? The answers depend on what we mean by cognition and knowledge: If empirically supported justifications essentially serve the discursive preparation for an intellectual intuition, then the intuitive grasp of the good will seem like the highest form of cognition. If all cognition is conceived discursively, prudential reflection on the good life becomes less compelling compared to cognition that is strictly deductively justified. If reason is understood as a productive faculty that gains the greatest certainty from a reflective "being-with-itself" [*Beisichselbstsein*], then morality can be justified based on rational self-legislation.

Kant follows Aristotle insofar as he uncouples practical reason from theoretical reason and denies the latter the possibility of objective knowledge. Yet at the same time, like Plato, he maintains the unity of speculative and pure practical reason and even accords priority to this faculty over the a priori principles of the faculty of desire. For in its practical use, reason proves to be the faculty of constitutive ideas that *determine* the will, whereas in its theoretical use, it turns out to be a faculty of regulative ideas that merely *guides* the cognition of the understanding. Since Aristotle's distinction between theoretical and practical philosophy, the dispute over the determination of moral "knowledge" is tied to the debate about the relationship between theoretical and practical reason. While Fichte derives theoretical reason from the practical reason of a self-positing ego and Hegel secured the primacy of self-encompassing speculative reason, Kant insists on distinguishing the practical from the theoretical use of reason without demoting practical reason as a faculty of judgment to a lower status as a faculty of cognition. This approach seeks to accommodate two intuitions that seem to me to be hard to deny.

On the one hand, expectations regarding moral behavior differ from other social norms such as customs and conventions in that they allow judging an action not only to conform to or violate a rule, but to be "right" or "wrong" with respect to the rule itself. The prescriptive sense of being "bidden" or "forbidden" is connected with the epistemic sense of being "warranted" or "unwarranted." Norms, which make possible such a cognitive evaluation of actions in individual cases, must themselves claim validity in a cognitively relevant sense. This is why moral norms would regularly be embedded in the context of an encompassing "doctrine" that would explain why they deserved to be recognized. All advanced cultures have been marked by doctrines of this sort, by world religions. Once these doctrines lost their universally binding character and public credibility in modernity, there arose a need for justification that could be met only by "reason," that is, by universally and publicly cogent reasons, if it could be met at all. Beginning with this genealogy suggests understanding moral knowledge on analogy with empirical knowledge.[1] This analogy is even closer than that between *phronesis* and *episteme.* For Aristotle connects prudence, which stems from practical judgment, with mere probability, so that the binding nature of moral duties cannot be translated into the categorical validity of moral judgments. It seems that a cognitivist interpretation of the normative validity of binding norms, which takes account of the inescapable sense of the "respect of the law" as a "fact of reason," is possible only if we conceive of morality on analogy with cognition.

On the other hand, talk about moral "knowledge" is askew because prima facie, no factual knowledge can be meant by this knowledge. The obvious difference between their senses of validity argues against an undifferentiated assimilation of moral convictions to beliefs with empirical content. Assertions say what *is* the case; injunctions or prohibitions say what *ought* or ought not to be the case. Knowing how things are connected "as a matter of fact" is different from demanding what should be done—or knowing how our actions "must" interlock in order for us to live together in the right way or justly. Moral knowledge is different from empirical knowledge, if only because of its reference to action. It says how people ought to act, and not how things are with objects in the world. The "truth" of descriptive statements means that the asserted states of affairs obtain, whereas the "rightness" of normative statements reflects the binding nature of the enjoined (or forbidden) ways of acting. Kant wants to do justice to this difference between epistemic and practical knowledge by differentiating between a theoretical and a practical use of reason with respect to the faculties of cognition and desire. Although theoretical reason is also productive in the transcendental sense, practical reason has legislative force in another "constructive" sense, as we might say with Rawls. The presupposed unity of a spontaneously generated world of objects of possible experience institutes continuity in the manifold of empirical cognitions, while the "kingdom of ends" that is projected from practical reason indicates how acting subjects ought to bring about or construct a world of well-ordered interpersonal relations—a "universal republic in accordance with the laws of virtue"—by means of insightful self-control of their own will [*einsichtige Selbstbindung ihres Willens*].

The Kantian determination of the relationship between theoretical and practical reason, which I cannot discuss further here,[2] depends particularly on the metaphysical background assumptions that support the architectonic of transcendental idealism in general.

As such, this determination offers no immediately persuasive occasions for drawing connections to contemporary discussions in moral theory. While the unstable relationship between theoretical and practical philosophy around 1800 set into motion the conceptual development from Kant to Fichte to Schelling to Hegel, it is rarely a topic of discussion today. Philosophy of language remains faithful to the set of problems it has inherited from theoretical philosophy, that is, from epistemology and metaphysics, even when it has to borrow from the normative vocabulary and basic conceptual apparatus of practical philosophy.[3] This corresponds to the complementary reserve of practical disciplines. The "free-standing" conception of justice that is independent of epistemological or ontological assumptions is the program, not just the result, of an advancing specialization.[4] If ever the question of the relationship between the justification and validity of moral norms and the justification and validity[5] of descriptive statements does arise, its answer is predetermined by the course that has been set more or less dogmatically. Thus, for example, Tugendhat allows for a pragmatic concept of justification (of something to someone) only for the practical use of reason, whereas he reserves a semantic concept of justification for truth-evaluable statements.[6]

In contrast, I want to show why the status and meaning of moral knowledge continue to be worthy of our attention (I) in order to go on to develop the perspective from which I want to approach the classical question on the basis of a pertinent discussion of the subject in psychology (II).

I

The question of the relationship between theoretical and practical reason can arise only for approaches that, on the one hand, grant morality a cognitive content of any sort and, on the other hand, do not reduce practical reason to a means-ends rationality. The familiar noncognitivist approaches seek to reduce the content of moral judgments directly to feelings, dispositions, or decisions of subjects who take certain positions.[7] These versions of ethical subjectivism draw a sharp line between judgments of fact and judgments of value, but they can account for why normative and evaluative sentences behave differently from sentences in the first person only by appealing to an "error theory." The expressions of feeling, preferences, and decisions lack the further claim to justification that we associate with "strong" evaluations (in the sense of Charles Taylor) and especially with moral judgments. The noncognitivist description of the moral language game is revisionary in that the participants themselves clearly presuppose that moral conflicts of interaction can be settled with reasons in light of intersubjectively recognized normative behavioral expectations. Yet on a noncognitivist account, these reasons, whereby the disputing parties seek to reach mutual agreement, are transformed into just so many errors.

Contractualism need not go so far. By reducing the validity of moral norms to a conventional agreement [*Vereinbarung*] among rational egoists, that is, to a happy coincidence of their respective interests, it preserves the cognitive content of moral disagreements. However, the sum of rational motives that brings each individual to concur in light of his or her own preferences does not suffice to explain the specific binding character of the agreed-upon norms—that is, the deontic commitment with which we expect a certain kind of behavior from one another as members of a moral community. Kant proposes a rational translation for the categorical sense of the validity of norms that is reflected in the phenomenon of "respect for the law." This unconditional validity claim of maxims that can be justified from the point of view of universalization is lost in the revisionary description of contractualism.[8]

At first glance, it may look like the fact that feelings play a constitutive role in moral disagreements is difficult to reconcile with cognitivism. The moral language game consists essentially of three grammatically interrelated kinds of utterances: judgments about how we ought to behave (or may or may not behave); assenting or dissenting responses; and especially reasons with which the disputing parties can justify their assenting or dissenting attitudes. However, the positive and negative stances are Janus-faced. On the one hand, they express a rationally motivated "yes" or "no" to statements that—in some truth-analogous sense—can be right or wrong; on the other hand they simultaneously take the form of emotive responses to a behavior that is evaluated as right or wrong. For in the case of norm violations, the anger of the hurt or insulted victim, the pain of the humiliated or dishonored party play as much a role as the stubbornness or the feelings of shame, guilt, and regret of the perpetrator and the anger or indignation of the family or community members who react by voicing their feelings. In the case of someone acting with impressive integrity or courage, we respond with feelings of gratitude, admiration, and reverence.

Because these feelings have propositional content, which goes hand in hand with the moral evaluation of thematic behavior, we can take them—like perceptions—to be implicit judgments. Particularly negative feelings have a cognitive content that can be made explicit in the form of value judgments in a similar way as the content of perceptions can be made explicit in the form of observation sentences. Put in explicit linguistic form like this, feelings, too, can take on the role of reasons that enter into practical discourses as observations enter into empirical discourses. Feelings of offense, guilt, and indignation serve as evidence that an action disturbs the presumed moral order of mutual recognition. As warning signals, they form an intuitive experiential basis relative to which we control the reflexive justifications of our actions and our normatively regulated ways of acting.[9]

Such an understanding of morality runs counter to the idea that moral sentiments are merely rewards or punishments that a community holds out in order to maintain an a priori normative accord [*Einverständnis*] or in order to reproduce an existing cultural form of life. This interpretation stems from an empiricist understanding of normative validity. On this reading, norms compellingly determine what a community's members may mutually demand of one another, and they do so such that the prescriptive meaning of norms lies in their enforcibility. Norms are "valid" to the extent that they can be enforced by means of the threat of internal or external sanctions. Yet this conception fits with neither the intrinsic validity of *moral* norms nor with the need to justify them. An empiricist description cannot even capture the complex mode of validity of the legal norms on which it is tacitly modeled. For it is part of the conditions of legitimacy of modern law, which is positively established and confirmed through sanctions, that it be *possible* to obey it out of "respect for the law."[10]

Even the psychological finding that moral insights commit us to doing "the right thing simply because it is the right thing to do"[11] suggests interpreting the validity claim that accompanies moral norms on analogy with truth. Psychological studies show that children learn early to distinguish unconditional moral injunctions from other social rules and mere conventions.[12] Kant conceived of "free will" as the ability to subordinate one's free choice to norms one accepts on the basis of moral insight. Interestingly, in research on motivation, it is precisely this assumption that opens the way for a contemporary alternative to traditional explanatory models.[13] The ability to distinguish true judgments from those taken to be true seems to correspond to the ability to distinguish valid moral judgments from those that are merely de facto accepted.

II

Cognitivist developmental psychology also conceives correct moral judgments truth-analogously and extends the epistemic concept of learning to the development of moral consciousness. Here, the venerable problem of the relationship between theoretical and practical reason, the dynamics of which unfolded in German Idealism, returns in deflated form. A person has "learned" something if she is capable of justifying the new insight in light of correcting a prior belief she now acknowledges to be mistaken. If this phenomenology of learning also applies to acquiring moral beliefs, then we must, on the one hand, assume that moral judgments can be true or false—or at least that they come with a similar, binarily coded validity claim. On the other hand, it is doubtful that there are "facts" that moral statements "fit" or to which they "correspond" in the way that descriptive statements do.

Lawrence Kohlberg refers to an "isomorphism" between forms of "logical" and "moral" judgment. He views the mastery of cognitive operations as a necessary condition for learning corresponding levels of moral judgment. However, this does not mean "that moral judgment is simply an application of a level of intelligence to moral problems. I believe moral development is its own sequential process rather than the reflection of cognitive development in a slightly different content area."[14] Without damaging the unity of reason, which ensures the analogy between cognition and moral insight, Kohlberg retains a distinction between theoretical and practical reason. But it remains unclear what distinguishes the two from one another.

Piaget places particular emphasis on the commonalities that come into view if we explain the development of cognitive abilities by means of the same learning mechanisms. He refers to a "parallelism" with regard to the development of the categories of the understanding and logical rules, on the one hand, and legal and moral norms, on the other. Piaget discovered that moral learning processes in general can no more be reduced to *contents* that children pick up at school or in everyday life than cognitive development can: "If, at every stage, the child chooses certain elements and assimilates them to her own understanding in a certain order, she is no more passively subject to the pressures of 'social life' than to 'physical reality'; rather she actively separates what is given to her from what she reconstructs in her own way."[15] Thus Piaget counts on the social world playing a similar role for the development of moral consciousness as the objective world plays for mental operations in general. In her practical dealings with her physical environment, the child, by a process of reflective abstraction, develops basic concepts and operations that are appropriate for taking in the objective world. She acquires the basic concepts and perspectives that are appropriate for morally evaluating conflicts of interaction in the same way in coping with her social environment.

In this way, developmental epistemology retains a realist core despite its constructivist approach. The universality of mature forms of cognition reflects the invariant *constraints* that an independently postulated objective world places on our active understanding in our practical attempts to master reality. Similarly, the invariant characteristics of the social world manifest themselves in the mature forms of moral insight and account for the universal validity of moral judgments. Conceiving of morality as analogous to knowledge certainly has the advantage of taking account of the intrinsic validity of moral judgments and of the distinction between moral norms being worthy of recognition and their being merely de facto recognized. However, if the social world is to play a similar role in the development of moral consciousness as the objective world plays in cognitive development, the question arises whether we can nonetheless escape moral realism of one sort or another.[16] This worry can be intuitively formulated as follows: Does the social world, which we presuppose in the same way as "independently given," constrain our sociomoral cognition in the same way and to the same extent as the objective world constrains the knowledge of facts? How can the symbolically structured world of interpersonal relations—which, after all, we produce ourselves in a way—determine whether moral judgments are valid or not?

Moral knowledge is obviously affected differently than empirical knowledge by the history and historical constitution of the social world. Indeed, this is the reason for the peculiar bilevel nature of the moral justification of actions. I am referring to the familiar point that well-grounded moral norms can claim only validity prima facie. For *ex ante,* only the consequences and collateral effects of *typical* cases, which can be anticipated, are considered. Unanticipated constellations of conflict situations that occur subsequently give rise to a further need for interpretation that must be met from within the altered perspective of a discourse of *application.*[17] During the process of application, the norm that is "appropriate" to the situation is selected from the plurality of warranted norms that might be applied in any given case. Hermeneutic insight comes into play in that the appropriate norm is made concrete in light of the particular characteristics of the situation and, conversely, that the case is described in light of what are determined to be the relevant norms. In any case, moral knowledge differs from empirical knowledge in that it is *internally* related to the solution of problems of application.

This striking asymmetry between the justification of actions and the explanation of events cannot be explicated in terms of the fallibilist proviso that applies to *all* knowledge. What accounts for the specific proviso according to which we may take well-grounded [*begründete*] moral norms to be valid only in an incomplete sense is not the universal cognitive provinciality of our finite mind relative to a better future knowledge. Rather, it is an existential provinciality, as it were, relative to the historical variability of the contexts of interaction themselves. Because a symbolically structured world of legitimately regulated interpersonal relations and interactions is constituted in a different way than the objective world of observable events and states of affairs, universal norms can determine future actions only to the extent that typical, probable circumstances can be anticipated—that is, in principle, incompletely.

Such differences between moral and empirical knowledge come face to face with a culturalist interpretation that questions the very analogy between truth and rightness. Neo-Aristotelian and post-Wittgensteinian approaches, for example, explain the fact that value judgments have the same grammatical form and cognitive appeal as truth-evaluable propositions in terms of a background consensus that is rooted in intersubjective forms of life and shared language games. In light of their evaluative vocabulary, members of the same linguistic community develop not only normative representations of themselves and the form of life with which they identify; they discover attractive and repulsive characteristics in everyday situations that they cannot understand without "knowing" how they ought to react to them. As the common property of a form of life, "thick ethical descriptions" of things that are "perceived" to be cruel, loving, or humiliating acquire a certain objectivity based on the unforced acceptance of routine language games. However, this objectivity in the sense of broad acceptance that is accorded to ethical knowledge from the "objective spirit" of the social environment ought not to be confused with truth-analogous validity in the sense of rational acceptability.[18]

The idea that moral judgments simply reflect the values and interpretations of intersubjective worldviews, that is, *culture-specific* historical constructs, has always been predominant in cultural anthropology and the historicist human sciences. This introduces a second-level empiricism that reduces evaluations not to mental events such as feelings and attitudes, but to cultural contexts. R. A. Shweder, for instance, criticizes Kohlberg's moral universalism from this relativist perspective.[19] Of course cultural constructivism does not stop with questions of value but extends to questions of fact. It tends toward a radical historicism according to which different traditions, forms of life, and cultures embody not only different morals and standards of value, but also different standards of rationality.[20] Today's prevalent contextualism contests the categorical sense of claims to truth no less than that of claims to rightness.

In view of the current state of the debate, not even the theoretical use of reason may be assumed to be unproblematic. Moreover, it is not advisable to take up the question of the relationship between theoretical and practical reason in its entire breadth, that is, from either an epistemological point of view or from the point of view of the theory of justification. The discussion of Piaget's and Kohlberg's premises illustrates the relevance of putting the question in terms of the theory of validity: To what extent does a cognitivist conception of moral judgments require assimilating the concept of "rightness" to that of "truth"? In German, the term *Geltung* is used rather than *Gültigkeit* with reference to moral judgments. Yet this blurs the clear distinction between the acceptance [*Geltung*] of a judgment that, as a matter of fact, is recognized and the validity [*Gültigkeit*] of a judgment that *deserves* to be intersubjectively recognized because it is true.[21] This linguistic usage betrays a certain hesitation about treating truth [*Wahrheitsgeltung*] and normative validity [*Sollgeltung*] as analogous without reservation. The weaker the ontological connotations of the concept of truth that we appeal to in the comparison, the easier it will be to establish the plausibility of a truth-analogous conception of moral validity. A conception that does justice to the realist intuition that there is a world independent of us without representing propositions as *corresponding* to facts fits with the project of clarifying the ways in which truth and rightness are alike and those in which they differ.[22]

My guiding intuition can be characterized as follows. On the one hand, we discover the rightness of moral judgments in the same way as the truth of descriptions: through argumentation. We no more have direct access unfiltered by reasons to truth conditions than we do to the conditions under which moral norms merit universal recognition. In either case, the validity of statements can be *established* only through discursive engagement using available reasons. On the other hand, moral validity claims do not refer to the world in the way that is characteristic of truth claims. "Truth" is a justification-transcendent concept that cannot be made to coincide even with the concept of ideal warranted assertibility.[23] Rather, it refers to the truth conditions that must, as it were, be met by reality itself. In contrast, the meaning of "rightness" consists entirely in ideal warranted acceptability. For we ourselves contribute to the fulfillment of the validity conditions of moral judgments and norms by constructing a world of well-ordered interpersonal relationships. However, this construction is subject to constraints that are not at our disposal; otherwise we could not talk about moral *insight*. The absence of ontological connotations must not impair the claim to universal or unconditional validity. That claim is assessed in terms of social conditions and relations of reciprocal recognition that merit being acknowledged as just by all parties.

Following a discussion of the relationship between "justification" and "truth," I shall first introduce a discursive concept of truth (III). Yet before undertaking a differentiation between truth and normative rightness, this epistemic concept of truth of course requires a pragmatic interpretation (IV). Against this background, we shall see that the meaning of the predicate "is right"—unlike that of the truth predicate—is exhausted by the notion of "ideal warranted assertibility." While the normative validity of moral statements lacks the ontological connotations of objective validity, the justification-transcendent relation to the objective world is replaced by the regulative idea of the mutual inclusion of the other in an inclusive—and to that extent universal—world of well-ordered interpersonal relationships (V). This projection of a single moral world is rooted in the communicative presuppositions of rational discourse. For under the conditions of the modern pluralism of world views, the idea of justice has been sublimated into the concept of the impartiality of a discursively attained agreement (VI). In responding to a realist reading of discourse ethics, I want to show why, regardless of the justification-immanent sense of "rightness," we may conceive of it on analogy with "truth" as an unconditional kind of validity. The key to this account lies in the demanding conditions of communication that attribute to participants in practical discourses the ability of generating a shared perspective of self-critical impartiality (VII). Of course the evidence for the possibility of a cognitivist understanding of morality does not suffice to explain why we *must* retain the concept of moral knowledge in the context of pluralism. A moment of convention seems to enter into the categorical sense of moral validity inasmuch as we impose, as it were, a binary schematization onto the dimension of the Good with this truth-analogous conception; only then do we separate the Just from the Good. Yet this "resolve to freedom" is not up to us because the moral language game that is inscribed in the communicative form of life could not be maintained in any other way (VIII).

III

The contexualist challenge to the realist intuition, which is connected to concepts like truth, knowledge, and reason, is the result of the linguistic turn. That turn shifted the standard of epistemic objectivity from the private certainty of an experiencing subject to the public practice of justification within a communicative community.[24] Today, there is broad consensus that language and reality are inextricably intertwined. Facts can be explained only by recourse to factual statements, what is real only by appeal to what is true. Since the truth of beliefs and sentences in turn can be justified or disputed only by means of other beliefs and sentences, we—as reflecting agents—cannot step outside the circle of language. This suggests an antifoundationalist concept of knowledge and a holistic concept of justification; and both seem compatible only with a coherence theory of truth. It is therefore a good idea first to clarify whether any sense of context-independent validity can be salvaged for the concept of truth itself before we return to the problem of adequately distinguishing between "truth" and "rightness."[25]

We cannot confront our sentences directly with a reality that is not already permeated by language. Hence we cannot identify a class of basic propositions that are self-legitimating and might therefore serve as the beginning and end of a linear chain of justifications. Yet if the semantic-deductive concept of justification fails to take hold, then the validity [*Gültigkeit*] of fallible propositions can only ever be justified acceptance [*Geltung*] by a given audience. We should therefore try to elucidate "truth" as an epistemic, that is, a three-place relation; truths seem to be accessible only in the form of what is rationally acceptable. This raises the question of whether the truth of a proposition, thus rendered epistemic, even still has a "value" that is independent of the particular context of its justification.[26] Within the linguistic paradigm, propositional truth can certainly no longer be conceived as "correspondence to something in the world." Otherwise we would have to be able to step outside of language by means of language. We would not even be able to compare a linguistic expression of a presumably "definitive" piece of evidence with a piece of uninterpreted or "naked" reality—that is, with a referent that would elude our language-bound inspection. The truth of a proposition, it seems, can be warranted only by its coherence with other propositions.

The requirement that a true belief "cohere" with already accepted beliefs, however, is insufficient. A coherence that is produced solely through a chain of reasons cannot explain why even the most thoroughly justified assertions can turn out to be false. Obviously we take "truth" to be a property of propositions that cannot be "lost." The "cautionary" use of the truth predicate, for instance, reminds us that the best reasons can be invalidated in light of future evidence. We therefore cannot avoid the ticklish question: "Why does the fact that our beliefs hang together, supposing they do, give the least indication that they are true?"[27] We are faced with the dilemma that we have nothing but justificatory reasons at our disposal in order to convince us of a proposition's truth, even though we apply the truth predicate in an absolute sense that transcends all possible justifications. While our practices of justification change in accordance with prevailing standards, we associate "truth" with a claim that *transcends* all potentially available evidence. This realist thorn prevents us from falling into a linguistic idealism that reduces "truth" to "warranted assertibility."

Nonetheless, there must be an internal relation between truth and justification. Although truth is not a "success term," we start from the assumption that a successful justification of p according to our standards indicates that p is true. Hence the question: "Given only knowledge of what we believe about the world, and how our beliefs fit together, how can we show that those beliefs are likely to be true?"[28] At first glance, a plausible way out is to distinguish "truth" from mere acceptability by means of the assumption of ideal conditions of justification: what is true is what would be accepted as justified under ideal epistemic conditions (Putnam) or in an ideal communication community (Apel) or in an ideal speech situation (Habermas). The moment of unconditionality that we intuitively associate with truth claims is here interpreted in the sense of a transcendence of local contexts. A proposition that is justified according to our standards differs from a true proposition in the way that a warranted proposition in a given context differs from one for which warrants could be provided in any possible context.

However, those versions of this suggestion to operate with presumed ideal *conditions* that derive from Peirce[29] run into difficulties. Such teleological constructs miss their mark because they put either too much or not enough distance between the determination of "truth" and warranted assertibility. The discursive conception of truth eludes these objections because it idealizes the formal and procedural properties of argumentation rather than its goals. On this reading, the practice of argumentation is introduced as a touchstone, and certain ideal requirements must be met *as* the practice is carried out. The *form* of communication is to ensure the full inclusion as well as the equal, uncoerced participation oriented toward reaching mutual understanding on the part of all those affected so that all relevant contributions to a given topic can be voiced and so that the best arguments can carry the day. Accordingly, a proposition is true if it withstands all attempts to invalidate it under the rigorous conditions of rational discourse.[30]

This proposal is also subject to a powerful objection: It is counterintuitive that a proposition that has been tested in this way should be true *on the basis* or as a result of its ability to survive in discourse. Epistemic conceptions of truth certainly do justice to the linguistic insight that, faced with controversial claims to truth, we depend exclusively on the better reasons because we are barred from direct access to uninterpreted truth conditions. Yet the truth of a proposition does not become an epistemically mediated state of affairs merely in virtue of the fact that we can determine whether its truth conditions (which we must interpret in light of the appropriate kinds of reasons in any given case) are fulfilled only by means of justification, that is, by means of discursively redeeming the corresponding truth claim. The gap between truth and justification cannot be closed even by idealizing the conditions of actual processes of justification. Since any real discourse that takes place in time will remain provincial relative to learning processes in the future, we cannot know whether propositions that today seem to us to be warranted even under approximately ideal conditions will indeed withstand attempts to invalidate them in the future. Nevertheless, we must content ourselves with rational acceptability under conditions as ideal as possible as sufficient grounds for truth. Thus the discursive conception is not straightforwardly false, but insufficient. It still fails to explain what *authorizes* us to take as true a proposition we suppose to be ideally warranted.[31]

Epistemic theories of truth in general suffer from locating propositional truth in the language game of argumentation—that is, precisely where problematized truth claims become the *explicit* topic of discussion. Yet truth claims become the hypothetical object of debate only once they have been pried apart from their everyday functional contexts and have been neutralized, as it were. In contrast, the pragmatic conception that I want to outline in what follows takes into account how truth claims function *within* the lifeworld. This is the sense in which the discursive conception of truth must be complemented if, even after the linguistic turn, it is to do justice to the weak ontological connotations that we associate with the "grasping of facts." This reading salvages the moment of unconditionality that continues to characterize even the understanding of truth that is accessible to us only by means of the discursive redemption of truth claims. This step provides me with the basis for comparing truth and rightness. The pragmatic interpretation of the "obtaining" of states of affairs serves as the foil for the "worthiness of recognition" of moral norms.

IV

Pragmatism makes us aware that everyday practice rules out suspending claims to truth in principle. The network of routine practices relies on more or less implicit beliefs that we take to be true against a broad background of intersubjectively shared or sufficiently overlapping beliefs. Everyday routines and habituated communication work on the basis of certainties that guide our actions. This "knowledge" that we draw on performatively has the Platonic connotation that we are operating with "truths"—with sentences whose truth conditions are fulfilled. As soon as such certainties are dislodged from the framework of what we take for granted in the lifeworld and are thus no longer naively accepted, they become just so many questionable assumptions. In the transition from action to discourse, what is taken to be true is the first thing to shed its mode of practical certainty and to take on instead the form of a hypothetical statement whose validity remains undetermined until it passes or fails the test of argumentation. Looking beyond the level of argumentation, we can comprehend the *pragmatic role* of a Janus-faced truth that establishes the desired internal connection between performative certainty and warranted assertibility.

The same mechanism whereby shaken performative certainties are transformed into mere hypotheses also allows for a retransformation of rationally acceptable assertions into performative certainties. From the perspective of agents who assume the reflective attitude of participants in argumentation only temporarily in order to repair or improve a partially shaken knowledge, the discursive redemption of validity claims acquires the sense of a license to return to the naiveté of the lifeworld. This change of perspective as such has explanatory power: What is an end in itself from the internal perspective of a participant in argumentation becomes a means for other ends from the external perspective of acting subjects coping with the world. Practical uncertainties arise when knowledge is problematized. The function of "dispensing" with such uncertainties explains why it no longer makes sense for interlocutors to carry argumentation further if, after having all the relevant information and considering all relevant reasons, they are convinced that the objections against p—or against substituting p with q—have been exhausted. The need to act in the lifeworld, in which discourses remain rooted, imposes temporal constraints on what is, from an internal perspective, "an infinite conversation." Hence it requires highly artificial measures to insulate rational discourses against the pressures of the lifeworld and to render them autonomous, as for example in the sciences, in order to establish continuing hypothetical thought. Only institutionalized science can confine itself to dealing with hypotheses and allow itself to adopt the kind of radical fallibilism that neutralizes the natural Platonism of the lifeworld.

On the other hand, this very dogmatic constitution of the lifeworld is a necessary condition for the fallibilist consciousness of participants in discourse who anticipate that they might be mistaken even if their beliefs are well grounded. The lifeworld, which extends into discourse, as it were, operates with strong, Platonist concepts of truth and knowledge that refer to practical certainties. Because of this Platonism, the lifeworld furnishes a justification-transcendent standard for orienting ourselves by context-independent truth claims—a standard that is always already presupposed in action. Within discourse, the difference between truth and warranted assertibility that is thus produced maintains the consciousness of fallibility and simultaneously requires participants in discourse to self-critically approximate ideal conditions of justification, that is, to increasingly decenter their respective justificatory community.

Moreover, the pragmatic roots of a Janus-faced everyday concept of truth that mediates between lifeworld and discourse accounts for the ontological connotations we associate with the illocutionary force of assertions. What we want to express with true sentences is that a certain state of affairs "obtains" or is "given." And these facts in turn refer to "the world" as the totality of things about which we may state facts. This ontological way of speaking establishes a connection between truth and reference, that is, between the truth of statements and the "objectivity" of that about which something is stated. The concept of the "objective world" encompasses everything that subjects capable of speech and action do not "make themselves" irrespective of their interventions and inventions. This enables them to refer to things that can be identified as the same under different descriptions. The experience of "coping" accounts for two determinations of "objectivity": the fact that the way the world is not up to us; and the fact that it is the *same* for all of us. Beliefs are confirmed in action by something different than in discourse.

In discourse, whether a belief that has become problematic turns out to be rationally acceptable depends solely on good reasons. The parties orient themselves by justification-transcendent claims to truth because, even as participants in discourse, they have not lost sight of the fact that true beliefs function differently in everyday practice than in discourse. As long as they were engaged in action, only their prereflexive "coping with the world" determined whether a belief "worked" or whether it succumbed to the pressure of problematization. Languages and practices are corroborated by their continuing "functioning" or "working," that is, by their successful performance itself. When they fail, the world stops cooperating as expected. Through failure, we experience in practice that the world revokes its readiness to cooperate, and this refusal gives rise to the concept of objectivity. The latter extends, on the one hand, to the resistance of a world that is not up to us, that opposes our manipulations on its own terms, and, on the other hand, to the identity of a world shared by everyone. Since in cooperating with one another, actors mutually presuppose that each refers to the same world from his or her perspective, the world "exists" only in the singular.

To be sure, at the level of discourse, this corroborating authority is suspended (or at best appealed to in experiments whose results merely count as arguments among others). Here, there is no pressure to take action and only reasons count. In the interpersonal dimension, where participants cast their objectifying regard away from the world and turn toward the objections of their opponents in a performative attitude, it is possible for as many worlds to vie with one another as there are interpretations. Yet even then, interlocutors continue to associate the connotation of "grasping facts" with the goal of discursively redeeming *unconditional* claims to truth— and thus they *keep* the objective world in view indirectly. They have not forgotten that, having finished their interpretive dispute, they will again refer to *the same* world together as actors as soon as they return to the lifeworld.

Once we properly understand the connection between the truth of propositions and the objectivity of what these propositions are about in this pragmatic way, the difficulty of articulating a conception that assimilates moral validity to truth becomes clearer still. For now not only the similarities but also the differences between the two claims to validity emerge. On the one hand, both depend on discursive redemption and hence on a practice of justification. Participants orient themselves toward the idea of "a single correct answer," although they know they cannot go beyond the "ideal warranted acceptability" of propositions. On the other hand, this analogy exists only on the level of argumentation. It cannot be transferred to the level of prereflexive "corroboration" of beliefs. For moral beliefs do not falter against the resistance of an objective world that all participants suppose to be one and the same. Rather, they falter against the irresolubility of normative dissensus among opposing parties in a shared social world.

To be sure, moral beliefs do guide (normatively) rule-governed social interactions in a similar way that empirical beliefs guide goal-oriented interventions in the objective world. However, they are implicitly *corroborated* in a different way—not by successfully manipulating otherwise independently occurring processes, but by consensually resolving conflicts of interaction. And that can occur only against the background of *intersubjectively shared* normative beliefs. Corroboration does not occur in a practice that can be readily differentiated from discourse. Rather it takes place from the outset in the linguistic medium of communication—even though people first "feel" the consequences of moral injury. Whether the certainties that guide our actions fail is determined not by the uncontrolled contingency of disconfirming states of affairs, but by the opposition or outcry of social players with dissonant value orientations. The resistance does not come from the objectively "given" that we cannot control, but from the lack of a normative consensus with others. The "objectivity" of an *other* mind is made of different stuff than the objectivity of an *unanticipated* reality. The resistance of "objective spirit" can be overcome by moral learning processes that lead the disputing parties to broaden their respective social worlds and to *include* one another in a world they jointly construct in such a way that they can assess their conflicts in the light of shared standards of evaluations and resolve them consensually.

V

Moral validity claims lack the reference to the objective world that is characteristic of claims to truth. This means they are robbed of a justification-transcendent point of reference. The reference to the world is replaced by an orientation toward extending the borders of the social community and its consensus about values. If we want to specify the difference between rightness and truth more precisely, we have to examine whether and, if so, how this orientation toward an ever more extensive inclusion of other claims and persons can make up for the missing reference to the world.

Rational discourses are constantly moving within the recursively closed cycle of arguments. With regard to descriptive as well as moral questions, a statement's rational acceptability must suffice for us to decide controversial questions of validity. However, a discursively attained consensus carries a different connotation for the truth of statements than for the rightness of moral judgments or norms. Under the assumption of approximately ideal conditions, all available arguments are taken into consideration and all relevant objections are exhausted. Therefore, a discursively reached agreement entitles us to take a proposition to be true. But with regard to the objective world, the proposition's truth signifies a fact—the obtaining of a state of affairs. Facts owe their facticity to their being rooted in a world of objects (about which we state facts) that exist independently of our descriptions of them. This ontological description implies that no matter how carefully a consensus about a proposition is established and no matter how well the proposition is justified, it may nonetheless turn out to be false in light of new evidence. It is precisely this difference between truth and ideal warranted assertibility that is blurred with respect to moral claims to validity. Whereas successful learning in the sphere of empirical problems may *result* in agreement, learning in the moral domain is *assessed* in terms of how inclusive such a consensus reached through reason-giving is.

If all those possibly affected in practical discourses together have reached the conviction that a particular way of acting is equally good for all persons with respect to some matter that needs to be settled, they will regard this practice as binding. For the participants, the discursively attained consensus is relatively definitive. It does not determine a fact, but "grounds" a norm that cannot "consist" in anything but that it "merits" intersubjective recognition—and the participants assume that they can determine whether it does just that under approximately ideal conditions of rational discourse. We do not understand the validity of a normative statement in terms of the *obtaining* of a state of affairs, but as the *worthiness of recognition* of a corresponding norm on which we ought to base our practice. A norm worthy of being recognized cannot be denied by a "world" refusing to "play along." Of course a norm whose worthiness of recognition is ideally warranted may not be recognized as a matter of fact—or such recognition may be withheld by a society in which *other* practices and interpretations of the world are established. Yet with the reference to the objective world, moral validity claims lose a touchstone that extends beyond discourse and transcends the insightful self-determination of the will of the participants.

An agreement about norms or actions that is reached discursively under ideal conditions has more than merely an authorizing power; it warrants the rightness of moral judgments. Ideally warranted assertibility *is* what we mean by moral validity; it not only signifies that the pros and cons of a controversial claim to validity have been exhaustively considered, but it exhausts the meaning of normative rightness itself as the worthiness of recognition. A norm's ideal warranted assertibility—unlike that of a justification-transcendent claim to truth—does not refer beyond the boundaries of discourse to something that might "exist" independently of having been determined to be worthy of recognition. The justification-immanence of "rightness" is based on a semantic argument: Since the "validity" of a norm consists in that it would be accepted, that is, recognized as valid, under ideal conditions of justification, "rightness" is an epistemic concept.

This conception in no way implies that we have to take our best possible moral insights to be infallible in any given case. Indeed, the agreement that is reached in two steps through moral discourses of justification and application is subject to a dual fallibilist proviso. In retrospect, we can learn that we were mistaken about the presumed presuppositions of argumentation and that we failed to anticipate relevant circumstances.

The idealization of the conditions of justification that we undertake in rational discourse forms the standard for the proviso regarding the degree to which our justificatory community has become decentered at any given point. Such a proviso can be invoked at any time.[32] For this community encounters, as we shall see, difficulties of a particular—not merely cognitive—sort with regard to moral problems. If those affected are excluded, certain topics suppressed, relevant contributions disregarded, evident interests not sincerely articulated or convincingly formulated, if others are not respected in their otherness, then we must expect that some rationally motivated positions do not get to play a role or even get expressed. If we—rightly or wrongly—suppose that an agreement has been reached under sufficiently ideal conditions of justification, then this fallibility can be reconciled with the definitive nature that such an understanding has *for us*. After all, we can correct mistakes only if we assume that it is possible to decide between what is "right" and "wrong" and orient ourselves toward finding the one right "answer" on the basis of the principle of bivalence. As already mentioned, another kind of fallibility is explained by the fact that all norms that are recognized as valid, no matter how well grounded they are, must be complemented by discourses of application. Here it may turn out that unforeseen circumstances or innovations require revisions that retroactively reopen questions of normative justification. The awareness of this existential provinciality vis-à-vis the future, however, need not interfere with our moral convictions as long as the circumstances presupposed in the discourses of justification are not recognizably proven wrong by history.

It is as yet unclear whether and, if so, how the constructivist sense of moral belief- and will-formation can make up for the lack of a justification-transcendent point of reference for "right" moral judgments. Kant translated the absolutely binding nature of moral duties into the categorical validity of moral judgments. If the concept of rightness now loses its justification-transcendent hold, which the concept of truth owes to its ontological connotations, the question arises of how the claim to rightness can preserve its moment of unconditionality.

A valid proposition lays claim to universal validity, that is, recognition not merely in local, but in all contexts. Looking at a truth-evaluable proposition p, we read it realistically from left to right. If p is true, the proposition is unconditionally valid and merits being recognized as true by everyone. In order for p to be indeed universally recognized in this way, everyone has to be able to convince herself of the truth of this proposition and *to know* that *p*. This knowledge in turn can rely on the truth of *p* because (and insofar as) true propositions can be supported with good reasons. This consideration rests on a familiar connection between truth and knowledge: someone knows that *p* if she (a) believes that *p* and (b) has sufficient reasons for believing that *p;* and if (c) *p* is true. Moral knowledge cannot meet these conditions if we take "rightness" to be an epistemic validity claim because this means that the nonepistemic requirement (c) cannot be fulfilled.[33] How can normative rightness still be conceived as a binarily coded unconditional validity claim if moral judgments can no longer be justified with reference to nonepistemic conditions of validity?[34]

Recall my earlier observation that the validity of moral judgments is *assessed* in terms of how *inclusive* the normative agreement is that has been reached among conflicting parties. By directing ourselves toward the goal of a "single right answer" even in moral controversies, we presuppose that a valid morality applies to a single social world that includes all claims and persons equally. Of course, like Kant's "kingdom of ends," this world is not so much a given for us as it is a mandate. The project of a fully inclusive world of well-ordered interpersonal relationships shared but one of the two determinations with the concept of the objective world that is "not made by us" and is "the same for everyone"—not that it is not up to us, but that it is the same for all of us. However, this identity is not modeled on the "sameness" of a formally presupposed objective world. The fact that the moral world is "the same for everyone" is due not to the coordination of various observer perspectives by means of a calibrated reference to the world, which is also reflected in the justification-transcendent orientation toward truth; rather, participants in the social dimension have to bring about an inclusive We-perspective by means of mutually taking one another's perspectives. G. H. Mead described this as a process of a step-by-step expansion of a reversible exchange of perspectives. Piaget talks about a progressive decentering: One's own perspective is all the more decentered the more the process of interlocking one another's perspectives approaches the limit of complete inclusiveness.

Following this constructivist conception,[35] the unconditional nature of moral validity claims can be accounted for in terms of the universality of a normative domain that *is to be brought about:* Only those judgments and norms are valid that could be accepted for good reasons by everyone affected from the inclusive perspective of equally taking into consideration the evident claims of all persons. The projection of a universe of self-legislation on the part of free and equal persons imposes the *constraints of this perspective* on the justification of moral statements. Insofar as we test the rightness of moral statements from such a universalist point of view, the reference point of an ideally projected social world of legitimately ordered interpersonal relationships can serve as an equivalent for the absent constraints of an objective world in the course of the presumably rational resolution of moral conflicts of interaction.

However, this shifts the burden of proof from the question of how to account for the unconditionality of a justification-immanent validity claim to the question of why we associate the concept of "moral validity" with a universalist program at all. Hence I must briefly address the circumstances in which questions of universality inevitably arise. This will allow me to show how the idea of justice recedes from the concrete contexts in which it is embedded into forms of an inclusive and impartial judgment formation. In other words, it takes on a proceduralist form. Thus the perspective of justice comes to coincide with a perspective assumed by participants in rational discourses in general. This convergence draws our attention to the fact that the project of a moral world that is equally inclusive of everyone's claims is not an arbitrarily chosen point of reference; it is due, rather, to the *projection* of the universal communicative presuppositions of argumentation *tout court.*

VI

Let me first clarify what is at issue in moral judgment. The fundamental question of morality consists in how we can legitimately regulate interpersonal relationships. What is at issue is not the representation of facts, but the appeal to norms worthy of recognition. These are norms that *merit* recognition among those to whom they apply.

Naturally this kind of legitimacy is assessed in accordance with its social context in terms of an existing consensus about what is considered to be just. The prevailing interpretation of "justice" determines the perspective from which certain ways of acting and interacting are judged to be "equally good for all members." For only then do such practices merit universal recognition and become binding for those to whom they apply. Based on such a background agreement, conflicts among disputing "parties" can be settled by appeal to reasons that convince both sides, that is, in a literally "impartial" or "nonpartisan" sense.

The belief in legitimacy varies with the multiplicity of substantive representations of justice. Historically, the expectation that practices are "equally good" for all members has hardly been understood a priori in an egalitarian let alone a universalist sense. These two implications have developed only gradually from concrete conceptions of justice that were embedded in comprehensive worldviews and forms of life. The function of explicating an increasingly abstract idea of justice accrues to an "impartiality" that is transformed by questions of application and justification only in the course of dealing with increasing societal complexity. The concrete representations of justice that initially make possible an impartial evaluation of individual cases are thus sublimated into a procedural concept of impartial evaluation that then in turn defines justice. The initial relationship between content and form is reversed in the course of this development. If at first substantive conceptions of justice served as the standard for whether norms underlying the evaluation of conflicts were worthy of recognition, what is just is assessed in the end in terms of the conditions for impartial judgment formation. This can be illustrated schematically with the following considerations.

Let's assume that there has already evolved a type of society that is hierarchically structured and, by today's standards, repressive as well as exploitative. At the same time, the members of this society are supposed to share a communal ethos and a worldview that justifies the prevailing distribution of competencies and roles in a manner that seems reasonable to them. Under the relevant descriptions, everything that maintains the societal structures is explained as a contribution to reproducing the "common good." And since this common good by definition expresses what is equally good for all, everyone in his function and in his place will feel that he is being treated equally—despite the unequal distribution of power, prestige, wealth and opportunity. Let us now simulate the transition from a traditional to a modern society. The mobilization of material and personal resources leads to a functional differentiation of society that radically alters living conditions. One of its consequences will ultimately consist in more and more people encountering more and more others in other roles and different situations as less and less familiar counterparts: They encounter one another as strangers, as persons of another sort and of different origin.[36] This change in turn has the consequence that the perceived multiplicity of collective forms of life and individual life projects can no longer be reconciled with the static framework of the concrete, universally binding ethos of a more or less homogeneous society. As the intersubjectively shared worldview is shattered and the traditional form of life disintegrates, the collective good that is intertwined with both of them becomes problematic.

This scenario of a pluralism of worldviews and of a disintegrating communal ethos is meant to remind us how members of modern societies can become aware of the fact that there can be rational dissensus about fundamental standards of value and why they might be faced with the task of making efforts *on their own* in order to reach an agreement *together* about norms for living together in justice. The moral universe loses the appearance of an ontological given and comes to be seen as a *construct*. At the same time, the pluralism of forms of life and life projects demands reaching an agreement about more abstract, general norms that are not tailored to specific cases in advance. However, given our premises, such norms can claim legitimacy only to the extent that they govern the broadened spectrum and greater variation of living conditions and options in the equal interest of everyone affected. If they have not done so already, the egalitarian implications of justice become evident now. The posttraditional need for justification raises the expectation of moral judgment formation and simultaneously alters the standard of impartiality itself.

As long as the communal ethos reflected the shared form of life, it was required for making one's own moral judgments only in isolated instances. With regard to typical conflicts of action and interaction, this ethos furnishes convincing reasons for the "right" solution about which disputing parties could reach an agreement—if need be by means of an "impartial third party." The model for impartial judgment was the discourse of the judge applying the law that is already in existence and specified with reference to any given case. However, the concept of impartiality must abandon this model as soon as the norms that are to be applied themselves are in need of justification. This is what allows us to differentiate between the justification and the application of norms. A judge's neutrality vis-à-vis conflicting parties—the blindfold of Justice—is now an inadequate model for the required practice of justification, since all members, insofar as they are potentially affected, must take part in this practice as equals. Thus there can no longer be a separation of roles between a privileged third party and the parties who are affected in the case. Everyone has now become party to the case and wants to convince everyone else in the competition for the better argument.

Nonetheless, modern natural law was for some time able to maintain the idea that even the norms that underlie application arise from the mere *application* of an encompassing conception of the good. The example of democratic nation-states in fact shows that the nationally shared form of life and the collective good embodied in it have at least some effect on the norms of equality of a society whose internal constitution is egalitarian. Yet these concrete conceptions of the good life in which abstract and universal norms are embedded stop being taken for granted as soon as friction between the various cultural forms of life—be they inter- or intranational—leads to conflicts that need to be adjudicated. What then occurs in cross-cultural debates is a renewed push toward reflection and abstraction, which now also brings to light the *universalist* implications of justice.[37]

The more the substance of a prior consensus about values has evaporated, the more the idea of justice itself amalgamates with the idea of an impartial justification (and application) of norms. The more advanced the erosion of innate representations of justice, the more "justice" comes to be articulated as a procedural, but by no means less demanding, concept. The expectation of legitimacy—that only norms that are "equally good for everyone" merit recognition—can be fulfilled only by means of a procedure that ensures the inclusion of everyone who is potentially affected as well as impartiality in the sense of equal consideration of all interests involved.

It is not all that surprising that the communicative presuppositions of rational discourse should meet the requirements of such a procedure. For moral knowledge, unlike empirical knowledge, is *inherently* used for purposes of critique and justification. Moral knowledge consists in a stockpile of convincing reasons for consensually settling conflicts of interaction that arise within the lifeworld. Hence the communicative model for deliberation about and justification of disputed propositions fits with a posttraditional, purged idea of justice. After the collapse of comprehensive worldviews and ethoi, this idea can be articulated only in terms of the impartiality of belief- and will-formation within an inclusive justificatory community. In practical discourses, "impartiality" as discursive vindication of criticizable validity claims coincides with "impartiality" as a posttraditional idea of justice.

Keeping in mind the pattern of moral learning processes that are triggered not by the contingency of frustrating circumstances but by the resistance of social players with dissonant value orientations, we can now better grasp the specific contribution that the communicative form of rational discourse makes to the translation of concrete representations of justice into an egalitarian universalism. Ascertaining norms that are equally good for all depends on the mutual *inclusion* of people who are (and may want to remain) strangers to one another just as it depends on the equal consideration of their interests.[38] This requires taking on the very perspective that participants in argumentation must assume anyway if they want to test whether statements are rationally acceptable under approximately ideal conditions.

The very perspective that Kohlberg describes as the "prior-to-society perspective" with regard to moral questions is constituted in the game of argumentation. This is a perspective that transcends the social and historical boundaries of one's affiliation with a given concrete community as well as the "member-of-society perspective" inscribed in it.[39] The gentle force of unavoidable presuppositions of argumentation requires participants to take on the perspectives and to consider equally the interests of all others. Thus the universality of a world of well-ordered interpersonal relations—the projection of a moral universe toward which the arguments are directed—is explained as a kind of reflection of the egalitarian universalism that participants in discourse must always already buy into lest they forfeit the cognitive import of their undertaking.

VII

The genealogy of the postmetaphysical need for justification I have outlined shows how the point of view of a posttraditional kind of justice coincides with a perspective embedded in the communicative form of rational discourse. And this ideal point of reference secures for moral validity claims the kind of context-independence and universality that truth claims have in virtue of the ontological connotations of their justification-transcendence. In this respect, the *projection* of a moral world and the *presupposition* of an objective world are functionally equivalent. However, this must not mislead us into assimilating the moral to the objective world. Cristina Lafont has sought to ground the cognitivist claim of discourse ethics in this way. She thinks that we make an existential presupposition in practical discourse that is akin to the one we make in empirical or theoretical discourse. A brief examination of this interesting suggestion will allow us to see the peculiarly constructive nature and the particular epistemic role of practical discourse.

With the orientation toward a "single correct answer" we presuppose a principle of bivalence that we interpret ontologically keeping in mind the pair "true" and "false"; a statement's truth depends on whether the state of affairs it represents obtains or not. Lafont claims that we schematize the same principle in a similar fashion with regard to the rightness or wrongness of moral statements: the rightness of a norm is supposed to depend on whether it is equally in everyone's interest. In this schematization, we start from the assumption that there *is* a domain of universal interests that can be attributed to everyone in the same way. This existential presupposition is supposed to play a similar role to the ontological presupposition of an objective world of obtaining states of affairs:

Just as the presupposition of the existence of states of affairs in the objective world is the condition of possibility for a meaningful discussion about the truth of statements, the presupposition of the existence of a domain of generalizable interests is the condition of possibility for a meaningful discussion about the moral rightness of norms. The existence presupposition is unavoidable in practical discourse not because it is necessarily the case that there is such a domain among all human beings, but because if we came to the conclusion that this presupposition makes no sense (which is, obviously, an open empirical question) the discussion about the moral rightness of social norms would become meaningless.[40]

There are a number of objections to this suggestion. First, it is not entirely clear to me how a determinate fact that is supposed to hold with regard to persons—that is, to something to which we can refer in the objective world—could support a reference system in turn, and how such a system could have the same function, albeit not the same extension, as the presupposition of an objective world without which we cannot so much as talk about a "domain of generalizable interests." Such a "domain" cannot simultaneously be an analogue to and an excerpt of the objective world. A *determinate* fact, the existence of shared interests, cannot do the same work in explaining the sense of validity of "rightness" as the *concept* of fact does for the ontological interpretation of the sense of validity of "truth."

Furthermore, the ontological sense of the "existence" of states of affairs corresponds to the "worthiness of recognition" of norms on the deontological side. Under the posttraditional conditions mentioned above, this sense of worthiness of recognition can no longer be substantively grounded in the "existence" [*Bestand*] of universal interests; it can be explicated only by appeal to a procedure of impartial judgment formation. This results in a different order of explanation.[41] The explication of justice as the "equal consideration of everyone's interests" lies not at the beginning, but at the end. The procedural sense of the "worthiness of recognition" is initially explained in terms of the discourse principle according to which only those norms may claim to be valid that could command the assent of all those affected in their role as participants in discourse. Not until we turn to the question of how to operationalize this notion, and introduce the principle of universalization to do so, does the idea of generalizable interests come into play. Yet Lafont relies on it from the outset for the constitution of a further object domain.

The ontologizing of generalizable interests presents a more serious problem. This move assimilates the participant perspective, from within which the required generalization of interests must be undertaken, to an objectifying observer perspective. The world of legitimately ordered interpersonal relations can be disclosed only from the perspective of someone who takes on a performative attitude—just as valid norms are recognizable as something that can be "violated" by those to whom they apply only if one takes on a second-person perspective. An interest that is thematized with normative intent is not some kind of given regarding which individuals might claim epistemic authority based on their privileged access to it. The interpretation of needs and wants must take place in terms of a public language that is not private property. The interpretation of needs and wants is just as much the cooperative task of discourse as is the evaluation of competing interests (which are ranked with reference to their possible consequences and side effects). Shared or coinciding interests only *show up* in the light of practices and norms in which they can be embodied. If we ontologize generalizable interests, we miss the moment *of producing* a world of norms that merit recognition. In the discursive generalization of interests, insight and construction interpenetrate. For the worthiness of norms to be recognized is based not on an objectively determined agreement of interests that are given, but on the participants' interpreting and evaluating interests from a first-person plural perspective. The participants can develop norms embodying shared interests only from a We-perspective. This perspective has to be *constructed* out of a reversible exchange of the perspectives of all those affected.[42]

This does not contradict the assumption that some of our needs are deeply rooted in our anthropology (e.g., physical integrity and health, freedom of movement, and protection against betrayal, insult, and loneliness).[43] There is a core of what we take for granted morally that we encounter in all cultures and that can no doubt also be traced back to such interests as can easily be recognized by anyone affected as her own. But before it can be considered as a general interest in public discourse, every interest that is to "count" morally in case of doubt must be convincingly interpreted and grounded as well as translated into a relevant claim *from the perspective of those affected.*

The ontologizing assimilation of the moral to the objective world ultimately blocks from view the additional function that rational discourse must take on with regard to practical issues: Participants must be mutually sensitized to one another's understanding of themselves and of the world. Among the necessary presupposition of argumentation are: complete inclusion of all those affected, equal distribution of argumentational rights and obligations, the uncoerciveness of the communicative situation, and the participants' orientation toward reaching mutual understanding. Under these exacting conditions of communication, all available information, suggestions, reasons, evidence, and objections that are relevant to selecting, specifying, and resolving an obvious problem are supposed to come into play such that the best arguments are introduced and that the best argument always holds sway. This epistemic function refers to sorting possible topics and mobilizing relevant contributions. What is expected from the participants is only sincere and unprejudiced testing of these contributions.

The latter presupposition, that people entering into argument in order to convince one another of something are truthful and unbiased, is unproblematic only as long as what is at issue are questions of fact. Disputes about practical issues, in contrast, involve one's own interests as well as those of others and thus require that every participant be honest with herself and unbiased toward others' interpretations of themselves and their situations. Since participants are also the ones affected in practical discourse, the relatively harmless presupposition of a sincere and unbiased evaluation of arguments is transformed into the tougher demand to be honest *with oneself* and unbiased *toward one another.* In the face of matters in which everyone is involved on her own, "sincerity" [*Aufrichtigkeit*] requires the readiness to distance oneself from one's situation and the strength to critique one's self-delusions. And with regard to the existential importance of these questions, openness to arguments means an exacting kind of impartiality: Everyone ought to put herself into everyone else's situation and take their understanding of themselves and of the world just as seriously as her own.

In view of moral questions, then, the conditions of communication do not have the epistemic sense anymore of merely ensuring that all relevant contributions get made and are directed through the right channels of argumentation. The conditions of communication that refer to the participants *themselves* fulfill an immediate practical function, which of course also has an indirect epistemic significance. The structure of rational discourse is supposed generally to guarantee openness and equal inclusion, uncoerciveness, and transparency and, on the side of contributions to the discussion, to help bring the better argument into play. Here, this structure functions as a model that demands a self-critical attitude and an empathetic exchange of interpretive perspectives from participants in argumentation.[44] In this regard, the communicative form of practical discourse can also be understood as a *liberating* arrangement. It is supposed to decenter the perception of self and other and enable participants to be affected by actor-independent reasons—the rational motives of *others*. The idealizing anticipation creates not only a space for letting the pertinent reasons and information float freely and thus generate insights; at the same time, it also creates room for ridding the will—however temporarily—of heterogeneous determinations. To be sure, moral insights make possible a kind of autonomy that Kant conceives as the insightful self-legislation [*Selbstbindung*] of the will. Yet at the same time, the transitory overcoming of heteronomy that is expected in practical discourse is a necessary condition for *acquiring* moral insights: "There is an essential connection between freedom and truth."

This explains why the impartiality presupposed in the discursive context has a motivational as well as a cognitive aspect. Participants in argumentation are enjoined mentally to anticipate the cooperative self-legislation [*Selbstgesetzgebung*] that would actually be exacted from them as acting subjects in the "realm of freedom." This anticipation that is structurally attributed to participants explains in turn why we can understand "rightness"—which reduces to ideally warranted acceptability nonetheless as unconditional validity—on analogy with justification-transcendent truth. For since the communicative presuppositions of discourse have normative content, the constraints that the projection of a moral universe impose on the practice of justification arise from discourse *itself*. In order to ascertain that moral imperatives are categorically binding, we need not be in touch with a world beyond the horizon of our justifications. It suffices to survey the "worldless" realm of discourse, because from a participant perspective our reference point is an inclusive community of well-ordered interpersonal relations. Yet this is a reference point that is no longer at our disposal as soon as we enter into argumentation.

VIII

What is not up to us is the communicative form of life in which we "always already" find ourselves as subjects capable of speech and action and which requires that we provide reasons when disputing about moral issues. Even in everyday events, the moral language game involves us in giving reasons in disputes. What is normally at issue in such disputes is how some conflict ought to be evaluated in light of basic shared normative beliefs. As soon as the dispute extends to this shared background, to whether the norms themselves are worthy of recognition, and hence to the formation of common interests, however, we commit ourselves to presuppositions that enjoin us to include the claims of everyone affected equally if we *continue* the argument. This point of reference that is embedded in rational discourse is not up to us. But there is one condition: We must take moral questions to be questions of knowledge even if the lifeworld's font of shared ethical background beliefs is depleted.

Only under these conditions can we make a confident attempt to bring about a discursive agreement in the face of intensifying disputes about basic moral issues. Here, our interest has been in whether this is possible not in terms of the theory of justification,[45] but in terms of the theory of truth. Our reflections were meant to show that the validity of moral statements *can* be understood on analogy with truth—without ontologizing the worthiness of moral imperatives to be recognized and thus assimilating "rightness" to "truth." But does it have to be so understood? What, if anything, *necessitates* understanding moral validity claims on analogy with truth claims? Are we still required even under the posttraditional conditions of a radical value pluralism to continue talking about moral *knowledge*? To be sure, the moral language game still imposes the analogy with truth. Yet do such grammatical facts not often disguise mere habit?

Since in a certain way, we construct our moral order ourselves, practical discourse is simultaneously the locus of both will- and belief-formation. Must not the connection of construction and insight, which we have traced all the way to the discursive generalization of interests, leave behind a conventional trace in the categorical meaning of moral validity? Even in Kant, the concepts of practical reason and free will are interdependent—albeit in the noumenal realm and not within the spatiotemporal bounds where real discourse takes place. In our sublunar world, the unconditionality of moral validity has to be brought into unison with the kind of existential provinciality relative to the future that manifests itself in the revisionary force of discourses of application, for instance. Practical discourses plug into lifeworld contexts in a different way than empirical or theoretical discourses or even moral-theoretical ones. Moral attitudes and feelings that regulate everyday conflicts of interaction are internally connected to reasons and discursive exchanges, but these discourses do not interrupt everyday practice; rather they form part of it. This on the one hand accounts for the immediate social effectiveness of moral judgments; yet on the other hand, it tests their context-independence. In view of this embeddedness, the supposition that every moral question *here and now* can in principle be given a "single right answer" is risky, to say the least. That a cognitive conception of morality is possible means only that we can know how we ought legitimately to govern our lives together if we are determined to take the sharply delimited questions of justice that—like questions of truth—are subject to a binary code out of the broad spectrum of conceptions of the Good about which it is no longer feasible to reach a consensus.

The binary coding of questions of truth is motivated, as I have shown, by the ontological supposition of an objective world that we have to cope with as agents. Yet the social world lacks the kind of in-dependence from us [*Unverfügbarkeit*] that could serve as the basis for a corresponding coding in the domain of values. The binary schematization cannot even be reconciled without qualification with the justification-immanent sense of "rightness." With no justification-transcendent point of reference for fulfilling validity conditions, rea-sons have the last word in practical discourse, conceptually as well as in fact. Now, there are always better and worse reasons; there is never the "one and only right" reason. Because the process of justifi-cation is guided by reasons alone, we ought always to expect more or less "good," but not unequivocal results. The choice between "right" and "wrong" risks becoming blurred because we can no longer eval-uate whether arguments are better or worse with reference to the justification-transcendent existence of states of affairs. Given the premise that "rightness" reduces to "rational acceptability," the bi-nary decision, which must be unequivocal, somewhat acquires the character of a posit. Evidently the "Good"—what is good for me or for us—forms a continuum of values that hardly suggests the choice between what is morally "right" and "wrong" by its very nature. If that is the case, however, then we have to slip (so to speak) the bi-nary schema over evaluative questions.

In this context, a phenomenon arises that suggests that the delim-itation of the "just" from the "good" derives from the "decision" to salvage the binding force of moral norms after the demise of strong traditions by means of a truth-analogous conception of moral valid-ity. We call certain actions *super*erogatory because "good" deeds in the sense of "the right thing to do" can be trumped by excellent deeds. Kohlberg's life-boat dilemma is an example: Three castaways know that only two of them can survive, but none can be morally *re-quired* to sacrifice himself. Enlightenment morality has done away with sacrifice. Nonetheless, supererogatory actions are ranked in the same terms as actions from duty: as "good" and indeed as *especially good* deeds. They fail to exemplify the "right" thing to do merely be-cause they cannot be expected from people *in general*. Irrespective of their high moral value, such actions cannot be required on the basis of valid norms. Because supererogatory actions cannot be equally expected of all people, no one is *obligated* to act that way. Otherwise the egalitarian sense of posttraditional justice—the injunction against unequal treatment—would be violated.

Thus the phenomenon of supererogation creates the appearance that a right action could be more or less good. In the face of this, "rightness" has to stand its ground as a concept of validity that cannot be *ratcheted up* like a concept of value. This argues in favor of the supposition that the distinction between morally mandated and supererogatory acts is based, as it were, on "positing" that rightness be binarily coded on analogy with truth. It seems as if the fact of pluralism (Rawls) requires the decision to maintain the moral language game and to bring about just conditions before it is possible to justify *how* we can legitimately coordinate our lives together. Indeed, despite the suggestive force of habituated practices, it is impossible to convince the radical skeptic that we ought to *hold fast* to the goal of finding "the one right answer" and to *impose* a certain order on our social interactions by means of a binary code once our ethical background beliefs and norms have come under dispute.

However, this consideration does not lead back to conventionalism, decisionism, or existentialism. The "decision" to maintain that practical questions are truth-evaluable even under conditions of a modern pluralism of worldviews is intertwined with pragmatic and ethical motives. We have good reasons to prefer a rationally motivated agreement that is brought about without coercion to the alternatives of force, threat, bribery, or deceit.[46] Nonetheless, talk about "decision" and "positing" points in the wrong direction. The skeptical move of opting out of the language game of *warranted* moral expectations, verdicts, and self-reproaches exists only in philosophical reflection, but not in practice: it would destroy the self-understanding of subjects acting communicatively. Sociated individuals in their everyday dealings with one another depend as much on a "knowledge" of values that they naively take to be valid as cooperating subjects dealing with reality depend on factual knowledge. Hence, they must rely on their own power of insight in reconstructing the core moral content of the traditional knowledge that has slipped away from them. Yet as soon as they seek to privilege a universally binding system of rules without the backing of a worldview, the only way open to them is that of a discursively produced agreement. The continuation of communicative action by discursive means is part of the communicative form of life, and this is the only form of life available to us.

In a certain way, the perspectival structure of a lifeworld that is spatiotemporally centered in our current interactions even creates the transcendental appearance of a moral realism.[47] For as long as we are participating in normatively unproblematic language games and practices, we do not distinguish moral beliefs from other value orientations in terms of *their structure*—except by means of a "weight" that gives priority to moral value orientations. The hypothetical principles and norms about which we dispute as participants in discourse from within a reflexive attitude revert, by way of a retransformation from discourse into the lifeworld, into binding values [*Wertbindungen*], that is, into normative beliefs [*Wertüberzeugungen*] that guide action and are precipitated in the evaluative vocabulary of a particular form of life. In light of this vocabulary, the relevant features of persons, actions, and situations are perceived as "good" or "bad" properties and represented in the grammatical form of indicative sentences.[48]

This observation is part of a phenomenology of the everyday that to this day feeds doubts regarding principle-based deontological ethics. Of course the knowledge of principles that has been accumulated in postconventional discourses of justification might by now have penetrated so deeply into the lifeworld that the network of concrete normative beliefs has not remained unaffected by this move toward abstraction. In our context, the Aristotelian description of moral everyday practice nonetheless makes an important point regarding the indispensability of the moral language game inscribed in every communicatively constituted lifeworld. It is not up to us to choose to code moral judgments binarily and conceive of rightness as a validity claim analogous to truth; for the moral language game cannot be maintained intact in any other way under the conditions of postmetaphysical thinking.

7

The Relationship between Theory and Practice Revisited

Questioning the meaning of philosophy and its right to exist is part and parcel of philosophy itself; it constitutes the medium of free, unchanneled thought. The question whether philosophy can become a practical discipline is as old as philosophy itself. What role can it play in the context of politics, culture, and education? I would like to begin by recalling the two ways in which ancient Greek philosophy has answered this question, one Platonic, the other Aristotelian (1). Today, neither answer is entirely convincing. The classical perception of the relation between theory and practice has changed along with changes in how philosophy thinks of itself. Under the conditions of modern, more or less postmetaphysical thought, contractualist theories of natural law and philosophies of history have led to different interpretations of the relation between theory and practice. The main strands are again affiliated with two figures, namely Hegel and Marx (2). But the dashed political expectations that were associated with these modern answers have, as far as I can see, prompted diametrically opposed responses in our times. On the one hand, there has been a renewed turn to a metaphysical or quasi-religious understanding of what philosophy can achieve. This is exemplified by Heidegger and some of his postmodern followers. On the other hand, the disappointment has led to a sobered philosophy that looks at its public function as situated within the framework of complex societies (3). This more modest understanding of philosophy goes hand in hand with the specification of various roles that philosophy can assume in the context of a culture shaped by science, in a society characterized by functional differentiation, and in relation to the members of such societies, each of whom feels increasingly strong pressure to lead her own individual life (4). In conclusion, I shall turn to the current debate about how to interpret human rights, to illustrate the more influential role of the public intellectual that philosophers can take on in promoting what Kant called "enlightenment" in the public sphere (5).

(1) In a nutshell, the Platonic answer to the question of what practical impact philosophy can have is: Nothing is more practical than theory itself. Plato believed that, in the final instance, immersing oneself in contemplation of the cosmos was not of scientific or epistemic but of religious importance. Theory holds the promise of a formative process that is the way to both knowledge and salvation. It triggers a catharsis that is to lead to a salutory conversion of the mind. For in ascending to the realm of ideas, the soul is purged of lower interests and passions. In that ascent to a noetic grasp of ideas, the soul detaches itself from its material shackles and frees itself from the prison of the body. In the Aristotelian and the Stoic traditions the *bios theoretikos* claims priority as well: the *vita contemplativa* ranks higher than any kind of *vita activa*.

Consequently, the ancient Greeks took the sage who devoted his life to contemplation as a model worthy of veneration. Yet unlike the figures of the itinerant preacher, the hermit, and the monk, the sage represents a path to salvation that is exclusive and can thus be embarked upon only by the educated few. If only because of this elitist touch, the public impact of philosophy could not keep pace with world religions that promised salvation for the masses. Thus, as of late Classical Antiquity, Greek philosophy entered into a close symbiosis with institutional Christianity, became more and more the scholarly organ of theology, forfeiting its own independent promise of salvation. Books with titles such as *De consolatione philosophiae* became increasingly rare, while religion relieved philosophy of the task of providing both consolation and moral education. In Europe, it was now the Church that helped people cope with existential crises, poverty, illness, and death. Meanwhile, philosophy, as the place-holder of secular reason, increasingly withdrew into the domain of its cognitive tasks and, in good Aristotelian fashion, understood theory to be the way to knowledge, rather than salvation.

Already in Aristotle we find a different answer to the question of the practical impact of philosophy: Theory, he claims, acquires practical significance only in the guise of practical philosophy. Uncoupled from theory in the strict sense of epistemology, this branch of philosophy specializes in questions about how most prudently to lead one's life. Ethical reasoning, in the Artistotelian sense of phronesis, relinquishes three classical claims of theory. First, profane instruction on how to lead a good life now takes the place of the promise of religious salvation. Second, such a reasonable orientation for our daily life must renounce any claim to the same certainty as knowledge secured by theory. Practical philosophy serves the purpose of prudence, not science. And, finally, ethical insights are now no longer reinforced by the motivating context of the formative process of a theoretical mode of life. Instead, ethics has to presume that its addressees can already look back on successful character development. Philosophy can teach how to pursue the good life only to those who have already acquired an intuitive knowledge of what a good life is.

Given the postmetaphysical thinking characterizing the modern condition, where ontological and theological background assumptions became more and more controversial, practical philosophy has gone on to sacrifice even its substantive content. For, in view of what is now considered as a legitimate pluralism of worldviews, modern philosophical ethics is no longer able to commend particular models for how to lead a good life and to hold them up as examples to follow. With Rawls, we might say that in liberal societies everyone has the right to develop and pursue her own conception of the good life, or, more cautiously, of a life that is not misspent. Given this premise, ethics (in the Aristotelian sense of teaching how to live a good life) must confine itself to the more formal aspects of the basic question of who I am and would like to be, and of what is good for me in the long run. As an existential philosophy, ethics merely explains the conditions and modalities of consciously or authentically leading one's life. In the form of a neo-Aristotelian hermeneutics, it

investigates how people clarify their self-understanding by appropriating traditions. And in the form of discourse ethics, it traces the
processes of argumentation that are necessary for attaining a clearer
view of one's own identity. Since Kant and Kierkegaard, the modern
versions of ethics—in the classical sense of a guidance for how to
live—have ceased to articulate publicly recognized models of exem-
plary life; they have, instead, counseled private individuals to opt for
a specific form of reflection in order to lead authentic lives of their
own choosing.

(2) Once the classical alliance of ethics and politics breaks down,
genuinely modern forms of political and moral theory develop with
contractualism and Kantian deontology. They replace the existential
question of what is good for me or for us in the long run with the
moral-political question of what are the just rules of social life that
are equally good for everyone. Such norms are considered "just" if
they are equally in everybody's interest and hence may be expected
to have the consent of all rational subjects.

Meanwhile, the concept of an "objective reason" embodied either
in nature or in world history had been transformed into a notion of
"subjective reason" as a mental capacity of individual actors. All participants are conceived as free and equal actors wishing to establish the
rules to govern their common life themselves, that is, autonomously.
Kant and Rousseau construe "autonomy" as the ability to bind one's
own will to laws, and only to those universal laws that are worth
adopting because they are equally good for everybody. In terms of
this egalitarian universalism, philosophy derived highly explosive
ideas "from reason alone." As Hegel already said, the French Revolution "was kindled by philosophy." He believed that with the contractualist tradition of natural law, philosophy had raised the hitherto
unprecedented claim "that Man place himself on his head, that is,
on his thoughts, and construct reality according to them."[1] In this
vein, the internal connection between modern natural law and revolution[2] spawns yet another answer to our initial question: The just society, which philosophy anticipates conceptually, should be realized
through "revolutionary" practice. Yet this relation between theory
and practice, as it was conceived by Marx, has in the meantime also
become deeply problematic.

This problematization is, if we focus on the conceptual rather than the empirical connections, due to the instrumental role played by the philosophy of history as it was developed during the eighteenth century. Those teleological concepts of history promised to compensate for the weakness inherent in the normativism of modern natural law. This is not to belittle the continuing relevance of straight normative constructions of a "just community" justified by reason. In light of such ideas, it is possible to denounce existing injustices and to make political demands for more legitimate institutions. However, those normative constructions, while providing rational grounds for what ought to be the case, say nothing about how, in practice, we ought to bring about what ought to be the case. In this context, Hegel spoke scornfully of the *Ohnmacht des Sollens* ("the impotence of the mere 'ought'"). It thus seemed plausible to scan history for tendencies that would, as it were, naturally buttress those normative ideas. As a consequence of a new, future-oriented historical consciousness, this sphere had been instilled with meaning and relevance so that history for the first time attracted the interest of philosophy. Kant took up this issue of the "realization of Reason in history." And Hegel went on to transpose the transhistorical operations of Reason as such into the processual concepts of a genesis of Reason that was now understood as giving structure to history as well as to nature.

With his dialectical philosophy of history, Hegel tried to bridge the gap between the normativity of abstract reason and the contingency of sociohistorical conditions. Whereas for Kant the moral practice of cooperating individuals had merely been encouraged by a philosophy of history, Hegel developed an all-encompassing conception of world history. Yet in view of a logic of world-historical processes that were fixed in advance, the Young Hegelians felt the need to break with such fatalism in order to make room for a form of practice that they could again attribute to the subjects engaged in history themselves. Both fascinated and repelled by their mentor's system, Feuerbach and Marx rejected the idealist form of philosophy—but wished to retain its rational content. They now wanted to abolish and sublate philosophy in order to realize it—not, like Kant, through individual moral action but by political means. Thus they finally turned the classical relationship of theory and practice on its head.

Theory now appears in a double guise: as false consciousness and as critique. In both respects, however, philosophy is embedded in the practice of a particular social context and remains dependent on it. While critical theory tries to uncover the context-dependency of a traditional theory that only imagined itself to be independent of any historical conditions, this critique becomes aware of its own social roots and becomes doubly reflexive: Gazing into the mirror of the historical context of its own genesis, it also discovers the addressee who can be spurred on to a liberating practice by means of the critical insights that the theory provides.

Thus, Marx transposed Hegel's theory into an economic critique that was supposed to trigger the practical overthrow of the capitalist foundations of society. He understood such a praxis to be the simultaneous sublation and realization of philosophy. But this exuberant idea was proved wrong long before the monstrous failure of the disastrous Soviet-Russian experiment. This version of theory becoming practice had already been criticized from within Western Marxism. Let me mention but three points in this regard.

Criticism was leveled first against the underlying assumptions of a materialist philosophy of history that in fact had not broken with the totalizing thrust of metaphysics, but had merely transposed the teleological figures of thought from nature onto history as a whole. Meanwhile, however, the fallibilist self-understanding of science had made its way into philosophy, too, and purged its thinking about history of any remains of metaphysics. The anonymous events and the structural changes in history could no longer be construed as manifesting some invisible hand. Second, the critique has targeted the projection of macrosubjects onto the screen of world history. Conceptions of collective actors such as "social class," "culture," "a people," or "*Volksgeist*" ("popular spirit") intimate something like subjects writ large. However, the divergent beliefs and conflicting intentions of different individuals can reasonably be integrated only by means of intersubjective processes of communication and deliberation. Political intervention in critical social developments therefore depends on democratic opinion- and will-formation. Third, the

avantgardist project of social revolution has directed critical attention to the overinflated claims of rational critique itself. It has become apparent that the interest in controlling social history, which
is inherently contingent and not at our disposal, has unfortunately
replaced the understandable moral impulse to liberate humankind
from the repetitive compulsions of a repressed history of suffering.
The conception of a practice informed by so-called laws of history
exceeds the boundaries of the finite human mind and fails to pay
due respect to the pluralist constitution of a form of practice that is
fueled by the "yes" and "no" of communicatively acting subjects. It
conflates the intersubjectively performed practice of socialized individuals with the technical interventions of a collective subject asserting itself.

(3) For Adorno, the post-Hegelian urge for theory to become
practical contained the totalitarian core of what he and Horkheimer
called instrumental reason. Is then the modern question, how can
philosophy become practical, perhaps wrongly put in the first place?
It would be somewhat hasty, I think, to jump to this conclusion.
Faced with the fact that philosophy today is but one among many
academic disciplines, most of us still have the nagging sense that
somehow an essential element is missing. It is hard to deny the feeling that a philosophy regressing into the self-sustaining discourses of
an academic discipline is no longer philosophy in the proper sense
of the word. It is not so much the absence of totalizing concepts, of
speculation about nature and history as a whole, that appears to be a
shortcoming. In modernity, particularly given the disasters of the
twentieth century, the ability for reason to disclose some metaphysical meaning appears to have been irrevocably lost. What philosophy
in the stunted form of a mere academic discipline lacks is something
else—namely, a perspective that would imbue its statements with the
power to give direction to people's lives.

After the fiasco of a theory that evidently became practical in the
wrong way, the Kantian distinction between academic and mundane
philosophy [*Schulphilosophie* and *Weltphilosophie*] is emerging in a
new form. Exoteric approaches that have the advantage of not responding exclusively to problems defined by and emerging from
academic philosophical discussion itself can easily be distinguished

from the highly specialized business of a remote discipline. The former have a public impact because they face up to the problems that confront philosophy from without, that is, from both private and public life. These diagnostic approaches respond to the particular need of modernity, which is, after all, bereft of any guidance by models of the past. For modernity has to develop a normative understanding of itself by its own devices. The philosophical discourse of modernity is a terrain occupied both by its defendants and by its postmodern critics, such as Karl Popper, Hans Blumenberg, or Karl-Otto Apel on the one side, and Michel Foucault, Jacques Derrida, and Richard Rorty on the other. This is not the place to get into the debate over which version of the critique of reason is the right one. However, in view of what we may expect philosophy to be able to accomplish today, what I find interesting is another tension that has arisen in the context of this dispute. Let me put it in terms of an opposition between a quasi-religious and a more pragmatic self-understanding of philosophy.

Following Nietzsche, Heidegger construes the history of Western civilization and society in terms of the conceptual history of Platonism and Hellenized Christianity. This is to say that he deconstructs the history of metaphysics in order to "overcome" the humanistic self-understanding of the moderns. According to his critique of the modern condition a new attitude of serenity [*Gelassenheit*] is to take the place of the possessive individualism of a self-empowering subjectivity. At the same time, Heidegger assigns to the enterprise of this critique of metaphysics a significance that is reminiscent of the original religious meaning of contemplation. However, the philosophical "remembrance" of Being is not so much to revive an anamnesis of ideas in the service of some personal salvation; it is intended to "overcome" an imminent apocalyptic fate of mankind. While promoting this "apocalyptic attentism," the later Heidegger appropriates the gesture of the chosen thinker who has privileged access to the epiphany of truth. He believes that a form of anamnestic thought tinged with mysticism has the magical and harrying power to accelerate the pending salvation of the Occident. In this vein the "thinker" is supposed to be able to affect the fate of a God-forsaken modernity. Marxism had endeavored to secure its relation to world history by means of revolutionary praxis. Heidegger preserves for philosophy a similarly fateful relation to the metahistory of Being by a kind of pseudo-religious revalorization of the spiritual powers of philosophical thought itself.

Thus philosophy continues to bear the fate of the world on its shoulders—precisely by providing the appropriate conceptual framework for modernity. Here, a strand of the Platonist tradition persists, one incompatible with the modern turn toward egalitarian universalism. A genuinely modern vision of philosophy, which wishes to keep standing with one leg in the business of science and academia and which hence cannot escape the fallibilist consciousness of any academic enterprise, is forced to drop the claim of holding the key to the Truth (what Arnold Gehlen once has referred to as the *Schlüsselattitüde* of the mandarins). To the extent that philosophy still seeks to provide direction for people's lives, it must do so in a less dramatic way. At this end of the spectrum, philosophy arrives at a more modest, pragmatic self-understanding by finding its place in the differentiated orders of modern societies. Philosophy thus no longer positions itself as a pretentious countervailing power against the entire modern world. Instead, it now tries to situate itself within this world at the same time as it interprets it, and it does so in such a way that it can take on various functionally differentiated roles and make specific contributions.

(4) The pragmatic roles played by philosophy that I shall outline in what follows result from a specific understanding of modern societies, which I have elaborated elsewhere.[3] On this reading, the *lifeworld* forms the horizon for a practice of reaching mutual understanding where subjects acting communicatively try to deal with their everyday problems together. Modern lifeworlds are differentiated into the domains of culture, society, and personality. *Culture* is articulated into the spheres of science and technology, law and morality, and art and art criticism in accordance with the validity aspects of questions of truth, justice, and taste. The basic institutions of *society* (such as family, church, and the law) have given rise to functional systems (such as the modern economy and state administration) that have taken on somewhat of a life of their own by means of their own media of communication (money and administrative power).

Finally, *personality structures* emerge from socialization processes that provide new generations with the ability to find their own directions in such a complex world.

Culture, society, and personality, as well as the private and public spheres of the lifeworld, provide us with points of reference for the functions that philosophy can fulfill in contemporary societies. Of course there is a tension between the social roles attributed to philosophy from without, on the one hand, and the perceptions from within the philosophers' own perspective, on the other. The totalizing view inherent in all philosophical thought—and be it only the view of the "whole" of some diffuse background of the lifeworld—resists any form of functional specification. Indeed, philosophy cannot completely immerse itself in any one of its social roles; it can only fulfill one or the other of its specialized roles by simultaneously transcending it. Were philosophy to correspond fully to one of those sharply defined functions based on a clear division of labor, then it would be robbed of its best, its anarchist heritage, namely of the strength of a kind of untamed thinking that is neither channeled nor fixed by any particular method.

The differentiation of the sciences from modern law, morality, and art has altered philosophy's overall position in modern culture as a whole. Until almost the seventeenth century, the specialization of knowledge took the form of differentiations within the framework of philosophy as the all-encompassing science. Even in the face of modern physics and its methodology, philosophy continued to claim that at least the "foundations" of knowledge remained in its purview. After Kant und Hegel, however, even foundationalist epistemology gives way to a philosophy of science that provides justifications after the fact. From now on, philosophy can do no more than respond to the independent developments of sciences that have become autonomous. It nevertheless retains its institutional position within the academy, in other words among the sciences and humanities, not merely out of habit, but for systematic reasons.

Since Plato, philosophy had practiced conceptual analysis by means of anamnestic procedures. Thus, today it still tries to reconstruct pretheoretical commonsense knowledge in order to elucidate the rational infrastructure of cognition, language, and action. Stripped of foundationalist claims and with a fallibilist sensibility, it enters into cooperation with other sciences. Frequently, philosophy serves only as stand-in for empirical theories with strongly universalist approaches.[4] Like the sciences, philosophy continues to focus on questions of truth; but unlike them, it maintains an *intrinsic* connection to law, morality, and art. It investigates normative and evaluative issues from the internal perspective of those domains themselves. By taking the logic of questions of justice or of taste seriously, by recognizing the structure of moral sentiments and aesthetic experiences, it preserves the unique ability to switch from one discourse to another and to translate from one expert idiom into another.

What we see here is that curious polyglot trait of philosophy which enables it to preserve a certain unity across all the disparate elements of reason, without thereby leveling the different aspects of validity—the truth of assertions, the legitimacy of moral or legal norms, and the convincing appeal of a work of art. Philosophy manages to maintain this formal unity of a pluralized reason not by virtue of some substantive notion of the totality of beings or by some concept of the universal good, for example, but thanks to its hermeneutic ability to cross the boundaries between languages and discourses, while remaining sensitive to their holistic background contexts.[5] However, it is never good for philosophy to abandon its collaboration with the sciences and to insist stubbornly on occupying a separate field with a method of its own, that is, a sphere above and beyond the sciences, be it "philosophical faith," "life," "existential freedom," "myth," or "Being" as it unfolds in a metahistorical dimension of "events." Without the interface with science and without working on the problems it generates itself as a specialized discipline, philosophy would lose the very insights of its own that it needs in order to fulfill its exoteric roles.

Before I go on to discuss how this place of philosophy within modern culture bears on the interesting role of the public intellectual (c), allow me briefly to address the role of the scientific expert (a) and the role of a therapist showing how to attain a "meaningful life" (b). Philosophy obviously has no exclusive claim to either of these roles. Philosophers must compete with other intellectuals and other types of knowledge that originate elsewhere.

(a) The functional systems of modern societies depend on specialized knowledge, which they source from experts, among other things. Because of their expertise, such professionals are expected to advise on issues that are presented to them from the perspective of those wishing to apply such knowledge. What is best suited to answer these "technical" questions is the applied knowledge generated by the relevant natural and social sciences. In such contexts, philosophical knowledge is called for as rarely as the historical or hermeneutic interpretations provided by the humanities in general. Nonetheless, philosophers are at least consulted on some issues, on questions of methodology in the critical evaluation of competing expert opinions, and, above all, on normative questions concerning ecology, medicine, or genetic engineering, and generally on questions having to do with the risks and consequences of using new technologies. In rare instances, the issue also has to do with the ethical self-understanding of the political community, as, for instance, in parliamentary discussions of the criminal nature of a political regime that has been overthrown or in debates about what are the best strategies for coping with an unmasterable past (trial and punishment vs. forgiving and forgetting). If we think, for example, of the by now fairly widespread practice of establishing ethics commissions for addressing difficult problems in, say, the gray areas of medical ethics, one cannot help but feel somewhat frustrated. There is obviously a cognitive dissonance between freewheeling philosophical thought and the constraints imposed by this kind of institutionalization of expertise. Acting as experts, philosophers will be able to avoid self-betrayal if, and only if, in response to the instrumentalization of their knowledge, they are able to maintain a keen awareness of the limits of any such expertise.

(b) By contrast, philosophy seems to be well equipped to meet people's private yearning to make their—increasingly isolated—lives "meaningful," as it were. Yet even here it cannot fulfill such expectations without reservation. Given that modernity is characterized first and foremost by the acceptance of a legitimate plurality of worldviews and absent the support of a universally recognized metaphysical framework, philosophers cannot take a stance for or against the substance of any particular way of leading one's life. They cannot slake the thirst of the sons and daughters of modernity by providing some surrogate for the lost certainties of religious faith or of a cosmological worldview. They have to leave it to priests to provide comfort and consolation in existential crises. Philosophy can rely neither on a knowledge of salvation nor on clinical knowledge and therefore cannot provide "advice for how to live" [*Lebenshilfe*] in the way that either religion or clinical psychology can. In the form of ethics, it can offer guidelines for how to attain a reasonable understanding of one's identity, of who one is and who one would like to be. However, today the "therapeutic" role of philosophical ethics consists at best in encouraging people to lead their lives *consciously*. Philosophical "advice" remains ascetic when it comes to demands for "making sense of life"; the responsibility for reflecting on the meaning of a person's life has to remain with that person.

(c) Philosophers have wider ranging, better circumscribed, and more historically grounded opportunities to intervene in the course of events in the role of public intellectuals than they do as experts or therapists. Intellectuals take part in those public debates through which modern societies seek to arrive at an understanding of themselves. Various public spheres from different places and dealing with specific topics overlap or converge at the national level in a cultural and political public sphere made possible and supported by the mass media. National public spheres are simultaneously traversed and complemented by the global flow of communication. This public space forms the sounding board for macrosocial problems that are no longer visible from the perspective of closed, self-referential functional systems. In other words, the diffuse network of a public sphere anchored in civil society is the place where highly complex societies become aware of significant failures and risks and can deal politically with those problems that push them to act on themselves. Certainly, many actors are involved in addressing and handling public issues. We are interested here in one group of actors who stand out in virtue of the fact that they have been neither asked nor delegated to intervene but instead make unsolicited use of their professional abilities to offer their more or less well-reasoned opinions on such issues of general interest. These intellectuals can at best rely on an authority they acquire by dint of making good on the ambitious claim to consider in each case all relevant points of view impartially and to take all interests involved equally into account.

There are some questions that philosophers are better prepared to handle than are other intellectuals, be they writers, professionals, or scientists. First, philosophy can make a specific contribution to the diagnosis of our times in terms of which modern societies come to understand themselves. Ever since the late eighteenth century, the discourse of modernity has been conducted primarily in the philosophical form of an auto-critique of reason. Second, philosophy can fruitfully tap into its ability to think in terms of the whole and its polyglossia to develop certain sorts of interpretations. Given that it maintains an intimate relation to both the sciences and to common sense, and that it understands the specialized idioms of expert cultures as well as it does the ordinary language of everyday life, philosophy can, for example, criticize the colonization of a lifeworld that has been gutted by trends toward commercialization, bureaucratization, and legalization, as well as scientization. Third, philosophy has an inherent capacity to address basic normative issues of the "just" or well-ordered society. Philosophy and democracy not only emerge from the same historical context of origin; they are also structurally dependent on each other. Philosophy has a special interest in the constitutional protection of the freedom of thought and communication, while, conversely, a perennially endangered democratic discourse also depends on the vigilance and intervention of this public guardian of rationality.

In modern European history, political philosophy from Rousseau, via Hegel and Marx, through John Stuart Mill and Dewey has established for itself a considerable influence on public life. A current example illustrating the political need for philosophical clarification is the cross-cultural controversy about how to conceptualize human rights.

(5) Today, as it grows ever more closely together, the community of nations is no longer compelled only to regulate "international" transactions. Under the pressures of economic globalization, politics, too, must develop into a transnational system. It is also gradually becoming necessary to transform national law into a "cosmopolitan" civil law on which people can rely in intrastate matters and to which,

if need be, they can appeal even in dealing with their own government. Human rights, as they have been codified in various declarations, are well suited for this purpose. Indeed, the controversy over the correct interpretation of human rights has intensified against the background of the United Nations pursuing its human rights policies more actively since 1989 and under the pressure of global initiatives on the part of NGOs. Since the collapse of the Soviet Union, differences in outlook among social systems have been reduced. In their place, however, cross-cultural differences have emerged—in particular between the secularized West and fundamentalist Islamic currents on the one hand, and between the individualistic West and communitarian Asian traditions, on the other.[6]

I cannot go into this debate in greater detail here.[7] However, the example shows how philosophy could have direct political influence. Allow me in conclusion to pinpoint three key aspects of this particular debate where I believe philosophical clarification is both desirable and possible.

I would first of all propose that we reflect on the hermeneutic situation of the human rights debate itself, as it involves participants of different cultural backgrounds. This would draw our attention to the normative content already implicit in the tacit presuppositions of any discourse aiming at reaching mutual understanding. For, irrespective of cultural background, all the participants intuitively know full well that a consensus based on insight is not possible if the relations between the participants in communication are not symmetrical—that is, relations of mutual recognition, of reciprocal perspective-taking, a shared willingness to look at one's own traditions through the eyes of a stranger, to learn from one another, and so on.

Second, I believe it would be useful to reflect on the notion of "subjective rights" used in the conception of human rights. In this way, our reading of the debate between individualists and collectivists could bring a double misunderstanding to light. For possessive individualism in its Western guise fails to see that subjective rights can be derived only from antecedent, intersubjectively recognized norms governing a legal community. Individual legal persons are, of course, endowed with subjective rights under the rule of law; however, the status of such persons as the bearers of subjective rights is constituted in the first place in a political community based on mutual recognition. Now, by jettisoning the erroneous thesis that there exists an individual with innate rights prior to all socialization we can at the same time abandon the antithesis that accords priority to the claims of a community over the legal claims of individuals. The purported alternatives these two theoretical strategies afford dissolve into nothing if, contrary to both strategies, we incorporate the *unity* of processes of individuation and socialization into the core concepts of an intersubjective approach to legal theory: Legal persons in general become individuals only through socialization.

Third and finally, it would be important to clarify the different grammatical roles played by ought-sentences and by value statements, as well as those played by normative and evaluative expressions in general. For deontological considerations of rights and duties must not be assimilated to axiological considerations of value preferences. Given that different directions in life are existentially irreconcilable, it is always difficult for two parties whose identities have been shaped in different ways of life and traditions to reach agreement—be it at the international level between different cultures or between different subcultural collectivities within one and the same state. Here, it is all the more helpful to remember that an agreement on binding norms (ensuring reciprocal rights and duties) does not require the mutual appreciation for one another's cultural achievements and life styles, but instead depends solely on acknowledging that every person is of equal value precisely *as* a person.

Notes

Translator's Introduction

1. See J. Habermas, *On the Pragmatics of Social Interaction*, trans. B. Fultner (Cambridge, Mass., 2001).

2. See J. Habermas, *Moral Consciousness and Communicative Action* (Cambridge, Mass., 1990).

3. See *The Theory of Communicative Action*, trans. T. A. McCarthy, vol. 2 (Boston, 1987), pp. 3–44.

4. For an excellent account of how to combine a direct theory of reference with the theory of communicative action, see C. Lafont, *The Linguistic Turn in Hermeneutic Philosophy*, trans. José Medina (Cambridge, Mass., 1999).

5. See J. Habermas, "Reflections on the Linguistic Foundation of Sociology," in *On the Pragmatics of Social Interaction* (Cambridge, 2001), pp. 1–103.

6. J. Habermas, "Wahrheitstheorien," in *Vorstudien und Ergänzungen zur Theorie des kommunikativen Handelns* (Frankfurt, 1984), pp. 127–183.

7. B. Fultner, "Idealization, Acceptability, and Fallibilism in Jürgen Habermas' Theory of Meaning," *International Journal of Philosophical Studies* 4, no. 2 (1996): pp. 233–251.

8. See also Charles Taylor's landmark essay, "Theories of Meaning," in *Human Agency and Language* (Cambridge, 1985), pp. 248–292.

9. D. Davidson, "On the Very Idea of a Conceptual Scheme," in *Inquiries Into Truth and Interpretation* (Oxford, 1984), p. 194. Although Davidson is arguing against postulating facts at all, this is arguably to be understood as an argument against *reifying* facts, that is, against treating them as *things*.

10. For an elaboration of the incompatibilities between Brandom's and Habermas's notions of objectivity, see C. Lafont, "Is Objectivity Perspectival?" in *Habermas and Pragmatism*, M. Abulafia, M. Bookman, and C. Kemp, eds. (New York, 2002), pp. 185–209.

11. A. Wellmer, "Gibt es eine Wahrheit jenseits der Aussagenwahrheit?" in *Die Öffentlichkeit der Vernunft und die Vernunft der Öffentlichkeit*, Lutz Wingert and Klaus Günther, eds. (Frankfurt am Main, 2001), pp. 13–52.

12. H. Putnam, "Antwort auf Jürgen Habermas," in *Hilary Putnam und die Tradition des Pragmatismus*, M.-L. Raters and M. Willaschek, eds. (Frankfurt am Main, 2002), pp. 306–321.

13. Ibid., pp. 317–318.

14. Ibid., p. 318.

Introduction: Realism after the Linguistic Turn

1. M. Dummett, *The Origins of Analytical Philosophy* (London, 1993).

2. K.-O. Apel, "Die Logosauszeichnung der menschlichen Sprache," in H. G. Bosshardt, ed., *Perspektiven auf Sprache* (Berlin and New York, 1986), pp. 45–87.

3. G. H. v. Wright, *The Tree of Knowledge* (Leiden, 1993).

4. M. Dummett, "Language and Communication," in *The Seas of Language* (Oxford, 1993), p. 166.

5. See K.-O. Apel's and my critique of J. Searle's intentionalistic approach in E. Lepore and R. v. Gulick, eds., *John Searle and His Critics* (Oxford, 1991), pp. 17–56.

6. M. Dummett, "Truth and Meaning," in *The Seas of Language*, pp. 147–165.

7. J. Habermas, "Toward a Critique of a Theory of Meaning," in *Postmetaphysical Thinking* (Cambridge, Mass., 1992).

8. A. Matar, *From Dummett's Philosophical Perspective* (New York, 1997).

9. J. Habermas, "Knowledge and Human Interests" (1965), in *Technology and Science as "Ideology"* (Frankfurt, 1968), pp. 146–168. K.-O. Apel, "Scientics, Hermeneutics, and the Critique of Ideology," in *Towards a Transformation of Philosophy*, trans. G. Adey and D. Frisby (London, 1980), pp. 46–76.

10. K.-O. Apel has pursued this interest more consistently since his program of a "transformation of philosophy" to this day continues to align itself with a Kantian transcendental philosophy. The deeper source of our differences, which Apel articulates in his *Auseinandersetzungen in Erprobung des transcendentalpragmatischen Ansatzes* (Frankfurt, 1998), chs. 11–13, I attribute to my opting for a "weak" naturalism. However, I cannot do justice to Apel's subtle objections in the context of this introduction.

11. For an elucidation of my doubts about the "premise that methodology and epistemology are suitable as the *via regia* for an analysis of the foundations of social theory," see the preface to the second edition of my *On the Logic of the Social Sciences*, trans. S. Weber Nicholson and J. A. Stark (Cambridge, Mass., 1988), pp. xiii ff.

12. A. Matar characterizes Michael Dummett's constructivism, which has been labeled "antirealist," as a linguistic Kantianism. His "antirealism" essentially feeds on the motives of rejecting a "metaphysical realism" and is compatible with "internal realism" as developed by Putnam. See Matar, *From Dummett's Philosophical Perspective*, pp. 53–57.

13. See my discussion of Richard Rorty's contextualism in "Rorty's Pragmatic Turn," in *On the Pragmatics of Communication*, ed. Maeve Cooke (Cambridge, Mass., 1998), as well as Rorty's response in Robert Brandom, ed., *Rorty and his Critics* (Oxford, 2000), pp. 31–55.

14. This essay first appeared in *Deutsche Zeitschrift für Philosophie*, vol. 46 (1998), pp. 179–208.

15. H. Putnam, *The Many Faces of Realism* (LaSalle, Ill., 1987) and *Pragmatism* (Oxford, 1995).

16. See J. Habermas, "Ancora sulla Relzione fra Teoria e Prassi," in *Paradigmi* 15 (1997), pp. 434–442.

17. J. Habermas, "Appendix" to *Knowledge and Human Interests*, trans. J. Shapiro (London, 1978), second ed.

18. R. Rorty, *Philosophy and the Mirror of Nature* (Princeton, N.J., 1979).

19. J. Habermas, "Morality and Ethical Life: Does Hegel's Critique of Kant Apply to Discourse Ethics?" in *Moral Consciousness and Communicative Action* (Cambridge, Mass., 1990).

20. Immanuel Kant, *Critique of Pure Reason*, trans. Werner S. Pluhar (Indianapolis, 1996), p. 64.

21. W. Sellars, *Empiricism and the Philosophy of Mind* (Cambridge, Mass., 1997).

22. On the stratification of behavior, see my "Handlungen, Operationen, körperliche Bewegungen," in my *Vorstudien und Ergänzungen zur Theorie des kommunikativen Handelns* (Frankfurt, 1984), pp. 273–306.

23. For an analysis of such rules, see P. Lorenzen, *Lehrbuch der konstruktiven Wissenschaftstheorie* (Mannheim, 1987).

24. K.-O. Apel, *Der Denkweg von Charles S. Peirce* (Frankfurt, 1975), pp. 106ff.

25. M. Sacks, "Transcendental Constraints and Transcendental features," *International Journal of Philosophical Studies*, vol. 5 (1997), pp. 164–186.

26. [The reference is to Kleist's despair in the face of the realization that, following Kant, all knowledge is ultimately subjective.—Trans.]

27. Ibid., p. 179.

28. J. Searle, *Speech Acts* (Cambridge, 1969); J. Habermas, "What Is Universal Pragmatics?" in *Communication and the Evolution of Society* (Cambridge, Mass., 1979), pp. 1–68.

29. A. Gehlen, *Man* (New York, 1988); see A. Honneth and H. Joas, *Soziales Handeln und menschliche Natur* (Frankfurt, 1980).

30. I did not pay sufficient heed to this difference between lived and research practices in *Knowledge and Human Interests.* See my appendix to that work.

31. On the construction of a "nature-in-itself," see my *Theory and Practice* (Boston, 1973), pp. 36ff. On its aporetic consequences, see T. A. McCarthy, *The Critical Theory of Jürgen Habermas* (Cambridge, Mass., 1981), pp. 111ff. My reply appears in *Vorstudien und Ergänzungen zur Theorie des kommunikativen Handelns* (Frankfurt, 1984), pp. 509ff.

32. A. Schmidt, *Der Begriff der Natur in der Lehre von Marx* (Frankfurt, 1962).

33. Based on other premises, M. Scheler establishes a similar connection in *Die Wissensformen und die Gesellschaft* (1925) (Bern, 1960).

34. The positivistic leveling of this difference formerly motivated my attempt to unearth the hidden pragmatic dimension of research processes. See the preface to J. Habermas *Theory and Practice*. See also A. Wellmer, *Methodologie als Erkenntnistheorie* (Frankfurt, 1997).

35. C. Lafont, *Heidegger, Language, and World-Disclosure,* trans. Graham Harman (Cambridge, 2000).

36. R. Rorty, *Philosophy and the Mirror of Nature.*

37. P. Dews correctly characterizes my account of the consistency of an uncommon combination as follows: "It is the combination of anti-idealism with anti-scientism *and* a propensity toward naturalism which makes for the distinctiveness of Habermas's work. It marks him out as belonging to a sub-tradition which ultimately derives from the world of Hegel's left-wing followers during the 1830s and 40s" ("Naturalism and Anti-Naturalism in Habermas's Philosophy," unpublished manuscript).

38. P. Winch, *The Idea of a Social Science* (London, 1958).

39. See my critique of Peirce's linguistically revised realism about universals in *Knowledge and Human Interests.*

40. L. Wittgenstein, *Tractatus Logico-Philosophicus,* trans. C. R. Ogden (London, 1992), §1.1.

41. P. F. Strawson, "Truth," in G. Pitcher, ed., *Truth* (Englewood Cliffs, 1964), pp. 32–53.

42. E. Tugendhat, *Vorlesungen zur Einführung in die sprachanalytische Philosophie* (Frankfurt, 1976), pp. 60–65; "Die Seinsfrage und ihre sprachliche Grundlage," in *Philosophische Aufsätze* (Frankfurt, 1992), pp. 90–107.

43. J. Mcdowell, *Mind and World* (Cambridge, Mass., 1994).

44. With regard to the following, see A. Mueller, *Referenz und Fallibilismus* (doctoral dissertation, University of Frankfurt, 1999).

45. H. Putnam, "The Meaning of 'Meaning,'" in *Mind, Language, and Reality* (New York, 1978), pp. 215–271.

46. H. Putnam, *Representation and Reality* (Cambridge, Mass., 1988), p. 108; also "Reference and Truth," in *Realism and Reason* (New York, 1983), pp. 69–86.

47. "Although we have to use a *description* of extension to *give* the extension, we think of the component in question as being the *extension* (the *set*), not the description of the extension" (Putnam, *Mind, Language, and Reality*, p. 270).

48. See R. Rorty's early engagement with "conceptual relativism" in "The World Well Lost," *Journal of Philosophy*, vol. 69, no. 19 (1972), pp. 649–665.

49. See C. S. Peirce, *Collected Papers*, vol. 5, p. 408; K.-O. Apel, "The A Priori of the Communication Community and the Foundations of Ethics," in *Towards a Transformation of Philosophy*, pp. 225–300; and "Fallibilismus, Konsenstheorie der Wahrheit und Letztbegründung" (1987), in *Auseinandersetzungen*, pp. 81–194; H. Putnam, *Reason, Truth, and History* (New York, 1981) and *Realism and Reason;* and J. Habermas, "Wahrheitstheorien" (1972), in *Vorstudien und Ergänzungen*, pp. 127–186, and J. Habermas, *Between Facts and Norms*, trans. W. Rehg (Cambridge, Mass., 1996), pp. 13ff.

50. See S. Knell, "Dreifache Kontexttranszendenz," *Deutsche Zeitschrift für Philosophie*, vol. 46 (1998), pp. 563–581. Knell misunderstands the motivation for introducing an epistemic concept of truth because he already reads a conceptual connection between the truth claims made with assertions and "compelling" reasons off the "grammar" of the concept of knowledge. But the "grammatical presupposition" that we have "compelling" reasons at our disposal when we claim to know something is characteristic only of certainties of action in the mode of engaging in habitual practices, that is, within the horizon of the lifeworld in which the philosophically interesting "questions of truth" do not yet arise. As soon as these practices are disrupted and the performatively embedded certainties are problematized, the presumed availability of "compelling" reasons is shown to be illusory. Through the in principle fallible processes of justification that are initiated by the transition from action to discourse, we can search only for "better" reasons, not irretractable ones.

51. According to the proceduralist conception of truth, the condition of the universal capacity to agree is fulfilled by the fact that justified truth claims prove to be resistant to objections in the course of argumentation (which can be resumed at any time). In contrast, see Knell, "Dreifache Kontexttranszendenz," note 51.

52. This argument has been raised by Davidson, among others. It also applies to the regulatively powerless concept of a "final opinion" to be developed (according to Peirce) by a spatiotemporally completely unlimited communicative community of inquirers "at the end of time," as it were.

53. On the following, see L. Wingert, *Mit realistischem Sinn: Zur Erklärung empirischer Rechtfertigung* (Frankfurt am Main, forthcoming).

54. See pp. 256ff. below.

55. See pp. 206ff. below.

56. See pp. 277ff. below.

57. K. Günther, *The Sense of Appropriateness: Application Discourses in Morality and Law*, trans. John Farrell (Albany, N.Y., 1993).

58. K.-O. Apel, "Auflösung der Diskursethik? Zur Architektonik der Discursdifferenzierung in Habermas' *Faktizität und Geltung*," in *Diskurs und Verantwortung* (Frankfurt am Main, 1988), here p. 754.

59. J. Habermas, *Moral Consciousness and Communicative Action* (Cambridge, Mass., 1988), pp. 57ff. and p. 65.

60. See my discussion of Klaus Günther's theses in *Justification and Application: Remarks on Discourse Ethics* (Cambridge, Mass., 1993), pp. 36ff.

61. See pp. 206ff. below.

62. J. Habermas, *Between Facts and Norms*. pp. 401ff.

Chapter 1: Hermeneutic and Analytic Philosophy

1. This text was the basis for the final of a series of lectures organized by the Royal Institute of Philosophy in London between October 1997 and March 1998.

2. C. Taylor, "Theories of Meaning," in *Philosophical Papers*, vol. I (Cambridge, 1985) pp. 248–292.

3. On the influence of linguists such as J. Lohmann and L. Weisgerber on Heidegger, see K.-O. Apel, "Der philosophische Wahrheitsbegriff als Voraussetzung einer inhaltlich orientierten Sprachwissenschaft," in *Transformation der Philosophie*, vol. I (Frankfurt, 1973), pp. 106–137.

4. See my reply to Charles Taylor in A. Honneth and H. Joas, eds., *Communicative Action: Essays on Jürgen Habermas's The Theory of Communicative Action* (Cambridge, 1991), pp. 215–222.

5. K.-O. Apel, "Wittgenstein und Heidegger," in B. McGuiness, J. Habermas, et al., eds., *Der Löwe spricht . . . und wir können ihn nicht verstehen* (Frankfurt, 1991), pp. 27–68.

6. W. v. Humboldt, "Über den Nationalcharakter der Sprachen," in A. Flitner and K. Giel, eds., *Werke*, vol. III, *Schriften zur Sprachphilosophie* (Stuttgart, 1963), p. 77.

7. Humboldt, "Über den Einfluss des verschiedenen Charakters der Sprachen auf Literatur und Geistesbildung," *Werke*, vol. III, p. 26.

8. Humboldt, "Über die Verschiedenheiten des Menschlichen Sprachbaus," *Werke*, III, pp. 224ff.

9. [Although Habermas is here clearly not following the Fregean distinction between sense (*Sinn*) and reference (*Bedeutung*) and uses the German terms interchangeably, the distinction will play a significant role below where he distinguishes between *Sinn* and *Referenz*.—Trans.]

10. Humboldt, "Über die Verschiedenheiten des Menschlichen Sprachbaus," p. 196.

11. Humboldt, "Über den Nationalcharakter," p. 68.

12. Humboldt, "Über die Verschiedenheit des Menschlichen Sprachbaus und ihren Einfluss auf die geistige Entwicklung des Menschengeschlects," *Werke*, III, p. 438.

13. Ibid., p. 229.

14. Humboldt, "Sprachcharakter und Literatur," *Werke*, III, p. 30.

15. This is supposed to be true also for the representation of perceivable objects: "The expressions for sensual objects are equivalent insofar as the same object is thought of in all of them, but since they express the specific way of representing it, their meaning, too, diverges in this respect." *Werke*, III, p. 21.

16. For the following, see C. Lafont, *Heidegger, Language*, and *World-Disclosure* (Cambridge, 2000), introduction.

17. J. G. Hamann, "Metakritik. Über den Purismus der Vernunft" (1784), in J. G. Hamann, ed., *Schriften zur Sprache* (Frankfurt, 1967), p. 226.

18. Humboldt, "Über das vergleichende Sprachstudium," *Werke*, III, pp. 20ff: "For what remains to be conquered is, essentially, always what is objective, and if man approaches it on the subjective path of a peculiar language, his second effort is to re-isolate what is subjective, if only by exchanging one linguistic subjectivity for another, and to re-abstract from it what is objective in as pure a state as possible."

19. Humboldt, *Werke*, III, p. 81.

20. Humboldt, "Über das vergleichende Sprachstudium," *Werke*, III, p. 12.

21. Humboldt, "Über die Verschiedenheiten des Menschlichen Sprachbaus," p. 156.

22. This is why C. Lafont, in her discussion of Heidegger, emphasizes the problem of reference. See Lafont, *Heidegger, Language, and World-Disclosure*.

23. Humboldt, "Über die Verschiedenheiten des Menschlichen Sprachbaus," p. 201; see also Humboldt, "Über den Dualis," *Werke*, III, p. 139: "Nor can language attain reality by the efforts of the individual, it can do so only socially, only by following up the attempt that was hazarded with another, new one. The word, therefore, must achieve its essence and language its expansion, in someone who is listening and responding."

24. Ibid., pp. 138ff.

25. Humboldt, "Über die Verschiedenheiten des Menschlichen Sprachbaus," pp. 147ff.

26. J. Habermas, *The Theory of Communicative Action*, vol. 2, trans. Thomas McCarthy, (Boston: Beacon Press, 1984/87), pp. 113–152.

27. Humboldt, *Werke*, III, pp. 202ff.

28. L. Wittgenstein, *Tractatus logico-philosophicus* (London, 1974), pp. 40–42.

29. M. Dummett, *The Origins of Analytical Philosophy* (London, 1993), ch. 4.

30. *Tractatus*, 5.4711.

31. This is what Dummett means when he claims that the philosophers of the Vienna Circle, *unlike* Frege and Wittgenstein, were interested in a philosophy of language not "for its own sake," but because this "armoury" could furnish weapons "that would arm them for combat in other areas of philosophy." M. Dummett, "Can Analytical Philosophy Be Systematic and Ought It to Be?" in *Truth and Other Enigmas* (Cambridge, Mass., 1978), p. 443.

32. L. Wittgenstein, *Philosophical Investigations* (Oxford, 1958), p. 88 (para. 242); see the interpretations of part II of this work in E. v. Savigny and O. R. Scholz, eds., *Wittgenstein über die Seele* (Frankfurt, 1995).

33. M. Heidegger, *Being and Time* (Oxford, 1980), p. 194.

34. Heidegger, *Being and Time*, p. 61.

35. E. Husserl, *Erfahrung und Urteil* (Hamburg, 1948), pp. 6–10, pp. 15ff.

36. See C. Lafont, *Heidegger, Language, and World-Disclosure*, part I.

37. On Heidegger's critique of Humboldt, see C. Lafont, The *Linguistic Turn in Hermeneutic Philosophy*, trans. José Medina (Cambridge, 1999), ch. 3.

38. M. Heidegger, *On the Way to Language* (New York, 1982), pp. 126ff.

39. L. Wittgenstein, *On Certainty* (Oxford, 1974), p. 16 (para. 105).

40. J. Habermas, "Coping with Contingencies," in J. Niznik and J. T. Sanders, eds., *Debating the State of Philosophy* (Westport, 1996), pp. 1–24.

41. D. Davidson, *Inquiries Into Truth and Interpretation* (Oxford, 1984).

42. D. Davidson, "A Nice Derangement of Epitaphs," in E. Lepore, ed., *Truth and Interpretation* (Oxford, 1986), pp. 433–446. For critical comment, see Dummett, "'A Nice Derangement of Epitaphs': Some Comments on Davidson and Hacking," in the same volume, pp. 458–476.

43. R. Rorty, *Philosophy and the Mirror of Nature* (Princeton, 1979), p. 261.

44. R. Brandom, *Making It Explicit* (Cambridge, 1994), p. 5: "We are the ones on whom reasons are binding, who are subject to the peculiar force of the better reason."

45. K.-O. Apel, *Die Idee der Sprache in der Tradition des Humanismus von Dante bis Vico* (Bonn, 1963), p. 27.

46. Ibid., p. 38.

47. M. Dummett, "Language and Communication," in *The Seas of Language* (Oxford, 1993), p. 182.

48. K.-O. Apel, "Die Entfaltung der sprachanalytischen Philosophie und das Problem der Geisteswissenschaften," in *Transformation der Philosophie*, vol. II, pp. 28–95.

49. K.-O. Apel, "Wittgenstein und Heidegger," in *Transformation der Philosophie*, vol. I, pp. 225–275.

50. H.-G. Gadamer, *Truth and Method*, trans. J. Weinsheimer and D. Marshall (New York, 1988), part III.

51. K.-O. Apel, *Transformation der Philosophie*, vol. I, p. 49.

52. Ibid., vol. II, p. 352. Since I share and support this critique of the hypostatization of world-disclosure from the very start, I disagree with the tenor of the second chapter of Lafont, *The Linguistic Turn in Hermeneutic Philosophy*. The problem of reference that we indeed neglected provides just one of the many objections that I have been putting forward. See J. Habermas, *Postmetaphysical Thinking* (Cambridge, Mass., 1992), pp. 42ff., 46ff., 57ff., 134ff.; and J. Habermas, *The Philosophical Discourse of Modernity* (Cambridge, Mass., 1990), pp. 294ff.

53. E. Martens and H. Schnädelbach, *Philosophie* (Hamburg, 1985), p. 32.

54. J. Habermas, *On the Logic of the Social Sciences* (1967), trans. Shierry Weber Nicholson and Jerry A. Stark (Cambridge, 1988), pp. 271–305; K.-O. Apel et al., *Hemeneutik und Ideologiekritik* (Frankfurt, 1971). Subsequent to the work, published at the same time, of G. H. von Wright, *Explanation and Understanding* (London, 1971), the controversy was continued and extended to analytic contributions: K.-O. Apel, J. Mannichen, and R. Tuomela, eds., *Neue Versuche über Erklären und Verstehen* (Frankfurt, 1978).

55. K.-O. Apel, "Scientistics, Hermeneutics and the Critique of Ideology," in *Towards a Transformation of Philosophy*, trans. G. Adey and D. Frisby (London, 1980), pp. 93–135; Habermas, *Knowledge and Human Interests*, trans. Jeremy Shapiro (London, 1978), second edition.

56. For my own work on the linguistic pragmatics, see J. Habermas, *On the Pragmatics of Communication*, ed. Maeve Cooke (Cambridge, Mass., 1998).

57. J. Habermas, "Appendix" in *Knowledge and Human Interests*.

58. J. Habermas, "Wahrheitstheorien" (1972) in *Vorstudien und Ergänzungen zur Theories des kommunikativen Handelns* (Frankfurt, 1983), pp. 127–183.

59. Apel, *Transformation der Philosophie*, p. 333.

60. K.-O. Apel, "The A Priori of the Communication Community and the Foundations of Ethics," in *Transformation of Philosophy*, pp. 225–300; K.-O. Apel, *Diskurs und Verantwortung* (Frankfurt, 1988).

61. Habermas, *Theory of Communicative Action*.

62. See my preface to the new edition of J. Habermas, *On the Logic of the Social Sciences.*

63. J. R. Searle, *Speech Acts* (Cambridge, 1969); J. R. Searle, *Expression and Meaning* (Cambridge, 1979); for a critique of Searle's intentionalism, see K.-O. Apel, "Is Intentionality More Than Linguist Meaning?" in E. Lepore and R. von Gulick, eds., *John Searle and His Critics* (Oxford, 1991), pp. 31–56; J. Habermas, "Comments on J. Searle: Meaning, Communication, and Representation," pp. 17–30, in the same volume.

64. M. Dummett, "What is a Theory of Meaning? II," in *The Seas of Language* (Oxford, 1993), pp. 34–93.

65. J. Habermas, *Theory of Communicative Action*, vol. 1, pp. 273–337, vol. 2, pp. 119–135.

66. M. Dummett, "Language and Truth," in *The Seas of Language*, p. 142: "What we have been considering are two alternative ways of explaining the meanings of sentences of a language: in terms of how we establish them as true; and in terms of what is involved in accepting them as true. . . . they are complementary in that both are needed to give an account of the practice of speaking the language."

67. See the theory of language of R. Brandom, *Making It Explicit* (Cambridge, Mass., 1994), based on the complementary relation of inferential semantics and formal pragmatics.

68. Habermas, *Theory of Communicative Action*, vol. 1, pp. 22–42.

69. J. Habermas, "Rorty's Pragmatic Turn," in *On the Pragmatics of Communication*, pp. 343–382.

70. See the objection by Michael Dummett in his *Origins of Analytic Philosophy* (Cambridge, Mass., 1994), pp. 7ff.

71. L. Wittgenstein, *Vermischte Bemerkungen* (Frankfurt, 1977).

72. J. Habermas, "Individuation through Socialization: On George Herbert Mead's Theory of Subjectivity," in *Postmetaphysical Thinking* (Cambridge, 1992), pp. 149–204.

73. W. v. Humboldt, "Über die Verschiedenheiten des Menschlichen Sprachbaus," *Werke*, vol. III, pp. 160ff.

74. Habermas, *Theory of Communicative Action*, vol. 1, pp. 363–365.

Chapter 2: From Kant's "Ideas" of Pure Reason to the "Idealizing" Presuppositions of Communicative Action

1. Thomas McCarthy, *Ideals and Illusions* (Cambridge, Mass., 1991), p. 2.

2. Ibid., p. 4.

3. David Couzens Hoy and Thomas McCarthy, *Critical Theory* (Oxford, 1994), p. 38. [Note that references to this work hereafter refer to the chapters written by McCarthy.—Trans.]

4. Ibid., p. 39.

5. Here I need not revisit the domestic dispute within the domestic dispute. See T. McCarthy, "Practical Discourse: On the Relation of Morality to Politics," *Ideals and Illusions*, pp. 181–199; "Legitimacy and Diversity: Dialectical Reflections on Analytic Distinctions," in M. Rosenfeld and A. Arato, eds., *Habermas on Law and Democracy* (Berkeley, Calif., 1998), pp. 115–153. For my reply, see "Reply to Symposium Participants," in *Habermas on Law and Democracy*, pp. 391–404.

6. J. Habermas, *On the Pragmatics of Communication*, ed. and trans. M. Cooke (Cambridge, Mass., 1998).

7. Hoy and McCarthy, *Critical Theory*, p. 38.

8. J. Habermas, "Some Further Clarifications of the Concept of Communicative Rationality," *Pragmatics of Communication*, chap. 7.

9. See Immanuel Kant, *Critique of Pure Reason*, trans. N. K. Smith (New York, 1929), pp. 98, 384ff.

10. On Putnam's theory of reference, which is relevant here, see A. Mueller, *Referenz und Fallibilismus* (Berlin, 2001).

11. For a discussion of Peter Strawson's investigations on this topic, see M. Niquet, *Transzendentale Argumente* (Frankfurt am Main, 1991), chaps. 4 and 5.

12. On Putnam's "internal realism," see J. Habermas, "Values and Norms," this volume, pp. 213ff.

13. Karl-Otto Apel, "Sinnkonstitution und Geltungsrechtfertigung," in Forum für Philosophie, ed., *Martin Heidegger: Innen- und Außenansichten* (Frankfurt am Main 1989), p. 134.

14. C. S. Peirce, *Collected Papers*, vol. V/VI (1934), p. 268: "The opinion which is fated to be ultimately agreed to by all who investigate, is what we mean by the truth, and the object represented in this opinion is the real" (5.407). See also K.-O. Apel, *Charles S. Peirce: From Pragmatism to Pragmaticism*, trans. J. M. Krois (Amherst, Mass., 1981).

15. See the critique of the discursive conception of truth in Albrecht Wellmer, "Ethics and Dialogue: Elements of Moral Judgment in Kant and Discourse Ethics," *The Persistence of Modernity*, trans. D. Midgley (Cambridge, Mass., 1991), pp. 145ff.; Christina Lafont, *The Linguistic Turn in Hermeneutic Philosophy* (Cambridge, Mass., 1999), pp. 283ff.

16. J. Habermas, "Richard Rorty's Pragmatic Turn," *Pragmatics of Communication*, chap. 8.

17. J. Habermas, this volume pp. 36ff., 252ff., and "Rorty's Pragmatic Turn," p. 369.

18. On the "hermeneutics of an always already linguistically interpreted being-in-the-world," see K.-O. Apel, "Wittgensetin und Heidegger," in B. McGuinness et al., eds., *Der Löwe spricht . . . und wir können ihn nicht verstehen* (Frankfurt, 1991), pp. 27–68.

19. Richard F. Bernstein, *Beyond Objectivism and Relativism* (Philadelphia, 1983).

20. The quoted phrase is found in Kant's *Grounding for the Metaphysics of Morals,* second ed., trans. J. W. Ellington (Indianapolis, 1981), p. 59 (Ak. 460).

21. J. Habermas, *Between Facts and Norms,* trans. W. Rehg (Cambridge, Mass., 1996), p. 5.

22. Kant, *Grounding,* p. 40 (Ak. 433).

23. This insight can already be found in Emile Durkheim, *The Rules of Sociological Method,* eighth ed., trans. S. A. Soloray and J. H. Mueller, ed. G. E. G. Catlin (New York, 1966).

24. Hans-Georg Gadamer, *Truth and Method,* second ed., trans. J. Weinsheimer and D. Marshall (New York, 1990). Because he has in mind the appropriation of classical works, however, Gadamer is misled to aestheticize the problem of truth; see J. Habermas, "Wie ist nach dem Historismus noch Metaphysik möglich?" *Neue Zürcher Zeitung,* 12/13 (February 2000).

25. See Wellmer's critique in "Ethics and Dialogue," pp. 160ff.

26. Kant, *Grounding,* p. 42, n. 28 (Ak. 436).

27. William Rehg, *Insight and Solidarity* (Berkeley, Calif., 1994).

28. On the following, see J. Habermas, "A Genealogical Analysis of the Cognitive Content of Morality," in *The Inclusion of the Other,* ed. C. Cronin and P. De Greiff (Cambridge, Mass., 1998), pp. 3–46, here pp. 43ff.

29. On the following, see J. Habermas, "Rightness vs. Truth," this volume, pp. 237–276.

30. [In German, the same term, *bestehen,* isused to say that a state of affairs *obtains.* See p. 91 above.—Trans.]

31. [Habermas does not differentiate systematically between *Sinn* (sense) and *Bedeutung* (reference) in the way that Frege did, that is, to indicate a distinction between the object of reference and its mode of presentation. Elsewhere, however, Habermas does appeal to this very distinction in terms of *Sinn* and *Referenz.*—Trans.]

32. E. Tugendhat, *Einführung in die sprachanalytische Philosophie* (Frankfurt am Main, 1976), pp. 35ff.

33. H. Putnam, "The Meaning of 'Meaning,' " in his *Mind, Language, and Reality* (Cambridge, 1975), pp. 215–271.

34. G. Frege, "Der Gedanke" (1918/19), in *Logische Untersuchungen* (Göttingen, 1966), pp. 30–53. Here, Frege concludes that thoughts are neither things in the

external world nor ideas, but that a third realm must be acknowledged: "Die Gedanken sind weder Dinge der Aussenwelt noch Vorstellungen. Ein drittes Reich muss anerkannt werden" (p. 43).

35. [The T-sentences that are thus generated give the meaning of expressions.—Trans.]

36. Donald Davidson, *Inquiries into Truth and Interpretation* (Oxford, 1984), p. xiv.

37. D. Davidson, "Radical Interpretation," in *Inquiries into Truth and Interpretation,* p. 137.

38. B. Fultner, *Radical Interpretation or Communicative Action: Holism in Davidson and Habermas,* Ph.D. dissertation, Northwestern University, 1995, pp. 178ff.

39. A. Cutrofello, "On the Transcendental Pretensions of the Principle of Charity," in L. E. Hahn, ed., *The Philosophy of Donald Davidson* (LaSalle, Ill., 1999), p. 333: "The principle of charity is supposed to be a universally binding condition for the very possibility of interpreting anyone at all." In his response, Davidson accepts the term "transcendental" in the weak sense of a de facto inevitability; in any case, he speaks of "the inevitability of the appeal to that principle" (*The Philosophy of Davidson,* p. 342).

40. D. Davidson, "A Nice Derangement of Epitaphs," in Ernest Lepore, ed., *Truth and Interpretation* (Oxford, 1986), pp. 433–446.

41. D. Davidson, *Essays on Actions and Events* (Oxford, 1980).

42. See Hahn, ed., *The Philosophy of Donald Davidson,* p. 600.

43. D. Davidson, "Could There be a Science of Rationality?" *International Journal of Philosophical Studies* 3, 1995, 1–16, here p. 4.

44. R. Rorty, "Davidson's Mental-Physical Distinction," in Hahn, ed., *The Philosophy of Donald Davidson,* pp. 575–594.

45. D. Davidson, "The Myth of the Subjective," in *Subjective, Intersubjective, Objective* (Oxford, 2001), p. 44.

46. D. Davidson, "The Conditions of Thought" in *The Mind of Donald Davidson,* Johannes Brandl and Wolfgang L. Gombocz, eds. (Amsterdam, 1989), p. 198.

47. Ibid., p. 199.

48. Post hoc, I have encountered the same objection in John Fennell, "Davidson on Meaning Normativity: Public or Social," *European Journal of Philosophy* 8 (2000): "The regularity in the environment, the identification of the common stimuli as *the* ones we are both responding to involves a normative similarity judgment. . . . In order to make the required judgment of normative similarity the interpreter must exceed what is available to an external observer. . . . Hence triangulation faces the problem of the identification of the common stimuli. . . . and triangulation, if it is understood in purely causal terms as the correlation of stimulus-response groupings, leaves this problem unanswered" (p. 149).

49. Wilfrid Sellars, *Empiricism and the Philosophy of Mind* (Cambridge, Mass., 1997), p. 63.

50. J. Habermas, *Theory of Communicative Action*, trans. Thomas McCarthy, (Boston, 1984/1987), vol. 2, pp. 3–42.

51. H.-G. Gadamer, *Truth and Method*, p. 294.

52. Ibid., p. 262.

53. On this, see K.-O. Apel, "Wittgenstein and the Problem of Hermeneutical Understanding," in *Towards a Transformation of Philosophy* (London, 1980), pp. 1–45.

54. M. Dummett, "Language and Communication," in *The Seas of Language* (Oxford, 1993), p. 181.

55. Ibid., pp. 182ff.

56. M. Dummett, "Language and Truth," in *The Seas of Language*, p. 143.

57. J. Habermas, "From Kant to Hegel: On Robert Brandoms Pragmatics of Language," pp. 131–174, this volume.

58. R. Brandom, *Making It Explicit* (Cambridge, Mass., 1994), p. 5.

59. Ibid., p. 4.

Chapter 3:   From Kant to Hegel

1. What springs to mind in the German context is the affinity with aspects of the constructivism of the Erlangen School, in particular in its Wittgensteinian development by F. Kambartel, and with K.-O. Apel's transcendental pragmatics. There are convergences, too, with my own efforts to develop a formal pragmatics, beginning with the 1970–1971 Gauss lectures on the linguistic foundation of sociology (Jürgen Habermas, "Reflections on the Linguistic Foundation of Sociology," in *On the Pragmatics of Social Interaction* (Cambridge, Mass., 2001), pp. 1–103) and the 1976 treatise "What Is Universal Pragmatics?" (in J. Habermas, *On the Pragmatics of Communication*, ed. Maeve Cooke (Cambridge, Mass., 1998), pp. 21–103.

2. Robert B. Brandom, *Making It Explicit: Reasoning, Representing, and Discursive Commitment* (Cambridge, Mass., 1994), p. 5. (Subsequent page numbers in the text refer to this edition.)

3. "Correctnesses of application are discussed under the general headings of assessments of truth or representation; correctnesses of inference are discussed under the general heading of assessments of rationality." Ibid., p. 18.

4. "Being a reason is to be understood in the first instance in terms of what it is for a community to treat something in practice as such a reason . . . [as] *reasons for claims*" (ibid., p. 253, my emphasis).

5. J. Habermas, "Action, Speech Acts, Linguistically Mediated Interactions, and the Lifeworld," in J. Habermas, *On the Pragmatics of Communication*, pp. 215–255.

6. Piaget talks about "reflective abstraction" in this context.

7. [Habermas treats Brandom's talk about *claims* consistently as talk about *truth* claims. For the sake of the integrity of Habermas's arguments, the translation preserves the reference to truth.—Trans.]

8. See the theory of meaning that I present in the first "Intermediate Reflections" (in *The Theory of Communicative Action*, reprinted in revised translation in Habermas, *On the Pragmatics of Communication*, pp. 105–213); it should be noted, however, that this was worked out in the context of the theory of action. Here I develop the thesis that we understand a speech act if we know what makes it acceptable. I already make the distinction (see *On the Pragmatics of Communication*, p. 130) between the "content" of an utterance, which we understand if we know the conditions of its correct application, and the "obligations relevant for the sequel of interaction," that is, the consequences that would ensue from the utterance's being accepted.

9. See R. Brandom, *Making It Explicit*, pp. 102–116.

10. See R. Brandom, "Pragmatism, Phenomenalism, and Truth-Talk," *Midwest Studies in Philosophy* 12 (1988): pp. 75–93.

11. This point is emphasized by Gideon Rosen: "Some counterfactual assessment must be intended. But now comes the crucial question: how is the idealization to be characterized?" G. Rosen, "Who Makes the Rules Around Here?" *Philosophy and Phenomenological Research* 57 (1997): p. 170.

12. Thus the license that an entrance ticket confers on its owner (see *Making It Explicit*, pp. 161ff.) is supposed to shed light on the truth claim to which the speaker is authorized by the acknowledged status of her assertion, whereas the role of the ticket giver who tears off the ticket, thereby performatively confirming entitlement to enter, is compared to the role of an interpreter who acknowledges a speaker's entitlement to make an assertion. Similarly, the performatively binding character of the "queen's shilling" (the reference is to the eighteenth-century British practice of offering drinking money to unsuspecting victims in taverns in order to recruit them as soldiers against their will) is supposed to illustrate the binding power that the status of an utterance attributed by the interpreter has for its speaker. As a consequence of the assimilation of norms of rationality to norms of action, Brandom also uses (see *Making It Explicit*, pp. 163ff.) a broad conception of commitment that embraces morally binding "promises" as much as speech-act-immanent obligations.

13. R. Brandom, "Heidegger's Categories in Being and Time," *Monist* 66, no. 3 (1983): pp. 387–409.

14. Ibid., pp. 403–404.

15. Ibid., p. 405.

16. I have benefited from remarks by Michael Williams in a discussion with Robert Brandom, Thomas McCarthy and Richard Rorty in November 1997 in Charlottesville, Virginia.

17. See Tugendhat, *Traditional and Analytic Philosophy* (Cambridge, 1982), pp. 212–227.

18. This is the objection raised by R. Rorty in "What Do You Do When They Call You a Relativist?" *Philosophy and Phenomenological Research* 57 (1997): p. 174.

19. See H. Putnam, "The Meaning of 'Meaning', in *Mind, Language, and Reality*, vol. 2, *Philosophical Papers* (New York, 1975), pp. 215–271.

20. [I have altered Habermas's orginial example (*Walfische sind Säugetiere*) in order to convey the philosophical point he is making.—Trans.]

21. R. Brandom, "Freedom and Constraint by Norms," *American Philosophical Quarterly* 16 (1979), here p. 190.

22. On this operation, see Donald Davidson's classic essay "Truth and Meaning," in *Inquiries Into Truth and Interpretation* (Oxford, 1984).

23. G. H. von Wright, "Die Stellung der Psychologie under den Wissenschaften," in *Rektorat der Universität Leipzig* (Leipzig, 1997), pp. 21–32.

24. This pragmatist alternative is also emphasized by I. Levi, "Review of *Making It Explicit*," *Journal of Philosophy* 43 (1996): pp. 145–158.

25. See K.-O. Apel, *From Pragmatism to Pragmaticism* (J. M. Krois, trans.; Atlantic Highlands 1995), part two.

26. There is a related train of thought in J. McDowell, *Mind and World* (Cambridge, Mass., 1994): lecture IV, pp. 66ff. See also the discussion between McDowell and Brandom in J. McDowell, "Brandom on Representation and Inference," *Philosophy and Phenomenological Research*, vol. 52 (1997): pp. 157–162; and R. Brandom, "A Precis of *Making It Explicit*", *Philosophy and Phenomenological Research*, vol. 52 (1997): pp. 153–156.

27. J. Habermas, *Postmetaphysical Thinking*, trans. W. M. Hohengarten (Cambridge, Mass., 1992), pp. 28ff.

28. I have put this as follows elsewhere: "What makes us stand apart from nature is the only thing whose nature we are capable of knowing: language." In J. Habermas, *Technik und Wissenschaft als 'Ideologie,'* (Frankfurt, 1968), p. 163.

29. M. Dummett, *The Origins of Analytical Philosophy* (London, 1993).

30. Of course, if we conceive of the world in the sense favored by me as the totality of the objects of reference of possible statements, the facts that we state about objects can be formulated only in "our" language. A contextualist understanding of competing descriptions does not necessarily follow from this: Putnam, for example, combines a theoretical pluralism of scientific descriptions with an internally realist theory of knowledge.

31. See J. McDowell, *Mind and World*, lecture V, pp. 87ff.

32. Brandom, "Freedom and Constraint by Norms," *American Philosophical Quarterly*, vol. 16 (1979): p. 192.

33. This dimly recalls N. Hartmann's stratified ontology; see N. Hartmann, *Die Philosophie der Natur* (Berlin, 1950) and *Der Aufbau der realen Welt* (Berlin, 1964).

34. See my "Remarks on J. Searle's 'Meaning, Communication, and Representation,'" in *On the Pragmatics of Communication*, pp. 257–275.

35. See my "Toward a Critique of the Theory of Meaning," in *On the Pragmatics of Communication*, pp. 277–306.

36. R. Brandom, in a letter to me dated November 16, 1997.

37. K.-O. Apel, "Die Logosauszeichnung der menschlichen Sprache," in *Perspektiven der Sprache*, ed. H. G. Bosshardt (Berlin, 1986), pp. 45–87.

38. E. Cassirer, " 'Mind' and 'Life': Heidegger," trans. J. M. Krois, *Philosophy and Rhetoric*, vol. 16 (1983): pp. 160–163.

Chapter 4: From Kant to Hegel and Back Again

1. Jürgen Habermas, "Conceptions of Modernity," in *The Postnational Constellation: Political Essays*, trans. Max Pensky (Cambridge, Mass., 2001), pp. 130–156.

2. As the subtitle of K. Löwith, *Von Hegel zu Nietzsche: Der Revolutionäre Bruch im Denken des 19. Jahrhundert.* (Zurich, 1941) puts it.

3. J. Habermas, "Labour and Interaction," in *Theory and Practice* (London, 1974), pp. 142–169.

4. M. Theunissen, "Die verdrängte Intersubjektivität in Hegels Philosophie des Rechts," in *Hegels Philosophie des Rechts*, ed. D. Henrich and R. P. Horstmann (Stuttgart, 1982), pp. 317–381.

5. J. Habermas, *The Philosophical Discourse of Modernity* (Cambridge, Mass., 1987), chap. 2.

6. For a systematic development of this perspective, see A. Honneth, *The Struggle for Recognition* (Cambridge, Mass., 1996).

7. Manfred Frank, *Selbstbewusstsein und Selbsterkenntnis* (Stuttgart, 1991), pp. 9–49, and the two readers edited by, him: *Selbstbewusstseinstheorien von Fichte bis Sartre* (Frankfurt am Main, 1991) and *Analytische Theorien des Selbstbewusstseins* (Frankfurt, am Main, 1994). On the debate between Henrich, Tugendhat, and myself, see B. Mauersberg, "Der lange Abschied von der Bewusstseinsphilosophie" (Ph.D. dissertation, University of Frankfurt, 1999).

8. See also R. Rorty, *Philosophy and the Mirror of Nature* (Princeton, 1979).

9. R. B. Pippin, "Kant on the Spontaneity of Mind," in *Idealism as Modernism* (Cambridge, 1997), pp. 29ff.

10. R. Brandom, *Making It Explicit* (Cambridge, Mass., 1994), pp. 614ff.

11. M. Theunissen, *Sein und Schein* (Frankfurt, 1978), chap. 1.

12. G. W. F. Hegel, *Jenaer Systementwürfe*, vol. I (Hamburg, 1986), fragment 20, pp. 203ff. ["Es ist vollkommen falsch, in der empirischen Anschauung so wie im

310

Notes to pages 175–212

Gedächtnis und im Begreifen diese Momente des Bewusstseins zu betrachten als zusammengesetzt aus den beiden Seiten des Gegensatzes, so dass jedes von ihnen einen Teil zu dem Eins beitrage und zu fragen, was in dieser Zusammensetzung das Tätige jedes Teils sei."]

13. Ibid., p. 205. ["Es muss eigentlich weder von einem solchern Subjekte noch Objekte die Rede sein, sondern vom Geist!"]

14. E. Rothacker, *Logik und Systematik der Geisteswissenschaften* (Bonn, 1948).

15. K. Ott, *Menschenkenntnis als Wissenschaft: Über die Entstehung und Logik der Historie als der Wissenschaft vom Individuellen* (Frankfurt am Main, 1991).

16. R. Koselleck, *Vergangene Zukunft: Zur Semantik geschichtlicher Zeiten* (Frankfurt am Main, 1989).

17. G. W. F. Hegel, *Phänomenologie des Geistes* (Leipzig, 1949), p. 229.

18. Hegel, *Jenaer Systementwürfe I*, fragment 15, p. 182. ["Was das Individuum für sich tut, (wird) unmittelbar ein Tun für die ganze Gattung; . . . und ebenso (wird) das Sein und Tun der ganzen Gattung zum Sein und Tun des Individuums; der animalische Eigennutz ist unmittelbar uneigennützig und die Uneigennützigkeit, das Aufheben der Einzelheit des Individuums, unmittelbar Nutzen des Individuums."]

19. J. Habermas, "Individuation through Socialization: On George Herbert Mead's Theory of Subjectivity," in *Postmetaphysical Thinking* (Cambridge, Mass., 1992) pp. 149–204.

20. L. Wingert, *Gemeinsinn und Moral* (Frankfurt am Main, 1993), pp. 179ff.

21. G. W. F. Hegel, *Jenaer Systementwürfe I*, p. 191. ["Ihre Einheit erscheint als eine Mitte zwischen ihnen, als Werk beider, als das Dritte, worauf sie sich beziehen, in dem sie eins sind."]

22. Hegel, *Jenaer Systementwürfe I*, fragment 18, p. 193. ["Jene erste gebundene Existenz des Bewusstseins als Mitte ist sein Sein als Sprache, als Werkzeug. . . ."]

23. Hegel, *Jenaer Systementwürfe* vol. III (Hamburg, 1987), p. 175.

24. Hegel, *Jenaer Systementwürfe I*, fragment 20, p. 208. ["Das Bewusstsein (organisiert sich) in der Sprache zur Totalität des Idealen."]

25. Ibid., fragment 20, pp. 202ff.

26. Hegel, *Jenaer Systementwürfe III*, p. 178. ["Die Übung des Gedächtnisses ist deswegen die erste Arbeit des erwachten Geistes."]

27. Hegel, *Jenaer Systementwürfe I*, fragment 20, p. 211. ["Das Werkzeug ist die existierende, vernünftige Mitte. . . . Es ist das, worin das Arbeiten sein Bleiben hat, was von dem Arbeitenden und dem Bearbeiteten allein übrig bleibt und worin ihre Zufälligkeit sich verewigt."] Hegel holds on to this insight; see G. W. F. Hegel, *Wissenschaft der Logik*, 2 vols. (Hamburg, 1951), vol. 2, p. 398: "In this sense the means is something higher than the ultimate aim . . .; the plow is more noble than immediate enjoyment. . . . The tool remains, whereas immediate enjoyment fades

and is forgotten!" ["Insofern ist das Mittel ein Höheres als die endlichen Zwecke . . .; der Pflug ist ehrenvoller als unmittelbar die Genüsse . . . Das Werkzeug erhält sich, während die unmittelbaren Genüsse vergehen und vergessen werden."]

28. Hegel, *Jenaer Systementwürfe III*, p. 190. ["Hier tritt der Trieb ganz aus der Arbeit zurück; er lässt die Natur sich abreiben, sieht ruhig zu, und regiert nur mit leichter Mühe das Ganze—List."]

29. On the level of objective spirit Hegel conceives language, following Herder and Humboldt, as the energy that is manifested in the linguistically articulated worldview of a people: "Language exists only as the language of a people. . . . Language is the ideal existence of spirit, in which it expresses itself, only as the work of a people!" Hegel, *Jenaer Systementwürfe I*, p. 226. ["Die Sprache ist nur als Sprache eines Volkes. . . . Nur als Werk eines Volkes ist die Sprache die ideale Existenz des Geistes, in welcher er sich ausspricht."] Need-satisfaction, labor, and technology assume an objective shape in the context of a conflict-ridden market society that requires political constraints: "Need and labor, raised to this level of generality, build up in a great people an immense system of common and reciprocal dependency, a self-moving life of something dead, which shifts blindly and elementally to and fro in its movement and, like a wild animal, requires continuous and strict control and taming!" (Ibid., p. 230). ["Das Bedürfnis und die Arbeit, in diese Allgemeinheit erhoben, bildet so für sich in einem grossen Volk ein ungeheures System von Gemeinschaftlichkeit und gegenseitiger Abhängigkeit, ein sich in sich bewegendes Leben des Toten, das in seiner Bewegung blind und elementarisch sich hin und her bewegt und als ein wildes Tier einer ständigen strengen Beherrschung und Bezähmung bedarf."]

30. Ibid., p. 193.

31. Hegel, *Jenaer Systementwürfe III*, p. 192. ["Jedes ist darin (in der Liebe) dem anderen gleich, worin er sich ihm entgegengesetzt hat. Sein Unterscheiden vom Anderen ist daher ein Sichgleichsetzen mit ihm."]

32. On "love," "law," and "civic solidarity" as the different stages of mutual recognition in Hegel's writings of the Jena period, see A. Honneth, *Kampf um Anerkennung* (Frankfurt, 1992).

33. Hegel, *Jenaer Systementwürfe III*, p. 232. ["Allgemeinheit in der vollkommenen Freiheit und Selbständigkeit des Einzelnen."]

34. M. Theunissen, *Der Andere* (Berlin, 1977) chap. 6; J. Habermas, "Reflections on the Linguistic Foundation of Sociology," in *On the Pragmatics of Social Interaction* (Cambridge, Mass., 2001), pp. 23–44; A. Honneth, "The Struggle for Recognition: On Sartre's Theory of Intersubjectivity," in *The Fragmented World of the Social*, ed. Charles W. Wright (Albany, 1996).

35. Hegel, *Phänomenologie des Geistes*, p. 141. ["Das Selbstbewusstsein ist an und für sich, indem und dadurch, dass es für ein anderes an und für sich ist; d.h. es ist nur als ein Anerkanntes."]

36. Ibid., p. 143. ["Sie anerkennen sich, als gegenseitig sich anerkennend."]

37. T. Pinkard, *Hegel's Phenomenology: The Sociality of Reason* (Cambridge, 1994), p. 57.

38. Ibid., p. 61.

39. Ibid., p. 62.

40. C. Taylor, *Hegel* (Cambridge, 1983), chap. 1.

41. H.-G. Gadamer, *Truth and Method,* trans. J. Weinsheimer and D. Marshall (New York, 1988).

42. G. W. F. Hegel, *Philosophie des Rechts* (Hamburg, 1953), Vorrede, p. 16. ["Mit der subjektiven Freiheit nicht in einem Besonderen und Zufälligen, sondern in dem, was an und für sich ist, zu stehen."]

43. Pinkard, *Hegel's Phenomenology: The Sociality of Reason,* p. 252.

44. Ibid., p. 222.

45. Ibid., pp. 222, 254.

46. G. W. F. Hegel, *Enzyklopädie der philosophischen Wissenschaften,* ed. E. Molden-hauer and K. Michelet, vols. 8–10, *Werke* (Frankfurt am Main, 1970), §381. ["Der Geist hat für uns die Natur zu seiner Voraussetzung, deren Wahrheit, und damit deren absolut Erstes er ist."]

47. Hegel, *Phänomenologie des Geistes,* p. 556. [". . . seinem vollständigen und wahren Inhalt zugleich die Form des Selbsts gibt."]

48. Ibid., p. 559. ["Die Zeit ist der Begriff, der da ist . . .; deswegen erscheint der Geist notwendig in der Zeit, (aber) er erscheint (nur) solange in der Zeit, als er nicht seinen reinen Begriff erfaßt, d.h. nicht die Zeit tilgt."]

49. Hegel, *Enzyklopädie der philosophischen Wissenschaften,* §§411, 458ff.

50. Hegel, *Wissenschaft der Logik,* "Teleologie," esp. pp. 396ff.

51. Ibid., p. 220.

52. D. Henrich, *Hegel im Kontext* (Frankfurt am Main, 1971).

53. Taylor, *Hegel.*

54. Hegel, *Phänomenologie des Geistes,* pp. 424ff.

55. J. Habermas, "Morality and Ethical Life: Does Hegel's Critique of Kant Apply to Discourse Ethics?" in *Moral Consciousness and Communicative Action* (Cambridge, Mass., 1990), pp. 195–215.

56. K. Günther, *The Sense of Appropriateness: Application Discourses in Morality and Law,* trans. John Farrell (Albany, 1993).

57. Hegel, *Philosophie des Rechts,* §144. ["Ein . . . über das subjektive Meinen und Belieben erhabenes Bestehen."]

58. Ibid., §260. ["... die ungeheure Stärke und Tiefe, das Prinzip der Subjektivität sich zum selbständigen Extreme der persönlichen Besonderheit vollenden zu lassen und es zugleich in die substantielle Einheit zurückzuführen."]

59. J. Habermas, *Between Facts and Norms: Contributions to a Discourse Theory of Law and Democracy*, trans. William Rehg (Cambridge, Mass., 1996).

60. Hegel, *Philosophie des Rechts*, p. 16. ["Fessel irgendeines Abstraktums, das nicht zum Begriff befreit ist."]

61. M. Neves, *Symbolische Konstitutionalisierung* (Berlin, 1998). L. F. Schwartz, *Die Hoffnung auf radikale Demokratie* (Ph.D. dissertation, University of Frankfurt).

62. Ulrich Beck, *Was Ist Globalisierung?* (Frankfurt am Main, 1997) and Ulrich Beck, ed., *Politik der Globalisierung?* (Frankfurt am Main, 1998).

63. Habermas, *The Postnational Constellation*.

Chapter 5: Norms and Values

1. This essay was the opening address for a conference entitled "Putnam and the Tradition of Pragmatism" in Münster, June 14–18, 2000.

2. This concluding reservation is at the same time meant to be a metacritical reply to objections that Putnam raised in a paper entitled "Values and Norms" on the occasion of my seventieth birthday in Frankfurt in 1999. See H. Putnam, "Werte und Normen," in *Die Öffentlichkeit der Vernunft und die Vernunft der Öffentlichkeit*, ed. Lutz Wingert and Klaus Günther (Frankfurt am Main, 2001), pp. 280–313. The English version appears in H. Putnam, *The Collapse of the Fact/Value Distinction and Other Essays* (Cambridge, Mass., 2002), pp. 111–134.

3. M. Horkheimer, *Zur Kritik der instrumentellen Vernunft* (1947; Frankfurt, 1967), p. 66.

4. Ibid., p. 80; on the double orientation of early critical theory, see Jürgen Habermas, *Theory of Communicative Action*, trans. Thomas McCarthy (Boston, 1984/1987), vol. 1, pp. 372–377.

5. H. Putnam, "Why Is a Philosopher?" in *Realism with a Human Face* (Cambridge, Mass., 1990), p. 116.

6. J. Habermas, "Rorty's Pragmatic Turn," in *On the Pragmatics of Communication*, ed. Maeve Cooke (Cambridge, Mass., 1998), pp. 343–382.

7. H. Putnam, *Pragmatism* (Oxford, 1992), p. 29.

8. H. Putnam, "Why Reason Can't Be Naturalized," in *Realism and Reason* (Cambridge, 1983), p. 230.

9. H. Putnam, "The Question of Realism," in *Words and Life* (Cambridge, Mass., 1994), p. 299.

10. Putnam, *Words and Life*, p. xxix.

314

Notes to pages 213–236

11. K.-O. Apel, *Transformation der Philosophie*, 2 vols. (Frankfurt, 1973).

12. Putnam, *Pragmatism*, p. 46; see also Putnam, *Words and Life*, p. 283.

13. H. Putnam, "Realism Without Absolutes," in *Words and Life*, p. 282.

14. H. Putnam, "Rethinking Mathematical Necessity," in *Words and Life*, p. 256.

15. H. Putnam, "The Craving for Objectivity," in *Realism With a Human Face*, pp. 125ff.

16. On the debate between Putnam and Rorty, see J. Habermas, "The Unity of Reason in the Diversity of Its Voices," in J. Habermas, *Postmetaphysical Thinking*, trans. W. M. Hohengarten (Cambridge, Mass., 1992), pp. 115–148, here pp. 135ff.

17. Putnam, "Why Reason Can't Be Naturalized," in *Realism and Reason*, p. 234.

18. H. Putnam, "Pragmatism and Moral Objectivity," in *Words and Life*, p. 174.

19. H. Putnam, "Beyond the Fact/Value Dichotomy," in *Realism With a Human Face*, p. 141.

20. Putnam, "Pragmatisms and Objectivity," in *Words and Life*, p. 170.

21. Putnam, "Pragmatism and Relativism," in *Words and Life*, p. 195.

22. Putnam, "Values and Norms."

23. J. McDowell, "Virtue and Reason," *Monist* 62 (1979), pp. 331–350.

24. H. Putnam, *Reason, Truth, and History*, pp. 174ff.; Putnam, "Pragmatism and Moral Objectivity," in *Realism With a Human Face*, pp. 170ff.

25. Putnam, "Objectivity and the Science/Ethics Distinction," in *Words and Life*, p. 171.

26. Putnam, "The Craving for Objectivity," p. 131: "Newton got it right when he said that the tides are caused by the gravitational pull of the moon and the sun. He got it right, even though his statement has been reinterpreted in an age of general relativity and may have to be reinterpreted as long as there continue to be scientific revolution in physics."

27. Putnam approvingly cites Wittgenstein's view "that religion has more to do with the kind of picture that one allows to organize one's own life than it does with expressions of belief." H. Putnam, *Renewing Philosophy* (Cambridge, Mass., 1992), p. 146.

28. J. Rawls, *Political Liberalism* (New York, 1993), pp. 54–58.

29. J. Habermas, "On the Pragmatic, the Ethical, and the Moral Employment of Practical Reason," in *Justification and Application* (Cambridge, Mass., 1993), pp. 1–19.

30. See Michael Walzer's "moral minimalism" in M. Walzer, *Thick and Thin* (South Bend, 1994).

315

31. H. Putnam, "Pragmatism and Relativism," in *Words and Life*, p. 191.

32. H. Putnam, *Reason, Truth, and History* (Cambridge, 1981), p. 200: "Belief in a pluralist ideal is not the same thing as the belief that every ideal of human flourishing is as good as any other. There are ideals of human flourishing that we reject as mistaken, infantile, sick, or one-sided."

33. J. Habermas, "Justice and Solidarity," in *Justice*, ed. Milton Fisk (Atlantic Highlands, 1993), pp. 98–100; as well as J. Habermas, "A Genealogical Analysis of the Cognitive Content of Morality," in *The Inclusion of the Other*, ed. Ciaran Cronin and Pablo De Greiff (Cambridge, Mass., 1998), pp. 3–46.

34. For my criticism of B. Williams, *Ethics and the Limits of Philosophy* (London, 1985), see J. Habermas, *Erläuterungen zur Diskursethik* (Frankfurt, 1991), pp. 120–125.

35. J. Habermas, "A Genealogical Analysis of the Cognitive Content of Morality."

36. H. Putnam, "Dewey's Logic: Epistemology as Hypothesis," in *Words and Life*, p. 205.

37. H. Joas, *The Creativity of Action*, trans. Jeremy Gaines and Paul Keast (Chicago, 1996).

38. H. Putnam, "Dewey's Logic," in *Words and Life*, p. 214.

39. On the following, see A. Honneth, "Zwischen Prozeduralismus und Teleologie," *Deutsche Zeitschrift für Philososophie*, 47 (1999), 59–74.

40. H. Putnam, "Values and Norms," p. 121.

41. H. Putnam, "William James's Ideas," in *Words and Life*, p. 225.

42. On the two aspects of moral vulnerability as "irreplaceable individual" and as "member with equal rights," see L. Wingert, *Gemeinsinn und Moral* (Frankfurt, 1993), pp. 179ff.

43. H. Putnam, *Renewing Philosophy*, p. 180.

Chapter 6: Rightness versus Truth

1. Jürgen Habermas, "A Genealogical Analysis of the Cognitive Content of Morality," in *The Inclusion of the Other*, ed. Ciaran Cronin and Pablo De Greiff (Cambridge, Mass., 1998), pp. 3–46.

2. Still a landmark contribution on this subject is D. Henrich, "Der Begriff der sittlichen Einsicht und Kants Lehre vom Faktum der Vernunft," in *Kant*, ed. G. Prauss (Cologne, 1973), pp. 221–254.

3. Robert B. Brandom, *Making It Explicit: Reasoning, Representing, and Discursive Commitment* (Cambridge, Mass., 1994), especially chaps. 1 and 4.

4. J. Rawls, *Political Liberalism* (New York, 1993), §2.

5. [Although Habermas here uses different German terms to refer to the justification and validity of moral norms and empirical statements (*Rechtfertigung/Geltung* and *Begründung/Gültigkeit*, respectively) to mark a distinction within the sphere of validity in general, he does not systematically apply such a terminological distinction throughout the text, but uses the terms interchangeably.—Trans.]

6. E. Tugendhat, *Probleme der Ethik* (Stuttgart, 1983), pp. 83ff.

7. E. Keuth, *Erkenntnis oder Entscheidung* (Tübingen, 1993).

8. Even Tugendhat's more complex theory falters on the attempt adequately to explain this phenomenon (see E. Tugendhat, *Vorlesungen über Ethik* [Frankfurt am Main, 1993]). This noncontractualist approach distinguishes three levels of justification. First, a system of norms is justified to potential addressees by showing that each of them has an equal interest in participating in a shared practice that is constituted in such a way. This operation can be understood as the application of a principle of universalization: "Here norms are justified in such a way that it is shown to be equally in everyone's interest that everyone be asked to obey them" (E. Tugendhat, *Dialog in Leticia* [Frankfurt am Main, 1997], p. 54). From the internal perspective of a justification to members of a moral community, only actor-independent reasons that refer to the respective interests of any given individual, but have to be plausible epistemic reasons to everyone, count: "These are no longer reasons in the sense of motives, but reasons for statements" (ibid., p. 48). At the next—and predetermined—level, however, the normative system that has been justified in a Kantian way, as it were, is again divested of its cognitivist import. For at this basic level, the fundamental contractualist assumption is brought to bear that actions (and normatively regulated ways of acting) can ultimately be justified only from the first-person perspective of an acting subject. With regard to the package of a shared practice that is well justified for the internal perspective, every individual ultimately has to decide according to her own preferences whether she has a rational motive—whether it is "good for her"—to "join" such a moral community. Yet if anyone at any time can determine from their egocentric perspective whether it is worth it for them to even enter into morality, then the moves that are possible within the moral language game lose their categorical binding nature. Moral judgments and norms change their illocutionary meaning if they can lay claim to validity only relative to the result of instrumental considerations. See my critique in Habermas, "A Genealogical Analysis of the Cognitive Content of Morality," pp. 33–38; see also L. Wingert, "Gott naturalisieren? Anscombes Problem und Tugendhats Lösung," *Deutsche Zeitschrift für Philosophie* 45, no. 4 (1997), pp. 501–528.

9. L. Wingert, *Gemeinsinn und Moral* (Frankfurt am Main, 1993), pp. 72ff.

10. J. Habermas, *Between Facts and Norms: Contributions to a Discourse Theory of Law and Democracy*, trans. William Rehg (Cambridge, Mass., 1996), pp. 28ff.

11. G. Nunner, "Zur moralischen Sozialisation," *Kölner Zeitschrift für Sociologie und Sozialpsychologie* 44 (1992), p. 266.

12. E. Turiel, *The Development of Social Knowledge: Morality and Convention* (Cambridge, Mass., 1983).

13. G. Nunner develops a "self-binding model" that "allows for uncoupling the formal structure of motives and the formation of judgments" in order to "capture what

is specific to morality theoretically in such a way that individuals conceive of their moral behavior by no means as a conditioned pattern of responding, but very much as a conscious realization of grounded and justifiable moral judgments" ("Zur moralischen Sozialisation," p. 266).

14. L. Kohlberg, "From 'Is' to 'Ought,'" in *Essays in Moral Development* (San Francisco, 1981), pp. 137ff.

15. J. Piaget, *Die Entwicklung des Erkennens*, vol. 3 (Stuttgart, 1973), p. 179.

16. See my confrontation with the realist reading of discourse ethics suggested by Cristina Lafont in section VII of this chapter.

17. K. Günther, *The Sense of Appropriateness: Application Discourses in Morality and Law*, trans. John Farrell (Albany, 1993), pp. 23–100. See also J. Habermas, "Remarks on Discourse Ethics," in *Justification and Application*, trans. Ciaran Cronin (Cambridge, Mass., 1993), section 4, pp. 35ff.

18. B. Williams, in *Truth in Ethics*, ed. B. Hooker (Cambridge, 1996), pp. 19–34.

19. R. A. Shweder, *Thinking Through Cultures* (Cambridge, Mass., 1991).

20. A. MacIntyre, *Whose Justice? Which Rationality?* (Notre Dame, Ind., 1988).

21. [As the very next sentence shows, Habermas does not distinguish systematically between *Geltung* and *Gültigkeit* to mark the difference between validity and acceptance.—Trans.]

22. This is my understanding of Crispin Wright's strategy of argumentation in "Truth in Ethics," in *Truth in Ethics*, ed. B. Hooker (Cambridge, 1996), pp. 1–18.

23. This is a point on which I differ with Crispin Wright, who is content with an epistemic concept of truth and talks about "superassertibility" if a proposition that may be justifiably asserted in a given context remains assertible regardless of future information and objections. See C. Wright, *Truth and Objectivity* (Cambridge, Mass., 1992).

24. R. Rorty, *Philosophy and the Mirror of Nature* (Princeton, 1979).

25. I am referring in what follows to discussions between Richard Rorty and Hilary Putnam without documenting them in detail here. For a more detailed discussion, see my "Rorty's Pragmatic Turn," in *On the Pragmatics of Communication*, Maeve Cooke, ed. (Cambridge, Mass., 1998), pp. 343–382.

26. R. Rorty, "Sind Aussagen universelle Geltungsansprüche?" *Deutsche Zeitschrift für Philosophie*, no. 6 (1994).

27. M. Williams, *Unnatural Doubts* (Princeton, 1996), p. 232.

28. Ibid., p. 249.

29. K.-O. Apel, *Der Denkweg von Charles S. Peirce* (Frankfurt am Main, 1975).

30. This corresponds to C. Wright's concept of "superassertibility"; see note 22 above.

31. Following Durkheim, incidentally, Piaget also arrives at a social conception of truth: "If one rejects all reference to an external or internal absolute, all that remains is agreement among minds as an (experimental or formal) criterion of truth" (*Die Entwicklung des Erkennens*, p. 237). He, too, faces the problem of how the claim to the objectivity of cognition can be reconciled with an epistemic concept of truth: "From the fact that what is true rests on a agreement of minds it has been inferred that every agreement of minds produces a truth, as if past or contemporary history were not full of examples of collective error." In light of his developmental epistemology, Piaget therefore explains the internal connection between rational acceptability and truth—not unlike Peirce with his doctrine of the synthetic syllogism—by means of formal operations that are rooted in a socially mediated practical coping with reality: "The agreement among minds that grounds truth is thus not the static harmony of a shared belief; it is the dynamic convergence that arises from the use of shared tools of thought." Here, Piaget is relying on the pragmatist assumption that all cognitive progress is connected to a "progress in the socialization of thought," that is, with a progressive decentering of the perspective of the cognizing subject: "The study of the development of reason demonstrates a close correlation between the development of logical operations and the formation of certain forms of cooperation" (ibid., pp. 237ff.)

32. The fallibilist proviso that is based on the idealization of procedure renders moot the alternative with which C. S. Nino confronts me in C. S. Nino, *The Constitution of Deliberative Democracy* (New Haven, 1996), p. 113. Rational discourse can be characterized as the *sole* access to moral insights—rather than merely as the "most promising" or "most reliable"—without elevating the de facto prevailing agreement in any given case to a criterion of the truth or rightness of moral judgments. Interpreted intersubjectively, "rational *acceptability*," if it is made to depend on an ideal procedure, is not tantamount to intersubjectively reached *acceptance*.

33. [Claim (c) is a nonepistemic requirement in that whether it is met is not a function of what we (can) know, but of how the world is.—Trans.]

34. Based on her persuasive critique of epistemic conceptions of truth, Cristina Lafont concludes that a cognitivist understanding of morality is possible only in the sense of a moral realism.

35. It is in this sense that Rawls speaks of Kantian constructivism in moral theory, in J. Rawls, "Kantian Constructivism in Moral Theory," *Journal of Philosophy* 77 (1980), 515ff. See also Rawls, *Political Liberalism*, lecture III, pp. 89ff.

36. On the phenomenology of interactions that have come under the pressure of societal complexity, see C. Offe, "Der Naturzustand im Kleinformat," in *Modernität und Barbarei*, ed. M. Miller and H. G. Soeffner (Frankfurt am Main, 1996), pp. 258–289.

37. J. Habermas, "Inklusion: Einbeziehung oder Einschliessen?" in *Einbeziehung des Anderen*, ed. J. Habermas (Frankfurt am Main, 1996), pp. 154–184.

38. J. Habermas, *The Inclusion of the Other* (Cambridge, Mass., 1998), pp. 39ff.

39. On the conception of "sociomoral perspectives," see L. Kohlberg, *The Psychology of Moral Development: The Nature and Validity of Moral Stages* (San Francisco, 1984), pp. 170–180.

40. C. Lafont, "Pluralism and Universalism in Discourse Ethics," in *A Matter of Discourse: Community and Communication*, ed. A. Nascimento (Hampshire, 1998), p. 68.

41. See my account in Habermas, "A Genealogical Analysis of the Cognitive Content of Morality," section IX, pp. 39ff.

42. The objection against ontologizing also applies to Tugendhat's conception, according to which "we"—as neutral observers or philosophers—can determine whether a given normative system is indeed in the equal interest of all participants. This is supposed to be the case if everyone has a rational motive to agree to thus constituted ways of acting. See Tugendhat, *Dialog in Leticia*, pp. 42ff.

43. M. C. Nussbaum, "Human Functioning and Social Justice," *Political Theory* 20 (1992), pp. 202–246.

44. This is how I would ground the "ontological thesis" cited by C. S. Nino: "Moral truth is constituted by the satisfaction of formal or procedural presuppositions of a discursive practice directed at attaining cooperation and avoiding conflicts" (*The Constitution of Deliberative Democracy*, pp. 112ff.).

45. J. Habermas, *Moral Consciousness and Communicative Action* (Cambridge, Mass., 1990), and *Justification and Application: Remarks on Discourse Ethics* (Cambridge, Mass., 1993).

46. See also E. Tugendhat, *Dialog in Leticia*, pp. 85ff.

47. I am grateful to Axel Honneth for the critical point I take up in what follows.

48. J. McDowell, "Virtue and Reason," *Monist* 62 (1979), pp. 331–350.

Chapter 7: The Relationship between Theory and Practice Revisited

1. Hegel, *Werke* (Suhrkamp), vol. 12, p. 529.

2. J. Habermas, *Theory and Practice*, trans. John Viertel (Boston, 1973) chaps. 2, 3, and 4.

3. J. Habermas, *Theory of Communicative Action*, trans. Thomas McCarthy, 2 vols. (Boston, 1984/1987).

4. J. Habermas, "Philosophy as Stand-In and Interpreter," in *Moral Consciousness and Communicative Action* (Cambridge, Mass., 1990).

5. J. Habermas, "Edmund Husserl über Lebenswelt, Philosophie und Wissenschaft," in *Texte und Kontexte* (Frankfurt, 1991), pp. 34–48.

6. See J. Habermas, "Vom Kampf der Glaubensmächte," in *Vom sinnlichen Eindruck zum symbolischen Ausdruck* (Frankfurt, 1997).

7. J. Habermas, "Remarks on Legitimation through Human Rights," in *The Postnational Constellation* (Cambirdge, Mass., 2001), pp. 41–58.

Index